Facing Death, Facing Oneself

Facing Death, Facing Oneself

AN EXPLORATION ON LIVING

First Edition

Francis D. Degnin

University of Northern Iowa

cognella®
SAN DIEGO

Bassim Hamadeh, CEO and Publisher
David Miano, Senior Specialist Acquisitions Editor
Michelle Piehl, Senior Project Editor
David Rajec, Editorial Assistant
Emely Villavencio, Senior Graphic Designer
Stephanie Kohl, Licensing Coordinator
Natalie Piccotti, Director of Marketing
Kassie Graves, Vice President of Editorial
Jamie Giganti, Director of Academic Publishing

Printed in the United States of America.

cognella® | ACADEMIC PUBLISHING
3970 Sorrento Valley Blvd., Ste. 500, San Diego, CA 92121

Brief Contents

SECTION IV

Love as the Ultimate Rational Act   301

Detailed Contents

SECTION IV

Love as the Ultimate Rational Act   301

Acknowledgments

THIS BOOK IS a labor of love. It is an attempt to share some of the resources I've come across for asking life's most difficult, yet rewarding, questions. It's certainly not a final answer, in part because I don't believe that there is a single and complete answer, but also because everyone's answer to these sorts of questions has to be lived in their own way. No one can replace another's journey, but such study can, as Morrie put it, help us decide what to pack along the way.

My own journey owes thanks to many people; there are too many to name here. I have had many wonderful teachers starting with my parents. My mother taught me the value of service for and love of others. My father taught me (with great difficulty!) the value of discipline in forming character. Our parents, for good or bad, are usually our most important teachers. I count myself lucky. The remaining acknowledgments are for teachers who left a particularly significant mark on my life. They are listed alphabetically within their respective institutions.

My parents

Carolyn Degnin
John Degnin

Whose values continue to serve as my inspiration.

Whitman College

Dr. George Ball

St. Thomas Hospital

Dr. John Johnson

Dr. Bruce White

Villanova University

Dr. Walter Brogan

Dr. John Caputo

Fr. James McCartney

Seattle University

Dr. Patrick Burke

Dr. James Risser

Dr. Ken Stikkers

Fr. John Topel

Vanderbilt University

Dr. John Lachs

Dr. Charles Scott

Dr. Richard Zaner

Introduction

Facing Death: Facing Ourselves

Facing death is more than an intellectual proposition. When one honestly faces death, there is a certain discomfort, a sense of uncanniness, and a feeling of uneasiness in the body. What would it mean to stay with those feelings, to see what they have to teach us? To do so, one must temporarily set aside any belief in an afterlife. Why? Because it is too easy to use such a belief to "hide" from the discomfort, to avoid the fundamental question raised by those feelings. What question?

If this is all there is, if nothing is there when I die, what is it that makes this life worthwhile?

Once a person figures this out, not just intellectually, but as an embodied being, their life changes. The "chaff" sort of falls away and we live for that which is really important to us. The question will need to be reassessed from time to time, but it provides a touchstone for living a rich and meaningful life.

Given this sort of central question, this book is more than a textbook. It's a compilation of ideas and resources about thinking about the meaning of life. While many will find the answers fruitful, they aren't final answers. That's true for several reasons.

Firstly, any real answer has to be worked out by each person in the context of their own lives, hearts, and bodies. The mind is important, but secondary. Why? Because the real answers to life's mysteries can only be lived and engaged, not intellectually solved. Life starts with experience, not thinking. Could one really understand, say, love, if one only had an intellectual knowledge of the concept? Experience is our first teacher.

This is not to say that intellect, or reason, should be discarded. Far from it. We need to live from our bodies and our hearts, but the mind can help to moderate the flights of fancy of the heart. The mind can also help avoid self-destructive decisions or repeated mistakes. More than this, the mind has a positive role to play in interpreting and constructing meaning from experiences, from giving us purpose and direction. The mind is our second teacher.

Yet, the mind can only capture minuet parts of the experiences available to us. For example, only a tiny portion of the electromagnetic spectrum is visible to the naked eye. Even then we can only store a tiny portion of what we do see into memory. (It's a myth that there are people who can actually see and recall "everything" they see. But some can recall far more than most.)

Instead, we learn from perceptual psychology that we sort of "construct" reality. We tend to focus on what we learn—via experience, family, culture—which is important to help us survive and flourish. Most other things are excluded. It is still grounded in the real world, but we only see and recall selective fragments of those experiences. Understanding why we remember some fragments and not others can help us to understand why different people can look at the same scene and see such different things. Understanding why different people can legitimately see different things can help us to become both more empathetic and open to personal growth.

Similarly, this book also is just a "slice" and "take" on reality. It would be foolish and arrogant to claim a certain and final answer.

In that case, what good is this sort of project? If one demands absolute answers, very little. These questions are not entirely of the mind. They are not amenable to absolute intellectual certitude. In this book, I discuss the nature of mystery. A mystery is a paradox which, while it cannot finally be "solved" intellectually, can be engaged. In that engagement, it deepens and enriches who we are. Love, for example, has the character of mystery. Such engagement uses the mind but is not just of the mind. One must also engage with the heart and the body. From the outside, love seems ridiculous. But from the inside, authentic love is powerful, meaningful, and life-giving. Such is also true of any project that explores the meaning of life. The "meaning of life" questions are not accessible by intellect alone.

"Final" answers don't really work. Only **lived** answers work.
"Lived" answers speak to a **process**, not a static solution.

This book is not about "final" answers. Instead, it explores a hypothesis as to the nature of those answers from a variety of perspectives. The unifying theme of these explorations is the question of facing death.

The fact that it can be helpful to set aside one's belief in a particular sort of afterlife doesn't mean that one doesn't return to such a belief. But, if my experience as a hospital chaplain is accurate, something changes. There is often a world of difference between both the psychology and the spirituality of a person who comes back to a belief in an afterlife **after** working through this question and a person who uses their belief in an afterlife to hold back the discomfort. Those who "repress" their fear are far more likely to be judgmental, anxious, and ideological. Those who have worked through their fear are usually more peaceful, joyful, and accepting of others. The same is often true on the deathbed.

What is the value of this project? In *Tuesdays with Morrie*, Morrie comments about being able to teach people "what to pack along the way." Exploring other insights—religious, philosophical, mythological, cultural, psychological, historical—can help us to deepen our experience and our insights into those experiences. It can give us tools to explore and engage, with which to deepen and enrich ourselves. No one can simply "give" us their answers, but they can help to light our way.

What Makes This Book Different?

Most courses on death and dying cover similar themes: how we die, what death has to teach about living, different traditions about death, stages and dealing with grief, etc. When I teach this course, I cover a lot of these same themes. The difference is in the depth and emphasis of the course. Most who teach the course spend perhaps a week explicitly focusing on philosophical and theological issues (meaning of life stuff). And while these issues may come up in bits and pieces elsewhere, they're not a major component of the course.

Teaching out of a philosophy and world religions department places these questions at the heart of the course. What has death to teach us about living? What are some of the answers offered by various religious traditions? What guidance might we find in mythology, literature, psychology, history, and philosophy? The depth in which these are explored, particularly in the last two-thirds of the book, go far beyond any other textbook of which I'm aware.

This is not, however, the only book I use for the course. I use a variety of other books as well as novels and films. This book covers about two-thirds of the course as I teach it. It has to do with those parts of the course that are unique, those which focus most on tools and questions about what makes for a rich and meaningful life.

How to Use This as a Textbook

This book is not a textbook for an entire course on death and dying. Rather, it is the distillation of the central themes and parts that, I feel, make my course unique. It can be read as just a book, not a textbook. In fact, I originally planned to write it as a general interest book. Here, I'd like to make a few comments about using it in a classroom setting.

When choosing the order of material for a class, I am often faced with a dilemma. The philosophical side of me wants to go in logical order. For instance, to start with the ideas and concepts we need to build on, then go to the richer stories and start applying them. This doesn't work with most students. Why?

Until they see the relevance of the "tools" or ideas and concepts we need to build upon, starting with these will just lose their interest. One needs to start with material that will engage them both emotionally and intellectually, which means holding off on at least some of the "tools" until later. It's also why I no longer start with the syllabus on the first day—it's dull—instead, I want to give them a taste of the topic in that first session.

I start class with the grief exercise. It personalizes the course, makes it clear that it's more than just an intellectual project, and engages them from the beginning. I've laid out the exercise prior to the first chapter, but feel free to modify it. I never really do it the same way twice.

What I do next is somewhat variable. If I were going purely by "interest," I would most likely go to chapter four, Lessons from Grief. Not only is the material relevant to most of our lives, the chapter is mostly told in stories, which makes it very accessible. My tendency, however, has been to use some of the "capital" I get from that first exercise to develop certain ideas and tools. That's really chapter one, which lays out the central themes of the course. In general, I try to alternate the more "interesting" and easy material with the tools or more difficult material.

Chapter two, which is about self-deception, is likely to be a bit dull for many. While I sometimes assign it as reading for outside of class, it's also worth considering having students access that chapter in "sections" with other readings. That way, they don't have to absorb it all at once.

Another way to make chapter two relevant is to assign a discussion group or journal, which asks students to identify and use an experience from their own life to explain one of the techniques by which we lie to ourselves. This makes the chapter more concrete. Also, if it's in an online discussion post, they see others engaged in the same experiences.

There are similar considerations with other chapters. For example, some of the critique of C.S. Lewis would be better to include after the discussion of the nature of truth. At the same time, the critique of Lewis can help to motivate the importance of that discussion. These are judgment calls.

I'd also note that the theological and philosophical issues really take off starting in chapter five, where we discuss the film *What Dreams May Come*.

Viewing Guides

There are three films discussed in the book. Why? Research suggests that we remember only 10 percent of what we read, but 20 percent of what we hear. It's also far easier to remember things when connected to a story than just a lecture. The three films bring up critical material for the course in an accessible format. But we don't just watch the films. If I'm showing the film in class, we pause at critical points to analyze scenes, draw comparisons to previously read/viewed material, or raise related psychological, philosophical, or theological issues.

The "Viewing Guides" serve this same purpose for someone who can't attend class or if the class is being taught as an online course. Students can either flip pages as they watch the movie, pausing the film when they need to read material, or read it after watching the film. Even for students who were in class, it can serve as detailed notes.

The film *Tuesdays with Morrie* deserves special mention. The primary three themes for the course are all drawn, directly or indirectly, from this film. Why the film rather than the book? In part, it has to do with the retention issues already mentioned. This is also a rare circumstance where I found the movie to be better, in some ways, than the book. In the movie version, there is a scene where the key lessons Morrie is trying to teach Mitch about the meaning of life are enacted in one place. In the book, there's no central moment that seems to pull it all together.

Tuesday's with Morrie is also a place for my favorite assignment for the course. After watching the movie, students are asked to reflect on what they would want others to be able to say about them at their eulogy. They are also to reflect, and write, about whether or not they are that type of person. They are then asked to reflect on what needs to change to get there. This sort of assignment draws together much of the course by asking the following question: What has facing the possibility of my own death taught me about the kind of person I want to be?

If it helps, I suggest that students use one of two incidents from the Viewing Guide to help frame their reflection.

Early in the movie, Morrie asks Mitch three linked questions:

Are you happy?
Are you giving back to your community?
Are you at peace with yourself?

Alternately, students could use the story of the Buddhist bird on one's shoulder. Each day, you ask the bird:

Is this the day that I'm going to die, little bird?
Am I ready?
Am I leading the life I want to live?
Am I the person I want to be?

Previewing

This book is ideally set up for the technique of "previewing." Previewing is a well-documented study technique that offers significant results with very little additional time.[1]

In previewing, I ask students to first read the study or reflection questions. In doing so, they are to think about what might be being asked of them, what the writer seems to think is important, and what questions it may raise for them.

I then ask them to review the headers and the "special print" (bold, italics) of each chapter. Don't read the text, just try to see the big picture of what the author is speaking to. Again, ask oneself what it looks like the author thinks is important. Try to see if any additional questions are raised for oneself.

This entire process only takes about ten minutes, but it needs to be focused time. Ideally, I ask my students to do so just before class, but if that's not practical, either earlier in the day or the night before. If earlier, the suggestion is to do it at a time when they don't need to immediately go on to something else, to let the questions "settle," so-to-speak.

Previewing cognitively primes the mind to receive information, reducing cognitive overload. With the study/reflection questions, it also primes the student to notice when we get to material that addresses a particular question. This means that they are more likely to notice the answer and include it in their notes. This applies to both in-class lectures/discussions and to reading the text, if it's an online class.

Following the class, students should then review the actual text more closely.

What makes this book ideal for previewing is not just that it has reflection questions, but the way in which topics have headers and key issues are highlighted in the text. In fact, when I learned of this technique, I edited the book to make it more accessible to previewing.

I also give students regular "reading quizzes" on the material. Since these are open book, the headings make it easy to locate material quickly. However, since the goal is to ensure that students are reviewing all of the material, the quizzes have time limits. There's more than enough time for a well-prepared student to do well, but not for someone going in cold.

---

1 For a fuller discussion and other tools, consider McQuire & McQuire, 2015, *Teaching Students How to Learn*, Stylus Publishing, Sterling, VA. Special thanks to Dr. Susan Hill, Director of the UNI Learning Center, for introducing me to this approach.

Other Texts

This is a list of the most important other texts I have students read for my class. Complete references can be found in the references section.

The Death of Ivan Ilych, Tolstoy
How We Die, Nuland
Stiff: The Curious Life of Cadavers, Roach
Seven Choices (pocket edition), Neeld
The Epic of Gilgamesh (any edition)
Siddhartha, Hesse
The Sacred Art of Dying, Kramer

Films: See the Viewing Guides

Wit
What Dreams May Come
Tuesdays with Morrie

Understanding Ourselves: What Do We Really Want?

Grief Exercise[1]

READINGS CAN BE interesting or dull depending upon how well we feel they relate to our lives. The insights of this course, in particular, only fully make sense if they are embodied, taken in not just to the mind, but in terms of feelings, physicality, and, for some, spiritually. Much of what we are doing is exploring other people's answers to life's most important questions. Ultimately, the only answer that really matters is the one each of us takes into our lives.

For this reason, I strongly recommend starting with the following short video and exercise. I do it in my classes as a group. For many, it is quite powerful. If reading on one's own, there will be no narrator, but one can still read, pause, close one's eyes, and reflect, before returning again.

Setting the Mood

Before starting the exercise, I start with a YouTube video by the Cleveland Clinic on Empathy. It can be Googled (Cleveland Clinic Empathy Video), or the URL can be typed in:

https://www.youtube.com/watch?v=cDDWvj_q-o8

---

1 I've seen various versions of this exercise used in places like hospice training and addiction classes. Just as I have developed some of my own twists from what I have previously encountered, others may wish to modify what I've written.

Preparation

Begin by dividing a sheet of paper into 12 boxes. Following the directions below, write something in each box (the explanation is below the sample):

Special Person	Special Person	Special Person
Defining Quality	Defining Quality	Defining Quality
Favorite Activity	Favorite Activity	Favorite Activity
Special Item	Special Item	Greatest Fear (NOT coming true)

Special Persons

Three boxes: Persons who are most dear and important to me
(i.e., parent[s], spouse, friend, child, pets, etc.).

Defining Qualities

Three boxes: Qualities that I feel are essential to who I am
(i.e., compassion, human, intelligence, athleticism, etc.).

Favorite Activities

Three boxes: Activities that make life worth living for me
(i.e., sports, dancing, conversations, service, romantic relationships, etc.).

Special Items

Two boxes: Items that have special significance or value to me
(e.g., a special gift from a loved one, the game ball from a sports event).

Greatest Fear

One box: My greatest fear
(e.g., drowning, cancer, dying childless).

One doesn't have to be rigid about how one fills out these boxes. If you have four special "people" and only one special "item" you can steal a box from the item list and use it for a person. However, please include at least one box from each category.

Once the boxes are filled out, clear off the table and cut them into a dozen separate boxes. Spread them out on the table in front of you. Sit comfortably but straight, close your eyes, and take several deep, slow, relaxing breaths. We are ready to begin.

General Instructions

Normally, I ask each person to listen to my voice and imagine they are in the situations I describe. Alternately, one would read it, then pause for a minute or two to close their eyes and imagine themselves in that situation. Pause for a few seconds between each paragraph or a bit longer where noted.

I let students know that I will ask them, at times, to open their eyes and choose which slips of paper to tear up. When they do so, that person, quality, or item is now gone from their life. The greatest fear, however, works in reverse. When that box gets torn up, it means the fear has come true.

Grief Exercise

Narrator

1. You're waiting in the doctor's office. It's a dreary day: cloudy, grey, and with a persistent drizzle. You're here because they "found" something—a lump. They performed a biopsy two weeks ago. Two weeks of waiting.

   The doctor enters the room. You stand and she invites you to sit. Her face is serious.

   You wonder, what does this mean? She tells you, "*I have bad news, it's cancer.*"

   You don't even hear the next three sentences.

   What is going through your mind? What are you feeling?

(Longer pause)

When you "return" to reality, you realize that the doctor has continued to speak.

What did you miss?

She goes on to say that this particular cancer has a fairly good cure rate, about a 60 percent remission after 5 years, but that the treatment is difficult and it needs to be started very soon.

Is there someone you wish you had brought with you? Who? Why?

(Longer pause)

Close your eyes and breathe, slowly and deeply.

2. You're driving home from the doctor's office. The road is slippery from the rain and you feel the chill in your bones.

   What are you thinking about?

   (Longer pause)

   You snap to attention to a blaring horn and screeching tires. You've run a stop sign and almost hit someone. **Your heart races.**

   You remember advice from your death and dying class: "When in shock or grief, do not drive alone." Now you understand why. You resolve to focus more on the rest of the way home.

   You arrive home safely and open the door. There is someone you want to greet you.

   Who?

   You call out but the halls resound in their absence. The place feels empty.

   Who did you want/need there? Why? What would you say to them? What would they say to you?

(Longer pause)

*Open your eyes, **tear up two slips of paper.***

These two are now gone from your life. Unless you choose to tear up your greatest fear, which means it came true.

(Longer pause)

Close your eyes and breathe.

3. You've started chemotherapy. Unfortunately, this is not one of the newer, gentler treatments.

   After the first treatment, you lose not just your hair, but your eyebrows and your eyelashes. The chemo also effects the cells lining your gastrointestinal tract, which results, on some days, in unrelenting vomiting.

   You lose 20 pounds in the first month, mostly of muscle. You find yourself wishing your state was one that allowed medical marijuana as it could have at least helped you to eat.

   Eight months like this.

   Who do you want to be with you? With whom do you want to talk, day by day? Who are you willing to let see you like this? What are you feeling? Besides your health, is there anything you're worried about?

   (Longer pause)

   *Open your eyes, **tear up two slips of paper.***

   Close your eyes and breathe.

4. The eight months is up and you're back at your doctor's office. By this time, for the important visits, you've gotten into the habit of bringing someone with you. Not only do you bring someone for support, but also to ask questions you might forget, and to remember information you might miss.

   Who is this person or persons you bring with you? Why them?

You've gotten to know your doctor pretty well in the last year and you know her facial expressions. When she walks into the room, you know it's not good.

"I'm sorry, the chemo has slowed the progression of the cancer, but it hasn't stopped it. There's nothing more we can do for you but keep you comfortable. You probably have three to six months to live."

(Longer pause)

What are you feeling?

(Longer pause)

What are your thoughts?

(Longer pause)

> *Open your eyes, **tear up two slips of paper.***

> *Close your eyes and breathe.*

5. The first couple of months are somewhat better, relatively. Without the chemo, you have only the pain and weakness of the cancer to deal with. Well, and the knowledge that death is not only certain, but near. While weak, you're no longer bedridden. You can even eat. You realize this might be your last chance to do some of the things you wanted to do with your life.

Are there some foods that you crave?

What activities might you hope to do in this time?

Is there something you want to finish or accomplish?

Where would you go? Who and what would you like to see?

(Longer pause)

> *Open your eyes, **tear up two slips of paper.***

> *Close your eyes and breathe.*

6. Your "respite" is passing and the cancer is relentless. While not entirely home bound, you again need help with many of the most basic activities of living. Your thoughts turn to relationships and regrets.

    Is there someone you need to forgive or to ask for forgiveness? Who? What?

    (Longer pause)

    What do you want to say to them, or them to you?

    Or just something which has been left, too long, unsaid?

    (Longer pause)

    > *Open your eyes, **tear up two slips of paper.***

    > *Close your eyes and breathe.*

7. They've moved a hospital bed into the living room since it was too hard to get it into one of the bedrooms. You're in constant pain, relieved only by the morphine drip attached to your arm.

    Each breath now requires effort. You just can't seem to get enough air. When you finally fall asleep at night, you wonder, *will I wake up tomorrow?*

    (Longer pause)

    Who is still with you? Who do you want with you at this time, why, and who do you want to stay away?

    (Longer pause)

    > *Open your eyes, **place the last two slips of paper facedown in front of you.***

    > *Close your eyes and breathe.*

    (Either the narrator walks around selecting and tearing up one slip of paper per person, or the student simulates this by randomly selecting one on their own.)

8. Open your eyes, look at the last slip of paper, and tear it up.

You have died.

Post-Processing

After a pause, the narrator invites students to take turns sharing any feelings, thoughts, or insights from the experience. *It's important to state that no one needs to share something for which they don't feel safe or that is too personal.* Start with volunteers, but make sure everyone has an opportunity to say something. Often, I prompt the group to start with the following:

What were your two last choices? Why?

Did you end up with the one you wanted? If so, why or why not?

What was your greatest fear?

What came up as "unfinished" business?

What struck you most about the exercise?

Did anything surprise you?

Did you gain any insights?

Results will vary, but some insights are quite striking.

Some find what they consider their priorities, or what they currently treat as their priorities, changes. They come to a realization of what they feel is most important.

For example, I've had students realize, much to their surprise, that they didn't actually want their partner of many years with them at or near the end. As a result, they realized that this was not a relationship worth continuing.

I've had persons who didn't want their loved ones to "see them like this," but then they realized (sometimes with the help of others) how rejected and upset their loved one's might feel for having not been allowed to care for them.

At some point in the discussion, the issue arises about the moment when the narrator selected the second-to-last loss. At that point, it's worth asking how many were angry at losing that choice? How many were relieved? There's always a division. Why?

The exercise and the video, together, end up serving several purposes:

The primary purpose is to engage, on more than a purely intellectual level, with what the fear of dying might teach us. In this case, it teaches us to gain a glimpse into what is really important in our lives.

The second purpose is to become more sensitive and thoughtful to what other people might be going through when faced with serious illness—empathy.

The third is to see and become more sensitive to the differences between people. We tend to assume that all people are like us when that's only partly true.

CHAPTER ONE

Facing Death
COMING TO KNOW ONESELF

The Peaceful Death

To rejoice at the opportunity of experiencing each new day is to prepare for one's ultimate acceptance of death. For it is those who have not really lived— who have left issues unsettled, dreams unfulfilled, hopes shattered, and who have let the real things in life (loving and being loved by others, contributing in a positive way to other people's happiness and welfare, finding out what things are really you) pass them by—who are most reluctant to die.

(Kübler-Ross 1975, xi; emphasis hers)

What if Believing in an Afterlife Makes One LESS Likely to Die Peacefully?

WHAT A PREPOSTEROUS *thought! It makes no sense!* Of course, those who truly believe in an afterlife, particularly if they believe in heaven and a loving God, go peacefully into that good night. It's not that they won't miss the ones they leave behind, or that we won't miss them. We know it's only temporary and in the end, we all (well, those who accept God's mercy), will be joined in a life (well, afterlife) of eternal bliss ...

Intellectually, this argument makes perfect sense.

Yet, oddly it doesn't appear to be true.

What if the belief in a positive afterlife isn't the main reason, or even necessary, for determining whether one dies a peaceful death?

Kübler-Ross, the pioneer of the modern-day study of death and dying, talks about something entirely different. Her work is confirmed both by my own experience as a night relief hospital chaplain and by some of the full-time chaplains with whom I've worked. The two factors that appear to correlate most with a peaceful death are a positive response to the following questions:

1. Have I lived a rich and full life? Have I explored life and experienced much of the richness this life has to offer?

2. Am I surrounded by those I love, or perhaps preceded by them, so that I feel a rich connection to others? Do I feel like I've contributed to their lives and happiness and they to mine?

Part of living a rich and full life is pursing and fulfilling at least some of one's dreams. Part of having rich relationships with others is to resolve those issues keeping us apart. Part of loving relationships is leaving a positive legacy through touching the lives and hearts of others, contributing to their happiness and welfare. These two principles, living a rich life and having rich, loving relationships, are another way of framing Kübler-Ross' insight.

Of course, there are other factors that affect how one dies, such as intense and untreated pain. Air hunger (difficulty breathing), while physical, can cause intense anxiety. But here, we focus on those factors relating to a person's life and life choices. Unless we are to argue that for those who believe in an afterlife but do not die in peace, it's due to a deficiency of their faith, it appears that there is something strange going on here.

What about atheists or agnostics? Atheists and agnostics, who have no professed faith (at least not in the conventional sense of the term), should have anxious and troubled deaths. Yet for many, that's simply not the case. Many atheists and agnostics die peacefully, just as many people of faith (Christian or otherwise) die in fear and anxiety.

While the thought that only a belief in a loving God and an afterlife can allow one to die peacefully makes a certain *logical* sense, it doesn't appear to hold up *empirically*, when we look at multiple and diverse real people. This will be one of the sub-themes to which we will attend: ***What does actual experience have to teach us, as opposed to intellectual formulations about what life "should" be about?*** *Facing the concrete realities of specific illnesses or death can, at times, be highly illuminating.* For each person, there will be some variation in what experience has to teach, but there will also be common themes.

For example, whether one's faith helps one to die in peace appears to depend, in part, on the nature of one's faith and beliefs. What if my view is that this life is only a prelude, a test, for the afterlife? What if I believe the only real value of this life is preparation for the next? In this case, I might disengage from fully living. If I spend my life walking on eggshells, driven more by what I shouldn't do than by what I want to do, if my actions come from a fear-based "should" rather than from the fullness of my heart and lived experiences, I may come to the end without having really lived.

If I come to the end of my life having given up so much for the hope of something I'm not truly certain of, I may look back and ask:

What if I have given it all up for nothing?

To be clear, it's not that all atheists die in peace. Likewise, many persons of other faiths go peacefully into that good night. But it seems that belief in an afterlife is less important than the two factors listed above. If one's faith helps one to have these sorts of rich life experiences—to have rich and loving relationships, to contribute to one another's lives and well-being—it appears that one's faith contributes to a peaceful death.

Heaven Can Wait

Later, we will examine the nature of faith. In the meantime, I have a suggestion:
Those who believe in an afterlife should set that belief aside.

As we will see, there appears to be *an enormous difference in both the psychology and spirituality of those who have faced their fear of death—the fear that, at the end of this life, "this" is all there is—and those who use their belief in an afterlife as a way to push away that fear.*

Facing one's fear of death, sitting with that sense of uncanniness and discomfort, has an enormous amount to teach us about living.

This speaks to the heart of what this book attempts to address.

This is not to say that there is no afterlife. *That's a belief each of us must discern for ourselves.* One goal of this book is to invite you to take the time to experience and engage with the fear that this is all there is, to find out what it has to teach you, and only then move on to considering the afterlife. *If this fear is fully engaged, rather than pushed away, it can be transformative.*

Engaging these fears is the first part of a rich, embodied understanding. What do I mean by an "embodied" understanding? It's a bit like love. While I may be able to learn the poetry and psychologies of love and be able to wax philosophically about it, how can I understand love unless I have actually experienced it? Biblically, perhaps this is part of what is meant in 1 Cor 13:1.

> *If I speak with the tongues of men and angels, but have not love, I am only a resounding gong or a clanging cymbal.*

Similarly, when it comes to questions of truth, Soren Kierkegaard writes:

> *... what good would it do me if truth stood before me, cold and naked, not caring whether I recognized her or not, and producing in me a shudder of fear rather than a trusting devotion? I certainly do not deny that I still recognize an imperative of*

understanding and that through it one can work on men, but it must be taken up into my life ... (Kierkegaard 1946, 5).

It's not that "abstract" truth is meaningless, but that the important truths, the ones that matter, are the ones that affect and change one's life.

Intellectual discussions of these sorts of issues, while helpful, are simply inadequate. These are meaning of life questions. ***Unless they are EXPERIENCED in the heart and body, the mind will never grasp an answer.***

Which brings us to the themes of this book:

Primary Themes

1. Only when one knows how to die does one know how to live.
2. In the end, love is the ultimate rational act.
3. Become more thoughtful and self-aware, self-honest, and self-critical in understanding oneself.

To achieve these, there are several sub-goals worth highlighting:

a. To develop a greater sensitivity to the differences between people and a greater empathy to the variety of human experience, particularly suffering.
b. To develop a concrete (embodied, as opposed to merely intellectual) understanding of the human experience, and in particular, of one's own experiences.
c. To gain an understanding of what some of the rich aspects of both western and eastern traditions have to offer us in addressing these themes.

The first two themes are consistent with Kübler-Ross's insights, but they are drawn more directly from the book and film, *Tuesdays with Morrie*. We will explore these themes using texts from psychology, philosophy, religious traditions, mythology, history, and literature. In essence, we are seeking to understand a variety of responses to the question of the meaning of life. Here, we lay the groundwork for that exploration.

Facing one's death, seeing what it has to teach us about living, is also seeing what it has to teach us about ourselves. For this reason, **coming to *honestly* know oneself**

(self-critical awareness and understanding) is critical to achieving the first two. Along these lines, consider the following exercise:

EXERCISE: EMPTYING THE MIND?

There's a joke about men and women that periodically makes the rounds via social media. In one form, it shows a man and a woman sitting on a swing. The "thought bubble" over the woman's head is full of thoughts. The thought bubble over the man's head is, well, empty. After a while, the woman asks, "What are you thinking about?" He replies, "Nothing." Her thought bubble, paired with an angry expression on her face, steams with the words, "He just won't talk about his feelings!"

Clichés aside, it's actually very difficult to truly still one's mind. In the case above, it was more likely that his mind was just unfocused, allowing what he saw or thought to come and go easily, rather than truly empty. That's still worthwhile and it can be a stage along the way. It's not quite the same, however, as truly emptying one's mind.

So, for now, sit comfortably, preferably with your back straight. Take several deep, slow breaths. Feel the breath move slowly in and out of your body. Breathe fully, expanding and contracting through both the lungs and the abdomen. Relax.

When you're ready, still you mind. Attempt to let go of every thought and image. Continue breathing slowly but attempt to keep your mind completely clear for at least a minute.

Were you successful?

Unless you're a person who practices some form of spiritual or relaxation meditation, it's very unlikely you'll be successful in this first attempt. But even this short attempt has something to teach us about who and what we are. This is what we will explore next.

Consciousness as a Dynamic "Space" for the Play of Possibilities

Think about your attempt to still your mind. We are rarely just "conscious." We are (almost) always conscious of something. In fact, while possible, it is very difficult without practice to intentionally quiet or "still" one's consciousness, to merely sit in that stillness.

Consciousness is, in a very important way, at the heart of who we are as persons. It is the voice in your head that tells you that you exist. It's where we think, decide, express our feelings, and "see" the world. In a fundamental sense, *we are our consciousness.*

Yet consciousness is, in another sense, *no-thing (nothing)*. It is an emptiness or a stage. What is a stage? A stage is a space where things can be seen and where stories can be played out. Following this metaphor, if the stage were "full" of some material, nothing new could be played out. So, we think of consciousness as the "space" inside of us. It is the space wherein things in the world can be projected and be seen. The space where things can be imagined, where stories can be told, and where we can "play" with our stories, possibilities, and ideas before projecting them back outwards into the world. Consciousness, because it allows a space (an emptiness) for change and play, is at the very heart of freedom, our capacity to make a choice, to be creative.

It's interesting that so many people also speak of "loneliness" or certain types of depression as an "emptiness." Could it be that the same capacity that gives us everything and makes us human—freedom, thought, creativity, etc.—is also at the heart of our capacity to be lonely or depressed? We will return to this later.

For now, just focus on this very odd sort of space. Returning to the idea that we are rarely "just" conscious, we are almost always conscious "of" something. That something typically involves a projection (as on a screen) of some possibility. For example, if I'm hungry, I may be thinking about when I can stop reading and go to dinner. I may be looking forward to a date this weekend, a conversation with a friend, or a birthday party. Similarly, perhaps I am dreading a confrontation or a difficult conversation with a friend or family member.

Consider another type of example. You walk out of a store and into a large parking lot. You look around. Some people will think, "Where is my car?" However, it's just as likely that one will think, "Where am I?" That's the point. We aren't just "looking" for our car, we are, in some way, projecting ourselves as already in that space, in the place where our car was left. At some point, but only when you have the thought involuntarily (if you try too hard, it will just be in the mind), attend to your body just after you think it. You may almost "feel" your body projecting itself forward into that space.

What we see is that consciousness is rarely a "passive" space, it is almost always an active *projection* into our future. Even when we look at the past, it's usually in terms of how it affects us now and in our future. Consciousness names a dynamic space in which the contents are constantly changing. Consciousness is almost always oriented and projected towards a future.

Consciousness is the dynamic space wherein we project our possibilities towards our future.[1]

How does this help us in thinking about death?

---

1   Those who have read Heidegger will recognize this as a simplification of dasein. For Heidegger, however, dasien refers to the ontological condition that makes consciousness possible, while we are applying this idea to consciousness itself. Heidegger would view this as psychologizing.

If consciousness is the ongoing projection of our possibilities (for action, ideas, relationships, and all the ways in which we move and engage our world), what happens when we *project the possibility of the "end" of all our possibilities?*

If we do this, not just intellectually, but in our feelings and in our body, it creates in us a sense of uncanniness. We feel this, vaguely at times, when we know someone who dies. We often forget it because it makes us uncomfortable and because we don't know how to name it or what to do with it. While we may grieve for someone close to us, even if we come upon the body of a stranger, it is likely to stir us in difficult and uncomfortable ways. What we are experiencing, in part, is the fear and uncanniness of the possibility that this is all there is. ***Death as the possibility of the end of our possibilities.***

What if Death Is Really Just the End?

To be clear, I'm not making any claims, pro or con, about an afterlife. But there is an important difference, both in psychology and spirituality, between people who use their belief in an afterlife to "escape" their fear of death and people who first face that fear, learn from it, and come back to that belief. My experience is that, for the most part, those who use their belief in an afterlife to escape their fear often show many of the basic features of **psychological repression**: rigid thinking, judgmental behaviors, lashing out at those who may believe differently. Those who face their fear, on the other hand, are more likely to be peaceful, tolerant, accepting of different beliefs, and less judgmental. This appears to be because of what facing that fear can teach them. *In doing so, they transcend that fear.*

Facing this question is what is meant by facing one's death. But one doesn't stop there. If one really, at least for a time, accepts that this life may be all there is, it raises a second fundamental question:

If This Life Is All There is, What Is It That Makes This Life, My Life, Worthwhile?

This is just a particular way of asking the more general question:

What is the meaning of life?

This question can't be answered quickly. Nor is it enough to come up with an intellectual solution. When we get to the discussion of *Wit*, we will meet a woman who has tremendous intellectual gifts. Yet, despite all her knowledge and intellect, she has never really experienced love. How can one really understand something like love with just the mind? Once must experience it in the heart, body, and very core.

If There Is Nothing More Than This Life, What Is It That Makes My Life Worth Living?

While for each person the answer is somewhat different, there are certain commonalities that appear throughout human history, religion, literature, and so forth. As we will see in the second theme, love as the ultimate rational act names what is perhaps the most common thread in these traditions. *These can serve as guides and resources but studying them will not give one meaning. Ultimately, the path of discovery for each person must be their own.*

One Philosopher's Answer: Happiness

> *When I was five years old, my mother told me happiness was the key to life.*
> *When I went to school, they asked me what I wanted to be when I grew up.*
> *I told them, "Happy."*
> *They told me I didn't understand the question.*
> *I told them they didn't understand life.*[2]

We will explore a number of responses to the question of the meaning of life. Here, we start with one of the oldest responses in western history: Aristotle's.

Why start with Aristotle? He is a bit "drier" than most of the other approaches we will explore. Part of the reason for that dryness is the systematic and insightful way in which Aristotle approaches all his thinking. My reason for beginning here is because **Aristotle, rather than starting with a grand idea of the nature of reality, starts by simply observing basic human experiences and behaviors.** The systematic way in which Aristotle thinks provides insights and resources which, while they can be used with other thinkers, are not directly provided by many of those thinkers. It is the "method" of starting with observations rather than grand ideas that will also be used in many key places in this text. Let us begin with a basic question:

Do You Want to Be Happy?

Aristotle tells us that *all people desire to be happy*. It's an empirical claim not founded in some grand metaphysics, but through simple observations of real people. Of course, while *physical pleasure*, the satisfaction of our physical needs, is part of happiness, it's not enough. Aristotle suggests that we also need *social (rich and satisfying interactions with others)* and *intellectual (a rich mental life)* fulfillment to be truly happy. We could

---

2   This appears in various forms on internet memes.

add other categories, such as satisfying our *psychological* and *spiritual* needs. The bottom line, however, is that each of us experiences and responds to these various needs in our own way. *For Aristotle, satisfying these needs allows us to be happy.*

Aristotle goes on to define, again through observation, the characteristics of persons who appear likely to achieve happiness. He observes that this correlates to certain *habits of a person's character*, which he calls the *virtues*. This is not a "moral" claim in the Christian sense. *A virtue is simply a habit of character (action, the moral virtues) or of the mind (intellectual virtues) that allows one to live a rich, fulfilling, and happy life.* What do I mean when I say it's not a "Christian" notion of morals? Monotheistic religions often focus more on "good" vs "evil." It's all about the grand, supernatural struggle. Aristotle's claims are humbler and rooted in observation. He's just asking: *What do I see in people who appear to be happy?*

Aristotle argues that these character habits operated on what he calls **the golden mean**. Rather than each virtue (good) being at the opposite extreme of an evil, virtue speaks to a life lived with passion that is "balanced." The balance is observed to take place in at least two ways. First, each virtue is a balance between the extremes of excess and deficiency of that particular virtue. Second, all of the virtues are held in balance with one another.[3]

A common example of such a balance is courage. A person deficient in courage could be called a coward, while a person with courage in excess could be called reckless. Recklessness may look more like courage than cowardice, but it also fails to serve the goals of living a rich and full life. Just as the coward fears doing what is needed to really live, the person who is reckless is likely to engage in destructive behaviors that are similarly averse to long-term happiness.

A second example could be regarding money or goods in which the virtue is generosity. The obvious deficiency here is greed or miserliness. Aristotle would also object, however, to the person who gives all their money or goods to the poor and ends up destitute. There's no clear word in English for this vice but, depending on the context, one might use wastefulness or prodigality. While Aristotle would likely argue that the greater vice is greed,[4] one is also expected to maintain sufficient income to care

---

3   More specifically, while some Christians simply go to the extreme of good vs evil, there is also a strong tradition founded by Aquinas. In this tradition, the "theological" virtues are seen in this way while the moral virtues continue to operate on the Golden Mean. It's worth mentioning that there are also intellectual virtues in Aristotle, but I don't deal with them here.

4   As with courage, one vice is closer to the virtue (recklessness) than the other (cowardice). In the case of generosity, greed is the more distant vice. Similarly, Aristotle would be highly suspicious of wealth amassed by a select few, not just for their sake, but also for the sake of the happiness of others and for the sake of the Athenian democracy. **For Aristotle, the purpose of government is to help create the conditions necessary for human happiness.** Since no society can guarantee the happiness of all its members, one of the best ways to judge a society would be to see whether it primarily serves a few

for one's family and other social obligations. Unless there are unusual and compelling circumstances, one should not give away so much as to become a burden on society.[5]

Notice that Aristotle refers to the virtues as "habits." This is important. Acting in a balanced, virtuous manner depends, at least initially, on cultivating decisions and actions via habit. It's a bit like muscle memory. Of course, this typically begins with the training and discipline we receive as children. But there comes a point where we also make choices that internalize and reinforce the "habits" of moral and intellectual virtues. At first, we do so because we have to. Over time, we do so because of the type person we have become.

Aristotle also makes a distinction between virtue (equity) and the law (rules). For Aristotle, the most important of the moral virtues is *phronesis*. Phronesis is often translated as *prudence*, though some prefer the translation "*moral perception.*"

For Aristotle, the nature of the universe and the rules by which we should live are ultimately generated out of experience. Instead of *deducing* ethics from some grand moral being, Aristotle is *inductive* in his approach, which means that he generalizes rules based on multiple experiences. For example, perhaps I notice that a flame is hot. After several such experiences, I generalize that everything that looks like a flame must be hot. While a good generalization is almost always true there are often exceptions that only become known over time. For example, there are "cool" fireplaces in which the flame is only an image. One could think of this as part of Aristotle's *theory of knowledge*, which is a just a formal way of saying it's about *how we know what we know.*

In terms of ethics and the law, this means that the "rules" (the generalizations of what works based on experience) only go so far. For example, it's a good rule not to kill other people. But what about self-defense? As time goes on, rules get increasingly complicated. For Aristotle, the rules can never be detailed enough to capture the richness of human experience—the world is too complex.

Put another way, the "rules" are here to serve us and we are not put on earth to serve the rules.

This distinction leads Aristotle to the role of a judge. A judge should know the law but should also have embodied the virtues so deeply that he or she "sees," as by a sort of moral perception (*phronesis*), when a particular law needs to be set aside or changed for a particular case. This sort of judgment is what Aristotle refers to

---

members (a ruling class) or the whole. (Of course, for Aristotle, this applied only to male citizens. Women and slaves were, even when born in the society, excluded. There is no reason, however, why his reasoning can't be expanded to include all people.) Democracy is not an end in itself, but a form of society that, when properly pursed, allows for the greatest opportunity for all of its members to achieve happiness. When a few people control too many of the resources of the society, they gain a disproportionate influence on the decision-making of that society. This undermines the equal say of the citizens, so that it may no longer be a true democracy.

5   Note the difference between this and Jesus's command to give all and follow him.

as equity; it is above the letter of the law, but it serves the deeper purpose (human flourishing) of the law.

To understand what Aristotle is getting at, consider a master artist. Perhaps she has spent her life mastering the techniques and knowledge of her craft, learning from the masters who came before. This knowledge is not just intellectual but it is embodied in her very self, including her muscle memory. Then, knowing so well what came before, she breaks with tradition. She sees and creates something new in art. Perhaps she creates not just another beautiful painting, but a whole new way of painting. Or maybe she recognizes the creative approach of a student that, while not following the "assignment," shows extraordinary promise.

This is how Aristotle views the truly virtuous person. A virtuous person knows and almost always follows the rules, but so richly embodies and understands the virtues that they don't follow them mechanically. They recognize when there should be an exception or when a new rule or law needs to be made. This is the definition of *phronesis*.[6]

Aristotle also recognizes that the circumstances of our lives are not entirely under our control. Luck and the actions of others, for example, also affect us. Being raised by parents who love and teach their children well is a huge advantage. Being born into a wealthy family creates more opportunities than being born poor. Yet Aristotle observes that, even in the face of adversity or hardship, some people appear to suffer less. Persons with well-developed virtues deal with adversity better than persons who are "deficient" (lack these habits of character) in the virtues. By contrast, those with underdeveloped virtues, even when they are "lucky," are still less likely to be happy. Consider the many modern-day stories of people who claimed that winning the lottery "ruined" their lives. Moreover, while the expression of these needs is unique for each one of us, true happiness requires each of us to find an appropriate *balance* in our expression and satisfaction over a rich and full life.

Aristotle's concern is not so much for momentary pleasures ("I won the lottery!"), as it is for happiness over the fullness of one's life. For Aristotle, it's not possible to say whether one is truly happy until the end of their life. Aristotle wants to understand and help us to experience the sort of life where we can look back say, "***My life has been rich and full, I can pass on in peace.***"

Aristotle is just our first approach to the question of the meaning of life. The answer to the question in this case is happiness. Others prefer the term "human flourishing." For some, the term "happiness" is too easily reduced to pleasure. Aristotle's understanding, however, is far richer than this. In terms of this study, I want us to remember the following characteristics of Aristotle's approach:

1. Aristotle's approach is empirical. He focuses on how real people live and experience their lives rather than making "deductions" from some grand idea of

---

6 Of course, when most of us make exceptions, it's more about self deception than about true *phronesis*.

the nature of reality. His conclusions are therefore rooted in concrete human experience as opposed to in ideas. We will be using this focus in much of our own analysis.

2. It involves what I call a "***moral psychology***," a description of what it means to be human that allows one to make choices about ethics, character, etc. (Note that if you change the description, you change the conclusions.) Aristotle also has an *inductive theory of knowledge*, which is why *phronesis* is the highest virtue.

3. Aristotle's approach is *teleological*, which means that it focuses on a goal. In this case, Aristotle argues that the goal people seek is happiness (human flourishing).

4. While the goal is happiness, the path to happiness isn't simple, nor is it the same as pleasure. Part of Aristotle's description aims to understand those human characteristics that are likely to lead to happiness and those that are likely to undermine it. Most other thinkers don't provide such detailed descriptions of these sorts of characteristics. Much of Aristotle's analysis can be applied to many other "ends."

5. The virtues make happiness possible, even though it is not guaranteed. There are many factors beyond one's control. Aristotle argues that only the virtuous person has the chance to be truly happy and that the virtuous person is able to handle setbacks with less suffering.

6. One is only truly happy when one can, at the end of life, contemplate a full life that has been richly lived. This includes not just physical pleasure, but also social responsibilities and connections, family, friends, and loved ones. It's a question that can only, in a sense, be answered when facing death. But one can still ask a related question much sooner: *What do I want to be able to say about my life when I reach the point of death?*

One might wonder, given the above, if the real goal is not happiness but perhaps a certain character. This is one of the ambiguities that makes life interesting. It appears, however, to be true. In many traditions, and in psychological research, it appears that "happiness," if pursued directly, is unlikely to be achieved. Instead, ***happiness appears to be a byproduct of pursuing other goals***.

Another Answer: Meaning

Victor Frankl writes, "***it is the very pursuit of happiness that thwarts happiness***" (Smith 2013). For Frankl, what is more central to our existence is a sense of meaning, a sense of being part of or serving more than just ourselves. Without this sense of meaning, we can't really be happy. If so, this is what we should pursue, not happiness directly.

When treating individuals contemplating suicide, Frankl discovered that a key to helping someone move beyond their suicidal thoughts was to help them to see where they could make a positive difference in the world or in another's life, and that perhaps no one else could make such a difference. It wasn't so much an intellectual "should," but an empathetic connection that moved these individuals beyond their own pain to something outside themselves. While we will analyze this is greater detail later, for now consider Frankl's words:

> A man who becomes conscious of the responsibility he bears toward a human being who affectionately waits for him, or to an unfinished work, will never be able to throw away his life. He knows the "why" for his existence, and will be able to bear almost any "how." (Smith 2013)

This doesn't mean that Aristotle and Frankl must be taken to conflict. Modern questions of finding a "meaningful" life depend, to a large degree, on the notions of autonomy and individuality. In our culture, these ideas developed centuries after Aristotle. So, what we call "existential anxiety," the anxiety one feels over the purpose and meaning of one's existence, would not have existed, at least for the vast majority of people, in Aristotle's time. What was left? Happiness.

More importantly, for both Frankl and Aristotle it appears that happiness, while greatly desired, is secondary to other goals. For Frankl, happiness is only possible in the context of a meaningful life, a life that in some ways goes beyond the desires of the self. For Aristotle, virtue alone cannot guarantee happiness, but only a virtuous person can become truly happy. In fact, there are many people who have chosen meaningful, but miserable, existences over "happier," easier ones. Both would argue that those who pursue only individual happiness are unlikely to find it.

For our purposes, we will continue to focus on both happiness and meaning. I suspect that most people want both. It's easier to relate to happiness, but I agree with Frankl. It seems that happiness, taken directly and on its own, seems unlikely. Why? *Because taken on its own, happiness points inward, toward satisfaction just of the self.*[7] Both the emphasis on virtue (character) and meaning turn us outward, towards more than just the self. This, as we will see when we discuss Scarry, helps explain why happiness cannot be achieved directly.

We've taken a foray into two different answers to the meaning of life. We still have much more to understand, in particular about ourselves, if we are to assess the value in their teaching and understand what we may want to learn from others. The remainder of this chapter, and the next, are devoted to better understanding our own

---

7   One example to whom this might not apply would be a sociopath. But then, there are reasons why we consider such a condition to be a mental defect.

nature: how we think, our limits, and, particularly in the next chapter, mechanisms by which we lie to ourselves. The remainder of this chapter focuses on an aspect of the "meaning of life" question. What does it mean to seek meaning?

Are We Meaning-Seeking and Meaning-Generating Creatures?

We approach the world with a variety of basic assumptions. Most of us assume, for example, that we tend to see the world just "as it is." Sometimes we make mistakes, but for the most part our minds are sort of like a mirror or a photograph (perhaps a video camera), taking in the world in all its detail.

Anyone who has studied perception knows that this is simply untrue. For example, we see only a tiny portion of the available electromagnetic spectrum. Even taking what we do see, we don't have anywhere near the memory or mental capacity to process more than a fraction.[8] Plus, there are differences not only in how different people process visual information in their brains, but also in what their eyes (or hearing, etc.) can take in. How do we overcome these limits?

The answer is that we become highly selective in what we perceive/remember. We also "construct" a large part of what we think we "see."

Example One: The Blind Spot

Let's start with a basic example. Each of our eyes has a blind spot where the optic nerve comes into the eye. Because the vision fields from our eyes overlap, the other eye always covers this blind spot. Even when we close one eye, we don't notice any gap in our vision. If we look at a wall, the wall appears to be entirely there.

The reason for this is that our brain fills in the "gap" where the optic nerve comes in. If there is material on both sides of the gap, your brain will fill in the gap with similar-looking material. I'm not sure whether anyone is capable of stopping this process. It is possible to see it, indirectly, in action.

When I was an undergraduate, I had to do an experiment. I was given a sheet of paper with a thick, black line running horizontally across the middle. There was a similar black circle on the page. The line had two "gaps" in it, where the page was white. Both gaps were equal distance from the center of the line.

I was told to cover one eye and to position the open eye directly over the dot. I was then told to move my head slowly closer and farther from the dot. *If the diagram was*

---

8 Person's with eidetic (photographic) memories are able to absorb more than the rest of us, but it's a myth that they absorb everything.

done correctly and your eyes were at the correct distance from the point on the paper, the white "gap" on one side of the line ended up entirely in the blind spot of that eye. At that point, you would suddenly see a solid line in place of the gap. The gap would disappear.

It worked. While I knew that there was still a gap in the line, at that point all I could see was a solid line.

There are a variety of studies demonstrating this phenomenon. For some samples of ways one can demonstrate this at home, visit:

https://faculty.washington.edu/chudler/chvision.html

There are also multiple studies and examples illustrating how we often see what we are "looking for" or expecting to see, and not what is actually there. For some fun experiments along those lines, consider watching some of following YouTube videos:

http://www.theinvisiblegorilla.com/videos.html

Other experiments demonstrate how people see and process perceptual information differently. This goes far beyond issues like color blindness and applies to all the senses. To offer some sports examples, part of what makes many running backs great is their ability to "see" more with their peripheral vision than most people. This allows them to see and avoid tackles further in advance than other running backs. The same is true of certain basketball stars. NBA star Steve Curry, for example, appears to "see" differently than the rest of us.[9]

This is only the beginning of the complexity of how our eyes and brain construct what we see. Illusionists study how different parts of our perception and our brains work, which is how many of their illusions work. For example, if an illusionist asked you for a number between one and ten, they have most likely "primed" you with various auditory and visual cues that make it almost automatic for you to select a particular number. In another example, one can construct two wheels that spin in opposite directions. Depending upon the visual clues built into those wheels, if you look directly at one the other will appear to be spinning in the SAME direction. If you shift your gaze to the other, both will shift to the other direction. This is based on knowledge of how the peripheral vision areas of the eyes process information differently (and in more limited ways) than the central area of the eyes.

9 http://nymag.com/scienceofus/2016/06/steph-curry-perception-performance.html?mid=facebook_nymag

Example Two: Corpus Callosum

The corpus callosum is a bundle of fibers connecting the two hemispheres of the brain. While there are some secondary pathways, almost all of the direct communication between the two halves of the brain takes place through the corpus callosum. When it is cut, interesting things happen.

Why would it be cut? There are a number of reasons the corpus callosum would be cut, the most common of which appears to be either a head injury or medical treatment for certain seizures. For example, there are people who experience extreme seizures that develop by "jumping" through the corpus callosum from hemisphere to hemisphere, gaining strength with each passage. If they cannot be controlled by other means, cutting the corpus callosum can stop the seizures and allow one to live a relatively normal life.

For our purposes, what is of interest is the fact that the two hemispheres of the brain perform different functions. In this case, since we are focusing on language, it is important to recognize that, for most people, language is controlled by the left hemisphere of the brain.[10] Similarly, each hemisphere tends to control the opposite side of the body. This is why when a person loses the ability to speak and has flaccid muscles on the right side of their face or other right-side impairments, we know that they probably had a stroke in the left hemisphere of their brain.

People who have had their corpus callosum cut usually operate normally, but oddities can be observed, even enhanced, through special experiments. For example, we can construct ways to communicate with just one side of the brain.

In the case of the eyes, it's not quite as simple as covering up one eye or the other, since different parts of each eye are controlled by each hemisphere. While each hemisphere controls parts of each eye, the parts they control are unique. One can create a lens that only allows information to be seen by one side of the brain when it is worn.

In this case, experimenters blocked out the parts of vision that went to the left side of the brain. Then, they held up instructions. For example, they might ask the subject to "get up and walk around." Though only seen by the right hemisphere, the subject was able to follow the instructions.

The experimenters then asked the subject, *"Why are you walking around?"*

This is where it gets interesting.

---

10   Note the conditional, "for most people." The more one works in medicine or psychology, the more one realizes that there are few rules that apply to all people. For example, I've known two patients whose "organs" were "backwards" in their bodies. The heart, for example, was on the right. I've had a student with three kidneys. I am missing two ribs. Most people have at least minor anatomical anomalies but just don't know it.

Remember that only the right side of the brain knows the real reason. Even though both sides of the brain hear the question, only the left side has the capacity to answer but it doesn't know why.

Often, *the subject will make up a reason* such as, "Oh, I'm thirsty, I'm going to get some water." The strange thing is that they will then be convinced that this was, in fact, the reason they got up in the first place. In reality, it's just something they made up on the spot.

Meaning-Seeking and Meaning-Generating Creatures

These are just two examples but they help us to begin to understand that *to be human is to be a meaning-seeking and meaning-generating creature*.

Why?

We can take in only a tiny part of what goes on in the world around us. Since we can only process a small amount of that data, it helps to have ways to organize it so as to figure out what's important to notice, or remember. Important in what way? If Aristotle is correct, this helps us to flourish, survive, and be happy.

Because we have only limited access to the world around us, we tend to organize the information we have in ways that make sense to us. These are ways in which we are taught and that we perceive to be useful. We don't have total "control" of what we see, but we have significant influence over what we notice.

We also tend to "construct" our world in ways that both reflect our upbringing and our personalities.

As one's vision diminishes with age (assuming that even glasses no longer completely correct it), some of these issues become easier to see. Have you ever seen a billboard and, while not looking all that closely, been entirely convinced of what it said?

Later, when you see it again, you look closer. It turns out to be completely different than your memory. It's not that they changed the billboard, it's that your brain and memory constructed it incorrectly based on limited cues. This sort of thing happens to us all. Most of us, however, just "forget" about these sorts of things when they happen in our lives and don't reflect on what they might mean.

Fortunately, there is the possibility of growth, of "correcting" one's course.

Example Three: Not Everyone Is Like Me

We all know, in a sense, that this is true but we often don't fully realize it. Most of us tend to construct our understanding of the world in ways that match up to a combination of our upbringing and personality. Focusing here on the personality side, it has profound implications.

For example, consider the Myers-Briggs personality type inventory or the related Keirsey Temperament Sorter. The Myers-Briggs sorts people out according to four temperaments or types. A person can be at various levels between the two poles of each measure. The four poles are:

1. Introvert–Extrovert
2. Intuitive–Sensate
3. Feeling–Thinking
4. Perceiving–Judging

One must be careful to understand the technical meaning of each of these terms as it's not always the same as the common meaning. For example, introversion-extroversion has little to do with shyness, but more to do with whether and to what degree one "recharges" one's emotional batteries. Introverts need time alone (or with one or two close friends) to recharge while extroverts get energy from being in groups.

Here, I want to focus on feeling and thinking.

For this test, this category does NOT measure one's capacity to think or feel. I have a PhD in philosophy, yet I am more a "feeler" than a "thinker." Instead, it measures a particular aspect of how we make decisions.

Assume that one is a teacher or a parent. When faced with an ethical or practical decision of what to do for a student or child, *a strong "feeler" would focus mainly on what is best for the child in a given situation.*

A strong "thinker," on the other hand, *would likely focus on the impact of that decision on all other children.* What if, for example, we allowed all kids to get away with a particular poor behavior without punishment? And what would it mean for developing character? For society?

A "feeler" focuses more on individual circumstances, while a "thinker" focuses on the general issues of justice and fairness.

Unless they understand these differences, *persons who rate high on the feeling or thinking scale when paired with the opposite may have great difficulty understanding one another.* If one parent is a "thinker," they may think their "feeler" partner, "just doesn't get it." With all the fuzzy ethics, our kid will grow up without character. There are times in which you need tough love. On the other hand, from the perspective of the feeler, the thinker may just appear to be "a cold-hearted b ..."

In reality, we need both "thinkers" and "feelers." Justice and fairness are equally important. To treat one child differently than another invites jealously and disrespect for law and the rules. At the same time, no two people are the same.

People are complex. People are different. This is an important point to remember. Understanding this will also be essential to helping one get along with other people. I'd also like to note, just for the future, the following:

Everything Interesting about Being Human Happens in the Grey between Extremes

What I mean by this is that life doesn't fit into black and white categories. People aren't just rules. We are all different and complex. Aristotle recognizes this in the role of judges in the law. He also acknowledges this when he writes, speaking of ethics, that it is irrational to expect precision for which the subject matter does not allow. Ethics is like that. Both "thinkers" and "feelers" have something valid to contribute.

For example, strong "thinkers," unless they have reflected on the issue, tend to confuse "justice" with treating all people the same, or "equally." Since people are different, justice may not be the same as "equality," in the sense of treating all persons the same.

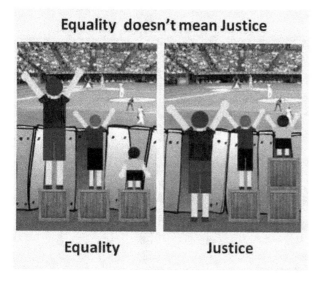

Equality doesn't mean Justice

Equality   **Justice**

FIGURE 1.1

As the meme suggests, if we slavishly follow rules for the sake of "justice," we, in fact, do them an injustice. At the same time, how we treat differences shouldn't just be arbitrary; developing character is also important. In this case, there is a clear reason for treating people "unequally."

My folks figured this out early in my childhood. If there is one thing I hated, it was having my dad lecture me. I'd much rather have a spanking and get it over with. My older brother, on the other hand, didn't react to lectures at all. As my mother would put it, it rolled off him "like water off a duck's back." Lectures were very effective for punishing me, but utterly ineffective for my brother. He got the spankings. I got the lectures.

We were, and still are, very different people. But we both turned out alright.

If we can become more humble in our assumptions and perceptions of the world, we gain the possibility of a richer understanding of both others and ourselves.

This is why critical thinking is important to coming to know oneself.

Figure Credits

Fig. 1.1: Source: https://www.wired.com/2016/09/birth-weird-life-afterlife-internet-meme/.

CHAPTER TWO

Self-Deception

DETECTING WHEN ONE IS LYING TO ONESELF

In the books, movies, and stories we refer to in this text, second only to the two primary themes of this book, you will be asked to notice **when and how persons lie, not just to others, but to themselves.** *This is why the third primary theme deals with self-honesty. The ultimate goal, of course, is not just to perceive when others are lying to themselves (a useful skill), but when we are lying to ourselves. Why? In part, because it is nearly impossible to be honest with another if one is not honest with oneself. Moreover,* **it is almost impossible to be happy, or even to know what it takes to be happy, if one is not honest with oneself.** For this reason, **the theme of self-honesty is as important as the first two.**

This is not to say that one can ever be perfectly self-honest. Again, reality is too complex for a mere human mind to grasp. Just as we can only understand aspects of the world in part, so too can we never fully understand ourselves. There are levels of understanding, however, and one can always improve. By analogy, that's part of what I love about dancing. It's not about being the best dancer, it's about the joy of the activity and the fact that one always has room to grow. **The activity can be its own reward.**

The first challenge with self-honesty, on the other hand, is overcoming one's initial resistance. *Most of us are not prepared to deal with the differences between how we see ourselves and who we really are.* This is part of the appeal of Christianity. We all know, deep in our hearts, this gap exists. We attempt to push it away. Christianity acknowledges the gap—it acknowledges our weaknesses, failings, inadequacies—and then tells us that we are accepted and loved despite it. For many, this notion of "redemption" is incredibly life-giving. It's the idea of "grace," or unconditional love, even if we don't deserve it. It is love as a gift.

"Grace" appears, in some form, in every major religion. There is something incredibly important about this gift. Consider the example of a life partner. If you marry wisely, you will be with a partner who, while encouraging you to grow and be self-honest, also accepts and loves you despite your flaws.

Such love is incredibly freeing. My best relationships make me want to be a better person, not because I'm judged, but because I'm loved. My best friends are those I can talk to and confess to when I feel I have done something "morally" wrong. *I can talk with these friends about what I find deeply embarrassing.*

Another theme that arises in every major religion is that of spiritual pride. **Spiritual pride**, we are often told, is perhaps the greatest barrier to spiritual growth. This is not "pride" in the sense of self-respect or honest pleasure in an accomplishment. This is "false" pride, based on some degree on a form of self-deception. It can even mask itself as humility. This will show up when we read C.S. Lewis and *Siddhartha*. Becoming *honestly* humble in the face of one's pride is key to self-awareness and growth.

To be clear, one doesn't have to be "religious" to learn from these insights. Recall Aristotle's notion of starting with observable human experience. We will develop a definition of spirituality that focuses on experiences we all share. Whether those experiences take one towards a particular religion, or somewhere else, is a question we each must discern for ourselves. Either way, we can view religious language as another way of talking about those basic human experiences.

While the exact origin is unknown, we know that one of the oldest Greek aphorisms, supposedly spoken by the Oracle at Delphi (Ancient Greece's most holy shrine), is the command to ***Know Thyself***. Again, if one lies to oneself, the very basis for true self-awareness is lost. If Aristotle is right, only a person who understands himself or herself, who has both schooled their passions and their mind, can truly be happy. "Schooling one's passions" is an odd phrase. What is mean by it is not that I make choices because I "should." Rather, it means that, for the most part, the "good" choice actually ends up giving me pleasure. It takes time, and mistakes, to reach that point. If I lack the "habit" of doing things for the greater (and long-term) good, I become a slave to my passions. In following those passions, I may achieve momentary satisfaction, but I damage the long-term happiness of myself and others.

For example, if I sleep with my neighbor's spouse, then I betray their relationship. I also run the risk of retaliation by the injured spouse. Perhaps I get great pleasure from sleeping in instead of going to work. If I end up penniless and on the street, however, that pleasure will be short lived. ***One becomes a slave to one's passions when one seeks immediate gratification, even when it will cause great long-term harm.***

Ever hear the term "retail therapy?"

Similarly, the more well-developed the intellectual virtues, the better one will see the whole and make choices that serve one's long-term good, as well as that of others. The two are linked. Often, when we want to follow our passions without regard for others, ***we use our intellectual abilities to forge false justifications for why it is the right thing to do. We often convince ourselves that a lie is the truth.*** If our habits and passions have been "schooled" so that we usually desire what is good, it is far easier to avoid these sorts of self-deceptions.

For this reason, this chapter is devoted to naming and recognizing some of the ways in which we lie to ourselves. We can't achieve perfection, but we can become more honest.

We begin with the overarching category I will be using for these sorts of self-deceptions. I call them **self-serving rationalities**.

Pretexts and Self-Serving Rationalities

For our purposes,

> A *pretext* is a truth, or a half truth, designed to hide a bigger lie.

> A *self-serving rationality* is a rational argument for which the real purpose is not the reason being argued.

Usually, the real purpose has something to do with the perceived self-interest of the one(s) proposing the argument.

Sometimes we treat something as a "neutral" truth (i.e., this is just how the world works and we can't do it any other way), when, in fact, it is merely a "useful" intellectual construct.

Other times, we don't just present these constructs as neutral, we present them *as if* they are for the sake of helping others, convincing ourselves that we are helping people even when we are really doing them harm.

Most self-serving rationalities are also pretexts, which is why I group the two together.

It's important to note the condition "perceived" self-interest. Often, we act against our interests. We just don't see it. *There are times we so strongly identify with a group* (say, liberal or conservative, Christian or Muslim) *that we uncritically assume that the agenda of that group is in our best interest. There are warning signs to watch for which can help one spot this sort of deception (or self-deception).*

The remainder of this chapter builds on these ideas in three ways. First, we talk more about the specifics and dynamics of self-identity. Second, we list and explain a series of psychological mechanisms that make it easier for us to lie to ourselves. Finally, we name some of the warning signs that can help one realize that one might be engaged in such a practice.

Throughout the text, there are also a number of "logical fallacies" highlighted in bold. For those who don't already understand logical fallacies, there is a partial list at the end of this chapter. The value of knowing these fallacies is, again, not just that it can help us to see problems in the reasoning of others, but that it can help us to clarify such reasoning in ourselves.

Not every logical fallacy is the result of some deep inner deception. It may be an attempt to manipulate someone else. It may just be sloppy thinking. Here's a way to tell the difference. If, once the fallacy is pointed out, it makes no difference to one's beliefs, there is probably something else going on. Often, we find ourselves selectively "using" reason to justify what we want. The loss of one set of reasons then just causes us to search for another (classic to **self-serving rationalities**).

Let's return to the issue of why is it so hard, at least initially, to face the "truth" about ourselves. In part, it has to do with whatever becomes our **self-identity**. Something that challenges my sense of self identity appears to challenge the very essence of who I am. We see this all the time in politics when "identity politics" trump "issues." But this doesn't just occur in politics. **By becoming aware of these issues, we also realize that** *we can make choices about and change our self-identity.*

Self-Identity and Identity Politics

Consciously or unconsciously, we all develop a sense of self-identity. In simple terms, it's who we think we are and the groups, activities, or ideals we most value. The term "politics" here includes, but is broader than, societal "politics." Politics has to do with functioning as a group, any group. Part of the reason many teenagers rebel is because they have to "separate" from their parents in order to find, or create, an identity of their own. At the same time, we don't do so in vacuum. We develop that self-identity by connecting with other groups, either wholeheartedly or in part. For many, even being a "rebel" has a distinct subculture for which a certain amount of conformity is required.

What is the value of such bonding? When does it start?

One of our first experiences with self-identity occurs with the development of gender identity, which is usually established by age two. Interestingly, the fact that women are still the primary caretakers in our society may account for part, though not all, of the differences between boys and girls. As Nancy Chodorow argues, since both boys and girls usually start off with their mother as their primary caregiver, boys have to "separate" from mom in order to find male role models. Young girls, on the other hand, may bond more deeply with their primary caregiver, since that is their gender role model. This might explain, *in part*, the stronger development of notions of autonomy in young boys (autonomy, separation) and the greater emphasis on relationship (connection, bonding) in young girls (Gilligan 1993, 7–10).

Identifying with and joining groups is a natural part of human development. Why do we join certain clubs or social organizations in college? It helps us make friends, it's fun, it looks good on our resumes for future jobs, etc. Additionally, social isolation is, for most, a painful experience.

When we are young, we often "try on" a variety of identities before forging a unique blend of these into an identity of our own. One problem is when the process gets "stuck." In other words, we may end up identifying with a particular group, religion, or political persuasion early in life, and that can become so important to our self-identity that we are no longer open to growth and change. In that situation, we may use our reason not to honestly figure out the greater good, but to "defend" that all-important sense of self-identity. From the outside, others may see our reasons as foolish, but the reasons aren't really for the sake of others. These reasons are for our own sake and the sake of our group.

There is great risk in defying one's perceived group. If I identify with a particular group, or subgroup, and I go against them, I may feel lost and I may not know who I am for a while. I may, deep down, fear becoming an outcast. Unless I can develop a new and richer sense of self-identity, I may reject even that which is in my real self-interest. This experience of loss has particular power in grief situations. This will be referred to later as the loss of one's "assumptive world." I'll offer two simple examples, followed by a more complex example from Denmark.

Sarah[1]

I had an older student in my class a few years ago. She was a delightful person and a strong Christian. As we began to talk about Christianity, however, she became very anxious. She even told me that she was afraid I would say something that would "take away her Christianity," by which she meant undermine her faith.

It's worth noting that her self-honesty about her "fear" meant that she wasn't closed off and that she was open to change. She also showed real courage in acknowledging and staying with that fear.

For my part, I reassured her that my goal was not to take away her spiritual beliefs. It was only to help her become more thoughtful and self-critical in those beliefs. How she ended up using those skills was up to her.

After the key classes devoted to the topic were over she came and thanked me. She told me that she was relieved! She felt that her faith, while changed, was deeper and richer than before. In her mind, the "critique" had enriched her faith rather than undermined it. It opened her up to other possibilities in her faith.

By facing her fear she transcended it. She ended up with a richer faith and self-identity.

Polly

Polly was in stark contrast to Sarah, although she was also a strong Christian. When we got to the point in class where we were "brainstorming" about the nature of faith,

---

1   As usual, not their real names.

all she could say was "Jesus Christ." I asked her if she would say something else about faith. What did faith do for her? What value did it hold? What might be some of its more general characteristics? The exercise was to put lots of ideas up on the board and to explore their connection, not to a particular religion but to how we experience them. She refused. She just kept repeating "Jesus Christ."

The exercise was too threatening. She dropped the class rather than consider possibilities outside of her comfort zone.

This happens on occasion but, fortunately, it's rare.

It takes time to develop a rich sense of self-identity and there are risks when one doesn't have a well-developed sense of self-identity. For one thing, it's hard to be happy. For another, it can make one susceptible to radical senses of self-identity.

Example: Denmark's Response to Radicalized Outcasts

During the battle with ISIS, many Western nations became concerned with immigrants and with people born into their own society who had been "radicalized" via internet propaganda. What causes some people to be susceptible to such radicalization?

There is no single reason but there are common elements between many of the cases. Most, if not all, feel left out and unwelcome. This may be due to mental illness, skin color, language, economic disparity, or desperation. It may also be due to family members who have died at the hands of perceived Western actions. The most common thread, however, appears to be that these people feel excluded in some way. This is to say that *they don't identify with the society in which they live*.

The result is that *these individuals cast around for some other sense of self-identity or purpose. The desire to know who we are and to have a sense of purpose is fundamental to us as meaning seeking and generating creatures*. This doesn't refer exclusively to a group like ISIS. It could also be a home-grown radical group like the KKK or even a very strong affiliation to a particular church. It could still end up a positive affiliation.

A city in Denmark recognized this dynamic and attempted a novel approach to preventing such radicalization. Instead of focusing purely on police action, which tends to confirm feelings of discrimination and anger (thus reinforcing radicalized self-identity), they reached out to individuals who appeared to be at risk for "radicalization." For example, they made it clear that instead of jailing them for travelling to Syria, they would welcome them home, help them get back to school or find work, find them a mentor or psychiatric help, etc.[2]

---

2 http://www.npr.org/sections/health-shots/2016/07/15/485900076/how-a-danish-town-helped-young-muslims-turn-away-from-isis?utm_source=facebook.com&utm_medium=social&utm_campaign=npr&utm_term=nprnews&utm_content=20160715

The program usually began with an invitation to coffee with a police officer in the program. As expected, it had a slow start. Once a few "at-risk" people came in and told others that it was safe, more and more got involved. People who had travelled to Syria to fight with ISIS and become disillusioned, but who felt trapped by the fear they would be prosecuted, started coming home. Other's planning to travel to places like Syria changed their minds.

The "mentor" was key, not just to the returning fighters, but to those who hadn't yet gone. It was a bit like a big brother program. The mentor would meet and talk with the young person. In one case, they met at coffee shop after coffee shop. Many of these were filled with light-skinned Danes, so it was uncomfortable at first for the young man with darker skin. After a while his attitude changed. While there were still instances of discrimination, he no longer attributed it to the society as a whole, but to individuals in the society. He eventually came to identify himself as "Danish" rather than as an outsider.[3]

The program has been a great success, but with three caveats. Firstly, it doesn't expect to prevent every at-risk person from being radicalized. In the article referenced, there were still people in their town who eventually went to Syria, just far less than from similar towns in the same time period. Still, to prevent a significant number of people from becoming "radicals" and instead help them to become happy, productive members of society is a phenomenal achievement. In fact, I worry now that it has made international news that ISIS will target that town in order to shut down the program. Secondly, Denmark has a far more developed social services network to fall back on than, say, the United States. This makes it easier to implement such a program. Thirdly, in the case of those who still become radicalized, the program made it easier to track them.

The bottom line is this: *Some individuals in Denmark realized that while some police action is still necessary, police action alone won't stop the radicalization of terrorists. It may, in fact, even reinforce it. Instead, they seek to win the hearts and minds of their citizens who might become radicalized by offering them alternative experiences, which lead to the development of a completely different sort of self-identity.*

They helped their citizens get "unstuck" from what was becoming a destructive self-identity, allowing them to choose another.

---

3 The story about the coffee shops comes from the radio version of the story; the written article above is abridged.

We all have this capacity.

EXERCISE: IDENTITY POLITICS

I mentioned that part of the problem with this process is that we sometimes get so bonded with a particular community that we are no longer open to growth and change. This is an exercise to help one see if that is the case. *Complete each step before reading about the next.*

First:

Write down those "groups" to which you feel the strongest affiliation. This could be anything from a fraternity to a political party. It could even be to a particular person.

Write down what you like about each of these groups and how they enrich or benefit your life.

Write what you contribute to them.

Second:

Write down what would be, where possible, the natural "opposing" group, party, or person. By the "natural" opposite, I don't mean another extreme. For example, if one identifies oneself as a political conservative, one might pick political liberals, not extremist groups like ISIS.

Write down your primary criticism of each of these groups or persons.

Third:

Under the groups you support and feel part of, write down two or three strong criticisms of those people/groups.

Under the groups that you disagree with, write down two or three strongly positive things you believe about those people/groups.

Your compliments and criticisms need to be significant and sincere. For example, unless the focus on the group is on fashion, criticizing the dress of the members is trivial.

Assessment:

If this is an easy exercise, it means that you are able to move between groups and see the strengths and weaknesses of each. It means that you are probably able to change and grow your self-identity as situations change and as you learn more about life.

If this is difficult for you, it may mean that you are so strongly bonded that you have difficulty seeing another side. It could indicate a propensity to get "stuck" in a particular self-identity.

Psychological Mechanisms of Self-Deception

Confirmation Bias

The need for thoughtful, careful, and empirical observation.

Intellectual beliefs, while often true, need to be "tested" by actual experience, preferably over multiple and diverse groups of people. For example, it's a common belief that wearing one's helmet saves health care dollars because one is more likely to survive; however, this may not be borne out of facts. *The only way to determine which of these beliefs is true is through examining the data in an empirical study.* Most studies, however, don't look at the data in these terms. **We tend to look at data or experience in ways that confirm what we already believe to be true.** This is called **confirmation bias**. Unless one is looking specifically for this bias it can be difficult to sift through the studies that appear to support the commonly held belief.

Consider the following scenario: People in motorcycle accidents tend to fall into three groups in terms of their injuries. Group A does fairly well with minimal interventions and minimal health care costs. Group C dies quickly, so medical costs are also limited. Group B, those that are severely brain injured and take significant or lifelong additional support, really drive up the bill. Since wearing a helmet means that one is more likely to survive and do well, how does this relate to medical costs?

Assume this is a graphic description of the breakup of riders not wearing helmets:

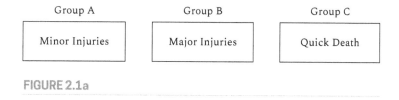

FIGURE 2.1a

The high-cost group is group B. So that's the group, from the standpoint of cost, one would want to reduce (preferably by moving them to group A).

What if once people start wearing helmets approximately the same number of people move from group B to group A and from group C to group B? In that case, group C would shrink, group A would expand, and group B would remain about the same. While funeral costs would go down, the effect on medical costs wouldn't be all that significant. This is still a good result, but it doesn't result in health care savings.

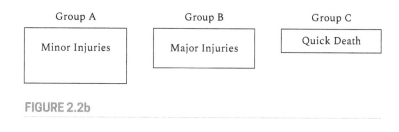

FIGURE 2.2b

It's an interesting argument, but is it true? Again, *the only way to determine which of these beliefs is true is through examining the data in an empirical study.* Most studies, however, don't look at the data in these terms. **We tend to look at data or experience in ways that confirm what we already believe to be true.**

This is not to claim that motorcycle helmets might not still save health care dollars if group B shrinks. That can only be determined, however, by looking at real data and cases. This can get even more complicated. For example, people who have been drinking are less likely to wear seatbelts. If the same is true for motorcycle helmets, then it might be drinking that is the primary culprit of increased accidents and injury and not the lack of a helmet. Someone who already believes that wearing a helmet reduces health care costs is less likely to explore the data to test these sorts of alternate explanations.

This aside on motorcycle helmets is not to prove the issue of whether wearing helmets saves health care dollars, but to illustrate the need to be thoughtful and self-aware of our assumptions.[4] It shows up in many places in our lives, particularly in politics.

For example, does increasing the minimum wage cost jobs, or does it generate more jobs because people have more money to spend? Does trickle-down economics work, or do the wealthy mostly keep the extra money?[5] There's some evidence on both sides of each of these two issues, though I believe that the best research suggests one side is significantly more true than the other. In each of these examples, only a decent understanding of both the data AND the biases of some of the researches will enable one to discover what the answer might be.

Some confirmation bias is simply due to the fact that we haven't asked the right questions. Other biases have to do with strong beliefs. For example, consider medical and recreational marijuana. The reasons against the medical use of marijuana should be no different than any other drug. Determining whether and how it should be used should be based on an analysis of risks versus benefits.

Most medicines have negative side effects. We tolerate the side effects for the sake of the benefit. For example, I may need a life-saving drug now, but in 20 years will develop cancer due to the drug. Since I would be dead now without the drug, clearly, the benefit outweighs the risk

Whether legalizing marijuana for medical purposes "opens a floodgate" to other uses depends not on medical criteria, but on how well the laws are crafted to regulate and enforce such usage. The fact that it has been restricted for so long, despite

---

4   For an example of someone sensitive to the complexity of this particular issue, consider https://www.sciencebasedmedicine.org/the-cost-of-repealing-mandatory-motorcycle-helmet-laws/.

5   For example, in 2016, companies were holding 25 trillion dollars in overseas accounts rather than reinvesting. When this happens, none of that money can "trickle down." http://www.businessinsider.com/us-companies-hoarding-25-trillion-of-cash-overseas-2016–9

obvious medical benefits to particular classes of patients, has more to do with bias than with medical fact. One can see this even more clearly with those who dismiss all medical value.

In recreational use, since it's not being used to treat a specific condition, there is no specific medical "benefit" to weigh against potential harms. A marijuana cigarette, for example, has more carcinogens than tobacco. There are also questions about impairment and driving. The question of recreational use is less obvious.

Knowing people on both sides of this debate, I see many look only to data that confirms their own point of view, dismissing data supporting the other side. This is basic confirmation bias. But there's a risk. If we restrict marijuana unnecessarily, we are impinging on people's freedom. If it does increase, for example, auto fatalities, we sacrifice lives. It's important to limit our bias and try to understand the true story.

Confirmation bias is a natural human reaction*. It is it not all bad. To an important degree, it acts as a sort of "shorthand," allowing us to move on to other issues. If we are going to address the deeper questions raised around what facing death teaches us about living, we will need to be more self-aware.*

Fundamental Attribution Error

Too often we judge others by their worst examples, while judging ourselves by our best intentions.

President George W. Bush
Dallas Police Memorial Service, 2016

The fundamental attribution error speaks to a basic way in which we tend to misjudge others. Basically, it means that we are far more forgiving of those whom we feel are part of our group, while far less forgiving of those we perceive as "different" than ourselves. It has to do with whether we "attribute" the motives behind the action to a person's basic character (internal to who they are) or to a mistake or moment of weakness (external to who they are, more about the situation). More specifically, it works like this:

We tend to shift the reasons for which we attribute behavior based on our sense of affiliation with the person or persons.

External: If a person does something bad but it is someone we like, agree with, or is part of our "group," then that is just a "mistake," an aberration.

Internal: If a person does something bad and is part of a group we oppose or dislike, we attribute the bad behavior to their "character."

This happens most often around things we passionately identify with (**identity politics**). For example, a comparative religion professor at Vanderbilt Divinity School would never allow his students to write a paper comparing his or her own religion to another. Why? The fundamental attribution error. For example, if I'm a Christian, then all the bad things that Christians do will likely be attributed to distortions in their understanding of religion, momentary weakness, responding to the persecution of others, etc. As the bumper sticker goes, "Christians aren't perfect, just forgiven." The problems are "external" to who they are and to the religion. On the other hand, if I'm looking at another religion, for example, Islam, my tendency will be to attribute the bad things that they do to the "internal" nature of the religion, not to the actions of people who distort, misunderstand, or make mistakes. One can find both beautiful and horrific sentiments expressed in the scriptures of both traditions, and one can find both deeply loving acts and atrocities committed by members of both faiths. Our tendency is to cherry pick those facts that fit into our point of view, a lot like confirmation bias.

Interestingly, we are likely to be outraged when we feel that someone else is distorting or taking our statements, actions, or scriptures out of context. We don't feel that it's at all problematic when we pick and choose from someone else's scriptures to confirm our beliefs about them. This is because we assume our biases to be "true."

This is why the Vanderbilt professor refused to allow those sorts of comparison papers. Too many of them would simply reaffirm the writer's biases.

The same is often true in politics. If someone of my party does something immoral, I'm far more likely to forgive, assuming it's just a moment of weakness based on some sort of (external) circumstance. If someone from the other party acts in a similar matter, well, it just goes to show that they are fundamentally corrupt.[6] It's part of their character (internal).

Of course, some may be fundamentally corrupt, but the issue is looking at the whole of the situation with balance and fairness. If we are aware of this bias, we are more likely to be able to moderate it and see the more of the truth.

---

6   There's another twist that has recently shown up in the literature. We all know that we tend to be far more critical of other's arguments than of our own. There is a study showing that, when people are fooled into believing that their own argument (given earlier in a different context) is not their own, but someone else's, they are 50 percent more likely to reject the argument: http://www.npr.org/sections/13.7/2016/08/01/488228453/the-selective-laziness-of-human-reasoning?utm_source=facebook.com&utm_medium=social&utm_campaign=npr&utm_term=nprnews&utm_content=20160801. Accessed on August 2, 2016.

Self-Fulfilling Prophesies

Self-fulfilling prophesies also relate to confirmation bias, in that *we act or make choices in ways that tend to bring about the situation we expect, particularly when it might not have occurred otherwise.*

This can become quite complicated, but an easy example is to accuse a person of being angry and/or defensive. You may not be angry when I start accusing you but, after a while, I am likely to make your angry. The result? Even though you weren't angry when I first accused you, you are now. I feel as though I have been proven right.[7]

In a second example, assume you are a Roman general for North Africa. You are loyal to the emperor; however, you are told that the emperor has become suspicious that you are planning a rebellion. You could return home and plead your case. If you do, you might be executed. To survive, you decide to stay in the province and start a rebellion.

Perhaps a more common example is one that many people experience in relationships. Assume that I am in a romantic relationship, but insecure about my partner's love for me. I worry that she is planning to break up with me. Instead of enjoying the relationship and my partner, I act out my insecurity. After a while, she becomes sufficiently alienated by my actions and insecurities that she does break up with me. My actions brought about the very circumstance I feared.

Psychological Repression

Psychological repression is one of the prime ways in which we lie to ourselves. In a sense, we "push down" those parts of ourselves about which we feel uncomfortable or pretend they don't exist.

Earlier, we noted the example of a person who, rather than facing their fear of death, used their belief in an afterlife to push away (hide from) that fear. *Some of the warning signs of repression are that a person is unable to accept or consider other points of view, so they become almost obsessively focused on a particular issue, irrationally angry, highly judgmental, and, of course, use logical fallacies to justify their position.*

---

7   For a much more complicated and life-altering example, see my article, "'Difficult' Patients, Over Medication, and Dangerous Group Decisional Dynamics," *The Journal of Clinical Ethics* 20, no. 1 (Spring 2009): 1–11.

Example: Gay Marriage and the Sanctity of Marriage

There are many people of faith who feel that a homosexual lifestyle is against their beliefs. Yet, just as with divorce, many are willing to accept the differences of others. Even if one believes that a gay lifestyle is "sinful," so long as it's not directly harming someone else, one can accept that it's an issue to be worked out between the persons engaged in the lifestyle and God. Pope Francis, from a church which has long opposed gay lifestyles, said that many Christians (Catholic and other) owe gays an apology for their mistreatment. It is possible to disagree with a lifestyle and still treat people with dignity and respect.

Once one comes to understand psychological repression, however, one is not surprised by the fact that many of the politicians and political leaders who most vocally opposed gay marriage have been caught in gay activities. For these people, their reaction is likely due to repression. They work so hard to "reject" those feelings and impulses in themselves that they feel they must overtly judge others who accept those feelings. The same appears to be true of many of the "sanctity of marriage" proponents who end up having multiple affairs.

How do people justify themselves when they act against what they claim is a core belief? I saw one answer when I volunteered for an outreach ministry for street kids in Seattle. Many of the "Johns" (men who picked up the girls engaged in prostitution) went to church on Sunday and considered themselves good Christians. When they were caught, they often blamed the girls. They would say it was her fault for being out there and tempting them. The girls led them astray by playing on their weaknesses.

Of course, these girls weren't coming to these men's homes or neighborhoods. Most of the girls were victims of abusive homes, pimps, and sex traffickers. At least with the population we served, they were mostly underage and on the street corners in nonresidential areas. *These men were going out of their way to find them. Still, it was the girls' fault.*

Example: Refusal to Listen

Have you ever been talking with a friend or family member who always has to be right? You raise an issue, and while what they are saying may be "true," in the sense that it is factually accurate, your feeling is that they just aren't hearing what you're trying to say?

The more you try to explain, the more it feels like some sort of strange argument where you are both talking past each other.

In my experience, one either has to walk away or try to change the dynamic. There's no "perfect" way to describe what is going on. Instead, I try to be honest, relatively neutral, and hope for the other person's good will. I might say something like:

"What you are saying is true, but I don't feel as though you are fully hearing what I'm trying to say."

If someone says this to me, my response is to stop my "thinking" on the path it has been going, start to review what was said, and to ask, *"I'm sorry, can you tell me more of what you mean?"* I try to become more receptive.

It may turn out that I've really missed something. It may turn out that I did hear them, but that the person just didn't feel heard. *Often, I realize it's because I was listening with my mind when the person needed me to listen with my heart.* Either way, it's a great strategy to nurture understanding and the relationship.

Not everyone will take this approach.

I have a friend who, in the past few years, has started to go on the attack whenever something comes up that makes him uncomfortable. Recently, when I told him that I didn't feel heard, he immediately argued that I was wrong, and proceeded to list, in detail, everything I'd said and accused me of being passive aggressive just for asking the question.

Never once did he ask, or allow an opening for, me to speak my heart.

Ever had that experience?

This sort of aggressive response could come out of a general attitude towards life. For instance, always having to be right.

It might also be more specific about a particular situation and person that is too threatening. In this case, it's not the person's general attitude.

My suspicion, in this case, is that it traces back to a series of occasions where he had failed to keep his word to me about money he had borrowed. If so, while I understand the stress that may have led to the lapses, at the time, he couldn't admit to himself that he broke a trust. Even though I had no intention of reminding him of that particular issue, any communication that threatened his "rightness" in any way took him back, emotionally, to that issue. Since it was too threatening to his self-identity, he lashed out.

This example highlights one of the characteristics of repression. While it is true that a person can be very "healthy" in some parts of his or her life and not so much in other areas, repression rarely remains entirely it's "box." When something comes up on a feeling level that might touch the repressed issue, the person often lashes out. Overreaction and anger are often indicators of repression.

That said, there's a danger in knowing just a bit about psychology. If not careful, one can just accuse someone of repression as a way to dismiss them. Ultimately, it's about openness and good will. The difference between my friend and I is that I was willing both to talk about it and to recognize that my assessment could be wrong. He, on the other hand, is willing to talk, just not about anything that threatens him. If we really talked, something totally different might emerge. Even if it turned out that I was right, it could generate a space for forgiveness.

At the same time, there's no point in bringing something up that another person is unable to hear.

Clues That One Might Be Lying to Oneself

i. The Inability to Critique One's Own Group

One of the most obvious clues is the inability to critique one's own group. If members are not allowed to have some disagreements, or if a person is completely unable to see any weakness in their position, it's a warning flag.

ii. All-or-Nothing Thinking

Of course, this can involve a host of other logical fallacies (**hasty generalizations, excluded middle, slippery slope,** etc.), but the point is to distract us from seeking a "balanced" point of view and to see an issue in simple black-and-white terms. This often shows up in debates that ignite people's passions, such as gun control in the US.

A common meme that shows up on social media is as follows:

> *"Cain killed able with a rock. It's a heart problem, not a gun problem."*

Of course, this is true. The ultimate issue is a "heart problem" in the sense that some people's hearts are so distorted by hurt and/or rage that they want to kill other people. That's the truth or the half-truth (**pretext**) that hides the greater lie.

First, there's an implication that a rock and a gun are the same and that any sort of regulation is fruitless since it doesn't get to the heart of the issue.

Clearly, however, the analogy is suspect (**false analogy**). For instance, while I can kill with a rock or a knife, I can kill far more quickly and easily with a semiautomatic rifle.

One might also respond to the argument by taking it to its logical extreme. That is, since it's really about a heart problem, why bother regulating bombs or nuclear materials?

The typical response continues along the all-or-nothing lines and commonly references events like the Oklahoma bombing. Though most of these materials were regulated, the claim is that the regulations are ineffective. Criminals will find a way so why bother?

The underlying assumption behind this version of the argument is that since regulations aren't 100 percent effective they are worthless. This is a **hasty generalization**. The key, which is usually unspoken, is the "100 percent." No regulation or law is perfect. *Every other major industrialized democracy in the world experiences a tiny fraction* *of the gun violence that we experience in the United States. Many even allow most of their citizens, if they wish, to own many types of guns.* They don't stop all gun violence, but they reduce gun violence to a fraction of what we experience in the US.

The solution, then, doesn't appear to be take away everyone's guns. Rather, we could look to how other countries have been successful in balancing gun rights with public safety.

Another example comes for a recent election cycle. I know Hillary and Bernie supporters who cannot acknowledge anything wrong about their candidate. Similarly, they have difficulty acknowledging anything "right" or good about their opposing candidate. Even the "worst" person is likely to do a few good things, just as even the "best" people do some wrong things. In this case, they were even on the same side of the political spectrum. Most neutral observers noted that what was directly said between them was probably the least negative in recent politics.

Yet, even after Hillary had won and Bernie eventually endorsed her, some Hillary supporters remained angry, even enraged, at Bernie Sanders. One might understand why Bernie supporters would take some time to come around; no one likes to lose. But the Hillary supporters? Why?

Some writers pointed out that some groups of Hillary supporters were voting based more on self-identity (identity politics) than the issues. For instance, he or she likes the Clintons and believes Hillary has paid her dues and is clearly qualified. At the same time, when it came to the "issues," some individuals were really closer to Bernie Sanders. If that dissonance made them too uncomfortable, they might repress it and lash out at the one creating the dissonance.

Whether this is true or not is above my pay grade. Also above my pay grade is whether this animosity was being fed by foreign election interference via social media. The fact is that when I talked to friends about their "reasons" for being so angry, they never really made sense. This sort of irrational anger and all-or-nothing thinking is a classic warning sign.

What is the real solution to dealing with these issues?

Thinking back to Aristotle, it's not about all-or-nothing. Instead, it's about balance. For example, when it comes to gun regulation, a meaningful conversation would be about how to balance the reasonable freedom to bear arms with the need for other citizens to be free from fear of mass shootings, or at least to make them a rare, rather than a common, occurrence. But that's another topic.[8] Here, the issue is to highlight the nature and importance of critical thinking.

---

8   For the gun issue, for example, the next step might be to ask why certain special interests appear dead set against even something as simple as truly universal background checks. The answer is often to follow the money. For example, who profits whenever there is a mass shooting?

iii. Non-Falsifiable Conditions

One could think of this as a variation of "all-or-nothing" thinking, but there are some important additional features. This term comes from the philosophy of science. Science, in part, works by trial and error. Some of the definitions, however, are very different than in common language.

For example, in common language, a "fact" is considered more certain and real than a "theory." This is not the case in science. A "fact" is the least useful and certain element of science. Without context, facts are relatively useless.

A scientific theory, on the other hand, is a description of some aspect of the world (dealing with large collections of "facts") that, by generating multiple hypotheses and lines of inquiry, has been tested, refined, and tested again. A "theory" is a set of hypotheses that have stood the test of time and experimentation. For that reason, it is considered more "real" than a simple "fact."

The generation of testable hypotheses is critical for something to be considered "science." If there is no test that could be done that, if it failed, could prove the hypothesis or theory wrong, it's not really considered science. This is why "intelligent design," or the idea that an intelligent creator either created each species on its own OR inserted a subtle guiding hand in evolution, isn't science. Some form of intelligent design may in fact be true. If it cannot be tested, *it is non-falsifiable*, it is not science.

There are even aspects that scientists work on for which the outcomes are unclear. Is string theory science or physical philosophy? So far, no method has been devised to test string theory.

Later, we will explore aspects of the relationship between faith and science. If it's an aspect of life that can be "tested," but those tests don't matter to one's beliefs, then that's a clue. It shows up in more than just religion. For example, the following is a comment a colleague made about conspiracy theories:

> It is a basic principle of conspiracy theorizing that anything that tends to disprove the theory is part of the conspiracy.[9]

This is a classic non-falsifiable condition.

iv. Sartre: Facticity versus Transcendence

Example: The Lady in the Paris Café
Sartre instigated my first real understanding of **bad faith** (his term for self-deception) with his famous story of the woman on a date in a Paris café.[10] There are two

---

9 Chris Fox, PhD, Department of Philosophy, Newman University, Wichita, KS.

10 The text doesn't actually say Paris, but it helps the ambiance of the story.

definitions I should mention before we start. *Facticity* is just a fancy way of saying **"the basic facts of the matter."** For instance, a piece of wood or metal or the wind blowing. Just the facts. *Transcendence* **has to do with the meaning we attach to those facts.** For example, "this wood is beautiful" or "the wind is delightful."

Of course, as soon as we notice or speak of any "fact" there is some meaning involved. It's not a perfect distinction. As we saw in chapter one, the distinction gets at the fact that *there is a "gap" between what is "real," what we see, and how we interpret the world around us*. We are meaning seeking and meaning generating creatures. Every set of "facts" is open to a variety of interpretations.

This does not mean that every interpretation is equal. A tree, for example, can serve a variety of purposes (such as lumber, shade, or fire), but it cannot become a human person. For Sartre, *one of the ways in which we engage in bad faith is to intentionally (though not necessarily consciously) refuse to reasonably integrate the "facts" with the "meanings" we attach*.

> Take the example of a woman who has consented to go out with a particular man for the first time. She knows very well the intentions ... the man ... cherishes regarding her. She knows also that it will be necessary sooner or later for her to make a decision. (Sartre 1956, 96)

What decision? Whether to allow the relationship to take on a romantic, physical element.

She isn't ready for that decision, so she seeks to delay it for as long as possible.

> *... She concerns herself only with what is respectful and discreet in the attitude of her companion. She does not apprehend this contact as an attempt to achieve what we call "the first approach." ... She restricts his behavior to what is in the present; she does not wish to read into the phrases which he addresses to her anything other than their explicit meaning. If he says to her, "I find you so attractive!" she disarms this phrase of its sexual background. ... (Sartre 1956, 96)*

The lady is caught in the middle. She enjoys the attention but hasn't decided about the suitor one way or the other. She's unsure if she wants to let a romantic relationship develop. Rather than simply admit this to herself, she pretends that there is nothing sexual about his intentions. Each statement is taken literally, divorced from its background, context, and future possibilities (recall the notion of consciousness as the projection of one's possibilities). At this stage, she lives only in the present moment, focusing on the immediate facts of his statements, "... which she imagines as objective qualities. The man speaking to her appears to her sincere and respectful as the table is round or square ..." (Sartre 1956, 96–97).

The difficulty is that she wants two things from the man. On the one hand, she wants to be respected and addressed "wholly to her personality." On the other hand, she also wants him to address her body as "wholly desire" (Sartre 1956, 97). Since she is unsure of what she wants and is unsure if he will do both, she wishes to postpone the decision for as long as possible.

Then, there is a moment of crisis. He takes her hand from across the table. This is a *physical* gambit. How will she respond?

> We know what happens next; the young woman leaves her hand there, but she *does not notice* that she is leaving it. She does not notice because it happens by chance that she is at this moment all intellect. She draws her companion up to the most lofty regions of sentimental speculation; the hand rests inert between the warm hands of her companion—neither consenting nor resisting—a thing. (Sartre 1956, 97; emphasis his)

Whereas previously, she focused almost exclusively on the bare facts of the situation, here, she shifts from the factual to the transcendent. She ignores the obvious fact of his physical advance by escaping into her mind. The hand? It's just sitting there. What's really going on is this rich, intellectual conversation.

This "careful" and deliberate jumping back and forth between "facts" and "what they mean," refusing to integrate them in a reasonable way, is Sartre's first description of how we lie to ourselves.

If we look back to our previous example of the gun verses the rock (*Cain killed able with a rock. It's a heart problem, not a gun problem.*), we see the same dynamic. *Instead of integrating all of the facts and meanings in a reasonable way, the argument depends on being highly selective about the facts and what they mean.* It's the essence of bad faith.

Example: AIDS

One of my favorite examples of bad faith comes from AIDS. Here, some people cherry pick their biology to match their religious beliefs. The argument runs as follows:

> When AIDS was first discovered in the 1980s, it was seen as a disease affecting gay men and intravenous drug users. In fact, its original name was GRID (Gay Related Immunodeficiency syndrome). For many who believed that a gay lifestyle was against God, this was said to be God's punishment. Similarly, intravenous drug users were also reaping the cost of their sins.

Is this what the biology supports?

Let us start with why HIV is so easily transmitted between gay partners. It has to do with anal sex. The virus has to find a way to get into the blood stream. The interior of the rectum tears easily, so when infected semen is deposited there, it finds its way into the blood stream of the recipient. All people can contract HIV, but anal sex has a higher transmission rate than (what is perceived as) conventional sexual activity.

So far, there is nothing to contradict the religious argument. Yes, other people can get HIV, but the higher transmission rate among gay partners would be consistent with their beliefs.

What sexual orientation has the second-highest transmission rate?

Turns out this group is heterosexual woman. In fact, the odds of a woman getting HIV during unprotected sex from a single encounter with a man with high viral load is about 1 in 10. Why not more? Because the vagina doesn't tear nearly as easily as the inside of the rectum.

The next-highest rate of transmission is heterosexual men. The odds of a man getting it from a woman during unprotected sex from a single encounter with a woman with a high viral load is about 1 in 100.

This hardly seems fair. Why are men only at one tenth the risk of women?

Does this mean that God loves men more than women?

Again, look to the biology. While the infected semen remains in the woman for some time, giving it greater opportunity to pass to her blood stream, the man doesn't usually take fluids internally from the woman. Plus, when he is done and cleans up, those on his exterior are also gone.

But now for the clincher. What about lesbians? It turns out that lesbians have the lowest rate of HIV transmission. Why? There are typically no infected sperm or other fluids to be deposited inside of the other woman.

This is strange. *If the claim is that the higher rate of HIV transmission between gay men is proof that God hates the gay lifestyle, then, if we are going to be consistent, the fact that lesbian woman have LOWER rates of transmission than heterosexuals would be proof that God prefers a lesbian lifestyle to a heterosexual one.*

Of course, in reality, this says nothing about what God prefers. The point is that one can cherry pick biology, selecting only those facts that confirm one's position while refusing to reasonably integrate facts with their meanings, to say almost anything one wants. The morality of sexual orientation is an entirely different sort of question.

v. The Conclusion Remains the Same, No Matter How the Circumstances Change

Example: Tax Cuts

When the second President Bush took office, he inherited a budget surplus from former President Clinton. At that point, he argued that the money should be returned

Some Common Informal Fallacies

Terms like "self-serving rationality" and "pretext" refer to a more general misuse of reason. These are some of the specific logical fallacies that might be used to support, for example, a self-serving rationality.

Note that it is not uncommon for a single statement to "fit" more than one logical fallacy.

Bifurcation: (also referred to as the *excluded middle* or the *false dilemma*)

J: You're either for the war and a patriot, or against the war and hate your country.

Very common, refusing to see that there are alternatives other than those presented.

Complex question:

This involves folding two questions into one, so that either way the question is answered, one answer is assumed. It's a form of begging the question.

J: Have you stopped beating your wife yet? (Only a yes or no answer is allowed.)

Note that the first question should legitimately have been, have you ever beat your wife? The complex question "assumes" the answer to the first question, thus begging that question. (Attorney's love using this fallacy on the witness stand.)

to the people; it was, after all, their money. If one ignores the fact that we still had a large national debt, it was a good argument.[11]

In this example, a warning sign comes from the fact that despite a fundamental reversal of the circumstances of the first argument, by Bush's second term a new argument was crafted such that the conclusion (that taxes should be cut) remained the same. Again, I'm less interested in the truth or falsity of the argument than in how the argument changed.

At the start of that term, Bush argued for even more tax cuts despite the fact that, due to becoming involved in two wars, we were now running a massive new deficit. Usually, when the country went to war, taxes were raised in order to pay for the war, though there would often be some borrowing in the form of selling bonds.[12] For these wars, however, there were no new taxes raised.

Remember that the argument for the first set of tax cuts was due to a surplus, returning the money to the people. Now the situation was entirely reversed. What was the new argument?

Bush's response to the issue of the national debt was classic Reganomics—trickle-down. In other words, by lowering taxes we increase the money for spending and investment so that the economy grows. This would, in turn, increase tax revenue, which would (assuming we

---

11   Here, it's important to understand the difference between the national debt and the deficit. The deficit refers to the budget each year: do we spend more or less than we take in? The national debt is the debt (and interest) accrued through decades of running the yearly budget in the red, spending more than we take in. Clinton finished his term with a budget surplus, which meant that, in terms of our yearly expenses, we were taking in more money than we were spending. It gives us the opportunity to slow or reduce the national debt. But unless the yearly surplus is greater than the interest spent on the national debt, the national debt will continue to grow.

12   A bond is basically a loan where the issuer promises to pay the purchaser back the money with interest.

didn't just keep lowering taxes) allow us to pay down that debt.[13]

_____

13 There is some truth to the Reganomics argument. Though "trickle-down" economics is not the same as stimulating the economy through reduced taxes. Let us separate the two. (1) Trickle-down involves reducing taxes, mainly on the wealthy, so that they invest and the effects of those investments "trickle down" to the rest of the people. (2) Tax cuts for the middle and lower economic classes depend more on them spending the money in the economy, thus creating a greater "multiplier" effct (i.e., if I have more money to spend, I purchase more food, etc). This helps pay for more people who work at the stores, who then also spend money, etc. Usually, a tax reduction goes to both groups. But the main difference between the two is whether the tax cuts go primarily to the rich or the working and middle classes.

Interestingly, when it comes to trickle-down from the rich, the opposite is often true. The claim is that taxing them less would cause them to reinvest more in their business, thus creating more jobs for the rest of us. If one looks at the data, the reality has been the opposite. It's not hard to understand why. If taxes are low, it is "cheap" for the owners to pull money out of their businesses. Money that is reinvested is not taxed. So, if marginal taxes are high, it becomes expensive to pull money out, but relatively cheap to reinvest that money into the business because the money, when reinvested, is not taxed.

The reason middle- and working-class tax cuts are often more effective is because of something economist's call "the multiplier effect." The multiplier effect is a measure of how much a particular change (investment, spending, tax cut) "ripples" through the economy. Some things have a much larger effect than others.

For this example, let's stay with the general issue of middle- and lower-class tax cuts, and not the trickledown version. While both depend upon the money being spent, the working and middle classes are more likely to actually spend the money, particularly on basic and durable goods.

Here, if we tax to either extreme, we end up without money for roads, schools, public safety, etc. Why? Obviously, if the tax rate is zero, the government gets no income. But if the tax rate is 100 percent, the same problem emerges because there would be no point in working.

Equivocation:

This fallacy is also the basis for most puns. It involves using the same word in an argument, but with two different meanings.

J: If we don't hang together, we shall surely hang separately.

L: Evolution is a theory. Therefore, it should not be taught in public schools as fact.

In the second case, there are actually two equivocations, though each of their terms is only said once and implied the second time. In scientific terms, "theory" is what is most certain, while "facts" are merely the building blocks for theories. In normal speech, "facts" are the most real and "theories" are the least real.

False analogy:

Also commonly used in humor, the false analogy depends on comparing two things as if they are similar when, in key ways that are relevant to the purpose of the comparison, they are not.

J: Cain killed Able with a rock. If you take away people's guns, they will just use rocks or knives.

J: The mind is like a river. With a river, the broader it is, the more shallow. So too with the mind.

Note that no analogy is "perfect." Thus, a good analogy is

referred to as "strong" while a poor analogy is referred to as "weak."

At issue is whether the key comparisons upon which one is making the analogy and drawing one's conclusion are apt or whether they are misleading, superficial, or implausible. The first example is weak because guns are not similar to rocks in a way key to the analogy. While you can kill someone with a rock, you can kill more and faster with a gun. Also note that one might think of the second example as equivocation due to the double meaning of "shallow" and "broad." Given that this is a comparison, it is clear that the words have two meanings.

False cause:
Attributing something as a causal event that merely happens to be coincidental in time.

> J: Becky went running this morning and won $100 in the lottery. Therefore, running in the morning will help you win the lottery.

Hasty generalization: (very common)
Drawing a conclusion about a generality on either too small a sample size or on a biased sample. This is also one form of **overstating one's case**.

> J: I dated two red heads who were air heads. All red heads must be air heads.
> J: Medical marijuana helps people. Marijuana must be good for you.

For the moment, let's set aside arguments about whether trickledown economics works since it's an empirical question. The point here is that *despite changes in circumstances, the conclusion always appeared to remain the same. This is a red flag that the argument is a pretext and that something else is really going on.*

Not every such situation is truly a self-serving rationality or a pretext, but it is a strong indicator. It suggests that the real reasons for arguing for a conclusion are not the reasons given. *This doesn't mean those other reasons are invalid.*

For example, Themistocles, the Athenian naval commander who kept the Persians from merely sailing troops behind the Spartans and other Greeks at Thermopylae, predicted shortly after the Greeks defeated the Persians at the earlier battle of Marathon[14] that the Persians would return. He realized that a strong navy would be critical to surviving that attack but he couldn't get his fellow Athenians to see the danger.

So, Themistocles lied to the Athenians. He convinced them that the island of Aegina, geographically much

---

Between these two extremes is an economic mechanism called the Laffer curve. As one gradually increases the tax rate above zero, tax revenues increase for a while. In fact, depending upon how that money is used (i.e., roads and infrastructure), higher taxes can stimulate economic growth. But if it gets too high, people lose incentive to work, don't have enough to spend, etc. In that case, it has the opposite effect.

Whether reducing taxes stimulates the economy and helps raise future tax rates is not a simple question. It depends on the specifics of the tax rate, who is being taxed, at what level, and how the tax money is spent. Interestingly, at the time of the second Bush administration, even one of Reagan's former economic advisors argued that we were on the "wrong" part of the Laffer curve to cut taxes, that it would just balloon the deficit. It appears he was correct.

14 This is where the tradition of running the "marathon" began. It was about 26 miles from Marathon to Athens. The Greek commander dispatched a messenger who ran from Marathon to Athens to deliver the news. He collapsed and died just after delivering the news.

closer, threatened Athenian shipping. This convinced them to give him the funds to build a larger navy.

The "300" Spartan's and the other Greeks at Thermopylae slowed the Persian advance and allowed Athens to be evacuated. It was Themistocles's naval victories, however, that forced the Persians to withdraw after burning Athens. The Persians had to be able to supply their troops and get them home if needed. Without naval superiority to protect their supply lines, they were forced to withdraw.

Unlike this case, more often than not, what is being "hidden" behind a pretext is not for the greater good. Only if one can discern whether there is a pretext or a self-serving rationality in progress can one seek, and perhaps find, what is really at stake.

Example: Gym Closure

Most examples of self-serving rationalities are more mundane. For example, I used to exercise at the university gym where I teach. They also had a small, secondary facility called Health Beat. The reason I finally went elsewhere is that they often closed for three to four days on holiday weekends and for between ten days and two weeks at the end of the summer. The latter was necessary to allow for major maintenance in the main gym. For example, that's when they refinished the floors. But I wondered, why they couldn't leave the small workout facility, Health Beat, open for those who wished to exercise.

Toward the end of one summer, I asked one of the regular staff members at the main gym whether Health Beat would be open at that time. She didn't know so she called back to someone else in the office. I heard her question and the reply, though I didn't see the other person. She then came back and said they would be closed.

Naturally, I asked why. Health Beat did not require the same sort of maintenance as the main gym, it was just a room with limited weights, machines, and cardio

Note the difference. The first example was from too small a sample size. The second example was drawn from a specialized group (biased sample) that may have been an exception.

A subclass of hasty generalizations is called **biased statistics**:

J: A poll of 1,000 Californian's showed that 60 percent of them believe that we should trust movie stars when it comes to politics. Therefore, 60 percent of all Americans believe that we should trust movie stars when it comes to politics.

The problem here is that different parts of the country likely have very different attitudes towards movie stars. Just looking at California might not reflect the country as a whole.

Slippery slope:
Don't do this because it will lead, eventually, to something horrible. Once you start down this slope, you won't be able to stop.

J: If we legalize marijuana, next it will be cocaine and heroin, and society will collapse.

There are multiple problems with this sort of argument, but one can also think of it as a version of bifurcation or the excluded middle. It claims that you can't find a decent place somewhere between two extremes, when, in fact, the best option may be somewhere in the middle (on the slope.)

Straw person:

Misrepresents the original argument in a much weaker form, then beats up the weaker argument while ignoring the real, stronger argument. (Very common.)

J: We should allow limited use of marijuana.

L: No, because societies which allow unlimited use of marijuana experience increases in crime, losses in productivity, and general decline.

Note that the second person changed the terms of the first person's statement, making it much more extreme and thus more subject to objections.

equipment. She said, "We close it since students like to have a break from work before school starts."

What an odd response! Remember, she didn't even know it was going to be closed. Since I heard the person's reply to her question, I also knew all he had said was that it would be closed. Why would she assert this sort of reason?

It's possible that she was extrapolating from a related conversation about the main gym. But while many students are needed for the desks in the main gym, it only takes one to watch the desk at Health Beat. When discussing this case in class, I've sometimes asked students to vote: If given a choice to work more hours and earn more money, or to have more time off, which would they want? There are always students who would rather earn more income for the coming school year than have the extra time off.

Empirically, then, the answer the staff member gave me was almost certainly false. Yes, some students like the extra time off but lots would also prefer to make more money. Health Beat, due to the small staff demand, could easily be staffed by students wanting extra hours. Why not leave it open?

My suspicion is that, perhaps drawing on some other conversations, she made up the reason. Why would she do this?

Here, she is giving me "bad" news. She is telling me something that would disappoint me. Most people don't like to deliver bad news, nor do we like to look bad. She may be a kind person by nature or she may just be someone concerned about her image. Either way, when we have to deliver news that might make us, or our organization, look "bad," we often search for ways to make it look better. In this case, she comes up with a noble-sounding reason for why she (or her organization) had to disappoint a client. She wants to look good.

Further, *her answer appeared to be designed to shut down any further questions.* Who am I to question such a noble and compassionate decision? *It would be selfish of me to object.*

The fact is, *we all engage in these sorts of rationalizations. Part of the problem with hiding behind false rationales is that, when things legitimately change with respect to the real reasons, we may be so locked into the false reasons that we become unable to adjust our behaviors. Moreover, failing to recognize the real reasons behind something means that one can't have a constructive argument or discussion and we end up talking at cross purposes.*[15]

What's also interesting about these sorts of self-serving rationalizations is that others often see right through them. Which means that, *often, we make ourselves look even worse in the eyes of others.* We just don't realize it.

I didn't tell the staff member that I saw through her rationalization.

---

[15] Again, the goal is not to eliminate these sorts of behaviors. That wouldn't be possible. But it is possible to engage in fewer of them.

Grief and the Physicality of Death

CHAPTER THREE

The Death of Ivan Ilyich

Tolstoy lived in a place and time when death was not hidden or sanitized in hospitals. What we now think of as a minor infection, easily treated by antibiotics, could, and often did, prove deadly. Tolstoy witnessed the deaths of 5 of his 13 children.

Living with death and accepting that it would happen to himself led Tolstoy to a crisis of faith. He railed against death, feeling that "he could not live if there was death" (Tolstoy 1981, 4; intro). Tolstoy eventually resolved his crisis. Upon facing his own fear and denial of death, he became a fervent Christian. But Tolstoy was less concerned with organized religions than with the power of love—love of one's neighbor, love of God—which he saw at the heart of all the great world religions. After serving in the Russian army early in life, he came to espouse nonviolence. Writings like Tolstoy's "Confessions" and "Letter to a Hindu" profoundly influenced social leaders and thinkers like Gandhi and Martin Luther King.

The Death of Ivan Ilyich was written towards the end of Tolstoy's crisis of faith. It stands as a classic in the literature of death and dying. Tolstoy's insights, which are expressed in the story, introduce ideas and themes that resonate throughout this book, helping us to understand other stories and traditions. Tolstoy allows us to reinforce the notion of happiness as a "byproduct" of other goals and to introduce two sets of "tools" to which we will repeatedly refer. The first is **Kramer's "Three Faces of Death."** The second is **Scarry's** discussion of **the relationship between pain and world**.

While the novelette begins with Ivan's death, the larger story follows the life of a man going through the motions, living day to day and doing what he believed he "should," but really only for himself. Ivan was caught up, in part, in what might be called the "saving lie," where we can see and accept another's death, but don't really believe or deal with our own fear of death (Tolstoy 1981, 6–7; intro). Yet, as the pain (the physicality) of his illness presses the fact of his death upon him, making it real in a concrete, embodied way, Ivan is pushed to address the lies he had told himself all his life. Ivan is forced to ask the uncomfortable question:

Since I am going to die, what is it, if anything, that has made my life worthwhile?

Sound familiar?

The Themes of Ivan's Life

1. *It's all about me:* My comfort, my happiness.
   Ivan skates along the surface of life. His relationships lack real engagement, connection, or intimacy. It's all about getting ahead and having a good, well-ordered life. It's all about himself. Surprisingly, this doesn't result in happiness.

2. *Life <u>should</u> follow a strictly prescribed order.*
   Ivan had a clear idea of how he "thought" the universe should operate. If he did the right things, he *should* get ahead. He lived more in his head, basing his choices on what he thought he "*should*" do, than in real life. For Ivan, life *should* not be messy or complicated.

3. *When Ivan is confronted by events or people that challenge his orderly view of the world, he adopts strategies of avoidance and denial.*
   When possible, he eliminated such people from his life. When he could not discard them, he "bracketed" or "compartmentalized" the offending parties. Ivan does what he perceives as his basic duties (the "should"), but no more. Ivan refuses to change or grow.

4. *The physicality of Ivan's illness presents a challenge he can't ignore.*
   For Ivan, he has done everything "right." He had the right sort of job, he did his job "well," he toadied up to the right people, etc. From his view, all should be comfortable and good. It wasn't right that he should be in terrible pain, ill, and dying. It wasn't right that life has become so messy. Worse yet, it wasn't right that no one seemed to care.

5. *Love and self-honesty*
   Just as Tolstoy concluded that the answer to the "meaning" of life is, in a sense, love, so the physicality of Ivan's illness presses Ivan to the same realization,

but only at the very end. But before Ivan can truly love, he must become honest with himself.

Theme 1: It's all about me

Which of Aristotle's categories best describes Ivan's relationships?

Consider Ivan's "friend," Fyodor Vasilyevich, upon first reading about Ivan's death. Is he stricken with grief? Is he concerned for Ivan's family? No, we see that his main concern, as with Ivan's other "friends" (who are primarily work colleagues), is how it might affect his prospects for a promotion and an increase in pay:

> And so the first thought that occurred to each of the gentlemen in his office, learning of Ivan Ilyich's death, was the effect it have on their own transfers and promotions or those of their acquaintances. (Tolstoy 1981, 36)

Ivan has surrounded himself with people like himself. For Ivan, friends serve two purposes. On a more generous level, they serve as pleasant companions. For example, colleagues with whom to play cards and pass the time. This fits with Aristotle's second level of friendship. Their service to Ivan was more important. Knowing the "right" people, being part of the "right" crowd was necessary for getting ahead, for getting the raise, and for getting the promotion. This is consistent with Aristotle's notion of utility.

This becomes clear as Ivan moves up the social ladder. For example, there came a time when Ivan was promoted to "examining magistrate," a sort of judge. Ivan's new post was a step higher up the bureaucratic and social ladder than his previous post. As such, Ivan's social standing was now clearly higher than that of most of his previous friends and colleagues. While he would never have been so rude as to dismiss his old friends directly, he gradually distanced himself from those friends and developed new friendships "from among the best circle of lawyers and wealthy gentry in town" (Tolstoy 1981, 54). He even adopted their social and political attitudes.

Aristotle on Friendship

Earlier, we made the suggestion that happiness, even if Aristotle was correct about it being the "goal" of human life, is really a byproduct of other goals, not an end that can be successfully pursued on its own. Again, while Aristotle might not have phrased the issue this way, the manner in which he describes what is necessary for happiness is consistent with this claim. For example, only a person of character (a person who has internalized the virtues) can be truly happy. These virtues must be pursued, not just as means to an end (happiness), but for their own sake. Let us expand this in terms of Aristotle's discussion of friendship.

Aristotle writes of three kinds of friendship. The lowest form is friendship built on **utility**, or mutual usefulness. The second is friendship built on **mutual enjoyment or pleasure** through, for example, simply enjoying one another's company. The highest is friendship built **on character or virtue**.

Even with utility, there may be a certain fondness for one's companion, but it's really about what the relationship does for oneself. These relationships are easily discarded when they no longer serve one's own goals. Friendships built on mutual companionship are stronger, but unless they transition into something more, are also easy to discard. Why? Because on both of these first two levels, it's still really about what the relationship does for oneself.

Friendships built on character are another matter. While they typically include elements of utility and mutual enjoyment, there is a deeper level of mutual respect and admiration for one another's character. This shifts the focus from being on what one "gets" from the relationship to, at least at times, on what one can "give" to the other. **There is a genuine and rich desire to support the other in their goals and development even without expectation of return.** If there is a setback in which helping would be inconvenient and offer no benefit to the helper, these are the friends who are most likely to step up and help the one in need.

So, for Aristotle, *the richest form of friendship*, which is also essential to happiness, *has to be pursed, not for the sake of happiness, but for its own sake.* Or, put another way, we must love others for their own sake, not just for what they can do for us.

Ivan's attitude towards relationships is also demonstrated by his marriage. Ivan strove to do everything expected by someone in his position. He worked hard, played the right card game, even his "affairs" as a young man were strictly what was expected by someone at his age and position. Because it was expected of him, he also learned dance. And since he was focused on getting ahead, he became a very good dancer.

Eventually, there came a time when it was expected that a man of his position and years should settle down. As a charming young magistrate and a good dancer, he won the heart of Praskovya Fyodoravna.

While it may be true that Praskovya fell in love with Ivan, it would be wrong to say that Ivan fell in love with Praskovya. "Praskovya Fyodoravna came from a good family and was quite attractive; she had a little money. ... It would be a good alliance" (Tolstoy 1981, 55). Thus, Ivan married Praskovya for two reasons. Firstly, "acquiring such a wife" would give him pleasure. Secondly, such a match would be looked upon favorably by "people of the highest standing ..." (Tolstoy 1981, 56).

It's clear that Ivan's relationships are based on utility and pleasure, not the deep mutual regard and appreciation that Aristotle characterizes in relationships based on virtue. In more modern terms, we might refer to a relationship based on virtue as a relationship based on real love. Ivan, however, had no concept, and perhaps no experience, of what love might be. One might hope that, over time, Ivan might find such a love with his family. Sadly, this did not happen in time for him to show his family any real love.

Theme 2: Life <u>should</u> follow a strictly prescribed order.

Tolstoy sets up the contrast between the "order" of the mind and the messiness of real life in the first few pages of the book. It begins with the obituary notice, which Tolstoy notes is a "fresh issue, still smelling of printer's ink" (Tolstoy 1981, 35). The mention of the smell was intentional. The paper was probably of a high linen content and the smell of the paper and ink is usually considered refreshing, enjoyable. Further, newspapers represent civilization and order. This is intended to contrast with the smell of Ivan's decaying body (Tolstoy 1981, 39). Tolstoy's readers would have been familiar with the sickly-sweet smell of decay. Unlike the clean, wholesome smell of the paper and printer's ink, this smell generates a visceral reaction of revulsion. Once experienced, it is difficult to forget.

The contrast between the two smells parallels a basic contrast of Ivan's life. Ivan views the world as a carefully ordered existence. Ivan lives primarily in his head; he believes that if he does all the "right" things he should be healthy, comfortable, and spared the "messiness" of other (lesser) people. Even his job reflects this. As an attorney and then a magistrate, his job is to punish those who fail to obey the "order" of society's laws.

The roots of this attitude go to his childhood.

Ivan was born the middle son of a mid-ranking Russian bureaucrat. Ivan is described as "clever, pleasant, lively, and respectable" (Tolstoy 1981, 50). He attended law school, where he is said to have acquitted himself "creditably." Tolstoy writes that law school shaped Ivan into the man he became:

> ... a capable, cheerful, good-natured, and sociable man but one strict to carry out whatever he considered his duty, and he considered his duty all things that were so designated by people in authority. (Tolstoy 1981, 50)

Ivan was strongly drawn to please and imitate those in authority. After all, these were the people who set the standard for success and the good life. Like Hannah Arendt's analysis of Adolph Eichmann, the German bureaucrat who, while never killing a single person, organized the transportation of thousands of Jews to concentration camps, Ivan deferred so strongly to those in authority that he was willing to ignore or still his own conscience if they felt it was acceptable.

> As a student he had done things which, at the time, seemed to him extremely vile and made him feel disgusted with himself; but later, seeing that people of high standing had no qualms about doing these things, he was not quite able to consider them good but managed to dismiss them and not feel the least perturbed when he recalled them. (Tolstoy 1981, 50–51)

Like Eichmann, who was a real person, Ivan was willing to simply adopt the values of whoever he felt was his "superior," whoever could help him get ahead. It wasn't that he lacked a conscience, it was that he simply suppressed it by telling himself that since these people were "moral" superiors, whatever they told him must be right.

There came a point, long before the pain of his physical injury, when Ivan's worldview was challenged.

Ivan's home life was on the rocks. He and his wife had children, though some had died. While he continued to receive promotions and raises at work, there never seemed to be enough money. Then the area of Ivan's life where his self-worth and order were most firmly anchored went sour. Ivan was passed over for a promotion that he strongly felt he deserved.

For Ivan, this was more than a simple injustice. It was a direct challenge of his very worldview. Ivan's life was built around an orderly, controllable world. Yes, there were some minor glitches here and there. For the most part, however, he believed if one does what one is supposed to do, if one performs one's duty, one is rewarded. He felt betrayed by those he served. Even so, he was confused and frustrated. His world was thrown into disarray.

Later, when dealing with models of grief, we will talk about the power and danger involved in the loss of one's **assumptive world**. Now, it is time to introduce the sort of *experiential* notion of the "world" that we will be using throughout the book.

We usually think of our "world" in fairly abstract terms, perhaps as a large blue ball floating in space. On a visceral level, a better **definition** might be as follows:

> *My world is the sum of my concrete possibilities for thought, action, and relationships beyond the physical body.*

Recall that we likened consciousness to a sort of dynamic "space." It was a "space" in the sense of a stage or an opening that allowed other things—ideas, images, etc.—to be seen. But, it's not passive. Consciousness also operates as a "project," in that *we are constantly projecting our possibilities for thought, action, and relationships into the future*. It could be something as simple as wondering what's for dinner, or as deep as wondering what one will do with one's life. In either case, **the sum of whatever you experience as *your* possibilities constitutes *your* world.**[1]

One's <u>*assumptive world*</u> *is the world as one has come to "assume" it to be. It has to do with our basic assumptions as to the nature both of reality and of our place in reality.* Recall that we tend to assume that reality matches up to a combination of our upbringing and personality. If one were to give Ivan the Myers-Briggs types inventory, I would suspect he would come up as an introvert, sensing, thinking, judger. For Ivan, there was a place for everything, and everything belonged in its place. Ivan's main concern in life was to attain and maintain a place in that world he enjoyed. When he was passed over for promotion, it called into question his every assumption about his world. *If that turned out to be false*, then it would question the very foundations of his life. *It would question his very identity.*

Things went from bad to worse. Ivan became angry and upset. He complained. But Ivan had surrounded himself with people like himself, people whose ultimate value was also pleasantness and propriety. Just as Ivan looked down on those who

---

1   This can get a bit complicated. For example, I might feel as though I can fly. While that feeling may be part of my world, it doesn't mean that the actual ability to fly is a real possibility. Still, the feeling can influence my behavior.

disturbed his peace, his colleagues and superiors began to look on him with disdain. The result is that he is passed over for promotion a second time.

In order to save money (and perhaps sulk), Ivan took a leave of absence and moved in with his wife's brother in the country. However, without work, Ivan "experiences for the first time in his life not only boredom but intolerable anguish" (Tolstoy 1981, 62). Without work, Ivan was forced to listen to his wife's nagging. More importantly, he has no distractions from himself.

The situation proved intolerable. Ivan decided to go to St. Petersburg and find a position with another ministry. Partly motivated by revenge, he would view success as repudiation of those who slighted him. He also wanted a salary of at least 5,000 rubles.

On the train to St. Petersburg, he met a colleague with whom he is on good terms. This colleague knew of a position opening up in St. Petersburg that not only paid the requisite 5,000 rubles and was in the same ministry, but was at a level two steps above his former colleagues. *Ivan is now their superior.*

Instead of seeking revenge, Ivan's resentment vanished (Tolstoy 1981, 63). Ivan was not a vindictive man. For Ivan, it was enough that they know he was now above them. Similarly, his wife was so pleased with the increased income that they forged a truce (Tolstoy 1981, 64).

Interestingly, ***being passed over for promotion gave Ivan a chance to rethink his life***, to get out of the "rut" in which he unconsciously remained. In this case, ***getting back what he wanted***, while offering immediate relief, also ***meant that he didn't have to face the challenge*** to his worldview that was instigated when he was passed over for promotion. For Ivan, the world was now set right and he could go back to the type of person he had always been.

Later, in the film ***What Dreams May Come***, Annie will use the phrase, "***Sometimes when you win, you lose.***" As we will see, in this case, "winning" (getting the job back) was also "losing" (since it meant that Ivan didn't learn what he needed to figure out).

Theme 3: When Ivan is confronted by events or people that challenge his orderly view of the world, he adopts strategies of avoidance and denial.

When Ivan was passed over for promotion, it threw him into turmoil. Again, this was more than just a normal sense of injustice, it challenged his very worldview. This didn't have to be a bad thing. The challenge could have pushed Ivan to rethink his worldview, and with it, himself and his relationships. Instead, he moved to the country (avoidance) and set out to prove those who had passed over him wrong (denial).

When Ivan was promoted above his former colleagues, he didn't seek revenge. That doesn't mean, however, that Ivan welcomed his old friends and colleagues back into his life. He was now above them on the social scale. Both he and his wife were never directly rude. If someone came around, they would be polite and civil, but not really welcoming (avoidance). After a time, they got the message (Tolstoy 1981, 71).

Another example of this strategy is when Ivan's marriage first went sour.

At first, Ivan's marriage went quite well. He and his wife enjoyed one another's company. For Ivan, it was a comfortable and pleasant reward for a life properly lived.

Then, Praskovya became pregnant. Like it is for many women, this is a time when she needed more support from her partner. Instead, Ivan saw her as jealous, demanding, unpleasant, and unreasonable. Ivan was a man who had spent most of his life cultivating the perfect public image. Even his marriage had been to further that image. Now, his wife was undermining the basic pleasantness of his life, "demanding he be more attentive to her, [finding] fault with everything, and [creating] distasteful and ill-mannered scenes" (Tolstoy 1981, 56).

"Ivan was horrified." The more he tried to ignore the problems, the more she lashed out, demanding that he be home and attend to her needs. She didn't respect his social time (usually whist, a card game similar to bridge), but she did appear to understand the necessity of his work. To fend her off, "Ivan Ilyich increasingly made work the center of gravity of his life. He grew more attached to his job and more ambitious than before" (Tolstoy 1981, 57).

Ivan really had three "areas" in his life: work, social (cards, time with friends), and family. Each could be bracketed or compartmentalized if necessary. If one became burdensome, his strategy was to shift his time to the others. He would do the bare minimum of the unpleasant duty and then ignore it while focusing on more pleasant pursuits.

Thus, when Ivan's family became a problem, instead of trying to understand and support his partner, he did the minimum that duty required. Ivan's married life was reduced to "only the conveniences it could provide—dinners at home, a well-run household, a partner in bed, and, above all, a veneer of respectability which public opinion required" (Tolstoy 1981, 58). It was perhaps the last that was most important to Ivan.

THREE FACES OF DEATH (KRAMER)

To deal with the dissatisfaction of his family life, *Ivan adopted a strategy of avoidance, choosing to "bracket" or "compartmentalize" the offending parties*. He still does what he perceives as his basic duties, but *he does not engage or seek to understand his wife's (or his children's) emotional needs*. Instead of attending to those needs, he pushed them away and denied the validity of those feelings in both himself and in his partner.

This is a good example of what Kramer refers to as *psychological death*. For that, we need some explanation.

On the surface, we have been talking about physical death. But death is far more than physical. While the awareness of physical death triggers both fear and a rich array of other possibilities for life, it's not the only way to think of death. Kramer refers to three kinds of death:

1. Physical

2. Psychological

3. Spiritual

1. **Physical Death** is the most obvious and refers to the cessation of bodily functions.

While this is physical, its implications are greater. As Becker puts it:

> The fear of death must be present behind our normal functioning in order for the organism to be armed towards self-preservation. But the fear of death cannot be present constantly in one's mental functioning, else the organism could not function. (*Kramer 1988, 15*)

2. **Psychological Death** "is the reversible termination of one's personal aliveness" (Kramer 1988, 18).

In other words, psychological death refers to emotional deadening, but one which can be reversed.

In this case, Kramer uses the example of Victor Frankl in the concentration camp, where people numb their emotions to avoid the trauma of how people were treated. This is a survival mechanism. But it doesn't have to be so extreme. "In modern culture, psychological death manifests itself as [some forms of] habitual behavior, such as taking one's partner for granted" (Kramer 1988, 19).

The key here is the emotional shutdown. It doesn't have to be total. Sometimes this shutdown is necessary. The problem is that once shut down, it can be difficult to turn back on.

Psychological death refers to the emotional numbing by which Ivan chose to cope with his family.

3. **Spiritual Death** is the death or transformation of old patterns, habits, roles, identities, and the birth of a new person (Kramer 1988 22).

This is perhaps the most important and the most easily misunderstood. It shows up with different language in every religion, but one doesn't have to follow a religion to experience this form of transformation. Becker writes that the fear of death cannot be present constantly in one's mental functioning. If one undergoes spiritual death, the facing of one's death overcomes the fear. So, the awareness of death can be part one's regular functioning. How?

> [*In*] Spiritual death ... the isolated ego dissolves spontaneously ... when the practitioner surrenders, or lets go, or gives up. In a special sense this complete sacrifice of any attempt to control or influence ..., this self-sacrifice, is life-giving. (*Kramer 1988, 23*)

Kramer uses the story of Abraham and Isaac as an example of spiritual death and rebirth. In fact, any time one releases or surrenders one's pride or ego in a truly profound way would be a sort of spiritual death and rebirth. Often, the language of becoming like a little child is appropriate.

This is far from clear. What is meant by "a special sense," "surrender," etc? While we will continue to develop the term spiritual death throughout the text, it can also be thought of, not in terms of some metaphysical reality, but as describing a basic human experience. One could then think of particular religions as offering interpretations of that experience. For now, we're just introducing the idea for later development. Our focus, early in the text, will be on the first two, while the later part of *Facing Death* will focus on spiritual death.

Theme 4: The physicality of Ivan's illness presents a challenge he can't ignore.

Ivan begins to experience an ongoing pain in his side. It's not clear from the text whether there is truly a relationship between the earlier fall and the pain, but it is possible. Over time, the pain increases. Ivan is often irritable, unable to sleep, develops a bad taste in his mouth, and starts producing a foul odor.

At the urging of his wife, they call a "celebrated" physician. The term "celebrated" refers to his status as he is highly regarded and travels in the best circles.

Tolstoy intends that the celebrated physician be very much like Ivan, forcing Ivan to see how others had experienced him. Just as when Ivan passed judgments in court, the physician exhibited an exaggerated sense of importance, often asked unnecessary questions, and exhibited a condescending attitude. Like Ivan, the celebrated physician was never intentionally cruel, but neither was he merciful. For example, regardless of extenuating circumstances, Ivan meticulously applied the law. He was unconcerned for the criminal or the victim and his judgments were really about himself, showcasing his own judicial prowess and intellect. It was the Ivan show. Except, in this case, it was the celebrated physician show.

But Ivan was now the "plaintiff" and not the "judge." This changed everything for Ivan:

> To Ivan Ilyich only one question mattered: was his condition serious or not? But the doctor ignored this inappropriate question. From his point of view it was an idle question and not worth considering. ... It was not a matter of Ivan Ilyich's life but a conflict between a floating kidney and a disease of the caecum. ... This was exactly what Ivan Ilyich had done a thousand times, and in the same brilliant manner, to prisoners on the dock. The doctor summed it up just as brilliantly, glancing triumphantly, even jovially, over his glasses at the prisoner. (Tolstoy 1981, 75–76)

When Ivan asked again, with great deference, if his condition was serious, the celebrated physician responded, "I have already told you what I consider necessary and suitable" (Tolstoy 1981, 76).

Why would the physician be so cold? In part, this was a physician whose primary concern was, like Ivan, his reputation and standing. To give a straight answer risked being wrong. Further, since the focus on this physician was, like Ivan, all about himself, he was simply insensitive to Ivan's pain. Later, when Ivan is crying in pain, we see the utter lack of simple human compassion when he says to Ivan's wife, "Yes, you sick people are always carrying on like this" (Tolstoy 1981, 110).

Ivan attempted to follow the physician's course of treatment, but other than moments of temporary hope, it was clear to him that the treatments were ineffective. Other courses proved equally futile. So, Ivan often gave up on them.

The effect of this was to give his wife the perfect pretext for her own lack of compassion towards Ivan. To be clear, the real reason she didn't feel sorry for her husband was because of how he had treated her throughout the years. It's not that he was abusive, it's just that he was never really there for her or concerned about her needs. Why should she feel concern for him?

Yet, here was a deathly ill man, often in terrible pain. How could she sleep at night if she didn't treat him with basic human compassion? She didn't want to think of herself as a monster.

Ivan's inconsistent following of his doctor's orders provided the perfect **pretext** for her lack of compassion. "Praskovya Fyodorovna's attitude toward her husband's illness was that he himself was to blame for it" (Tolstoy 1981, 81).

Why? ***She told herself that, if only he would follow his doctor's orders, he would get well.*** It was his own refusal to follow his treatments that caused his pain. She had come up with a classic **self-serving rationality**, in this case, by attributing a **false cause** to his remaining ill. Why should she suffer and feel sorry for him when he refused to take care of himself?

Theme 5: Love and self-honesty

It's possible that Praskovya loved Ivan when they were first married. If so, it was clearly over long before Ivan became ill. Praskovya's pregnancy was both a trial and an opportunity. If Ivan had handled it well, they could have developed a rich relationship. Instead, as we see with her lack of compassion for Ivan's suffering, Ivan "remade" her in his own image.

Ivan's daughter also reflected his attitude and values. For example, once, when Ivan is screaming in pain, instead of feeling sympathy, she says to her mother, "Why is he torturing us like this?" (Tolstoy 1981, 126). Just as it was all about Ivan, for his daughter, it was all about her.

It soon became clear to Ivan that those around him were mostly waiting for him to die. Despite this, they maintained the lie that he was just ill and that he would get better over time. The lie, instead of comforting Ivan, only became a greater source of distress. "Ivan was tortured by this lie" (Tolstoy 1981, 103). Why? Because it served as an excuse to dismiss his real suffering, to instead focus on the sorts of light social calls that had so characterized his own life, it "degrade[ed] the awesome, solemn act of his dying" (Tolstoy 1981, 103). "Nothing did so much to poison the last days of Ivan Ilyich's life as the falseness in himself and of those around him" (Tolstoy 1981, 105).

Anyone who has experienced serious pain knows that, if others dismiss, belittle, or refuse to take it seriously, it seems to make the pain worse. On the other hand, honest sympathy, here in short supply, has the effect of reducing pain.

Without the illness, Ivan could have continued indefinitely in his preferred lifestyle. *The illness, and the increased suffering and isolation that his lifestyle created, pushed Ivan to face the truth of his life.* It pushed him to question whether his view of the world, and his life, was a good one. Throughout the text, he fights this realization, but suffers all the more because of his denial.

There was one ray of light that entered Ivan's life. As his bodily needs became more extreme—and, for many, repulsive—a servant[2] was assigned to help with his bowel movements, washing, and other basic functions. Gerasim was utterly unlike anyone in Ivan's circle. While normally below Ivan's notice, Gerasim became Ivan's only source of real comfort.

It began when Ivan attempted to apologize for the unpleasantness of Gerasim having to carry out and clean his chamber pot, particularly since the stench was far worse than with normal excrement. "Oh no sir!" said Gerasim as he broke into a smile, his eyes and strong white teeth gleaming. "Why shouldn't I help you? You're a sick man" (Tolstoy 1981, 100).

That was the crux of the matter. While others pitied Ivan and looked down on him, Gerasim looked upon Ivan's illness as matter of fact, worthy of compassion, but not condescension. Gerasim understood that we will all one day die and that we will all be in need of one another. It's just part of life.

Gerasim, as the only person both emotionally and intellectually honest with Ivan, became a source of relief. Regular doses of morphine and opiates gave some direct relief to the physical side of Ivan's pain, but Gerasim's presence, and particularly his touch, did perhaps even more to relieve Ivan's actual suffering.

Ivan Ilyich had Gerasim sit down and hold his legs up, and he began talking to him. And, strangely enough, he thought he felt better while Gerasim was holding up his legs.

---

2 Gerasim's position is variously translated as the "pantry boy," "peasant boy," "servant," "butler," etc. Here, in this translation, he is the pantry boy. In any of these translations, the intent is the same. He is a peasant boy and a servant.

After that, Ivan Ilyich would send for Gerasim from time to time to have him hold his feet on his shoulders. And he loved to talk him. Gerasim did everything easily, willingly, simply, and with a goodness of heart which moved Ivan Ilyich. (Tolstoy 1981, 102)

Somehow, ***receiving honest compassion, even touch, on the part of another person went a long way to reducing Ivan's suffering***. Ivan's experience with Gerasim becomes the first major turning point of the book. It helps Ivan to awaken from his psychological numbness, or psychological death. But it's more than that. To understand, we need additional tools.

SCARRY AND THE RELATIONSHIP BETWEEN PAIN AND WORLD

We know, through experience and observation, that having someone like Gerasim in one's life tends to reduce the experience of suffering, even if the physical pain is unchanged. Similarly, relationships like those with Ivan's family, friends, and physician tend to actually increase the experience of suffering. This suggests that suffering is not just about the pain and that something else is going on. Elaine Scarry, in her study of pain, not just in medicine but in circumstances like torture and war and even in the courts, provides a rich way of thinking through this observation.

Let us begin by formalizing the difference between pain and suffering. While Scarry tends to use the term "pain" in both cases, the analysis is easier if we use "pain" to refer to a physical manifestation and "suffering" to refer to how we experience that physical manifestation. Note that there will still be places where, following common usage, we will return to using these two terms interchangeably. But for the sake of understanding, it's helpful to separate them here.

We also need to remind ourselves of our definition of world:

> *My world is the sum of my concrete possibilities for thought, action, and relationships beyond the physical body.*

This leads to one of Scarry's central insights:

> **Pain and world exist in an inverse relationship** (*Scarry 1985, 37*).

An inverse relationship, simply put, means that as one side increases the other decreases. The relationship is symmetrical in that it works in both directions. This has profound implications for both pain management and for understanding ourselves. But first, we need to understand it.

Let's return to our central insight of consciousness as a dynamic space, projecting itself forward into possibilities for action, thought, and relationships. These experiential possibilities are what make up each of our worlds. Again, no two person's worlds are identical. But there is a great deal of overlap, based in the experience that the "objective" part of reality, which forms a large part of each of our worlds, appears to be the same for us all. A second reason that our worlds overlap is that we are all human and we bring a similar set of precepts and capacities to our side of seeing those possibilities. This also means that our worlds differ, for at least two reasons. First, while we are all similar, none of us is identical. What I bring to understanding a situation is a bit different than what someone else brings to the same situation. Second, whatever "reality" is, it appears to be far more complex than any one mind (or set of ideas and possibilities) can capture. This is why, as we know from psychology, we each "select" small subsets of the data of our perception. This helps to account for the fact that many people, witnessing the same event, may see very different things.

A good example of this phenomena is the difference between Christians and Jews watching the film, **The Passion of Christ**. There was a great deal of controversy when the film came out. Some claimed it was anti-Semitic, while others felt that the claim was just foolishness. In reality, most people from the two groups saw what was almost two different "films." If you were a Christian your focus was on Jesus and his experience. If you were Jewish, you watched the crowds and how they were depicted. The Christian's identified, and many only really saw, the experiences of Jesus. Many of those of Jewish heritage identified with the crowds as their ancestors and focused their attention there instead. Just as the Christians noticed aspects of Jesus's portrayal that the Jews missed, so the Jews saw aspects of the portrayal of their people that the Christians missed. Both were true, but only in part. Both experienced **confirmation bias**.

Let's return to the relationship between pain and world. If consciousness, by its very nature, is always *projecting possibilities for the future for and beyond the physical body*, then a state of consciousness that shuts down those projections would also shut down one's "world."

This brings us to Scarry's definition of pain:

> **Pain is a state of consciousness without external reference** (*Scarry, 1985 5*).

Most people have struck their thumb or a finger when attempting to hammer a nail. If not that experience, perhaps consider when you have dropped something heavy on an unprotected toe. In either case, for the next minute, *nothing exists except the pain of that thumb or toe*. Abstractly, you are unchanged and all of your future possibilities remain the same (well, perhaps you won't be playing baseball the next day ...). *For you, in that moment, all of your possibilities vanish. Nothing exists except for the pain.*

Extreme pain is a state of consciousness without (that destroys) external reference (the experience of one's possibilities that constitute their world.)

Understanding this is one of the reasons why the US Military no longer considers it a "betrayal" when a service person signs a false confession under torture. In certain extreme situations, a person's world can be so narrowed that it's almost as if their "country" or family no longer exist. How can you betray something that doesn't exist?

This study also has profound implications for **palliative care** (care focused on relieving pain and suffering). Torture, for example, uses pain to destroy a person's world. What if we can reverse this process? What if, in cases of chronic pain, we can help people feel better by increasing their experience of their world? *As their world increases, their suffering should decrease.*

Why not merely treat all pain with medications? Some types of pain are easily treated in that way. But not all. In some cases, the only way we can keep someone out of pain is to sedate them into unconsciousness. Drugs also have side effects, including the possibility of addiction. If we can help someone manage their pain with fewer drugs, that would seem a significant win.

Returning to Ivan, we see that he has, thus far, experienced two basic strategies for increasing his world. We will also explore a third strategy, which we name here but will discuss when we get to the end of Ivan's life. These are:

1. Distraction

2. Connection to others by receiving compassion

3. Giving compassion and caring more for others or something beyond oneself

Have you ever had a headache or a nagging pain but you got so engrossed in a game, a movie, or a conversation that you simply no longer noticed the pain? When the event was over, you might have again felt the headache (if it hadn't passed), but you completely forgot about it while distracted. This is distraction.

While we all use it in a variety of ways, in the case of Ivan Ilyich, we see Ivan use it to deal with psychological pain. Recall that, when his home life came to be a disturbance, he threw himself into his work. By doing so, he would "forget," for a time, the troubles at home. Through expanding his world into his work, he could avoid the pain of his home life.

At times, this form of pain relief can be quite powerful. In general, it is probably the least effective of the three forms that we focus on in this text. As Ivan's pain became greater, his ability to ignore it (by throwing himself into his work) diminished. This brings us to the second level.

One of the most powerful ways to increase one's world appears to be through rich, deep, honest human connections. When we feel a deep connection to another person, somehow, we find ourselves transformed. In part, this is how Gerasim decreased Ivan's world. By approaching Ivan with honest compassion, Ivan felt accepted and valued, even in the state of whimpering patient. Touch reinforced that connection. Gerasim didn't "physically" diminish Ivan's pain, but Ivan felt it less. His suffering was reduced.

His family, by contrast, had the opposite effect. Tolstoy focused in part upon the lies. They would pretend he wasn't really dying. The main issue, however, was really the human connection. Lying, in this case, reduced Ivan's already tenuous connection to his family even more. But this is still secondary to Ivan's own self-deception, which, as we will see, was the strongest factor in reducing his world and increasing his suffering.

As Ivan moves closer to death, the physical pain of his illness pushes him closer and closer to asking fundamental questions about his life. Each time he pulls back, what he would have to admit to himself is too frightening. He struggles to accept two truths. First, the fact that he is dying. Second, and more importantly, the truth about how he has lived his life. Ivan asked himself, "What if my entire life, my entire conscious life, simply was *not the real thing*?" (Tolstoy 1981, 126; emphasis his).

This second lie thus breaks down into two related parts. The first was that his understanding of life was "correct" and that he had lived life as he should. The second was that he was good man for doing so. The fact that bad things (the illness and poor treatment by his family) kept happening to him challenged this self-deception. But as it was also at the heart of Ivan's self-identity, it was extremely difficult for him to let go.

By "the real thing" Tolstoy is asking the question of *what really matters* in life. This brings us back to Frankl's claim that *meaning is even more important than happiness*. Ivan has spent his entire life focused on getting ahead. To do so, he has curried favor from those in power, suppressing any internal criticisms, objections, or feelings that might go against their interests. "The doctor said that his physical agony was dreadful, and that was true; but even more dreadful was his moral agony, and it was this that tormented him most" (Tolstoy 1981, 126).

Ivan's moral pain was based on the fear that he had made the wrong choice(s) in life; that he had suppressed, from his youth, those impulses and actions that really mattered.

> It occurred to him that those scarcely perceptible impulses of his to protest what people of high rank considered good, vague impulses which he had always suppressed, might have been precisely what mattered. ... (Tolstoy 1981, 126)

He feared that he was taking leave of this life after "squander[ing] all that I was given ..." He saw his reflection in his wife and daughter, how he had made or remade them in his image, resulting in a "dreadful, enormous deception that shut them out of both life and death." He wondered, fearfully, is there "no possibility of rectifying matters?" (Tolstoy 1981, 127).

This phrase, "shut them out of both life and death," is telling. One of the themes of *Facing Death* is that only by facing one's own death does one learn how to live. Here, Tolstoy is naming that theme in reverse. **To numb oneself to death, to hide from what the fact of death has to teach us, is also to numb oneself to life**. To numb oneself to death is to be psychologically dead. There's a corollary principle that is similarly telling; *to numb oneself to pain is to numb oneself to joy*. In other words, **psychological death** doesn't just work in one direction. Only by authentically accepting the appropriate place of pain can one be fully open to joy. They go hand in hand.

This reminds me of a former professor, Patrick Burke, at Seattle University. When he married, I asked what attracted him to his wife. He answered: "She is not afraid to suffer." This took some explaining!

What Dr. Burke meant was that she was a woman who was radically open to life in all its textures. She was a person who could be profoundly present to someone in their pain and suffering. She didn't seek suffering, but she didn't run from it either. When suffering came, she allowed herself to experience it. By not resisting it, it passed through her, it didn't stop and fester. As it passed through, it was as if it had hollowed out a greater space in her spirit for joy. She was a profoundly joyful person.[3]

Meanwhile, Ivan's interaction with the celebrated physician changed. Instead of asking his physician if he was dying, Ivan stated it as a matter of fact. This approach, where Ivan began with his own honesty, changed everything.

Previously, the celebrated physician would not give Ivan an honest answer to the question of whether he would survive. This could be for a variety of reasons. It could be because, earlier, he didn't want to risk being wrong. It could be because he hated

---

3   I've experienced this to a lesser degree. For example, I'm aware that that, if I feel depressed and resist those feelings, they will often get stronger over time. But if I let myself simply feel them, perhaps for a time in the quiet of my home, often, they will pass within a day. At times, they will even leave a gift of some insight or greater capacity for feeling.

giving bad news or because he believed that telling someone that they were dying actually caused them to suffer more.

However, the celebrated physician was willing to affirm, *once Ivan asserted his dying*, rather than asking if it was fact. It took the responsibility off his shoulders. It also illustrated a basic psychological mechanism. It's a mechanism I saw when working with street youth. It's also a trick often used by police.[4] *We are more likely to affirm a truth when stated than to admit a truth when asked.*

At this point, Ivan has only admitted to the first lie. What about the second?

At the climax of the book, we see Ivan dying in intense pain. He screams incessantly, but the real pain is more moral than physical. The pain was so great that, at times, Ivan's world ceased to exist, along with time itself. That pain also pushed him to face the truth about his life.

> ... *he felt that with every minute, despite his efforts to resist, he was coming closer and closer to what terrified him. He felt he was in agony because he was being shoved into that black hole, but even more because he was unable to get right into it. (Tolstoy 1981, 131)*

The "black hole" was the truth about the lies he had been telling himself all his life. It was also the feeling that he had never really lived, that he had wasted his life. Like

---

4   Police use it in the following way: Let's say that they are searching for the person who committed a crime. They aren't at all sure if you committed the crime, but you might be a suspect. Instead of asking you, "Did you commit the crime?" they will say, "Why did you kill him?"

Technically, they have just committed the logical **fallacy of a complex question**. A complex question is really *two questions rolled into one, with the answer to the first question already assumed*. Thus, I might ask, "have you stopped beating your children?" Particularly if I insist on a yes or no answer, you're stuck. If you answer no, then it means you are still beating your children. But if you say yes, you have stopped, then you are admitting to having beat them in the past. What if you never beat your children?

The question is "complex" because there should really have been two questions and not one. The first question would have been, "Have you ever beat your children?" Only with an affirmative answer to that question would the second question, "Have you stopped beating your children?" make sense.

As an aside, this is also closely related to the **fallacy of bifurcation**, also called the **excluded middle**. The fallacy of the excluded middle gives one only two options when there is clearly *at least* one additional option. In this case, the excluded option is that you never beat your kids.

Let's return to the police. Why would they ask you, "Why did you kill him?" when they really don't know if you committed the murder? It could be because they know that, if they ask the first question, you will almost certainly say no. But if you committed the murder, and if they just state it as a matter of fact, you are far more likely to tell them why, and so confess.

I saw this mechanism over and over again while working with street kids in downtown Seattle. Most of them used drugs, usually to numb the pain of a terrible existence. If I asked them, "Do you take drugs?" the answer would almost always be no. But if I just asked them "So, which drugs do you use?" I would often get an answer.

most pain, it was all the worse for the fact that he resisted it. A bandage pulled off quickly hurts, but only for a moment. Pulled off slowly, the pain goes on and on.

> *What prevented him from getting into it was the belief that his life had been a good one. This justification held him fast, kept him from moving forward, and caused him more pain than anything else. (Tolstoy 1981, 131)*

When he finally enters fully into the darkness, something strange happens. He sees something at the bottom, something that he could not see until he accepted the lie of his life. It was something shining.

That shining thing was hope. It was the possibility that, now that he had accepted the truth, he might, for at least the last moments of his life, choose the "real thing" and focus on what was really worthwhile.

The problem was that he had no idea what "the real thing" was (Tolstoy 1981, 132).

Ivan grew quiet. This does not mean that he stopped screaming, the pain was too great. But a part of him stopped. Perhaps for the first time since childhood, if not the first time in his life, he really listened.

> *This took place at the end of the third day, an hour before his death. Just then his son crept quietly into the room and went up to his bed. The dying man was still screaming desperately and flailing his arms. One hand fell on the boy's head. The boy grasped it, pressed it to his lips, and began to cry. (Tolstoy 1981, 132)*

Ivan's son was still young enough not to be fully "remade" in his father's image. The compassion and pain of his son showed Ivan what he needed to do, what was real.

> *At the very moment Ivan fell through and saw a light, and it was revealed to him that his life had not been what it should have been but that he could still rectify the situation. … Just then he felt someone kissing his hand. He opened his eyes and looked at his son. He grieved for him.*
>
> *His wife came in and went up to him. He looked at her. She gazed at him with an open mouth, with unwiped tears on her nose and cheeks, with a look of despair … He grieved for her.*
>
> *… I'm torturing them, he thought …*
>
> *… it will be better for them when I die. (Tolstoy 1981, 132; formatting modified, emphasis mine).*

For the first time in Ivan's adult life, he cared more about someone else than himself.

The result?

> *… suddenly it became clear to him that what had been oppressing him and would not leave him suddenly was vanishing all at once—from two sides, ten sides, all sides. He felt sorry for them, he had to do something to keep from hurting them. To deliver them*

and himself from suffering. "How good and simple!" he thought. "And the pain?" he asked himself. "Where has it gone? Now, then, pain, where are you?"
  He waited for it attentively.
  "Ah, there it is. Well, what of it? Let it be." (Tolstoy 1981, 133)

For me, one of the saddest parts of this story is that Ivan, in attaining this insight so close to death, never really got to help his family in any substantial way. The realizations and the change in intention—coming to care for others—changed him, in fact, it transformed him, but it may have been too late for them. It's worth noting that it was the moral pain that was gone, while the physical pain remained. Yet, he suffered less. In a way far more powerful than the previous two, Ivan's world expanded. This is the third level we listen to in our discussion of Scarry:

Giving compassion, caring more for others or something beyond oneself.

This appears to be the most profound way in which we expand our world.

Taken another way, we can think of this in terms of one of Nietzsche's more famous phrases:

He who has a why to live for can bear almost any how.

The "why" is world expanding, or living for someone or something more than oneself. If we have found what we are living for something beyond ourselves, that connection dramatically expands our world.[5]

For Ivan, he finally came to love his family.

---

5   Sadly, to some degree, even a violent cause can be world expanding. But the claim here is that it's not the richest form, nor the ultimate way to joy. For Tolstoy, the best of all religions focus on the nature of love. It's this kind of living for something greater than oneself that, I would argue, speaks to the heart of our spiritual and most fundamentally human selves. To get there, one must also undergo a sort of reversal, as Ivan does when he fully enters into the darkness (Tolstoy 1981, 132). This reversal is the shift from a focus on oneself, from one's fear of death and pain, to a sense of joy and welcoming, and to care more for others. In the Hebrew Scriptures, for example, the stranger could be the terrorist bringing pain and suffering. While one isn't expected to act without caution, the basic attitude is one of welcoming the stranger, the poor, the widow, or the orphan.

For Tolstoy, there also appears to be a metaphysical turn here. Part of the bliss that Ivan feels may in fact be that he is being welcomed, now repentant, into heaven. Death no longer exists for Ivan (Tolstoy 1981, 133). There are many ways to look at this insight, and one must remember that, while Tolstoy was a Christian, he didn't believe that Christianity was the only way to truth.

While there is a danger in focusing on the metaphysical, danger can be instructive. We've started the argument that happiness is a byproduct of other goals. We are also starting to get a sense of what some of those goals might be. If we stay with Aristotle's notion of happiness, as the product of looking

Final Observations

This story provides an example of how happiness, even if it is the ultimate goal, cannot be achieved directly. For Tolstoy, it appears that happiness is a byproduct of caring for more than just oneself. In this claim, Tolstoy appears to be more in line with Frankl's claim that meaning is more important than happiness.[6] In other words, while having a meaningful life doesn't guarantee happiness, one cannot be truly happy without a deeper meaning to one's life. For Tolstoy, this meaning is found in loving others, which foreshadows the second theme of the course, that love is the ultimate rational act.

Running away from necessary pain and fear, including the fear of death, only makes that pain more powerful.

Ivan finally broke free of his moral pain when he was (1) honest with himself and (2) began to care more for others than just himself. However, it is unlikely that he could have reached that understanding if not for Gerasim's gift of compassion to Ivan. *We need to receive compassion to learn to give it.*

Of the forms of world expansion we discussed, *caring about others (love, compassion) appears to be the most powerful.*

While we do not yet have the tools to fully understand it, Ivan experiences not just a psychological rebirth, but a spiritual death and rebirth as well.

---

back on a rich, full life, the suicide bomber, while satisfying the "why," is not hoping for the happiness of a full life. At least, not in this life.

Moreover, even the "why" of the terrorist or suicide bomber is suspect. While they may believe that they are seeking to serve their God, they aren't really doing it for love, but for what they will receive in the end. In an important way, *they are still primarily focused on themselves.* They are like Ivan Ilyich, seeking to please someone they believe has power over them. Ivan didn't break through until his love was sincere, until his concern for his family was purely for their sake. (The importance of the idea of loving without expecting a return will be more fully explored when we discuss C.S. Lewis.)

For us, whether we take the conclusion as suggesting a metaphysical heaven, or just a fundamental experience we share in our common humanity, the message is clear. While these lessons have value at any point in our lives, what would it have meant if Ivan had come to understand this, and himself, at a much earlier age? *Do we want to wait until the end of our lives to become aware of what is really worthwhile?*

6 Living a "meaningful" life wasn't a category for Aristotle's culture, otherwise he might have drawn the same conclusion.

CHAPTER FOUR

Anger, Depression, Suicide, Forgiveness

LESSONS FROM GRIEF

Healing doesn't mean that the damage never existed.
It means that it no longer controls our lives.

Akshay Dubey

WHAT IF DEPRESSION could be a good thing? Not just in a trivial way, like suggesting that the contrast makes one appreciate the good times. *What if depression is fundamental to our humanity?*

Of course, no one actually wakes up in the morning thinking, "Wow, I feel depressed, isn't that great! Maybe I can keep this going for the whole week!" As Aries points out, society has made it almost a moral obligation to be happy. Part of that obligation is that we refuse, in our hearts, the fear and anxiety of fully accepting our mortality. Aries's conclusion? "And surprise! Our life is not as a result gladdened!" (Aries 1974, 106).

What if the same is true of feelings like depression? Perhaps depression is not always bad. Perhaps it carries gems that, when properly understood, can actually help us lead a richer and fuller life, allowing us to truly "gladden" our lives.

Elizabeth Kübler-Ross concluded that there were five stages most pass through on the way to "accepting" and finding peace in their deaths. These are denial, anger, bargaining, depression, and finally, acceptance (Kübler-Ross 1975, 10). One doesn't have to pass through them in strict order, nor does everyone reach the final stage. But Kübler-Ross gives us a strong hint of what depression, anger, and other so-called "negative" emotions might have to teach us:

> *To rejoice at the opportunity of experiencing each new day is to prepare for one's ultimate acceptance of death. For it is those who have not really lived—who have left issues unsettled, dreams unfulfilled, hopes shattered, and who*

have let the real things in life (loving and being loved by others, contributing in a posi-
tive way to other people's happiness and welfare, finding out what things are really you)
pass them by—who are most reluctant to die. (Kübler-Ross 1975, xi; emphasis hers)

If this looks familiar, it is. It's from the opening chapter of this book. It also names again the first two themes of this book. Rephrased to make the connection more obvious, they are:

Only by facing one's death, not just as a prelude to an afterlife, but the fear and anxiety that perhaps this is ALL there is, can one really figure out what is important in this life.

The answer to what makes this life worthwhile, on its own terms, appears to have something to do with living a rich life (in terms of what you do, not money) and fulfilling relationships with others.

However, when it comes to dealing with the loss of a loved one after death or divorce, there are other models, such as Elizabeth Neeld's *Seven Choices: Finding Daylight after Loss Shatters Your World*, which I find more helpful. What I like about Neeld's model is its greater focus on identifying the differences between those who get "stuck" in their grief and those who heal and go on to live a rich, full life. I find Neeld's model, which identifies seven stages and the sorts of *choices* that differentiate those who move on from those who get "stuck," more helpful to those working through grief. Moreover, as Neeld points out, Kübler-Ross's stages are often misunderstood. This is particularly true of acceptance.

... acceptance **is the booby prize** *in the active grieving process because most people, when asked their definition of acceptance, will indicate that the word means something like resignation. (Neeld 2003, 23; emphasis mixed)*

Neeld realizes that resignation is not what Kübler-Ross means by acceptance. She believes that there is a great deal that these stages can teach us about living, including, as Neeld loves to say, recovering a "zest" for life. Neeld's worry is for those people for whom "acceptance" is really reduced to "resignation."

The purpose of this chapter is to explore Kübler-Ross's stages in such a way as to illustrate their importance in creating and recovering not just that "zest" for life, but in deepening and enriching our very persons. Just as Kübler-Ross holds that these stages have something to teach the living, so the stories and analysis of this chapter are focused not only on the process of dying, but on what each stage can teach us about living in general. In the end, we will understand that this can be positive value in each of these states, the limits of that value, and most important, some indications of how these states can be used for personal transformation.

Before we begin, I need to offer some caveats. Most people who are not clinically depressed undergo situational depression at some points in their lives. Both the

American Medical Association and the American Psychological Association now recognize that several periods of extended depression are normal throughout the course of one's life.

This is not "clinical" depression. **There are levels of clinical depression for which there may be no "redemptive" value, for which the only hope is medical treatment.** For depression at this level, the stories that follow may not apply. *However, those who experience clinical depression typically also experience, albeit even more intensely, other levels of depression experienced by most other people. For that reason, these thoughts may be of value to them as well.*

A second caveat is that **some grief is never entirely "resolved."** For example, we will look at how, for some of us, the very fact that we miss someone so intensely can be a testament to how rich it was to have them in our lives and to how much we valued that time together. Over time, the bittersweet nature of this insight shifts more towards the sweet and less the bitter. But how does one really say that about, for example, the death of a child? It's easier (but still not always effective) to argue for this sort of strategy in the case of, for example, a married couple who shared 20+ years together, than for the case of a young child whose life was cut tragically short.

In cases like the death of a child, people may never entirely "work through" or gain "closure" on their grief. If we think about the value of "meaning" in one's life, what can happen is that we find a way to honor their memory. For some, it might be fighting for research funds to cure other children of the disease that took one's own. For another, whose child was killed by a drunk driver or active shooter, it might be getting involved in ways to reduce those risks to other children. Yet another might take it as a lesson to treasure the other children or people in their lives. The value, here, appears to be in **creating some sort of enduring meaning or value to the death. The grief is never entirely gone, but it gives a meaning to their loss.**

A third caveat is that **depression is too general a term**—there are many levels of feeling and mood that are part of us, even when one is "depressed." Similarly, there are types of grief that have nothing to do with death. But that doesn't make them unreal. It's important to remember that **there is no "one size fits all" answer.**

Still, there are things we can learn from one another. I recall a student I'd known since his freshman year, who came to me one year just after Christmas. He was talented, intelligent, good looking, but had also had a very challenging life. When we first met, he was cynical and unhappy. Having come from an impoverished childhood, his stated goal in life was to make as much money as possible. I could tell that the cynicism wasn't really where he wanted to be, he wanted something richer.

Over time, we would talk, and occasionally he would ask me, "When does all this stuff you're talking about kick in?" That's not a question to which I could give a firm answer. Like love, one had to be open, but one cannot force the moment. Transformations occur when outside circumstances meet our readiness to change.

This particular year, he had a difficult fall term, even undergoing a hospitalization. To top it off, over the break, his girlfriend cheated on him. For the first time facing this sort of betrayal, however, he wasn't angry. He didn't want to hurt her back. Between the combination of appropriate medication and the deep personal work he had been doing, he instead realized that this was her issue. Her actions weren't intended to hurt him, nor was it an indication of his failure. Instead of anger, he found himself feeling compassion for her. Then he said something I'll never forget. He said, "For the first time I can remember, I felt happy."

Who would have thought that the first moment, perhaps in years, where he felt "happy" was when someone "betrayed" him? Yet, if we recall the insights from Scarry and Ivan Ilyich, we shouldn't be surprised. Compassion requires that we move and care for others beyond ourselves.

Just as the feelings and solutions vary, so does what many describe as the hoped for outcome. Neeld writes of recovering a "**zest**" for life. *Others argue that happiness isn't the goal, that for many who are clinically depressed, the real goal is simply to feel "alive,"* to experience some sort of "**vitality**." This makes sense to me. But it also reminds me that each of these terms means somewhat different things to different people. Even with my aforementioned student, his experience of "being happy" was a product of certain other goals and transformations. Vitality or zest, and what brings it, seems a rich way to explore this experience.

Stage One: Denial

One of my former teachers used to say, "Denial, it's not just a river in Africa." Someone engaged in denial is unable, at least for a time, to accept and deal with reality. Usually, we view that as a bad thing. But can denial offer us a benefit? If so, how can one tell whether one's denial is beneficial or harmful?

The positive role of denial is that it helps one to continue to function in the face of news or an event that would otherwise be overwhelming. For example, a father finds out that his spouse has died, yet he still must care for their children. If the emotions of the initial impact completely overwhelm him, then he will be unable to care for their needs. This is not to say that one can't show feelings, but that *one may only be able to accept it in bits, in smaller doses. By spreading it out over time, one can still perform essential functions.*

Billy Bud

One of my experiences with the positive role of denial came with the loss of my cat, Billy Bud. Billy Bud was a sweet orange tabby. Very loving, but extremely timid and afraid both of strangers and of strange surroundings. He could become so paralyzed with fear that he would not even respond to my voice.

In April 2003, I was getting ready to take a job at the University of Northern Iowa. I lived in Nashville, Tennessee and travelled to Iowa to look for housing. While I was gone, my house was in the process of being painted. My main concern was that the painters would leave a window open and Billy Bud might get out. If so, and if I wasn't there to let him in, he would likely get lost, either due to hunger or due to being chased by another animal. If that happened, I feared I would never see him again.

I was absolutely clear with the painters that they must not leave the doors open. More importantly, since I knew they would have to open windows to avoid having them painted shut, I told them that they couldn't be left open more than a couple of inches, so that the cat could not escape. I didn't just leave instructions, I explained to them why it was important to me.

When I got home, Billy Bud was gone.

My first feeling was a sort of impotent rage. How could the painters have been so careless? Impotent, however, since being angry at that point would do nothing to rectify the situation.

Then it was grief. I knew I'd probably never see Billy Bud again.

The only thing I could think of was to put up posters and walk the streets and alleyways of the neighborhood calling his name. I knew the odds were poor of him coming, as he was likely too frozen in fear to come even when I called him. He was so timid that he would also unlikely find another home. Even so, it was the only thing that would give him a chance.

The problem was my own grief. Have you ever felt so much grief that your voice cracked, that you were unable to speak with any volume? That's how I felt whenever I thought of my poor companion. Yet, if I couldn't speak, if I couldn't project my voice, I would lose even what little chance I had of bringing him home.

I chose denial. In order to be able to call him, I told myself, again and again, that he was fine, that he would come home, and that there was nothing to worry about. It worked most of the time. I was able to walk the alleys and streets and call his name. When I got home I would let go and cry.

I never found Billy Bud. I expect he died a painful and lonely death. Denial allowed me to function well enough to give him a chance.

That's the positive role of denial.

Carman and Ishmael

Nuland tells the story of Carman and her husband, Ishmael. Ishmael was a decent father, but not a decent husband. Either from affairs or IV drug use, he contracted HIV. Because he didn't like the side effects, he often skipped his medications, progressing to full-blown AIDS. Carman, a woman of strong Catholic convictions, took him back to care for him as he was dying (Nuland 1985, 163–172).

The problem is that so long as Ishmael was alive, Carman refused to get an AIDS test for herself. It was only upon Ishmael's death that she asked the nurse for a test. Why? Nuland does not explain, but we can speculate.

The fear, of course, is of a positive result. It seems unlikely that she refused the test because she wanted to spare Ishmael's feelings before he died. For that, all she had to do was to refuse to tell him the results or even that she had gotten the test. More likely, she chose to remain ignorant because she felt it was her duty to care for Ishmael. If she tested positive, she may have feared that she would become so angry as to be unable to carry out that duty. *The positive value she gained from denial was that she was able to fulfill what she saw as her duty.*

But there is a serious risk in Carman's case. Just as Ishmael's refusal to take his medications caused the disease to advance rapidly, Carman's delay in being tested, if positive, meant a significant delay in treatment. We don't know the results of that test. If it was positive, given the state of medicine at the time, she likely gave up years of her life.

This is the negative side of denial. It can place oneself or others at significant risk. Denial, in the short term, rarely entails significant risk. But the longer it goes on, the greater the risk. In this case, Carman faced at least two major risks. The first risk is the loss of years off her life. The second risk is a relational loss. The cost of her life is also time taken away from raising her three girls.

The risk can be physical, psychological, relational, financial, etc. **The bottom line, not just for this stage, but for each stage, is that if remaining in a stage places oneself or others at significant risk, or causes significant problems in the process of living one's life, that stage is no longer healthy.**

Stage Two: Anger

Most of us think of anger as a bad thing. At best, we think that the positive role of anger is either to

(1) get the stuff "out" so as to experience a release (*catharsis*) or
(2) give us the strength to go through with something important.

While both of these points can be true, *these two points barely touch the surface of the real value of anger.*

Consider a richer notion of catharsis. *In psychology*, catharsis is not just an emotional release. Rather, *catharsis is an emotional release that brings insight*. What sort of insight? As a counselor once told me:

"Anger tells us that something needs to stop, something needs to change."

Discerning what needs to stop or change is the insight that anger is trying to bring to light. *Of course, we usually think of that change as needing to occur in the person or situation about which we are angry, when in fact,* **the change usually needs to occur within oneself.**

This is not to say there aren't changes one might appropriately hope for in another. For example, when married to an alcoholic, one might hope that he or she gives up drinking and enters a good recovery program. As a counselor will often end up telling the non-alcoholic spouse, "He or she is not going to change, so what are YOU going to do about it?" This is the crux of the issue. Do I just accept the behaviors and try to make my peace with them, or do I ask myself WHY I'm putting up with a clearly unhealthy situation and seek to change myself? Since it is unlikely that I will be able to change someone else, how can I change myself? *Once I make the changes,* either by finding my peace with the situation or by changing it, *I no longer need to be angry.*

In practice, of course, it's not that simple. I recall, while attending a divorce support group, the story of a woman on her third divorce. Three divorces is sad, but not that odd. *Then I realized that all three divorces were to the same man. What,* I thought to myself, *has she not figured out?*

Her situation is more obvious, but not all that uncommon. Most people, when they move from relationship to relationship, choose the same type of person and make the same sorts of mistakes. (*Same play, different characters.*) That's when I realized that it wasn't enough to merely accept the insight that since my partner wasn't going to change I needed to leave the marriage. I needed to understand why, given the abundance of warning signs, I married her in the first place. I needed to learn from my first marriage so that I didn't repeat the same mistakes in a second.

For example, I recognized that I needed to look much more closely at actions than words. My former spouse spoke of all of the values I held dear—service to others and living a life for more than just oneself—but rarely had any time to volunteer or otherwise act on those values. There were always excuses. Similarly, it is easy for someone to learn to live on a budget for a short while to please someone else, but that's not the same as someone who is able to do so for themselves over the long haul. Those criticisms, however, are focused mainly on her. In terms of my own life, I needed to be cured of my naïve belief that people would both follow their stated beliefs and wouldn't act in self-destructive ways. I also had to ask why I didn't have enough self-esteem to feel as though I deserved better. There were plenty of warning signs before I got married, I ignored them. These are a few of the many lessons I learned from my marriage. When I learned to accept and listen to the sources of my anger, it had much to teach me.

Anger can also give us the strength to make necessary changes. For me, one of my greatest fears lies in hurting another. In my marriage that merely allowed for manipulation by my spouse. We both enabled one another's dysfunctions. She would play the victim and I would rush to "rescue" her. I needed to realize that until I accepted that standing up for myself would mean that she would characterize me in the role of the villain, I would always be "hooked." Anger gave me the strength to accept that she would characterize me as such and to stand up and get out of the marriage. I am a much happier person as a result, and hopefully, so is she. That is, if she too took the time to learn what she needed too.

However, I also made a fateful mistake. I decided that, in order to have the strength to avoid "repeating" the same mistakes in another relationship, I would hang on to just a bit of that anger. This would have been fine for a short while. But eventually, I forgot that I was hanging on to it. This brings us to the nature of healthy anger: forgiveness.

Forgiveness: Anger's Necessary Partner

Hanging onto anger is letting someone live rent free in your head.

We usually start off thinking that forgiveness is about the person who needs to be forgiven. This is partly true. Far more profound, however, is the fact that forgiveness is a "letting go" on the part of the one doing the forgiving. It's a process of releasing anger, hurt, resentment, and letting go of some of the choices and emotions that get in the way of happiness. That said, it's worth highlighting that *forgiveness is not the same as becoming a doormat. It doesn't mean abdicating responsibility or allowing someone to run over you again and again.* When my ex over-drafted her credit cards she used the argument that, (1) if I took away her credit cards she would never learn to be responsible, and (2) if I didn't trust her with them, then I didn't love her, since trust is essential to love. While I didn't really believe her argument, I repeatedly helped her pay them off. The pattern then repeated.

I laugh at these arguments now. I'm a pretty honest person, but I know I have a weakness for chocolate. If you put an open bowl of chocolate on my desk, it will eventually get eaten. For that reason, I'll tell you to take away the bowl. It's not really an issue of trust, but an issue of understanding oneself and adjusting for one's weaknesses. Trust is not an all-or-nothing proposition. The same should have been true for her credit cards.

The best example I can think of for balancing forgiveness with responsibility comes from a friend of mine in Tennessee, who we will call Mary. Mary was a woman of rare courage and insight.

Mary and Paul[1]

Mary lived in the country. Paul was married with kids, but his marriage was strained so he was living in a trailer on Mary's land while he and his wife tried to work through their marital issues.

One night, when Paul was under particular strain, he snapped and beat up his sister. It was bad.

The police came and Paul was taken to jail. Needless to say, Mary got a restraining order. Paul was no longer welcome on her property.

The wheels of justice turn slowly. About a year after the incident, Mary made the decision to forgive her brother and move on. She called Paul and they attend counseling together. As a result, their relationship began to mend.

The assistant DA heard about their reconciliation. He called Mary, upset, and told her that he wouldn't drop the charges and expected her to testify. He was concerned, justifiably, with the pattern of abused spouses (mostly women) who go through cycles of forgiving and taking back their abuser, only to be abused again. It's very common.

Mary, however, told him that she would be testifying. She said that Paul needed to take responsibility for his actions, but that she needed to forgive him in order to heal and move on with her life.

On the day before the trial, Mary received a call from Paul. He was clearly distraught. Having reconciled with his wife, he was now back with his wife and kids. He explained that his attorney had told him that he was facing up to two years in jail. He said something like, "*Mary, I just got my kids back and I can't bear to be away from them again.*"

His purpose in calling was to explain what was going to happen in court. His attorney insisted that his best chance of avoiding jail was for him (the attorney) to attack Mary and to make it seem like the assault was Mary's fault. Paul wanted to prepare Mary for the tactic and to tell her that he knew it wasn't true, but that he was just too afraid of going to jail to say no.

Mary took a deep breath and said, "Paul, if you do this, I will forgive you, but it could be a long time." They hung up.

The next morning, on the way into court, Mary got another call from Paul. He said, "I almost lost my sister once; I couldn't bear to lose you again. I'll tell the truth and take my medicine."

When Mary forgave her brother Paul, she let the pain and the hurt heal. But she didn't take away the responsibility or the consequences of Paul's actions. In the end, she also helped Paul take responsibility for himself.

---

1 As with most stories, names and some details have been changed.

This is part of the lesson of forgiveness. It's about what we need to do to let go and heal. If that involves the other person, then all the better. But if it's not safe, or they aren't willing, one should not place oneself at risk for a cycle of violence or other forms of abuse.

It's also important to note that Paul was not habitually violent. This is why Mary could both forgive and have a relationship with him. Had the situation been different, she would still have needed to forgive him, but she would have needed to stay away. In fact, in such cases, it is often best to let go without telling the other person.

What finally happened? Mary testified honestly. Paul pled guilty. But they also told the judge about what had happened since. The judge realized this was not a typical case and sentenced Paul to a fine, probation, and counseling. Paul did not go to jail.

What of my mistake? Recall that I hung onto a bit of my anger towards my ex as a means of avoiding repeating the same mistake with a different person. Eventually, I forgot (**repressed**) that I was hanging onto it. What conclusion did we draw when a stage becomes unhealthy?

> ... the bottom line, not just for this stage, but for all of them, is that if remaining in a stage places oneself or others at significant risk, or causes significant problems in the process of living one's life, that stage is no longer healthy.

A few years after my divorce, I was dating a very nice woman. After the second or third occurrence of a particular event, I suddenly found that I couldn't break up fast enough. For some reason, all I wanted to do was get out of that relationship. The very thought of staying in the relationship generated intense anxiety, even panic.

It wasn't until about a year later that another event triggered an insight as to why. This woman had acted in a way that reminded me of my ex. The anger I had kept did exactly what I had held on to it for: it said, "never again." But I had only wanted it to keep me from repeating the same mistakes. Instead, it was triggered by a vague similarity between someone I was dating and my ex. I broke up without real choice or understanding. That's when I realized that I needed to finish forgiving my ex. Not for her sake, but for mine. Unless I forgave her, I would be unable to give myself in healthy relationships in the future.

> The day a child realizes that all adults are imperfect, he becomes an adolescent.
> The day he forgives them, he becomes an adult.
> The day he forgives himself, he becomes wise. (Alden Nowlan)

Stage Three: Bargaining

This is the stage where I have the least to say. As Kübler-Ross notes, most often, the bargaining is with God and rarely does one follow through with his or her promises. To me, bargaining seems a form of denial, for which much of the same analysis applies. Perhaps it can also, at times, allow one to clarify their values and what is important to them in life. That is accomplished far more richly in the next stage, depression.

Stage Four: Depression

Depression is perhaps the richest and most intriguing of Kübler-Ross's stages. My experience is that **people who have struggled with depression and come out the other side are among the richest and most peaceful people I know.** Why? Recall the first theme of the course, that only when one knows how to die does one know how to live. Facing one's death, facing the possibility that this might be all there is, pushes one to ask the question: "What makes this life worthwhile?" To get there, one must face death in an embodied sense, which I refer to as a certain anxiety and uncanniness within one's body. The question, once answered, transforms[2] one's life. Once one figures out, not just intellectually but emotionally and physically, what's most important to them, the chaff seems to fall away. We live our lives differently.

Depression can enable the same sort of questioning. While it includes a variety of feelings and states, depression includes a sense wherein *all the things in which most others find value and meaning appear empty, dry, and meaningless.* **This death of meaning can function very much like the facing of one's physical death.** Because all things seem empty, **it invites one to search for that which might be more richly meaningful.** Once this is found, life is transformed. However, I should also be cautious not to imply that one simply finds an answer and is "done." Rather, it takes one in a new direction, allowing one to engage life and oneself in a new and richer way. The process must be nurtured.

This does not mean depression automatically tends in this direction. As I noted earlier, sometimes we need help. In many cases, that help may be chemical. Yet, I am troubled by the sheer number of people who are on antidepressants in our society. I am also troubled by the gender differences; three times as many women are reported

---

2   I've used the term "transform" or "transformation" a number of times. It doesn't necessarily mean that one has entirely lost one's fear of the dying process, just as one doesn't typically enjoy pain. What it means is, as in the case of Ivan Ilyich, that fear (or pain) no longer dominates and that something more important has taken over.

to be on antidepressants as are men. In part, is it because we'd rather medicate people than talk with them and help them work through their concerns? It's not that antidepressants are bad. But when they replace other resources and merely suppress feelings rather than work through them, we lose the growth and insights that personal work could achieve. Acceptance, without the work, is a booby prize.

Melinda

Melinda was one of my housemates while I was pursuing my PhD. Our other roommate was a psychiatrist, also there for some advanced work. She was a psychiatric nurse practitioner in her early 20s who was full of life and richness. She had a presence that was admirably suited to her chosen profession. Melinda could be right there with you in almost any state, whether you were angry, sad, anxious, or joyful. It was as if there was a deep still pool of water inside her, a reservoir from which she drew strength and contentment.

One night, Melinda didn't come home. The next morning, we got a call from her work saying that she had not shown up. Her car was gone and she didn't answer her cell phone. We called the police. Then we called her family, who lived in a neighboring state.

It took a couple of days to find her car at a wilderness park where she liked to jog.

It took three more days to find her body.

It was some hikers who provided the clue. They were far from the immediate search area, but they reported a strange smell. When they directed the police to the area, they followed the smell.

Given the high heat and humidity, her body had undergone significant decay. Animals had gotten to her and pulled an arm away from her body. I'm glad to say I didn't see her in that state, though our psychiatrist housemate, who had also done a residency in pathology, did see her. What I saw was a blackened outline on the ground where her bodily fluids had sunk in and killed all vegetation. The unforgettable sickly-sweet smell of death lingered for months. I knew this because we returned several times to guide family, to grieve, and to put a stone marker on the spot so she would be remembered.[3]

At least a thousand people came to her funeral, many travelling, as we did, to her home state. When her family was with us in Tennessee, I asked her mother if Melinda had ever experienced depression. She looked at me, surprised, and asked, "How did you know?" I told her about what I noticed in Melinda and that I'd usually only seen

---

3   It turns out there was no foul play. Melinda was allergic to bee stings. Apparently, while running on the trail, she left the trail to answer the call of nature. In doing so, she tripped over a nest of yellow jackets buried in the leaves. With so many stings, even an EpiPen would have been unlikely to save her.

this sort of deep inner stillness and richness in people who had undergone depression, addiction, or some other great trial and come out the other side.

Her mother told me Melinda's story:

When Melinda was young, she suffered from depression. Of course, medications were more limited than they are today. Nothing that was available appeared to help nor did counseling or any other avenue they tried. They were getting desperate for some way to help their daughter until they got her involved with horses.

It was working with horses that drew Melinda out of her depression. Just as when Ivan Illyich started to care more about his son than about himself, caring for the horses drew Melinda out of herself and her own pain. As she came to love and relate to the horses, she also came to love and relate to others caring for the horses. The process continued until she became the vibrant, rich woman I had come to know. Her depression lifted when she became able to care for others and to engage in rich, loving relationships.

Oddly, much the same happened with one of my own nieces. I can still remember driving with her when she was young, it was like trying to connect to an empty space. She wasn't really there, she was anxious, angry, depressed, and sort of "absent." Her mother also got her involved with horses and experienced similar results. She is now a vibrant, thoughtful, self-aware, and confident young woman.

This is not to say that "horses" are the answer to all depression. There are many different paths to overcoming depression. Some people also benefit from medication. What this story illustrates is that finding meaning beyond oneself and finding a connection can take one outside of one's pain. Caring more, to some degree, about someone or something more than oneself is a key to passing beyond depression. For many, depression, or something like it, is necessary before they even start to look.

People who experience depression often feel as though there is something wrong with them. Yet as we noted above, the American Psychological Association and the American Medical Association both acknowledge that several periods of significant depression are normal in a person's lifetime. For most of us, these last no more than a year. For others, anxiety and/or depression are more fundamentally part of their life experience. For those of us who undergo the more temporary life events, it's far easier to simply forget them when they are over. For others, it's not so easy. In both cases, however, there is also opportunity.

Juan

Juan was born in the Dominican Republic and raised in the Bronx. He dropped out of high school and was working at a gas station when his girlfriend got pregnant. At that point, he took stock of his life. He didn't want his child to grow into the sort of person he felt he was becoming. So, he got his GED and applied to college. He went on to play minor league baseball. When I met him, he was working on his PhD at Vanderbilt.

Then came the accident. There was a crash on the highway. When he swerved to avoid it another car swerved in front of him. When he swerved again, trying to keep the crash away from the side of the car with his fiancé, the car flipped. The roof crushed down on his head, causing a severe spinal injury. Juan was paralyzed from the neck down.

Most people who become quadriplegic want to die for at least the first year after the accident. After a time, about 80 percent find joy in life again and are happy that they lived (Wilder 2006, 63). His fiancé, as is often the case in such accidents, couldn't handle his condition and left him. Juan often wanted to end his life.

His mother and some of his family moved to town to help care for him. We spent a lot of time together, but this was no one-way street. It only takes one party to make a divorce nasty, Juan was also helping me cope with that process. One day, Juan told me of an event that had helped him decide to live. It was a conversation we had some time before.

At the time, he was telling me about wanting to let go, to die. I looked at him and replied something like:

"Juan, I can't begin to understand what you have to endure and I would probably feel as you do were I in your situation. All I can say is that I'd really miss you if you were gone, and that you've really helped me deal with my divorce."

Even more than my missing Juan, I think *it was the fact that he was helping me that helped pull him out of his depression.* This is a generous, thoughtful, and caring man. But in his state, he felt that he was nothing more than a burden to others and that he had nothing left to offer. This was a concrete example of how he could still make a positive difference in another's life. He continues to do that for others today.

Four Pillars of Meaning

Most will note a common theme in these stories that the positive "fruit" of depression is that one finds what is meaningful for them. To expand on this, I am grateful to one of my former students, Elijah Evans, for referring me to the following TED talk:

https://www.ted.com/talks/emily_esfahani_smith_there_s_more_to_life_than_being_happy#t-433741

In this talk, Smith discusses a five-year study interviewing hundreds of people about how they found meaning in their lives. From these interviews, as well as an extensive review of existing literature, she came up with what she calls the **four "pillars" of meaning**, or ways in which people find meaning in their lives. These are:

1. **Belonging**: This refers to being part of ongoing relationships where we feel valued and value others just for who we are. This is not being valued primarily for one's beliefs or being part of a group that defines itself in opposition to other groups. This is more peaceful and positive. Smith refers to this as founded in love.

2. **Purpose**: This refers to those who find ways to use their strengths to serve others or a purpose beyond themselves. Her data suggests that it only really works if turned outwards. In other words, the purpose of becoming rich (or even happy) doesn't really serve to give someone meaning in life.

3. **Transcendence**: This refers to "rare" moments that take one beyond oneself, perhaps forgetting oneself, in such a way as to feel a connection to a greater reality.

4. **Storytelling**: This last one refers not just to stories in general, but to the story "we tell ourselves about ourselves." These narratives clarify who we are to ourselves. It's important to notice that, while the "facts" may not change, how we interpret and use these facts can. ***Changing one's story can change one's life.***

The story I told of Melinda seems to emphasize belonging, or being part of and accepted by the community of those who loved and cared for the horses. It also seems to involve purpose. Her purpose became increasingly to care for the horses, those who cared for the horses, and outward. It wouldn't surprise me if there were also moments of transcendence that contributed to her life. I just don't know about them.

The story of Juan emphasized purpose. He was surrounded by people who loved him, but he was afraid that he had nothing more to offer them. He found peace when he realized he did have something to offer. Feeling he had something to offer also allowed Juan to feel like he belonged and that he was more than just a burden to others. Though I will not describe them here, I can say that he also had profound experiences of transcendence.

The part that I want to emphasize here, however, is storytelling. As Smith says, we can't change the facts in our lives, but we can change how they impact us and what they mean. This reminds me of ***Rational Emotive Behavioral Therapy***, which suggests that it's not primarily the traumatic event that impacts us over the long-term, but how we interpret and react to the event. The "story" we tell ourselves about the event and how it fits into our lives is what carries us forward and determines whether it will continue to traumatize us or become a force for good.

For example, my parents were overprotective when we were young. My mother had to know where we were at all times. During my teenage years, I "interpreted" this as a lack of trust. It undermined my sense of self and self-confidence.

One night, I was with a group of other high school students at the debate coach's house working on a new debate plan for the next tournament. My parents had his phone number, so I expected a call when 9 p.m. rolled around.

The phone didn't ring. Soon it was 10 p.m. Still no ring. On the one hand, we were with a responsible adult. But still, as time went on, I kept looking at the phone. A warm feeling grew insight me. *"They trust me, they really trust me."* By the time my friends dropped me off at home (shortly after midnight, probably the latest I'd ever been out), I was filled with gratitude and love. I marched into their bedroom, ready to wake them up and tell them (well, gently) how grateful I was and that I would endeavor to live up to this new trust.

> They weren't home.
> Well, not so bad. They would have found a way to call me if they wanted to.
> When they did get home, I found out the truth.
> My debate coach had changed his number.

When I got home, they were at the coach's house. Later, I found out that my mom was screaming at him from his walkway, the neighbors lights were coming on, and he had threatened to call the police.

(Of course, what I didn't know is that my parents had reason to believe that this coach was not a responsible adult.)

> So, when they got home, they unloaded on me.
> As they lectured and yelled, I felt that new warm feeling in me dying.
> The feeling that my parents loved and trusted me was based on a lie.

What Has This to Do with Storytelling?

Before I lost the feeling entirely, I thought to myself: this feeling and belief, even if not entirely true, feels healthy and life giving. I decided that, even if it wasn't entirely true, I would hang on to as much as I could. I could still benefit from what I experienced, even if it wasn't entirely true.

As I got older, I realized (reinterpreting the events) that it wasn't about not loving me, or even trusting me. It was about their concerns about the coach and their wanting to protect me—which was also proof of their love.

I have reviewed and changed my story of myself many times over my life. I can also say, with certainty, that Melinda and Juan have as well.

Suicide

It's hard to talk about depression without making a few remarks about suicide. These are in no way comprehensive. This is a complex and difficult topic. Here, I'm only dealing with a few specific questions.

Is Suicide the Ultimate Selfish Act?

When I read student journals about friends who have committed suicide, they are often split between those who experience compassion and those who experience anger, feeling that suicide is the ultimate selfish act. There's truth in both positions.

If I am angry at someone for committing suicide, what insight does that anger offer me? While there will be a lot of variation, in many cases, I am probably angry about two things:

1. the fact that the person hurt so many people who cared for him or her; and
2. feeling helpless, even guilty, for not having recognized the problem and helped the person or anger at the person for not having called for help.

Unaddressed, these feelings fester.

There is a degree of truth in the claim that suicide is a selfish act, but not (typically) in the way one thinks.

Recall our discussion of the relationship between pain and world. Recall also that our world, our concrete world, is not some abstract idea. Rather, my world is my concrete sense of my possibilities for thought, action, and relationship beyond my physical body. Scarry tells us that pain and world exist in an inverse relationship—as one increases, the other decreases. "Intense pain is world-destroying" (Scarry 1985, 29). Consider, for example, if you hit your thumb with a hammer while driving a nail. For the next few minutes nothing exists except the pain. Your world, at least as you experience it, is gone.

What I'd like to suggest is that, in cases of suicides that are due to depression, the person considering suicide is more *self-absorbed* than selfish. By this I mean that their emotional pain is so great that their "world" is almost gone. Scarry writes, "*Psychological suffering*, though often difficult for any one person to express, *does* have referential content ..." (Scarry 1985, 11; emphasis hers). It's not quite the same as physical pain. In fact, at times, the world-destroying nature of physical pain is used by persons suffering mental anguish as a way of stilling that pain (Scarry 1985, 33). (For example, consider a person who cuts themselves. The physical pain of the cutting helps to still the psychological pain.) The "world" of the person considering suicide is similar to the person experiencing extreme physical pain in that the "pain" of their psychological world obliterates most references to a (real) world outside of that pain.

My sense is that, in many cases, it's not that the person attempting suicide intends to harm others, it's just that the others have almost ceased to exist for them. All that exists is the pain and those objects upon which it is focused. They know of others abstractly, but their pain so dominates them that nothing else really seems real.[4] Their entire world "warps" around this experience. Alverez writes:

> The logic of suicide is different ... Once a man decides to take his own life he enters a world where every detail fits and each incident reinforces his decision. An argument with a stranger in a bar, an expected letter which doesn't arrive, the wrong voice on the telephone, even a change in the weather–all seem charged with special meaning ... (EtKind 1997, 33)

From the outside, the thought process of a person considering suicide may seem absurd. For them, even with the contradictions, there is a sense of crystal clarity. Recall the claim that *we are meaning seeking and meaning generating creatures*. This is an example of that process taken to an extreme, into what psychologists call constriction, or we might call a sort of tunnel vision.

This illusion of clarity on the part of the person who has made the decision leads to another important fact those who wish to help him or her need to know. **Often, when the emotional turmoil appears to pass, so that the person appears calm, almost at peace, we assume that the crisis has passed.** It has, but not necessarily in the way we might think. We assume that they have found a reason to live. **Instead, they may have made the decision to die and are just going through the final arrangements.** The "crisis" of the decision has passed, but not necessarily in terms of a choice for life. For a time, their friends or loved ones may need to watch over them a bit more closely.

David Wallace has a powerful description of what some individuals are going through and why we shouldn't take their death so personally:

> The so-called "psychotically depressed" person who tries to kill herself doesn't do so out of quote "hopelessness" or any abstract conviction that life's assets and debits do not square. And surely not because death seems suddenly appealing. The person in whom its invisible agony reaches a certain unendurable level will kill herself the same way a trapped person will eventually jump from the window of a burning high-rise. Make no mistake about people who leap from burning windows. Their terror of falling from a great height is still just as great as it

---

4 It's worth noting that the old technique of having them promise to "call" before acting on such feelings tends not to be effective. I think it's still worthwhile as an indication of caring, but even if they promise, if their "world" vanishes, the promise will vanish with it.

would be for you or me standing speculatively at the same window just check-ing out the view; i.e. the fear of falling remains a constant. The variable here is the other terror, the fire's flames: when the flames get close enough, falling to death becomes the slightly less terrible of two terrors. It's not desiring the fall; it's terror of the flames. And yet nobody down on the sidewalk, looking up and yelling "Don't!" and "Hang on!", can understand the jump. Not really. You'd have to have personally been trapped and felt flames to really understand a terror way beyond falling.[5]

What if the Person Committing Suicide Is Angry, Even Leaving an Angry Note?

What if the person dies angry? What if the person leaves a note or commits the act in such a way as to suggest revenge? How many people, even when grown, never let go or heal from childhood traumas? How many suicide notes refer to abandonment, perhaps by a romantic interest?[6] These are more complicated, and *I don't think any generalization can cover every person*. But while anger may be a source of insight, when bottled up it can also become a source of depression, anxiety, rage, or reinforce sim-ilar sorts of feelings already present. Recall that, even when another is legitimately responsible for some injustice, the changes we need to make are usually in ourselves. In the case of a child from an abusive or neglectful home, this is particularly diffi-cult since the events happen well before they have any chance at emotional maturity. There is still a choice, eventually, to see what might be good in one's parents, or to at least let go of the anger and learn from it. We also often don't know the whole story. If I am in mental anguish, I might be unable to hear or empathize with another's story.

This brings to mind a close friend who struggled with depression for decades. One of the things his psychiatrist regularly asked him was, "How is your irritabil-ity index?" (i.e., the more depressed and anxious he became, the less he was able to be patient and empathize with others). His level of irritability served as a measure

---

5   http://www.goodreads.com/quotes/200381-the-so-called-psychotically-depressed-person-who-tries-to-kill-herself, accessed December 22, 2016.

6   While no generalization is absolute, there appear to be differences in the content of suicide notes based on age. In this case, suicide notes focusing on the loss of a romantic interest or relationships tend to come from persons in their 20s and 30s. The next stage, usually in the 40s, appears to indicate a sense of failure, of having not risen up to life's demands. Oddly, many people in their 50s tend to leave instructions, but not reasons. And after 60, notes more often express tiredness, loss, and pain. These last notes tend to focus on having outlived loved ones and being ready to move on. This is a reason why Nuland considers this category acceptable for physician-assisted suicide.

of his depression. Sometimes anger, bottled up, leads to depression. Sometimes it's the reverse.

My point here is that one should always take the contents of a suicide note with a great deal of reservation. Even angry notes are still usually, and primarily, expressions of pain. In anger, that pain is projected outwards. While there may be some basis in truth, it is not ultimately rational. At best, it usually reflects only a small part of reality. For the most part, studies of suicide notes show that they are "bizarre, rambling, angry and above all, sad documents of disturbed minds" (EtKind 1997, viii).

Joe

Joe was not a good man. He was an alcoholic and was physically and emotionally abusive. For their own self-preservation, his kids and relatives completely shut him out of their lives.

I never got to talk with Joe. I was the hospital chaplain who was called in when he was close to death. He never woke in my presence. But he was surrounded by love.

Joe wasn't a good man, but he became a good man. From the story his "adopted" family told me, I came to learn that he was raised by a father much like himself. As an adult, he continued the cycle of alcoholism and violence. When his kids and family left him, he hit bottom. He stopped drinking. Eventually, he started to take in others who were also hurt, damaged, or at the "bottom." He helped them get back on their feet. *These were his acts of healing and redemption.*

Among others, I met a newly married woman, whom Joe had taken in when she and her kids were homeless, thrown out by an abusive spouse. He took care of her and her kids, helped them get on their feet, and helped them buy a home. Eventually, he gave her away at her wedding.

His biological family never saw this side of Joe. In fact, *had they not left him, had he not hit bottom, this side might never have existed.* They did what they needed to do to protect themselves at the time. The first inkling any of them had of the change was when we called to tell them he was dying. My hope is that these two "families," old and new, talked, and that his biological family might also have had some healing. Of course, it's also possible that they might end up resenting the fact that he treated these others so well after treating them so poorly. I don't expect I'll ever know.

Facing one's depression, addiction (which involves depression), or other emotional pain can lead one to find what is really meaningful for one in life. It worked for Joe. **But there is a risk. It can also lead one to decide that there is nothing for one in this life, so that suicide becomes the only option.** This is not to say that it's a good option. **It cuts off any future chance to find those richer, more fulfilling options.** By ending one's life, one also ends the possibility for healing and redemption, at least in this life, on the part of one committing the act. Because Joe didn't take that option, he eventually found love and fulfillment. But it wasn't a short or easy road.

The bottom line? We need to forgive those who commit suicide, and we need to forgive ourselves if we feel guilt. Take the event as an opportunity to learn and grow. Feeling compassion for those who commit suicide may not help them, but it can be a great help to those of us left behind.

What Time of Year Do Most Suicides Occur?

Most people believe that suicide is most common in the winter months or over the holidays. There is good reason to think this is true. The cold and dark of winter can increase depression. The holidays can be particularly difficult for people who don't have good family or friends to be with. There are few things so lonely as being in a room with people and not feeling at all connected.

Yet this belief isn't borne out by the data. For some reason, the highest rates of suicide are in the spring, not the winter. I'll venture two guesses as to why.

When a person is at their lowest there is no energy, no hope. Even the act of suicide is, in a sense, an act of hope, hope for relief. But it takes energy to carry it out.

Just as the French Revolution didn't take place when the French peasants were experiencing their worst oppression, suicide is not most likely when a person is at their "lowest." The French Revolution occurred when the conditions actually improved. This allowed the peasants to look up and hope for more, instead of using all of their energy just to survive. In the case of depression, suicide might become more likely not when things are at their worst, but as the depression begins to lift. We generally experience more energy, and a bit more light, with the coming of spring. Therefore, we have more energy to act.

But it seems likely that it's more than just an increase in "energy." There is also data that suggest that, for a short period, suicide may become more likely after someone has started certain antidepressants. While this may be purely chemical, I suspect it also has to do with what Neeld calls the loss of one's "assumptive world." When dealing with the loss of a spouse, for example, the loss of one's assumptive world would be the "recognition that the future we assumed we would have would never happen now." In this context, however, it's also critical to recognize, *"One of the uses of our emotions is that they regulate our lives, give as a sense of coherence. ..."*[7]

My emotions are a key part of my assumptive world. They "regulate" and create "coherence" in how I make decisions, interpret experiences, and how I see and define

---

7 Elizabeth Harper Neeld, *Grief and Loss: What Helps When We Are Experiencing the Unthinkable*, http://connect.legacy.com/inspire/page/show?id=1984035%3APage%3A5112, accessed on February 2, 2016. Emphasis added.

my very self. When depression first starts to lift, if that is all I have known for years, perhaps even my entire life, I may no longer know who I am in this world. If my depression is fundamental to how I see myself, I may be entirely lost, confused, and unable to cope. My assumptive world has collapsed. But now, I have the energy to end it.

The loss of one's assumptive world can result from any profound life transition. In grief work, it's more likely to be due to the emotional upheaval of a loss. This can be so powerful that even a person one would think is well prepared to cope can succumb, at least for a time, to making risky and poor decisions.

Sarah

Sarah was going through a difficult divorce. She had been married for many years and had never expected to become a single mother. She was also a marriage and family therapist. If anyone would know how to handle the loss with grace and good sense, it would seem to be her.

Yet, one night she found herself at a bar. She let a stranger "pick her up." Not only did they fail to use protection, but she also loaned him $200 when he said he had forgotten his wallet at home. He was going to pay her back the next day. Of course, she never saw him again.

This sort of behavior was completely against her character. She was fortunate that she didn't become pregnant or contract a sexually transmitted disease. But the "against her character" is exactly the point. For a time, with her emotions in disarray and her assumptive world lost, she didn't know who she was any more.

If it can happen to someone like Sarah, with all her experience and training, think of how powerful it can be for the rest of us.

Jerry

Jerry had struggled with depression and anxiety all his life. When younger, he was good looking and athletic, but also thoughtful and richly reflective. The latter was, in part, a product of his melancholy. He is both one of the smartest and most humble men I know.

He married a good woman, though they weren't really suitable for one other. They both wanted very different things in life. It was just that, deep down, he felt that she was his only chance at marriage.

So, in an effort to hold onto her, he changed his life to suit her. After almost finishing a masters at a prestigious university, he was offered a full scholarship, including living expenses, to study with one of the top professors in his field in the South of

France. He would be expected to work with this professor four days a week. The other three, he and his wife would be free to explore the countryside.

> He turned it down, didn't finish his degree, and went to work to start the sort of life she wanted.
> He was very successful at making money.
> At the same time, his depression grew.
> He ate to deal with his unhappiness.

After 19 years of marriage, she had enough. She filed for divorce. In the next 18 months, he lost his job, his mother died, his best female friend died, and his dog died. He was depressed, morbidly obese, out of work, and felt that he had thrown his life away. He was convinced that no woman could ever love him. At times, he told me that he was calculating how long it would take for him to hit the ground if he were to jump from a particular spot on an I-90 bridge.

He struggled in this state for about two years.

Part of what him got him through it was what *Neeld named as the most important indicator of whether one will work through grief; to have at least one person that you can call almost any time of the day or night, who will just be with you in how you need to be.* Fortunately, he had more than one such person. There were times when someone might be on the phone with him for hours almost every night for a week.

Returning to the distinction between pain and world, Jerry's pain was so great that he came close to ending it. He had to reconstruct himself and his assumptive world nearly from scratch. In the beginning, his lifeline was his friends and family. *As in "The Death of Ivan Illyich," that which first helped Ivan cope with his pain was receiving honest compassion from Gerasim,* the peasant boy hired to care for him. The more profound change, however, was when Ivan began to really care for his family, to love them as much as, or even more than, himself. At that point, while his pain remained, it no longer dominated him. He rose above it. For Jerry, his friends and family were his "Gerasim," those giving him compassion. There was also an element, as there is for most going through a divorce, where one needs to experience what it is to still be romantically desirable by others. **But he didn't really emerge from the crisis until he too was able to turn outward, to see that he still had gifts to offer others.** The desire and the ability to **give** appears to be far more world creating, much stronger for overcoming grief or depression, than even receiving love and support. It gave him meaning and joy.

It's now been years since he seriously considered suicide.

Stage Five: Acceptance

Early on, I noted that Neeld felt that, in many cases, acceptance was the "booby prize." This is when a person, instead of working fully through their grief, essentially gives up. They are perhaps resigned to death or to life alone, but they haven't really worked through the stages. On the other hand, if one really works through the stages, be they Neeld's or Kübler-Ross's, then something very different can happen. One can rediscover and reinvent oneself, finding again a certain "zest" or "vitality" in living.

In the case of grief due to loss, this doesn't mean that we forget our loss. But there are several ways to face the pain of losing a loved one. For instance, one can say to oneself, "This hurts so much, I never want to go through it again." If so, one may never love again. One numbs oneself to life and to happiness. This is Kramer's notion of psychological death (Kramer 1988, 18).

Another way is to find some sort of meaning in the loss, as in working to change to protect others from that same sort of loss.

Another is to take grief as a testament to how rich the relationship was and to how much you meant to one another. Over time, it's not that the person is forgotten or lost, but that one gradually starts to remember the good times. While there may always be a tinge of sadness, of bittersweet, there also arises a certain joy in those memories, at having known one another and having been part of one another's lives. We then carry that person with us into the future, in who and what we are, and in what we become in future relationships.

CHAPTER FIVE

Viewing Guide

WIT

Introduction[1]

Wit is another example of what the physicality of illness has to teach us. *Wit* is a play about a woman, Vivian, who discovers she has cancer. She is one of the world authorities on the 17th-century poetry of John Donne, which she selected in part because of its difficulty. She is well respected in her field and somewhat feared by both her colleagues and students due to her demanding and uncompromising attitudes towards her (and their) work.

In this film, we will be focusing mainly on four comparisons/themes between Vivian Bearing and Ivan Ilyich. These are:

1. the lives and relationships of Vivian and Ivan,
2. the attitudes and the relationships with their physicians,
3. identifying the use of "self-serving rationalities," and
4. exploring major turning point(s) of the text in terms of Scarry's analysis of pain and world.

In addition, we will highlight other issues related to health care, particularly cancer.

---

1   Instead of standard parenthetical references, I will use time codes from the DVD (hh:mm:ss) to show where the conversation appears in the film. To make it easier to transcribe quotations, I've often quoted from the English subtitles, which at times vary slightly from the spoken text.

Primary characters:

Vivian Bearing (PhD)	The cancer patient
Harvey Kelekian (MD)	The attending (the physician in charge)
Jason Posner (MD)	The fellow (getting a year of patient experience before going to a lab)
Susie (RN)	Charge nurse
E.M. Ashford (PhD)	Vivian's teacher

Just a Number

Healthcare is changing. Thus the attitudes one sees in the play are not true for all hospitals. I can say, from personal experience, that many of the "odd" moments Vivian experienced are true, at least in the case of some large teaching hospitals. For example, Vivian comments about the standard greeting, "How are you?" While fairly innocuous, she finds it strange and insensitive that she is asked that question while throwing up or as she emerges from an intensive surgery with "a tube in every orifice" (00:05:21). She comments, "I am waiting for the moment when I'm asked this question and I am dead" (00:05:26).

Large teaching/research hospitals can provide the best cutting-edge therapies but, due in part to their size, a patient can be reduced to just a number.

Example: Kidney Stones

For example, the first time I went into Vanderbilt Hospital with kidney stones, the intern asked me if I was allergic to morphine. I said I didn't know, as I'd never had it. He checked the box and we moved on.

It took large doses of morphine to allow me to relax. But there was a side effect. So long as I lay perfectly still, I was fine. If I tried to move, or if they tried to move my bed, I experienced intense nausea.

I threw up in the ER, in my room, in the hallway, and in radiology.

The next time I had kidney stones, I told the resident during my intake, "Don't give me morphine, it causes me intense nausea." She merely looked at me and said, "No problem, we will just give you something for the nausea." After that, I was fine.

So here's my question: Why didn't anyone give me the other medication when I was throwing up in room after room?

The answer? Because the box had already been checked and it wasn't anyone's job, at least at that time, to call the physician for an order for the other medication. I wasn't really a person, I was just part of their routine. When I came in for the second time, they started over. Since the box had not been "checked," the issue could now be addressed.

Example: Bedsores

A second case that comes to mind is that of a close friend who, due to an auto accident, ended up quadriplegic. This means that he is unable to move his arms or legs. He stayed in Tennessee because he wanted to finish his doctorate at Vanderbilt, which, despite the difficulty of being unable to move his hands to type or hold a book, he did. Unfortunately, because Tennessee did not have the best social services, he periodically developed bedsores.

A bedsore is an area of skin and tissue that, due to too much pressure over time, becomes necrotic. Necrotic comes from the Greek, "stinking death"; it means that the flesh has died and is starting to rot. In terms of patients who cannot move themselves, it often results from inadequate attention to repositioning their bodies.

Once a bedsore has advanced to the point of necrosis, the treatment is surgical. They cut out the necrotic tissue and sew or graft the wound, allowing healthy tissue to bond with healthy tissue.

However, whenever my friend came back from a surgery, he was in incredible pain. Just because his limbs didn't move didn't mean that he couldn't feel pain. The surgeons, despite his requests, didn't bother to move him gently or support him once they had him under anesthesia.

Finally, we hit upon a possible solution. They tended to ignore my friend's requests. We weren't sure if it was because he was quadriplegic or because of some sort of racism (he was part African American, part Latino). I, on the other hand, was a student with the ethics department, had a hospital badge, and was older than the typical student.

I went with him the next time he went to the hospital. In preparation, I put on a white shirt and tie. I placed the badge in the front shirt pocket. People could tell it was there, but they couldn't quite tell my status.

Whenever someone asked me a question, I redirected them to my friend. He was, after all, the patient. At one point, I was asked if I was doctor. I said no, but didn't elaborate. My task was to be a presence and to alert the hospital personnel to listen to this patient.

Because they were nervous as to who I was, they did.

When he came out of surgery, for the first time, he came out without pain.

It's sad we had to go to such lengths for basic humane care.

In general, my experience is that one is more likely to be treated humanely at a midsized or smaller hospital. Which is why, unless I have a condition that requires the resources of a really large hospital, I tend to steer towards the midsized facilities. But there are no fixed rules. Some large hospitals do a great job treating patients as persons, some smaller hospitals do not.

Viewing Guide: *Wit*

Informed Consent

The play opens with Vivian sitting in Dr. Kelekian's office, where she is being "thoroughly diagnosed." This is her first meeting with Dr. Kelekain, a well-known research physician. She was sent to him because there were no standard treatments for stage four ovarian cancer. Stage four is very late detection. It had metastasized (started growing in other areas) to multiple other areas of her body. As she says, "There is no stage five" (00:05:55). Dr. Kelekian is prepared to enter Vivian into a trial for an experimental combination of drugs.

For our purposes, there are at least two issues to note from this first conversation.

The first is fairly common. At one point, Vivian zones out and stops attending to what Dr. Kelekian is saying. This is a natural reaction. It is also why it is a good idea to have someone with you if you suspect you may be receiving bad news. Another alternative, if one is in the hospital and no family members are around, is to ask the nurse to come into the room during the conversation. That way, one can ask questions of the nurse after the physician has left.

The second is more troubling. While far subtler than with Ivan's "celebrated" physician, Dr. Kelekian still avoids what most would feel is the most important question. If you recall, the most important question Ivan wanted answered was whether he was going to die or get well. As with the celebrated physician, Dr. Kelekian also avoids his this question and hides behind medical terminology. For example, he states:

> *... the most effective treatment modality is a chemotherapeutic agent. We are developing an experimental combination of drugs designed for primary-site ovarian, for the target specificity of state three and beyond administration. (00:01:11)*

While it sounds as though the treatment is intended to help Vivian, he never actually says this and Vivian, overwhelmed, doesn't think to ask.

It might be that this was just an oversight on the part of the attending. It's easy, talking to patient after patient, to forget some detail. But Dr. Kelekian also has a professional interest in getting Vivian to sign up for the clinical trial. Without patients, he cannot test new therapies. Though such treatments hope to benefit future patients, they also serve to enhance his reputation and income. This means that there may be a self-serving motive on the part of Dr. Kelekian. It may be that the treatment isn't expected to help Vivian at all, but some other patient in the future. Dr. Kelekian might not want to tell Vivian this for fear she will refuse the trial.

This is further suggested by the psychological ploy Dr. Kelekian uses before and after Vivian signs the consent form. Consider his description of the possible side effects just before she signs:

> *The first week of each cycle you'll be hospitalized for chemotherapy. The next week you may feel a little tired. The next two weeks will be fine, relatively. (00:03:00)*

Immediately after she signs, he shifts emphasis:

> *The important thing is for you to take the full dose of chemotherapy. There may be times when you wish for a lesser dose, due to the side effects. ... You must be very tough. (00:03:45)*

Earlier, he mentioned some of the specific side effects, including a reference to relying on her resolve "to withstand some of the more pernicious side effects" (00:02:00). But he appears to downplay this just before he asks for consent. The ploy here is simple. The rosy picture is to get her to sign. He also probably knows that, once a person has signed an agreement, they are far less likely to back out. Then, once he gets her signature, he needs to back off from his overly rosy description. Why? To protect himself from legal liability.

This is a trick well known to sales people. Think of the car salesperson who has you sign something, even though it's not binding, to take and talk over with his or her "manager."

Simple Human Truth, Uncompromising Scholarly Standards

The next scene takes place in the hospital room, apparently after the first round of chemotherapy. We know this because Vivian's hair is gone, and she is unable to eat due to nausea. Older forms of chemotherapy target cells, in part, based on their speed of replication. Cancer cells reproduce more rapidly than most other cells. The cells of the hair follicles and lining of the stomach and intestines also reproduce very rapidly so older chemotherapies attack them as well.

Vivian narrates:

> *It appears to be a matter, as the saying goes, of life and death. I know all about life and death. I am, after all, a professor of seventeenth-century poetry specializing in the Holy Sonnets of John Donne, which explore mortality in greater depth than any other body of work in the English language. And I know for a fact that I am tough. A demanding professor, uncompromising. (00:06:05)*

Vivian then recalls an encounter with her teacher, E. M. Ashford. Ashford gives her back a paper and says, "Your essay on Holy Sonnet VI Miss Bearing is a melodrama with a veneer of scholarship unworthy of you. ... Do it again" (00:06:55). Ashford objects, in part, because Vivian has used an edition that is "inauthentically punctuated" (00:07:20). Vivian attempts to object that the better translation was checked out of the library, but Ashford brushes that aside. There are no excuses.

Following a stern lecture on the importance of scholarship and the meaning of the passage, Vivian thinks she sees the point:

> *Life, death, I see. It's a metaphysical conceit, it's wit. I'll go back to the library ...*
> *(00:09:40)*

Ashford cuts her off:

> *It is not wit, Miss Bearing, it is truth. The paper's not the point.*
>   *... Vivian, you're a bright young woman. Use your intelligence. Don't go back to the library, go out. Enjoy yourself with friends. (00:09:48)*

This is a very odd change in tone. What might Ashford mean? She shifts from a stern lecture on rigor and scholarship to a comment about going out and being with friends, about using one's "own" intelligence?

We then see Vivian walking on the quad. Other students are there, laughing and talking. She thinks to herself:

> ***Simple human truth. Uncompromising scholarly standards. They're connected.***
> *I just couldn't ... I went back to the library. (00:10:35; emphasis added)*

What an odd event. Most students would happily take the advice to go out with friends. Vivian retreats to the library. Vivian doesn't understand it, but perhaps we can. What was her professor trying to tell her?

> ***Simple human truth. Uncompromising scholarly standards. They're connected.***

How are they connected?

Think back to Aristotle. All knowledge, thus all truth, begins with experience. Vivian, like Ivan, lives in her head. She doesn't really engage with the world. Recall again our example of love. A person growing up in our culture can read about it, research it, do studies on it, but that's no replacement for actually experiencing love. Experience is the foundation for all truth.

John Donne, as a poet, is writing about profound but simple *human experiences*. If Vivian never lives life enough to share in those sorts of experiences, she can never really understand John Donne. That's what her teacher is trying to tell her. She needs to experience simple human truths.

What of the "uncompromising scholarly standards?" While experience is our first teacher, we all know of people who make the same mistakes over and over again, never seeming to learn from those experiences. Scholarly standards build on experience, allowing us to learn and expand upon it. With such standards, we would never advance very far, in science or in life.

Scholarly standards, without being rooted in rich human experience, are hollow. But human experience, without scholarly standards, is meaningless. We need both.

Vivian has lived her life in denial of these simple human truths, which begin, to a large degree, in our existence as physical beings. Her illness, as with Ivan's, presses her to move out of her intellect and into her fuller experience—embodied, emotional, social, perhaps spiritual.

Medical History

When Vivian first meets Jason and Susie, it's in the context of Jason getting her medical history and performing a medical examination. Jason, it turns out, had taken a class from her as an undergraduate. He hadn't taken this class out of any particular interest in the subject matter. He took it because he knew that medical schools were less likely to take students who only took easy courses outside of the sciences. Now more than ever medical schools want well-rounded applicants. The ploy was successful. The fact that he did well in such a tough course was even mentioned in his medical school interview.

It doesn't take long to figure out that Jason is utterly inexperienced. It appears, in fact, that he has spent even less time with patients than, say, the typical fourth-year medical student. Most "fellowships" are completed after one completes not just medical school, but a three- to four-year residency. Fellows are usually quite experienced. What is different about Jason?

While an MD, Jason is not going into clinical medicine. He wants to work in a lab. At some point, if he discovers a promising treatment, he will have to be able to talk with clinical physicians. In Jason's case, the fellowship is not to prepare him to be a better clinical physician, but to give him some awareness and ability to work with actual clinicians. Unlike most fellowships, this fellowship is more like an "internship."

Why is this important to know? First, so that the play will not scare the viewer away from being treated by most fellows. It is also important to understand something critical about teaching hospitals. In such a hospital, one is likely to meet third- and fourth-year medical students, interns (another name for an R1, a first-year resident), more advanced residents (R2, R3, sometimes R4, where the number refers to the year of their residency), attendings (physicians in charge), and others. Who do you really want to treat you?

For example, if you are examined by an intern, particularly in the months from July to September, this is a student just out of medical school. Despite the fact that their work is reviewed by more advanced residents and the attending physician, the odds of a "mistake" are much higher than if you are initially examined by more experienced physicians. Why? Because even when the more experienced physician comes in, they may rely too heavily on the assessment of the intern.

You have the right to insist on a more experienced resident, even an attending, though you may have to wait a bit longer.

Similarly, not everything being done in the hospital is for your benefit (though you may still be charged for it.)[2] For example, in the film, Jason wants to take a clinical history from Vivian. Initially, she objects, saying, "I believe Dr. Kelekian has already done that" (00:15:29). Jason replies, "I know, but Dr. Kelekian wanted me to do one too" (00:15:32).

What isn't mentioned is why, and for whom, the medical interview is to be repeated.

There are good reasons for having more than one person taking a medical history. The first is that the patient may remember something important that wasn't mentioned previously. The second is that an experienced clinician may ask a question or notice something unusual that the first interviewer missed. For example, the patient may have failed to mention travelling to a part of the world where they may have been exposed to something rarely seen in the US. In this case, however, it's really just for Jason's education. While that has value, it should have been said.

This conflict between what is said and what is intended shows up in multiple points of the physician–patient encounter. It highlights a basic dilemma of health care and ethics. On the one hand, new physicians need to "practice" their craft in order to become experienced. On the other hand, do you really want to be the one upon whom they are "practicing?"

Consider another example. Say you are scheduled for a difficult surgery. You have travelled to a major hospital and are being seen by one of the finest surgeons in the country for your condition. Most likely, that surgeon is also teaching surgical residents.

In the actual operating room, it may turn out that the experienced surgeon is not the person actually performing the surgery. He or she will be supervising it, though there are also excellent odds that he or she will be out of the room supervising another surgery for part of that time. Some of this is benign; once the delicate part of the surgery is done, another surgeon can be left to do the routine closing and finishing. This allows the expert physician to help more patients.

---

2   For example, there is a major teaching program that got in trouble because, if a patient died on the operating table, the attendings would sometimes delay declaring the patient dead in order to allow the residents to practice additional procedures. Part of the reason they delayed "calling" the patient was the same reason they may have been caught: they sometimes charged insurance companies for procedures done after the patient should have been declared dead.

Unless you know to ask, there is no guarantee that even the delicate part of the operation will actually be performed by the expert rather than the trainee. You have the right to ask that the attending do the actual surgery, but you have to know to ask.

After the interview, as Jason is about to start the exam, he suddenly realizes that he needs to have a nurse in the room. Since this is a pelvic exam, he has already placed Vivian in the awkward stirrups. He leaves her in that position.

Here, we see Jason's first moment of **bad faith**. When Susie comes in, she asks, "Why did you leave her like this?" Jason replies, "I had to find you, now come on" (00:21:49). Here, Jason answers Susie in a manner that is, in the strictest sense, true. But he entirely misses the point. Why? In part, he has poor people skills. It may also be because, if he did hear her, he'd have to recognize that he had done something wrong.

The insensitivity here, and at other points, becomes extremely painful for Vivian. After Jason finishes the exam and almost flees the room, she narrates how the experience was "thoroughly degrading" (00:24:47).

Friends, Colleagues, and Gerasim

Following a session of dry heaves, Vivian comments:

> *If the word went around that Vivian Bearing had barfed her brains out, first my colleagues, most of whom are my former students, would scramble madly for my position.* (00:27:03)

Vivian's colleagues', like Ivan's, first concern upon her death would be how it could improve their positions. Given that, for academics, publishing assists in their career, the next thing they would do was still really about themselves:

> *And then their consciences would flare up. So to honor my memory, they'd put together a collection of their essays about John Donne.* (00:27:20)

Similarly, when Susie comes into the room to measure her "emesis," Susie notices that Vivian hasn't had any visitors. When Susie asks if there is anyone she can call, Vivian replies that she doesn't want visitors (00:29:07).

Vivian has shut down most of her emotional and relational life. Like Ivan, she is psychologically dead.

A difference between Vivian and Ivan is that Ivan had a family. Ivan's family provided little comfort, since the relationships offered no real connection. Remember the comment about being even more lonely in a crowded room? Since Vivian would likely have also lacked real connection, it was actually easier for Vivian not to have family around.

Susie reaches out to Vivian, starting a relationship that will eventually parallel the relationship between Ivan and Gerasim. "I'll tell you what. I'll come in every once and a while to see how you are doing. Make sure you're okay. If you need anything, you just ring" (00:29:15). A moment later, to emphasize the point, she puts her hand on Vivian and says, "You just call" (00:29:30).

Shake and Bake

Vivian is now far along in her treatment. She comes into the hospital with "fever and neutropenia" (00:38:51), what Jason will call "a shake and bake" (00:40:11). Fever, of course, is when one's temperature rises above the norm. Neutropenia is the loss of certain white blood cells (below 1,500 per microliter of blood) that fight infection. In this case, the cancer treatment has also damaged her immune system.

Why does the body raise one's temperature when fighting infection? Why does one often feel "chilled" and shake during this process?

Raising one's temperature is a way to fight infection. Usually, a bacteria or virus that infects humans operates more efficiently at around our base body temperature. By raising one's temperature, the bacteria or virus has more trouble replicating, slowing down its ability to attack the host. Meanwhile, our body's own immune system is set to operate at this higher temperature.

We get the "chills" because once our immune system has triggered the body to want to be at a higher temperature, we feel cold until we reach that temperature. The shaking generates additional heat, which helps the temperature to rise.

If the body reaches a temperature above 105 degrees, most viruses lose the ability to replicate. If they are at that temperature at that point in their lifecycle, they die. There is a problem, however, with such high temperatures. The body can sustain serious damage if the temperature is high for too long.

Some of this is brain damage, but there are other risks as well. For example, I once saw a patient whose temperature ended up denaturing his eyes; it was like hard-boiling an egg. It left him blind.

So, limited increases in temperature, for limited amounts of time, can be good. Higher temperatures, or moderate increases sustained for too long, can be dangerous.

This provides support for an interesting home remedy. In old movies, one will sometimes see a person with a cold holding their head over boiling water, covered with a towel and breathing in the steam. In part, the steam helps with congestion. More importantly, it raises the temperature of the lungs without raising the temperature of the entire body. If the lungs are held above 105 degrees for about 20 minutes, a significant portion of the virus on the surface of the lungs will be killed.

Returning to the film, we see another "**self-serving**" rationality on Jason's part. Jason gives the order for medication and reverse isolation.[3] As he walks into the

---

3   For some, "reverse isolation" also requires an explanation. In part, it is a metaphor for her life. She chose to be isolated from others. It's also a metaphor for her treatment. Her immediate condition is not

hallway, Susie asks him to talk with Dr. Kelekian about reducing the dose. Susie believes that the current dose is causing Vivian too much suffering.

Jason responds:

No way, she's tough, she can take it. Full dose. Wake me when the counts come from the lab. (00:40:35)

Note how, as before, Jason dismisses the nurse's concern without even giving it due consideration. Why?

The reason Jason doesn't want to lower the dose is because it would affect their research. They need the data from a person who made it through all eight cycles. Thus far, as we can tell from other parts of the film, no patient has made it through. Vivian is their best bet for good data.

Jason wants her to continue at the full dose, not just for the sake of the research, but also to please his mentor, Dr. Kelekian.

Jason, while socially insensitive, is not a monster. He has to be able to sleep at night. If he really thought that he might be torturing someone to death, it might raise moral anxiety. So, he simply dismisses it as a problem. "She's tough, she can take it." He tells himself (**repression**) that there is no issue.

Once she is in reverse isolation, we see a similar attitude from Dr. Kelekian:

Full dose? Definite progress, everything ok? ... You're doing swell. Isolation is no problem, couple of days. Think of it as a vacation. (00:41:20)

Progress for what? Her? Or the research? He leaves that ambiguous, trusting that most patients will assume it is the former.

Moreover, what patient would think of laying sick in a hospital bed as a "vacation"?

The statement isn't really for Vivian's sake. It's most likely part of Dr. Kelekian's own self-deception, which allows him to sleep at night.

---

directly a result of her cancer, but of the damage to her immune system done by the cancer treatment.

Moving away from this metaphor, isolation is normally a way of protecting health care workers and family from a dangerous infection carried by a patient. Sometimes this just means gowning up. At other times, it means a special *negative air pressure room*. That is, a room wherein, if one opens the doors, air from the outside is sucked in and no air from the room escapes into the hallway. That way, airborne infectious agents cannot escape to infect others in the hospital.

Reverse isolation works in "reverse." In this case, the fear is not for other patients, but for the patient in the room. In Vivian's case, her immune system is so weak that even a common cold, benign to the rest of us, could kill her. So the *air pressure in her case was positive*: the goal was to protect her from germs in the hallway. Actually, it looks as though she has a dual room. The room in the middle, with two doorways, likely has strong fans pulling the air through filters. The room functions with positive pressure from where Vivian sleeps but negative pressure from outside the second set of doors.

Dr. Kelekian is clearly out of touch with his patient. At the same time, while the answer will not become explicit until later, we have gotten some clarity as to the question of whether this was really expected to help Vivian. Earlier, during grand rounds, Jason reports to the students examining Vivian:

> *Evidence of primary site shrinkage. Shrinking in metastases has not been documented.* (00:32:32)

He lets the cat out of the bag. The treatment is likely to help patients with this form of cancer if caught before it metastasizes, not after. Since Vivian's cancer has metastasized prior to starting treatment, there is no real expectation of it helping Vivian.

Vivian is just research.

It's Not Supposed to Be Now! (00:46:22)

Vivian is in her room, lost in her imagination. In the moment, she doesn't feel sick. In her imagination, it feels as though she is in front of the classroom doing what she loves.

Susie comes in and tells her that she needs another test. She resists, petulant. She wants to stay in her dreams. Susie gives her a stern expression and Vivian relents.

When she arrives for the test, we see part of the reason she was resistant. It wasn't just that she was enjoying the "break," it was that she knew, from experience, that there was no real need to rush. When she arrives at the lab, the clinician checks her in and goes on break.

While frustrating, it is worthwhile to see this from the clinician's point of view. Tests vary with patient needs. Some days one is running every minute. Other days, one is sitting around. It's probable that Vivian was just the next in line on a busy day. At some point, the clinician would have to keep someone waiting just in order to use the bathroom or get something to eat.

Seeing the other point of view often helps to calm our own frustration. I know of a woman who complained that a nurse for whom she had a question, but was typing on a computer, didn't stop typing to answer her question right away. The person felt that whatever was on the computer should wait, that the nurse's first priority should be people.

She's right, overall. But what if the nurse was entering complicated medication orders from a physician? If she made a mistake, the patient could suffer. She could also lose her job. In this case, stopping to talk with a family member might have put a patient at risk.

We often see only the stresses on ourselves and our loved ones, and not on those taking care of them.

I Could Order a Test … or … the Touch of Human Kindness

Vivian comments that she has been reduced to a specimen jar. Having survived eight treatments at the full dose, Dr. Kelekian and Jason are "delighted" at the paper they will be able to publish about the results. The scene shifts to her room, where Jason comes in to check her "I and O" (inputs and outputs, in this case, fluids in versus fluids out.) Vivian asks questions about what Jason is doing, and Jason explains that he is simplifying the complex kidney function for her. She comments that this is part of "bedside manner" (00:52:50). Jason continues:

There's a whole course on it in med school. It's required. Colossal waste of time for researchers. (00:53:00)

Vivian tries to shift the conversation. So long as the conversation centers around medical and scientific topics about which Jason is comfortable, he responds. At one point, he even explains why cancer is "awesome" (00:53:53). As soon as Vivian tries to talk about a more personal issue, such as her anxiety around dying, Jason shuts her down. In several cases, Vivian starts to ask the question she really wants to ask, then switches it to something more comfortable for Jason. Finally, she blurts out:

What do you say when a patient is apprehensive, frightened? (00:55:50)

His response is entirely incredulous: "Of who?" (00:55:54). The question doesn't even penetrate. Vivian, seeing this, is defeated and backs down. "I just … never mind" (00:56:02).

Jason returns to another of his basic strategies for dealing with that which he might not understand. He asks her questions to see if she is confused and offers to order some additional tests. Whatever goes on, he pushes it into categories with which he is comfortable. As a result, he does not have to grow, but he also doesn't really help his patients.

It doesn't stop here. As with Ivan Ilyich and the celebrated physician, Vivian realizes that her life and Jason's are really very much alike:

So, the young doctor, like the senior scholar, prefers research to humanity. At the same time, the senior scholar, in her pathetic state as simpering victim, wishes the young doctor would take more interest in personal contact. Now, I suppose we shall see how the senior scholar ruthlessly denied her simpering students the touch of human kindness she now seeks. (00:57:00)

The scene retreats into a memory from the classroom. At the end of the class, a student comes to her and asks for an extension on a paper. His grandmother has just died. Vivian is cold and demanding. "Do what you will, but the paper is due when it is due" (00:59:45).

As with Ivan, Vivian is looking back on her life and asking whether the choices she made were really the right ones. The illness, with its subsequent weakness and dependency, is forcing her out of her comfortable isolation.

The classroom situation raises another interesting issue. I often comment that *everything interesting about being human happens in the grey, in the space between extremes*. In part, this will also be raised in *Tuesdays with Morrie* under the phrase "**the tension of opposites.**" Here is a concrete example.

Recall the dilemma we raised with Aristotle regarding justice versus equity. On the one hand, fairness dictates that teachers treat and grade all students equally. Moreover, to help prepare them for the working world, we should also push them to work hard and have high expectations.

Why? Because in the working world, failing to meet deadlines or failing to do good work won't just mean a poor grade, it could mean a loss of promotion or a loss of employment.

Interestingly, follow-up surveys of University of Northern Iowa students five years after graduation indicate that they wish their teachers had pushed them harder, even though they resented it while in school. This is because they came to know its value.

On the other hand, no two people are the same. Equality and equity mean different things to different people. Thus, there need to be exceptions for special circumstances. The "rules" are there to serve us, not for us to serve the rules.

At one extreme, we are rigid and fail to adjust to legitimate differences. At the other, we are too easy and fail to prepare students for when they leave college.

The ethical choice is not to cop out to either extreme, but to try to negotiate the differences when appropriate. There are a variety of strategies for attempting this, but no easy formula.

They Never Expected Me to Get Better

It's 4 a.m. and Vivian is wide awake in her hospital room, awash with anxiety. As with Ivan, the trigger for the anxiety is the fact that she is dying, but the source of her anxiety is the life she has led. Like Ivan, she senses that there is something wrong with the life she chose. Also, like Ivan, she isn't able to fully admit it. She feels confused. She wants comfort, but she feels too vulnerable to press the button and ask for help. She pinches her IV line, setting off an alarm, which brings Susie to the room. They start to talk.

Susie:	"What's the trouble, sweetheart?"
Vivian:	"I don't know."
Susie:	"Can't sleep?"
Vivian:	"No, I just keep thinking."
Susie:	"You do that too much, you can get kind of confused."

Vivian:	"... I can't seem to figure things out ... having these doubts."
Susie:	"... it's like it's out of control, isn't it?"
Vivian:	"Yeah. I'm scared"

Susie begins to rub Vivian's arm, saying, "Honey, of course you are."

Vivian:	"... I don't feel so sure of myself anymore."
Susie:	"And you used to feel sure, didn't you?" (01:01:30)

Susie spends time comforting Vivian, both verbally and physically. Here, she acts very like Gerasim. Eventually she offers Vivian a popsicle. Vivian offers Susie half and they sit and talk more.

Susie raises the issue of Vivian's code status. This is the question of what Vivian wants the doctors to do when her heart stops. A code can be a great benefit; it can save a person's life. But it can also be a highly invasive and painful procedure.

Codes are also far less successful than TV shows have led most people to believe. In Vivian's case, a code might extend her life for a short time, but not really save it. In fact, this is what some physicians call "extending the dying process." Is the pain and trouble of a code worth a short extension of what is going to be a potentially very painful end?

Vivian asks Susie, "My cancers not being cured, is it?" She goes on, "They never expected it to be, did they?" (01:04:44). As with Ivan, she has to state the truth for it to be affirmed to her. Susie is surprised and asks if she was told. Vivian replies, "I read between the lines" (01:05:28). She was not told, but she guessed.

Vivian agrees to become a no code (DNR: Do Not Resuscitate).

Then, she asks Susie a question that is on the mind of a great many seriously ill patients: "You're still going to take care of me, aren't you?" (01:08:23). In this case, Vivian is afraid that if she goes against what she thinks her doctors would want (by becoming a DNR), she might be abandoned.

As a caregiver, it is important to anticipate and calm this fear.

She's Earned a Rest

From the standpoint of **self-serving rationalities**, this next scene is the clearest and most obvious example in the play. The primary research is complete, but Vivian is still alive and in terrible pain. Susie calls Dr. Kelekian to begin aggressive pain management.

Despite the fact that Vivian is obviously overwhelmed with pain, Dr. Kelekian asks her, "Dr. Bearing, are you in pain?" (01:13:55). He orders a morphine drip. Susie protests, asking for patient-controlled analgesic. Dr. Kelekian replies: "Ordinarily, yes. In her case, no. ... She's earned a rest" (01:14:03).

What is going on here?

First, what is patient-controlled analgesic? The patient is hooked up to an IV drip that is controlled by a machine. The patient has a button. Whenever the patient feels pain, he or she can press the button and a small dose of morphine (or some other pain medication) is sent through the IV. There are limits on how much medication the pump will provide at any given time.

It works very well, except in those sorts of cases where the pain is so great that the only way to manage the pain is to sedate the patient into unconsciousness. If this is true, even if the pump allowed the patient to sedate themselves to unconsciousness, once asleep, the medication would stop. The patient would have to wake up in intense pain to press the button.

We aren't sure which situation applies here. It's worth noticing, however, that Dr. Kelekian never asked Vivian what she would want. She might have done fine under patient-controlled analgesic. If not, she could have later been moved to a stronger morphine drip.

Dr. Kelekian gives a reason for his decision, "She's earned a rest." It sounds compassionate. But is this really what's going on?

Consider Dr. Kelekian's attire. He's wearing a tux. This suggests that he was at some sort of formal event, from which he had been called. He had to leave to take care of Vivian.

His research on Vivian was done. If he put her on patient-controlled analgesic, she would remain awake. If she was awake, chances were good that he might be called out of some other event in the future. If she was sedated into unconsciousness, particularly given that she was a DNR, he was unlikely to be bothered again.

If it was really about Vivian, he would have asked her. In fact, to not ask her, given that she was competent, is against medical practice and the law.

Still, he needs to sleep at night. So he gives a reason that is not just any **self-serving rationality**, but one that made it sound as if it was for the sake of the patient. In terms of the underlying **pretext**, the truth is that she has earned a rest. The truth that is hidden, even from himself, is that his real reason is for his convenience.

Cancer Doctors and Hope

Lest this maneuver—telling oneself that one is doing something for the sake of a patient when it is really for oneself—seem an isolated incident, one has only to look at studies about cancer doctors and hope in the 1960s and the 1980s.

Up until the 1960s, very few physicians would tell a patient that they had cancer (Oken 1961). The family might be told, but something else would be made up to justify bringing in a patient for treatment. Physicians of the time argued that cancer, which had an extremely low remission rate at the time, was so devastating that it would take away hope. Hope, it was argued, had two values. Firstly, hope was therapeutic. If a person lost hope, they were more likely to die. Secondly, even if a person was dying, it was depressing to know the fact. By not telling them, they would suffer less.

By the 1980s, this pattern reversed. Today, we almost always tell every patient if they have cancer. What changed?

While part of this is likely due to increases in respect for patient autonomy, the main reason appears to be improvements in medical treatments for cancer. In the 1960s, cancer was usually a death sentence, with remission rates at no more than one in five. The treatments for cancer were worse; they were so terrible that many patients suffered more from the treatments than from the cancer. At the same time, these treatments were rarely successful. Thus, *if I was an oncologist in the 1960s, the only way that I could hope for a reasonable success percentage was to force as many patients as possible into treatment.* The result, in effect, was that we tortured many patients for the sake of saving a few.

Again, these people weren't monsters. They went into medicine hoping to help people. They told themselves the story about hope, and taught it to their residents, so that they could sleep at night.

By the 1980s, things had changed. While many of the therapies were still quite painful, they had much higher cure rates for many cancers. It was no longer necessary to press every possible patient into painful treatments in order to get a decent percentage into remission. Attitudes changed.

Surgeons and Hope

A similar issue continues among surgeons. The government keeps statistics on surgeries in the US. One of the key statistics is mortality, which is set at 30 days from the surgery. In other words, if a patient dies within 30 days of a surgery, *regardless of the cause*, it counts against the surgeon. This can affect a surgeon's reputation and income. If they die on day 31, however, it doesn't count.

Due in part to this economic and professional incentive, surgeons often have far more difficulty letting go of patients who are near death.[4] I've only known a couple of surgeons who would say this directly. I doubt most believe it. Instead, they are often taught a self-serving justification from residency.

A founding story for this attitude is often about the case of a patient whom everyone else was ready to give up on. The story would likely speak to how the surgeon

---

4 Another reason is that, after spending many hours trying to put a person back together, it can be difficult to let go.

stood up to the other physicians, insisting that he or she had a chance. The surgeon would be proved right when the patient left the ICU and did well.

The lesson? What is said is something like: "It takes a long time for the patient's body to declare itself. We need to give them that time."

What's not looked at are the patients who, being forced alive on machines for periods of days or weeks, are being tortured at the end of their lives.

Nothing is said about 30 days.

Fini

There is much more that could be uncovered from this film/play, but these are some of the points that work best with our themes. Some of them showed up repeatedly:

Various self-serving rationalities.

Vivian and Ivan were alike, not only to each other, but in their relationships with their colleagues and their physicians. Both fail to engage in real relationships and believe that life should conform to their "shoulds." Illness forced both to question their lives.

While Susie is a strong parallel to Gerasim, there is no clear analogue for the events at the end of Ivan's life with his son. We know that Vivian was changed by her illness and her interactions, particularly with Susie, but we don't know if she achieved the level of insight that Ivan achieved in the end. However, it is clear that her contact with Susie, like Gerasim, helped to reduce her suffering.

There is also the situation where Vivian's former teacher comes to see her. Since Vivian was doped up, we can't be sure if this was real or a dream. Since Vivian died immediately after the visit, some believe that the teacher was really meant to be an angel come to call her to heaven.

Religious and Philosophical Resources

CHAPTER SIX

Viewing Guide

WHAT DREAMS MAY COME: *VISIONS OF HEAVEN*

AND THE AFTERLIFE

Introduction

What Dreams May Come[1] follows the life, love, and afterlife of a pediatrician, Chris, and his wife, Annie. Their children die as teenagers. Chris dies a few years later while trying to help others in a multiple-car collision. The film moves back and forth between their lives and a vision of the afterlife.

The vision of heaven has elements that have been described as New Age, Wiccan, and Christian; I even have a colleague from Iran who says that it matches closely with the vision of an Islamic mystic. The reader of this text will notice, for example, elements consistent with both C.S. Lewis's Christianity and with Hinduism. It creates a rich opportunity for philosophical and theological reflection on various notions of the afterlife.

One way to focus on the film is in terms of its "metaphysical" implications. For example, does the version of reincarnation suggested by the film actually make sense? Once in this type of heaven, why would anyone come back? Or why, given that each can have their own private heaven where anything they want comes instantly to reality, do they also appear to long for a "common" space where they lack total control?

However, as with our other texts, what's even richer about the movie is what those reflections suggest about ourselves. Even if one steers clear of any suggestion that the "metaphysical" might be more than just a story, the very nature of the story has rich insights into our own nature.

We will raise questions on both of these levels.

---

1 Instead of standard parenthetical references, I will use time codes from the DVD (hh:mm:ss) to show where the conversation appears in the film. As this one lacks English subtitles, I did my best to transcribe the spoken words.

As we go through the film, pay special attention to the following themes:

1. the lives and relationships, mainly between Annie and Chris,
2. the exploration of a variety of psychological and theological implications raised by the story/film,
3. the use of "self-serving rationalities,"
4. the exploration of major turning points in Annie's life in terms of Scarry's analysis of pain and world, and
5. the comparison of those two major turning points with the two key turning points in Ivan Ilyich's life.

Primary characters:

- Chris Nielsen   Pediatrician, spouse
- Annie Nielsen   Art Director, spouse
- Albert Lewis   Physician/mentor to Chris "Doc"
- The Tracker   Guide
- Ian Nielsen   Son
- Marie Nielsen   Daughter

Viewing Guide: *What Dreams May Come*

The film begins on a sweet note. Annie and Chris meet by "accident" when their small sailboats collide on a lake bordering Switzerland. This part of the movie is really only significant (for our purposes) because it sets up the later claim that they were "soul mates." They later marry, have two kids, and enjoy a rich life together. There is a sense of joy and lightness to their lives.

Tragedy strikes when their two children are killed in an auto accident. However, while we see moments of the funeral, the important details about both the accident and their relationships with their children are shown later as flashbacks. The guide starts four years later.

"Christy, I've Got Meltdown ..."

Chris is at the office caring for a child when Annie calls. She's at the studio hanging art for a showing. She calls Chris on the phone, "Christy, I've got a meltdown ..." (00:09:43). Some of the paintings for the next day's show didn't arrive, and she isn't sure what to do. On top of this, it is their "double D" anniversary, their special day (the meaning of which will become clear later), and she is unsure when she will make it home. "… I'm ruining everything …" (00:10:02). Chris suggests some alternative paintings, including her own. He offers to drive to where they are stored and to bring them by the gallery on the way home.

Watching the scene, one immediately notices a certain fragility that wasn't there before the death of their children. Chris and Annie clearly share a deep affection, but Annie appears to have lost her lightness, joy, and confidence. There is a certain sadness about her. She feels fragile.

On the road that night, a car cuts Chris off while entering a detour in a tunnel. The aggressive driver hits another car head on and initiates a multicar collision. Chris manages to stop in time, grabs his medical bag, and rushes to help the wounded.

Somewhere in the line of wrecked vehicles, he finds a car upside down with a woman trapped inside. While he speaks to her, another car, speeding and cutting through traffic, crashes into the rear of the pileup. It flies through the air and lands on Chris.

The meltdown has just begun.

The Gravesite

Chris initially has trouble accepting that he has died. In fact, his "guide," Doc, has to tell him directly. For our purposes, the next scenes of importance are at his funeral and at the gravesite. Both have to do with his interaction with Annie.

At the funeral, Chris walks among the grievers as the pastor speaks. He moves to the first pew, where Annie sits. He touches her face tenderly and she reacts, subtly. It's not that she knows that he is there, but she senses something. A tear rolls down her face.

A couple of scenes later, they are at the graveside. Clearly time has passed as Chris's tombstone is in place and the ground does not look newly disturbed. The next exchange is telling:

Chris:	Christ, when does it end? (00:22:57)
Doc:	There's no rules, Chris. It ends when you want it to.
Chris:	Where were you?
Doc:	Someplace else. What do you think? I'm a figment of your imagination? It's real, she's real, you're real, it's all real. It's the point.
Chris:	There's a point?
Doc:	*Reality is it's **over when you stop wanting to hurt her**.* (00:23:22)[2]

---

2 When there is dialogue going back and forth like this, I may just include either the final time mark or the first and last time marks. Since there are no pages, the goal is just to make it easy for the reader to find the dialogue on the DVD version of the film.

What an odd statement! It seems to come from nowhere.

Annie kneels by the graveside, flowers in hand. She is clearly sad, but not overwhelmed. She brushes flower petals from the stone. Chris reads the word "Forever" on the stone.

Chris kneels behind her, puts his arms around her, and says:

Don't worry baby, I'm not leaving you alone. I'm not going anywhere. (00:24:03)

Annie screams, she wails. She is completely overwhelmed by her pain.

Chris pulls back. Standing up, he says:

> **Goodbye, babe.** (00:24:30)

and walks away.

Chris vanishes. Annie stops wailing and looks around. We're not sure what the expression on her face means, but her pain appears to have lessened.

What just happened here? One moment, Chris is telling Annie that he will never leave her. The next, he says goodbye. Why? It has to do with different ways in which we process loss.

Two Approaches to Loss

We respond to death in different ways. We all need to grieve at the loss of a loved one. For some, that grief is itself a sign of the gift they received in the time they spent together. The focus, over time, shifts more and more from the loss to the sense of gift. These people are far more likely to move on and live rich lives.

Some focus almost entirely on what they have lost. It's not that they aren't aware of the gift, it's just that the sense of what is lost is such that, in some cases, they can't move on. It's all about having lost the gift. That appears, at least at this point in the story, to be how Annie is experiencing her grief. Moving on is far more difficult.

It's not all that uncommon for people to feel a "sense" that their loved one is communicating with them, touching them, and wishing them well. I've known elderly people who have felt that their spouse's spirit stayed with them until their own death. For some, it can be a great comfort. For others, that sense only reinforces their feeling of loss.

My closest familial experience involves my sister, who lost a fiancée in a climbing accident. They were repelling down a mountain to a "shoulder" of a steep shale slide. He went down first. When she got down, he was nowhere to be seen. *The terrain where he slid down the shale was so rugged that it took rescuers seven days to recover his body.*

My sister was in torment. Then, one night, she felt his presence. It was almost as if he was telling her that he was alright. She felt as though he was visiting her to tell her that he was ready to move on and that she should move on as well. After that, she grieved, but in different way. He will always be a part of her, but she moved on, married a wonderful man, and lives a rich and happy life.

In terms of this story, *Doc was telling Chris that Annie would be unable to move on so long as he hung around. Chris loved her so much that, despite the fact that he wanted to stay, he left. He realized that his "presence" was making her miserable.*

When you truly love someone, you want them to be happy, even if that means being without you.

Near-Death Experiences as Proof of an Afterlife?

Chris enters the "tunnel."

The light at the end of the tunnel is perhaps the most universal of near-death experiences. It should be noted that this isn't true of all near-death experiences. For example, Aries mentions that the experience of "one's life passing before one's eyes" wasn't first recorded until around the 12th century (Aries 1974, 38). It coincided with two changes in western beliefs about death. Firstly, before the 12th century, salvation wasn't focused on the individual. Instead, unless you were a particularly great saint (or sinner?), whether you rose depended upon being part of the Christian community. Secondly, until the 12th century, most Christian's placed the resurrection with the second coming, not the moment of death.

Beliefs changed around the time of the 12th century. Now, the determination of whether one went to heaven or hell (or, perhaps, purgatory) happened for each individual at the moment of their death. At that time, it was thought that one stood before God, with the heavenly hosts on one side and the satanic hosts on the other, and a record was read of one's life in order to make the crucial determination.

This idea of a "record" of one's life may, in fact, be the origin of the experience of "one's life passing before one's eyes." If so, it suggests that near-death experiences are influenced, perhaps in substantial ways, by one's expectations. This doesn't address whether there is an afterlife. It only suggests that the evidence isn't clear.

Similarly, Nuland provides a possible biological explanation for the light at the end of the tunnel. In many cases, a loss of oxygen to the brain causes a loss of consciousness. Remember that consciousness is a sort of space, a place where things can been seen, perhaps "lit" up? As that space narrows due to the shutting down of consciousness, some may experience it as a light moving into the distance, perhaps the end of a tunnel (Nuland 1995, 16).

This is not proof. The afterlife remains an issue of faith. But it is interesting.

My Own Personal Heaven

Chris awakens in what he comes to understand as his own, personal heaven. At first, given his close connection to his wife's painting, he imagines everything as "paint" including flowers, stems, and birds, His dog, Katie, joins him there. "Doc" joins him there, still acting as guide. But now, as Doc has become solid, Chris can clearly see him as Albert Lewis, the physician who mentored Chris through residency.

This heaven looks a lot like Annie's paintings, in particular, the one she was working on for their Double D anniversary. She had painted a house on an island that was her image of the home they might retire to. But before looking at the home, Doc has to help Chris understand the nature of the place.

Chris comments, "Nice place you got here!" (00:29:20). To which Doc replies:

> *Oh no no no, nice place you've got here ... you're making all of this. See, we're all pretty insecure at first, so we see ourselves somewhere safe, comforting. We all paint our own surroundings, Chris, but you're the first guy I know to use real paint. (00:29:25)*

Chris:	There's so much here she didn't paint, like that bird. (00:29:40)
Doc:	Annie gave you a start, sort of like holding on the handrails. Now you're creating an entire world here, from your imagination, from paintings you love, anything you want. (00:29:55)
Chris:	Why doesn't it move?
Doc:	*It'll move when you want it to. (00:30:02)*

Heaven, in this vision, is whatever you want it to be. How perfect is that!

Note, however, the establishment of the sub-theme that will run throughout this vision of heaven.

> *It'll get clearer when you want me too, Chris.*

> *It'll move when you want it too.*

Or later, while at Chris's house:

> *No windows, what aren't you ready to see, I wonder? (00:32:46)*

Or when Chris claims he wants to see his children, Doc replies:

> *When you do, you will (00:42:42).*

If you have that sort of power, can anything really be blamed on anyone else?

You become totally responsible.

Dual Controls

Some people believe that we control everything in our lives. This is usually, though not always, connected with a notion of reincarnation. One version suggests that you "choose" this life according to what you feel you need to experience in order to grow. Whatever happens to you in life happens as a result of that prearranged choice, though modified by how you respond to the trials of this life. Thus, for example, if we respond to adversity by feeling sorry for ourselves and giving up, the "universe" will send more negative experiences of failure; because that's the energy we're putting out into the universe.[3] Whatever one puts out comes back.

The strength of this sort of metaphysical belief is that it pushes us to take responsibility for our lives. In fact, most of us probably have more "influence" over our lives than we believe. The exact same circumstance can be a roadblock for one person and an opportunity for another. The only difference may be the "person" and their attitudes.

But it seems a far stretch from the claim that we have more "influence" over our lives than we realize to the claim that, if we but understood enough, we would have total control. (This is the idea that we always have control, but it's rarely conscious.) First of all, that doesn't really match up with our experience. The next passage of the film provides a very straightforward refutation of "total" control.

Chris calls for the bird to move. He changes the color of its wings. Then, it moves in a way Chris doesn't expect. It swoops down and excretes a large glob of "pain" on Chris's head. "I didn't do that!" (00:30:52).

Doc replies:

> *No, I did. You see, when we're together, it's like dual controls. (00:30:57)*

In other words, for the new age idea (that we have "total control") of what happens in our lives to be true, that would also mean that all other "people" would also be under our control. In most of these versions of reality, other people are also acknowledged as being in control of their realities. So, unless there are no other independent people, the notion of "total control" is just a myth.

Interestingly, both the belief in "no control" and in "total control" utilize the same logical fallacy of **hasty generalization**. One overgeneralizes the side of our experience of limits, while the other overgeneralizes the side of our experience of control. Reality is in the middle.

---

3 This version appears to be more new age than Hindu, though there are close parallels to karma. I've also seen it expressed with the Unity (not to be confused with Unitarian) Church.

What Am "I"?

The next philosophical "issue" arises as they try to walk across the water to where Chris has imagined his "home." While Doc moves easily along the surface, Chris initially drops to the bottom.

Chris:	Am I really here? (00:31:35)
Doc:	What do you mean by "you" anyway? Are you your arm or your leg?
Chris:	Hardly.
Doc:	Really. If you lost all your limbs, wouldn't you still be you?
Chris:	I'd still be me.
Doc:	So, what is the me?
Chris:	My brain, I suppose.
Doc:	Your brain. Your brain is a body part. Like your fingernail or your heart. Why is that the part that's you?
Chris:	Cause I, sort of a voice in my head, the part of me that thinks, that feels, that is aware that I exist at all. (00:32:10)

At this point, Chris rises up from the bottom of the lake, able now to stand on its surface.

Doc:	So, if you're aware you exist, then you do. That's why you're still here. (00:32:20)

Anyone who's familiar with the history of philosophy will see Descartes's most famous argument: *I think, therefore I am.*

Descartes's more precise formulation of this argument was in the negative: I doubt my existence. But to even doubt that I exist demonstrates that I must exist, at least, as a doubter.[4]

The negative form is a much stronger argument than the positive. But the next leap, taken a few minutes later, is much weaker:

Doc:	Why is it so hard? Look, your brain is meat, it rots and disappears, did you really think that's all there was to you? Like you're in your house right now. You're in your house, it doesn't mean you are your house. House falls down, you get out and walk away. (00:33:08)

---

4 While this seems fairly common sense, Sartre has an interesting refutation of the argument. Sarte argues that Decartes's claim requires that we equivocate on the term "I." One "I" refers to consciousness as a process, the other takes that same consciousness as an object of consciousness. So they aren't really the same.

Chris: But it looks like I rebuilt. (00:33:22)

Doc: You see a body because you like seeing one. We're seeing what we choose to see. (00:33:30)

Doc goes to a wall, traces a shape with his hand, and pushes it out, making an opening. The exterior of Chris' world, while still of the same appearance, is no longer paint. It has become "real."

Doc: Thought is real, physical is the illusion. Ironic, huh? (00:34:17)

While certainly not shared by most, some people have drawn this conclusion. It's really just an interpretation, an explanation, of experience. Does it bear out?

There are multiple other ways to look at the same experiences. For example, there is an idea in psychology called **gestalt**, *the idea that an organized whole can be greater than, or at least different from, the sum of its parts.* If this is true, then one could draw an entirely different conclusion from that "voice" inside one's head (i.e., *even though consciousness isn't just about the physical, it might still only exist within a certain physical organization.*

Process philosophy and theology make this argument. The idea is that, for every "thing" in existence, there is both a mental and a physical "pole," like two sides of a single coin. At most levels of organization, the physical pole dominates, while the mental pole has only a limited role. In the case of a rock, for example, the mental part might do little more than reinforce the "stability" of the rock. But with complex organisms, the mental pole can be concentrated and even dominate. Trees, therefore, would have a more complex mental pole than a rock, but less than a cat. Self-consciousness would appear to be the highest level of which we are aware.

As the mental pole reaches various states of consciousness, it can become very flexible and adaptive in how it "imagines" and in how it directs the physical. That doesn't necessarily make it independent of the physical.

For example, I remember when I was first learning to do proofs in metalogic. It was a lot like real analysis (theoretical mathematics). One day, I caught a mild cold. In most things, I felt perfectly normal. But I suddenly found that the same proofs that I was able to grasp just the day before were now entirely out of reach. Until the cold had passed, that part of my higher brain function seemed to shut down. My "mental" pole was diminished.

It seemed consistent with the claim that, *while the mind is not "reducible" to the physical, it may not be able to exist independently either.*[5]

---

5 Lest this worry certain Christians, consider the notion that Christians are to have "risen" bodies.

The Mind-Body Problem

The notion that the mind and the body, while not reducible to one another, are part of every possible thing avoids one of the most famous philosophical and theological puzzles in Western thought: **the mind-body problem**. IF one claims that the body is purely physical, with no inherent mental (or spiritual) element, and IF one claims the mind/spirit is entirely nonphysical, then how could they interact? For example, if the mind/spirit can pass through walls without any touch (unlike a physical body passing through water or air, where matter is displaced), how could it move any matter at all? How could it control the body?

Process philosophy gets around this problem by supposing that all things are both mental and physical (as in energy and matter). The problem becomes one of figuring out the exact nature of that interaction, not of how there could be such a connection. The connection is always there.

Two final comments on this notion of reality, both having to do with logic. To claim that either the physical or the mental is an "illusion" appears to be based on looking at only one side of our experience. In either case, again, it requires a level of **bad faith** and a number of other logical fallacies, including **hasty generalization**, **excluded middle** (only the physical or the mental can be real, not both), etc. The other is a form of **confirmation bias** that might be further characterized as a **positional bias**.

This last one is probably the least obvious but the most important. To what do I pose the question "do I exist?" Using process philosophy, for example, I can only pose the question by and to the mental pole. So, of course, it will affirm its existence as primary and all else as secondary. Since the question is "mental," the physical side hasn't got much to say. That doesn't actually mean that the "mental" is independent of the physical.

Soul Mates

The next scene is where the term soul mates is first used. Annie paints a new tree on a canvas, which appears in Chris's heaven. Chris realizes this wasn't his doing (more evidence of "dual controls"). At first, Doc is confused, then concludes (mainly due to the fact that her actions in the world bleed through to Chris, though he also mentions the short courtship) that they must be soul mates. He goes on to say that it's incredibly rare, like nothing he's ever seen before. "Sort of like twin souls tuned into each other, apparently even in death" (00:38:54).

Flashing back to Annie, we hear her say to herself: "Why do I believe you can hear me? Why do I think you can see this?" (00:35:40). But later, she shifts: "You can't see it, can you. And you never will" (00:39:07). Weeping, she destroys the painting. On the hillside in his personal heaven, Chris also weeps.

Suicides Go Somewhere Else

Chris starts to remember times with his daughter, Maria. Initially, he doesn't recognize her when he meets her. She comes as another guide when Doc is away and doesn't reveal herself until Chris sees through her appearance. Later, back at the house, he sees Doc and thanks him for finding Marie. Doc's face is grave.

While Chris was reuniting with his daughter, Annie committed suicide. As she is preparing, we see a flash of her wrists. There are scars indicating this is not her first attempt. Chris, distracted by the joy of seeing his daughter, didn't key in to the event.

When Doc breaks the news, Chris is at first sad, then hopeful:

Chris: But she's ok. You know, because, her pain's over ... she won't cling like I did ... when do I see her? (00:55:05)

Doc: *Never. You never see her. She's a suicide. Suicides go somewhere else.* (00:55:14)

Chris is in shock. What is the fairness of this? Why is she being punished? Why do suicides go to hell?

Doc: There are no judges or crimes here, everybody's equal. It's just reality and the way things work. (00:55:33)

Chris becomes angry. Doc goes on:

Doc: *What you call hell is for those who don't know they're dead. They can't realize what they've done, what's happened to them. Too self-absorbed in life ... Suicides don't go to hell because they're immoral or selfish. They go for a very different reason. Each of us has an instinct that there's a natural order to our journey. And Annie's violated that. She won't face it. She won't realize, accept what she's done, and she will spend eternity playing that out. ... The real hell is your life gone wrong. ...* (00:56:00)

It makes perfect sense that, if we have "total control" of our individual heaven, the same would be true for hell. Further, we will see *how similar this idea is to C.S. Lewis's notion of hell—we are not there because God judged and condemned us to hell, but only because we were unable to choose heaven.* Even in the grey town, whatever you wished for appeared, though in that case, in very poor quality.

Note also the importance of self-honesty. The passage makes it clear that if Annie could have been honest with herself, she would never have chosen hell. Many of us are unwilling to face the pain of self-honesty. This idea shows up with Ivan Ilyich,

Vivian, Lewis, and again, with every major religion. What's not yet clear is the specific lie Annie is telling herself.

Chris insists that he can find Annie and get her back. Doc tells him that he's never seen anyone return from hell. Chris, in turn, quotes Doc, "There are no rules," and points out the appearance of the tree. Doc agrees to help Chris by finding him a tracker.

The Tracker

The tracker agrees to help Chris but tells him that it's not for the reason Chris thinks. He tells Chris that nothing he can say will cause Annie to recognize him, that her denial is stronger than her love. In fact, he tells Chris, it's reinforced by her love (remember this when you read of Lewis's account of the mother seeking her son). All he can do is find her, tell her what's in his heart, and leave. "Then you'll have the satisfaction that you didn't give up. That has to be enough" (01:00:42).

The Gates of Hell

At the gates of hell, we see symbolism from a variety of traditions. We see shipwrecks, one with the name Cerbeus (the three-headed hound that guarded the gates of hell in Greek mythology). We see people trying to scream through mouths sewn shut (symbolizing those who failed to speak out in life and are now unable to speak out for themselves in death). We see people carrying suitcases (baggage from life they were unable to let go). We see a field of people, with just their heads sticking out of the ground, grumbling and making excuses for their lives (reminiscent of the story from Lewis of the woman who had become a "grumble").

There are also a number of inversions, suggesting that whatever our mind suggests about the afterlife, it is probably wrong. The elevator to hell goes up instead of down. When Chris breaks through to find Annie, he falls down through what is clearly an image of an upside-down cathedral. As they move to her "house," they are in fact struggling forward on the ceiling.

First, they are stalled at the gate. Chris was thinking of his son. Doc is about to rush into one of the crowds guarding the entrance to a ship. Their weapons are raised. Chris stops him just in time: "*Your mother's not in there, Ian*" (01:10:48). Chris saved Ian at that point. Had Ian gone forward, he might have **lost his mind**. If so, he would have been unable to recognize his father or to leave that place. **That is**, in fact, **the real danger of this notion of hell** (01:02:50).

"Doc," however, wasn't really Doc. It was Chris's son there to help him but waiting for Chris to penetrate his appearance to reveal himself. At that point, the Tracker sends Ian away. Ian is too much of a distraction for Chris and he doesn't think they will be able to find Annie unless Chris is fully focused. Still, Ian gives Chris a piece of advice:

> *When you get there, don't listen to him. You find her. And you bring her back. You can do it. I believe in you. ... Think about mom, think about what happened when we died. Think about what you said to her to bring her back. (01:12:50)*

As they rise on the elevator to hell, Chris thinks about Ian's suggestion. He thinks back to the asylum, where Annie had been living. This was from her first suicide attempt, following the death of their children. Annie brought up the issue of divorce. Chris says, at least "it beats the statue thing." The statue thing is when Annie goes "catatonic," perhaps staring at a wall or a tree, refusing to respond or react to any inquiry.

Annie says she wonders why they are different. After all, why aren't they both there? Chris feels he has to be strong, perhaps for her, or perhaps on "general principle." "I loved them Annie, but they're gone. You got a choice. Life either goes on, or not" (01:15:37). Annie replies: "And you choose life" (01:15:45). And then:

> ***Sometimes when you win, you lose.*** *(01:15:49)*

This statement, and it's reverse, will be repeated. As we go further into the experience of spirituality, we will see it as another way of expressing a mystery at the heart of being human.

We return to the trip through hell. Just outside the house, when Chris is about to see Annie, the Tracker reveals his true identity. This is the real Albert, his real teacher. He has been waiting for the chance to watch out for Chris. He advises Chris to go in for no more than three minutes and then to return. Any longer and "you could lose your mind" (01:23:25). When Chris asks what this means, Albert replies: "Once her reality becomes yours, there's really no way back" (01:23:32).

Their Double D

Chris enters the wreck of their former house. Annie is there, disheveled and lost. She doesn't recognize Chris. To avoid raising her defenses, he pretends to be a new neighbor. He talks about seeing the dead. She insists that, "When you're dead, you disappear" (01:27:30).

Chris describes the scene that explains the Double D. He is back visiting Annie at the asylum. She has not spoken a word in over a month. At this point, he's ready to give up.

Chris: I need to talk to you. And you don't have to respond. (01:28:30)

Chris sits on the grass beside Annie:

> Chris: This is a one-way ticket. For me. My hanging around here is not help-
>   ing you. And it's killing me. So, today is kind of a D day. D for decision
>   I guess, about divorce. (01:29:00)
> Annie: That would be two Ds, wouldn't it? (01:29:08)
> Chris: I stand corrected. Look what happens when you don't say anything
>   for a month? (01:29:24)

The very fact that Annie has spoken at all is a shock to Chris and tears roll down his
face. Chris goes on to explain a conversation he had with the people at the museum.
They asked when Annie might be ready to come back. Chris told them that, somehow,
Annie felt that if she had been driving, she would have been able to save her kids.
Instead, she was at a meeting at the museum. If she came back, Annie would feel
that it would mean that she wasn't sorry, that "she would be betraying her children"
(01:30:00).

This is the lie Annie won't let go of. Some might call it survivor guilt, but a better
description may be that she so strongly felt it was her role to protect her children that
the failure was too great to bear. She felt that she could have, and should have, done
something different.

Control

This reminds me of a conversation I had with a friend who always blamed herself
when a guy broke up with her. Part of that would be self-image, but in her case, not
all. I suggested to her that it was really about control and about not being hurt in the
future.

At first, she was confused. Then, a light went on. She realized that she was always
trying to "fix" herself so as to keep the guy from leaving her when it was really about
controlling him by controlling herself. To really become happy, however, she had to
let go of the illusion that she could ever develop that level of control. She had to accept
herself and wait/look for the sort of man who would do the same.

This appears to be part of what was going on with Annie. Part of her was convinced that she should have been able to control what happened. In part because
of real grief, but also because her worldview was shattered as a result of the failure of that control. The first part is terrible but would have healed with time. The
second part was why she got "stuck." She was unwilling to let go of her illusion
of control, and with it the guilt. It was safer just to stay in the asylum. This is her
self-deception.

It plays out again because she was the one who sent Chris to pick up the painting.

On the one hand, the film, at least as far as heaven is concerned, suggests the possibility of "total control." On the other hand, it continues to undermine that prospect. Chris goes on:

> What's true in our minds is true, whether some people know it or not. That's when I realized that I'm part of the problem. Not because I remind you, but because I couldn't join you. So, I left you alone. (He leans forward, kisses her on the forehead, and, tears in his eyes, rises to leave.) Don't give up, ok? (01:30:52)

As Chris stands to leave, Annie grabs the ticket from his hand. She tears it up. They reconcile. Annie returns home.

What was it that changed Annie?

Jim and Vickie

I remember a day when my roommate was trying to break up with his girlfriend. Jim was a great guy—thoughtful, self-aware, and well-educated. Vickie was a great woman—well-educated, caring, and thoughtful. Neither had done anything terrible. Rather, it was just that there are some people with whom you can be great long-term friends, but not long-term romantic partners. Jim had come to this conclusion, Vickie had not.

They had been in the living room for what seemed like, and may have been, hours. Finally, Jim came into the kitchen to talk with me. He told me that he was trying to break up with her, but she wouldn't talk to him. All she would do was sit on the couch, frozen in emotion, a tear periodically rolling down her face. Jim asked what I thought.

Jim actually knows a lot more about psychology than I do. He's also very insightful. But it is often easier to see what is going on when one isn't directly involved. I knew that Jim cared deeply for Vickie. Even if that weren't true, he had such a strongly developed sense of compassion that it hurt him deeply to feel as though he was hurting another person. Vickie, on the other hand, had been to boarding schools and was even sent out of country. As a result, she had a strong fear of being abandoned. Breaking up triggered her fear of abandonment, while her tears triggered his fear of hurting her.

I suggested to Jim that the reason she wasn't talking was because, since he wouldn't "finish" the breakup without hearing her needs and concerns, it kept the breakup from actually happening. Moreover, other than this brief moment talking with me, it kept him there, on the couch, trying to comfort her. She didn't want the breakup. Consciously or unconsciously, this was a strategy that gave her exactly what she wanted. It both kept him there and kept the breakup from happening.

What, Jim asked, would change the dynamic? I answered that, at some point, Jim was going to have a meeting or a class. At that point, he would have to leave. The moment would be broken. That was the moment when she would get "unstuck," when she would start to talk, because that meant that the silence and the tears were no longer able to hold him.

However, it also meant that the time would be so short that Jim, being Jim, would be unable to "finalize" the breakup.

The situation went as predicted. When Jim finally told her he had to leave, she stared to talk. But it was only for a few minutes. The situation was unresolved, so they were still "together."

Gerasim: Receiving Compassion

How does this relate to Annie?

As long as Chris is willing to hang around, Annie can afford to wallow in grief and self-pity. While there is the loss of the day-to-day opportunities, she knows that Chris is waiting for her. She doesn't need to take action. There is no real "cost" to staying, at least, for a "few more days."

But when Chris is about to give up, two things change.

First, it's a sign of vulnerability. Chris has been the strong one, too strong, so Annie has been able to simply give up and be weak. In a sense, as Chris says later, "He pushed away the pain so hard he disconnected himself from the person he loved the most" (01:32:06). By sharing in her vulnerability, he reconnects with her and so helps her to leave the asylum and return to life.

Second, it forces her to decide. As with Jim and Vickie, **Annie was forced to make a choice**. If she continued to refuse to speak, if she continued to wallow in her grief, she would face an additional and profound loss: Chris. Annie chooses to leave the asylum rather than lose her husband.

Watching their dynamic, I'd guess that, while both are important, the second reason played the more critical role in her returning to life. *While she loved Chris, she returned, to a larger degree, not for him, but for herself.* She returned so that she wouldn't lose Chris. If she were returning for Chris's sake, for his happiness, she would likely have returned much sooner.

This means that, in terms of our comparison with both Scarry and Ivan Ilyich, this is a bit more like the circumstance with Gerasim than with Ivan's son. **Here, Annie's return is more based on what she might lose than for the sake of who she loves.** Of the levels of world we dealt with in chapter one, this is more about receiving love and compassion than about giving it.

This also explains, in part, why Annie's return is so fragile. She hasn't expanded her world into the power and fierceness that could be hers if it were instead founded on care for another. As with Ivan, receiving compassion helps, but it's not enough.

Descent into Hell

Annie, even upon hearing her own story, fails to recognize herself or Chris. Chris tries another tactic. He gets her to imagine her wedding. A light comes on in her eyes. As he tries to tell her that this is real, that he is real, she panics and bolts. She accuses him of trying to steal (even the memory of) her husband away from her (01:33:53).

She flees to another room. Chris follows her and, taking Albert's advice, tells her all the things he needed to say. She listens, quivering, with her back to him. He returns to Albert.

It's not what Albert expects. Chris has returned, not to leave with Albert, but to send him home.

He is giving up, but in a different way:

Chris: Go home Al. Will you tell my children I love them, and I won't leave
            their mother? (01:36:46)

Chris goes back inside, sits at Annie's feet, takes her hand (she grimaces and pulls back), and speaks:

Chris: In a minute, I won't know you any better than you'll know me. But we'll
            be together. Where we belong. Good people end up in hell because
            they can't forgive themselves. I know I can't. But I can forgive you.
            (01:37:15)
Annie: For killing my children, and my sweet husband? (01:37:33)
Chris: No, for being so wonderful a guy would choose hell over heaven just
            to hang around you. (01:37:40)

The flashback repeats from their last moments in the asylum. *This time, however, it appears to come from Annie's memory.*

> **Not because I remind you, but because I couldn't join you. So, I left you alone.**
> *(01:37:52)*

The light of recognition begins in her eyes. She murmurs his name, seeing him for the first time. But it may be too late. He comments that the room has gone cold. It turns dark. The light goes out of his eyes. Chris stares out into nothing. He no longer recognizes her (01:38:43).

Annie panics.

Christy? Oh God no no no no ... Don't give up. Don't give up. Don't give up Christy. ...
(01:38:58)

There's an image of Chris falling into water, along with flashes of memories from his past. He wakens alone, back in his private heaven. He has a moment of sadness. Why is he back here, alone?

But not for long.

Annie is there. She has come out of hell. They both made it. They hold one another. Annie speaks.

Annie:	***Sometimes when you lose, you win.*** (01:40:27)
Chris:	I tried everything, nothing worked. (01:41:45)
Annie:	Until you tried joining me. (01:41:54)

What Happened Here?

The simple answer is the one Annie gives, that Chris had joined her. While true, that seems too easy and it sends a dangerous message. What else is going on?

Looking back at the story of Ivan Ilyich, Ivan experienced his most profound release from suffering, and from self-deception, when he finally began to care more about his son and family than about himself. The two seem to go hand in hand. Gerasim was more about receiving compassion, but far more world expanding is the capacity to give love, to give compassion. **When I truly care deeply about others, my world includes them, and expands, in a profound way.** It also helps me to let go of my self-deceptions because the self-identity they support becomes less important.

Chris was about to lose himself and his mind to her world. Her hell was about to become his. This was perhaps the only thing that could have stirred Annie out of her self-absorption, out of being lost in her pain and in her telling herself that all these deaths were her fault, being unable to forgive herself. **The fact that he too was about to be lost stirred the embers of her love for him to life. They rose into a flame that rescued them both. Her love for Chris, as with Ivan's love for his son, overcame her suffering and self-deception.**

We also see, in Annie, the return of the sense of richness and confidence that characterized Annie at the start of the film. This recovery was not, like the first one, fragile.

But there is a danger in how one reads this happy ending. Though the characters emphasized again and again the rareness of this circumstance, we all too easily can apply it where we shouldn't. In the case of Chris and Annie, there was a deep and rich foundation of love that, eventually, carried them through their trials. But it would be far too easy to "assume" such a foundation and put up with, for example, abuse, telling oneself that, if only one tries hard enough, if only one loves enough, that love will get through to one's partner. *This should not be a rationale for accepting an abusive partner* or for staying in a relationship that isn't truly life giving.

Reincarnation

Later, after the reunion with the kids, Chris and Annie are talking:

> Annie: I want us to grow old together. Can we do that here? (01:44:02)

Chris murmurs assent.

> Chris: But what about going back? Being reborn? See, that's the one thing we can't have here. Finding each other. All over again. Falling in love. (01:44:30)
> Annie: Make different choices? (01:44:37) Try again? (01:44:43)
> Chris: Yea. Avoid sharp objects. (01:44:48)
> Chris: Don't worry about the kids ... a whole human life, that's just a heartbeat here in heaven. Then we'll all be together, forever. (01:45:00)

While sweet and romantic, there are at least two troubling aspects to this passage.

If they are in heaven, it seems odd that they would want to return to the earthly plane. Not just because they are in heaven, but because the return comes at a cost.

First, that first kiss and finding one another, the newness of it all. That's what draws them.

But, while it didn't end well, they already had that wonderful beginning. If they want it again, why only this once more? Why not again and again?

This suggests that there might be something fundamentally unsatisfying about this sort of heaven.

It gets worse.

Is there a danger in going back? What is the risk?

On this trip, they just barely managed to avoid ending up in hell.

If they go back, they risk ending up back in hell forever.

Why Would Anyone Risk It?

It's worth noting that this criticism does not apply to, for example, a typical Hindu notion of reincarnation. I'll raise different questions there. But we can take this criticism in two ways.

First, we can simply reject this as an adequate notion of reincarnation and the afterlife. There might be elements that work, but not this notion as a whole. We might then continue to assume that there is a notion of the afterlife for which there will be no such problems.

The second is the one that I want us to keep in mind.

As we continue our exploration, ***it is possible that we will find that every characterization of the afterlife, or of ultimate reality, will prove inadequate***. Remember, even the perceptual world is far richer than our minds can grasp. How much more inadequate will our ideas be when we try to grasp all of reality? Instead of feeling that this inadequacy is a failure, we can think of it as an opportunity. When we turn, with Lewis, to explore the nature of freedom and creativity, we may find that this "inadequacy" is essential to both.

CHAPTER SEVEN

Three Theological Questions

ANALYZING C.S. LEWIS'S THE GREAT DIVORCE

1. **If God is all-loving, how could God condemn his or her children to hell?**
2. **If God is all-powerful, how could evil (as a power other than God) even exist?**
3. **If God is all-knowing, how could we have free will?**

Lewis was an exceptional thinker and writer, in part because of the grace and clarity by which he could simplify complex theological and philosophical ideas. In this chapter, the main focus is on his allegorical story, *The Great Divorce*, which speaks to the "divorce" between heaven and hell. We pursue this study in three parts. We provide an introduction to some of Lewis's key ideas and their origins in medieval Christian thought. Second, focusing specifically on the text, we expand these ideas to understand how Lewis resolves three key questions from Christian theology. We conclude with a critique of Lewis's "answers" along the lines of his notion of freedom and provide an alternative understanding of freedom that, at least in part, responds to that critique.

Lewis on the Relationship between Faith, Reason, and the Law

Like all enduring literary works, *The Great Divorce* speaks to us on a number of levels. On a psychological level, Lewis speaks to how and why we often make choices that, on the surface, seem self-destructive. The study of how we lie to ourselves would, on its own, make this a worthwhile study. But while we will refer to these stories, we are more concerned with how Lewis responds to some of the most difficult questions in Christian theology. I'll begin with a short introduction to Lewis's thought.

In a time when reason and science are loudly denounced by some Christian sects, it is important to realize that such denouncements do not speak for all Christians. Lewis is sympathetic to the notion, which he roots both biblically and in medieval theology, that faith and reason "perfect" one another. After all, reason is a gift of God and science is a product of observation and reason. To deny either, from this view, would be to deny God. The problem with reason (or science) is not with reason itself, but with the misuse of reason. For example, while science can tell us a great deal as to the "how" of the world, it can say very little as to the "why," or the meaning behind the world (Lewis 1980, 22).

Lewis, as a medievalist, was deeply conversant in medieval scholarship on the following question: How could reason be misused? The simplistic answer is to deny God or subvert God's ends. That, however, is only part of the story. Christians often argue about those ends and about what laws we are to follow. The second part means that we cannot reduce reason to blind obedience about given ends. Rather, *reason takes a central role in understanding those ends and our relationship with God.*

The second point, that we need reason not just to follow God's will but also to discern that will, means that *each of us must use our gifts and faculties to engage with and understand our relationship to God, to one another, and to our world.* Like Aristotle, Lewis believes that any set of abstract rules or principles, while helpful, are at best partial guides. We can't just rest on our laurels. The ongoing need to engage and reflect, including the use of reason, is an essential part of our earthly existence. "Real things are not simple. ... It is not neat, not obvious, not what you'd expect" (Lewis 1980, 40–41). God, as the greatest reality, is even less simple. Because of this, Lewis writes, "It is no good asking for a simple religion" (Lewis 1980, 40).

So what is the proper role of reason? What are the proper rules for us to live by? Thomas Aquinas, one of the great medieval scholars, argued that before there could be human law, there was eternal and natural law. Both were designated by God. Eternal law is that part of the law that is only available by the light of revelation, while Natural Law is available to all by the light of the conscience and of reason (i.e., Romans 2:12). God "placed" an awareness of natural (moral) law in the heart of all people (Lewis 1980, 29). Human law

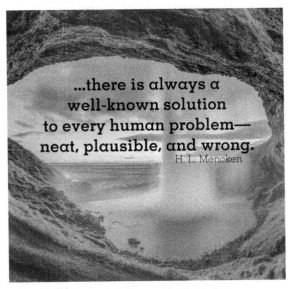

...there is always a well-known solution to every human problem—neat, plausible, and wrong.
H. L. Mencken

FIGURE 7.1

is good to the degree to which it is consistent with natural and eternal law and bad or wrong to the degree that it is not.

This distinction has a long and rich history. In modern times, Martin Luther King Jr. used this distinction to argue for when to "break" a human law, even when most should be respected.[1] Perhaps of equal importance, thinkers like King and Lewis also argue for limits even when "breaking" an unjust human law. The fact that an "unjust" law can, under some circumstances, be disobeyed does not mean that one can disobey other natural or eternal laws (i.e., murder) in that disobedience. For King, this is used to justify and explain the method of nonviolent protest. For Lewis, it serves several functions. It helps us to understand and resist part of the "nature" of evil. It also helps us to understand the proper role and relationship between faith and reason.

Lewis is profoundly aware that most who perform evil acts convince themselves that they do so for a greater good (Lewis 1980, 3). Various "self-deceptions" are exhibited again and again by the "ghosts" in *The Great Divorce* as reasons not to enter heaven. For example, consider the mother who appeared to "love" her son too much, while in reality, she wanted to control her son and live through him. For Lewis, "She loved her son too little, not too much" (Lewis 1974, 102). For Lewis, the road to "hell" is not found so much via a great sin, but through the little steps and choices made day by day, where we deceive ourselves one small step at a time until we can no longer even see the truth. Even when we "break" a human law in order to serve natural or eternal law, Lewis notes a peril. Part of the nature of evil, for Lewis, is to mistake a partial good for the whole of the good (God) and to distort the balance of the goods and the virtues. The danger is greater in the case of the "higher" goods or virtues, such that even one's professed love of "God" can become, in a sense, an idol, when one's beliefs become more important than the reality of God itself.

> ... the higher and mightier it is in the natural order; the more demonic it will be if it rebels. It's not out of bad mice or bad fleas that you made demons, but out of bad archangels. The false religion of lust is baser than the false religion of mother-love or patriotism or art: but lust is less likely to be made into a religion. (Lewis 1974, 96) (See also Lewis 1980, 49).

It's notable that, immediately following this passage, we see the one story of a ghost who is able to give up his "sin" and enter heaven. It's not a person who holds onto mother-love, to patriotism, or to art. It is the person whose life had been characterized by lust.

Thus, for Lewis, as for Aristotle and the Greeks, it's important to keep the virtues in balance. We can't use one virtue to justify violating all others.

---

1   For example, see King's *Letter from a Birmingham County Jail*.

Lewis uses this distinction to help us to understand why other religions and philosophies hold similar ethical truths to Christianity (Lewis 1980, 35). Natural law is available to all. Thus, all religions contain some truth and are worthy of study. The difference is that Christianity, in the person of Jesus, is the only religion to embody the "complete" truth.[2] But that "complete" truth is not immediately apparent, even to Christians. There is also much to learn, even for Christians, from other religions, cultures, and philosophies.

For Lewis, faith that is divorced from reason is likely to fall into dogmatism. Lewis believes that reason, without the light of God, is inadequate not only to "answer" our questions, but also to serve as a complete guide to human behavior and fulfillment. Natural law, even when properly discerned via one's conscience and the light of reason, can only get one so far. *The goal of human life, according to Lewis, is to love God. This alone allows one to rise into one's full humanity, one's "personhood."*

This does not mean that Christians are stamped from a single mold. Like John Stewart Mill, Lewis holds that our task is to develop and use our (God-given) human faculties. This means that, even within Christianity, there will be significant variation. Christians are not to rigidly follow a single set of rules, but to obey a living God who created each of us uniquely and gave us a banquet in the earth for which we must both be good stewards and, in that stewardship, we should take joy.

Turning now to *The Great Divorce*, Lewis applies this blending of faith and reason to answer three "metaphysical" theological questions:

1. If God is all-loving, how could God condemn his or her children to hell?
2. If God is all-powerful, how could evil (as a power other than God) even exist?
3. If God is all-knowing, how could we have free will?

Lewis's Answers to These Three Questions

1. If God Is All-Loving, How Could God Condemn His or Her Children to Hell?

Lewis not only believed that there is a hell, but that the existence of hell is essential for there to be human freedom. Why? If God is going to offer us a "real" choice, we must be able to refuse God. But the hell of *The Great Divorce* is not a place of fire and brimstone. Rather, it is simply what happens to us when we refuse God. Hell is where

---

2 Note that Lewis assumes what we will call, in the next chapter, the "correspondence" notion of truth. This allows one to question a number of Lewis's arguments in terms of the deeper notions of truth presented there.

we are and what we are when we place ourselves "away" from God. Lewis answers this dilemma directly when he has George MacDonald (Lewis's "guide" in the book) reply to a question:

> There are only two types of people in the end: those who say to God, "Thy will be done," and those to whom God says, in the end, "Thy will be done." All who are in Hell choose it. (Lewis 1974, 72)

Note the key role of freedom for Lewis. God gives us freedom to choose to follow God or to turn away. God, in loving us, would never condemn us to hell. ***It's not even that God condemns us because we have sinned and failed to repent. Rather, in the end, we CHOOSE to turn away from God. God, respecting our freedom, allows us the choice.*** As long as one might be able to make that other choice, God would welcome one back. ***God condemns no one to hell.***

This raises an interesting side question for those who believe in purgatory. In fact, MacDonald mentions that those who choose to stay in heaven could think of the Grey Town as purgatory. As with hell, God does not send one to purgatory, it's a state for those who are not yet fully ready to accept God's love and mercy. What does it mean to face God when one hasn't been purified?

Consider the ghosts' fear of the sunlight. IF the sun were to rise directly, it's beams would be like solid shafts of light. In their insubstantial state, it would burn the ghosts to a crisp. It would be agony. So, purgatory is not a punishment. Instead, it's about us not being ready to stand in the presence of the divine. God's mercy will always take us back once we are ready to accept God's mercy and forgive ourselves.

Even this becomes more complicated. One might ask, why, if the decision was made on earth, are these "ghosts" getting a second chance? There are at least two answers Lewis gives to this concern. First, at the end of the book, he notes that this is only a dream, it is instructive but not literal. We can take it for what it teaches us without expecting it to answer every question. But Lewis also has a richer response. For Lewis, God is outside of time. So, the "choice" one makes, ultimately, becomes one of an eternal present.

> ... ye cannot in your present state understand eternity ... both good and evil, when they become full grown, become retrospective. ... Heaven, once attained, will work backwards ... (so that) the Blessed will say, "We have never lived anywhere except in Heaven," and the Lost, "We were always in Hell." And both will speak truly. (Lewis 1974, 67–68)

The "choice," from God's perspective, is not made in a single instant, either on the earth or afterwards. Applying those categories just doesn't work. Whichever choice is finally made, it ripples forwards and backwards through time.

This reminds us of another question. At the start of *The Great Divorce*, the "damned" are allowed to take a holiday from hell. They are brought to the foothills of heaven where, if they want, they can stay. The choice seems so easy: stay and be happy or return and become miserable. In fact, of those who made the current trip, only one chooses to stay. Much of Lewis's thought is about the nature of how we deceive ourselves into making such choices.[3]

Lastly, this question raises one of Lewis's central strategies for founding his argument for the truth of Christianity. In *Mere Christianity*, Lewis argues that the very fact that we make "moral" arguments, rather than fighting like animals, means that we must assume some sort of higher, universal, moral standard or law that is, to some degree, accessible to all persons. This argument is central not just to the heart of Lewis's theology, but in a very personal manner as well. Early in life, Lewis was an atheist. Lewis found the notion of a loving God, given the fact that the world was full of pain and suffering, morally repugnant and unjust. Later, he realized that his very sense of injustice implied, at the very least, some higher standard or being that called us to justice. Otherwise, he had no "moral" grounds from which to object to pain and injustice (Lewis 1980, 38-39). Atheism, for Lewis, was too "simplistic." Many of Lewis's most basic arguments depend upon this same assumption. For example, Lewis argues that the nature behind reality cannot be dualist. Why? Because we still have a moral sense that one side is right and the other is wrong. If all we had were two equal and opposed powers ruling creation, how could we choose between them? Where would this sense come from? For Lewis, "the standard that measures two things is something different from either" (Lewis 1980, 13). This "third thing ... will be the real God" (Lewis 1980, 43).[4]

The notion that there must be a highest thing, God, in turn leads us to one of Lewis's key arguments for why Christianity contains the "highest" truth. For Lewis, it is the highest truth because God itself chose to come down, in the form of human flesh, to both teach and redeem us. How can we be sure of this? There are a number of related arguments, such as the one for a universal standard.[5] The most straightforward argument, however, is that because Jesus himself claimed to be God he cannot just have been a "great human teacher." Because of this claim, Lewis argues that Jesus must be either "a lunatic ... or the Devil of Hell" or exactly what he says he is (Lewis 1980, 52). Lewis goes on to argue that the first two do not apply, concluding

---

3 Lewis's *The Screwtape Letters* is also devoted to this question.

4 Again, keep this argument in mind when we get to the discussion of truth. Lewis's argument against dualism depends on a correspondence notion of truth.

5 Some of the other elements needed to get to this argument include recognizing that (1) "there is a real moral law," (2) "a power behind the law," and (3) that we have broken the law, which places us in violation of the law (Lewis 1980, 31). Only here can one start to talk about Christianity and forgiveness.

that Jesus must in fact be God. If Jesus is God, then Jesus's teachings must be the highest form of truth.[6]

2. If God Is All-Powerful, How Could Evil (as a Power Other Than God) Even Exist?

This question is a bit less obvious than the first. Because most Christians are raised to believe in both God and a devil, many are so used to thinking about both that it doesn't even seem to be an issue. Consider this: If God is truly all-powerful, how could there be any power other than God? How could any power exist outside of God? The notion of God being all-powerful seems inherently in conflict with the notion of a devil or an evil one. Of course, at this point we're skipping over other options, such as dualism (the notion that there are two independent powers, though they may not be equal) and pantheism (the notion that God is part of nature without also being separate from it). Lewis argues that both fail because of the lack of a "standard" by which either would be measured. Here, we are only considering how *The Great Divorce* responds to the question of how there could be a power (by definition, evil, if God is also, by definition, all of the good) outside of God *if* God were all-powerful.

Lewis, again following medieval thinkers like Aquinas, argues that "evil" is not a power in itself. Consider, for example, Aquinas's convertibility thesis. Aquinas argues that, from the human point of view, it appears that goodness and being (existence) are different. In fact, "being" appears primary (that which is most real) while goodness is more abstract, insubstantial. The insubstantial sense of "goodness" has to do with free will. We can't change the mere fact of matter's existence (although we can move things around a lot), but we can make choices between good and bad in how we use the things of the world.

However, from God's perspective, no such distinction exists.[7] Rather, goodness and being are like two sides of the same reality, two sides of one coin. Aquinas calls it the "convertibility" thesis because each is, ultimately, convertible into the other, a bit like matter and energy in the physical world.

---

6 There is a significant problem with Lewis's approach here. He assumes that the Bible is the literal word of God, something rejected by most nonfundamentalist scholars. In fact, Christians, during the first few centuries, generally believed that the Bible, while inspired, was not literal. While much was loosely based on historical events, the inspiration was more about what the stories were intended to teach, not the literal truth of the stories themselves (much like the parables). Literal notions became more common with the start of the medieval era. Lewis is thus engaged in the *bifurcation fallacy*, also called the *fallacy of the excluded middle*. Note that even though there are three alternatives, the fallacy applies because there is an alternative "between" the extremes that is being excluded. (Many Christian denominations believe in the divinity of Jesus without taking a literal approach to the Bible.)

7 Aquinas also argues that, from God's perspective, the good is primary.

This allows Lewis to argue that "evil" is not an independent power at all, but a mere diminishment or distortion of goodness. To us, evil seems quite powerful. But from God's perspective, the more one turns away from God's goodness, the more one's very being, one's very essence, is diminished. To turn entirely away from God would be to cease to exist. Evil is not an independent power; it is a loss of real power and being. In the end, it is nothing.

The metaphor Lewis uses to illustrate this point is central to *The Great Divorce*. Consider the "Grey Town." For someone in the town, it seems vast and endless. But from the perspective of heaven it is so small that it would be unable to disturb even the smallest atom of heaven. Even from within, there are hints of the lack of substance, that it's mostly illusion. For example, the roofs don't actually keep out the rain. Moreover, the "ghosts" of hell, when visiting the foothills of heaven, "grow" in size but not in substance. By the time they are large enough to interact with the spirits and angels sent to greet them, they are so insubstantial as to be almost entirely transparent.

> *Now that they were in the light, they were transparent—fully transparent when they stood between me and it, smudgy and imperfectly opaque when they stood in the shadow. … I noticed that the grass did not bend under their feet: even the dew drops were not disturbed. (Lewis 1974, 28)*

Other stories reinforce this solution. Consider the case of the grumbler. Lewis asks MacDonald, what is so bad about the lady? After all, all she is doing is complaining. Mac replies:

> *Aye, but ye misunderstand me. The question is whether she is a grumbler, or only a grumble. If there is a real woman—even the least trace of one—still there inside the grumbling, it can be brought to life again. If there's one wee spark under all those ashes, we'll blow it till the whole pile is red and clear. But if there's nothing but ashes we'll not go on blowing them in our own eyes forever. They must be swept up. (Lewis 1974, 74)*

In the end, when we turn away from God, the source of both goodness and our existence (being), we diminish ourselves. In the end, if we fully turn away from God, there are but ashes to be swept up. We no longer exist.

Thus hell, while real, is not literal in the same sense as most modern Christians are brought up to believe. I use the term "modern" Christians because beliefs about hell, as with many other Christian beliefs, changed over the centuries. For example, most modern Christians believe that the determination of heaven and hell takes place at, or just beyond, the moment of death. This notion of judgment taking place prior to the second coming, along with the belief that judgment is "individual" (rather than, for all but the great saints or sinners, judgment of the community as a whole), wasn't common until around the 12th century. For over half of the time since Jesus, Christians not only believed that one wasn't raised until the second coming, but also that resurrection was based more on the community rather than the individual. Additionally, most early Christians also believed that those who weren't Christian simply weren't "raised," not that they were sent to a place of suffering (Aries 1974, 28–39).

> The wicked, that is to say those who were not members of the Church, would doubtlessly not live after their death; they would not awaken and would be abandoned to a state of nonexistence. (Aries 1974, 31).

Saying what Christian's "believe" is actually quite complex. But for Lewis, hell, at least until one has entirely been lost, is a state of mind, as opposed to a state of "reality."

> *Hell is a state of mind. ... And every state of mind, left to itself, every shutting up of the creature within the dungeon of its own mind—is, in the end, Hell. But Heaven is not a state of mind. Heaven is reality itself. All that is fully real is heavenly. (Lewis 1974, 68)*
>
> *The whole difficulty of understanding Hell is that the thing to be understood is so nearly Nothing. (Lewis 1974, 74)*

Heaven is a state of being, of the fullness of reality, and when we enter into heaven, we become fully ourselves. When we shut out God, when we focus only on ourselves (or our own "states of mind"), that diminishment becomes hell.

Thus, the primary answer is that evil does NOT exist as a power separate from God, it only exists as a loss of diminishment of that power. Once something is fully evil (has completely rejected God), **it ceases to exist** (the ashes are blown away); **for nothing can truly exist outside of God.**

Again, we see the centrality of freedom to this answer. Without freedom, it would be impossible to turn away from God, and so "evil," even as diminishment, could never begin.

3. If God Is All-Knowing, How Could We Have Free Will?

This is the most difficult question to spot, as it is only *indirectly* addressed in *The Great Divorce*. Instead, Lewis alludes to the issue at the end of *The Great Divorce*, where he talks about how we see only through "the lens of time." This is also a place where Lewis cautions us not to take him too literally. His guide reminds him that this is only a dream and that he must not represent it as otherwise. Here, Lewis exhibits a profound humility about his thinking.

> *Do not ask of a vision in a dream more than a vision in a dream can give. (Lewis 1974, 124)*

Lewis is profoundly aware, as are the practitioners of many other religions, that the mind is limited. We can only go so far; ultimate reality is beyond our pale. Any idea or principle we come up with is only, at best, a partial truth. For Lewis, if we fail

The Nature of Mystery

Moving beyond Lewis, I'd argue that even the notion of **mystery** is generally misunderstood. A real "mystery" is not something that disengages our intellect and curiosity. Rather, while it may not give rise to a "complete" solution, *the very act of engaging that mystery is its value. Everything that is truly interesting about being human is mystery.* For example, we cannot read one another's minds. Yet somehow, we figure out how to understand (sometimes to a profound degree) one another. Love? That too is mystery. Can anyone entirely explain or understand love? If so, I've not seen it. Yet *the very act of love teaches, reveals, deepens, and enriches us.* Yes, we also use our minds in the process. But even as we develop richer understandings, it deepens who and what we are, and calls us to richer mysteries. *Mystery, by being engaged, deepens and enriches our personhood.*

For example, in *Wit*, Vivian complains that her students "flounder" when presented with paradox. Jason was clearly an exception, as he found Donne's poetry profoundly helpful for studying cellular dynamics. Jason argues that instead of trying to "solve" the puzzle, the "puzzle takes over. You're not even trying to solve it anymore. ... Great training for lab research. Looking at increasing levels of complexity" (01:19:55). When Susie asks whether the puzzle is ever solved, he replies: "No, when it comes

to recognize this, we are likely to end up replacing the living God with our own "ideas" about God.

This can be quite subtle. For instance, consider the example of some biblical literalists. Is it possible that the "book" (or their reading of it) can become more important than what the book is intended to guide? Can the Bible itself become an idol? It's also about allowing for freedom, which will take some explanation.

Again, this does not mean that one gives up on reason. Rather, reason itself can help us to understand its limits. *There is a world of difference between one who "engages" these questions with his or her entire being—including reasoning—and those who merely "cop out" by using phrases like "the Lord works in mysterious ways" to disengage.*

The Centrality of Free Will

Returning to *The Great Divorce*, Lewis recognizes the value of thinking and reasoning, but also their limits. He uses stories to help us think more deeply about our nature and place in the universe, but he doesn't claim literal insight into the mysteries of the afterlife.

The centrality of the question of whether, if God is all-knowing, there can be free will, is evident from Lewis's answers to the first two questions. In both cases, without real human freedom the answers fall apart. Here, we directly address a key objection to the possibility that God could be both all-knowing and we could have free will. For if God knows all our future choices before we make them, how are we really free? Are they, instead, predetermined?

> *Time is the very lens though which ye see—small and clear, as men see through the wrong end of a telescope—something which would otherwise be too big for ye to see at all. That this is Freedom: the gift whereby ye most resemble your Maker and are yourselves part of eternal reality. ... every attempt to see*

the shape of eternity except through the lens of Time
destroys your knowledge of freedom. (Lewis 1974 122)

The reference here is to Boethius (Boethius 1999), who argues that the problem is that we see such choices only through the lens of time. God, on the other hand, exists as an eternal presence throughout and beyond all of time. To put it crudely, imagine that time is a "bubble" existing within eternity. Since God exists simultaneously through (and outside of) all of time, from God's perspective, our future actions are as much a part of God's past as they are part of our future. In a sense, God "remembers" what we chose, because God is as much in our future as in our present and past. Our choices are "remembered" by God, but not caused by God. Our freedom remains intact.

Boethius: God exists both inside and outside the bubble of time.

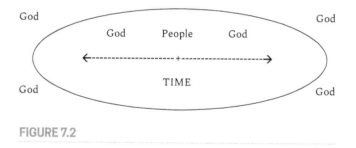

FIGURE 7.2

Why Do Bad Things Happen to Good People? A Problem with Lewis's Notion of Freedom

Lewis answers each of the three primary theological dilemmas addressed by *The Great Divorce* in terms of the single quality (love, power, knowing) of God that most directly generated the dilemma. But a solution that works in reference to a single attribute of God may be less attractive when considered in the context of all three. This, in turn, may require us to either reject those solutions or, at least, to rethink what we mean when we refer to qualities like freedom, power, knowing, or

down to it, research is just trying to quantify the complications of the puzzle" (01:20:14).

Jason argues that Donne's poetry is about salvation anxiety. We know we are sinners, but we have the promise of salvation. But Jason doesn't think that the "promise" stands up to scrutiny. He argues that Donne is trying to deal with ever deeper levels of complexity of the problem, until one "forgets" the original insolvability.

Something similar is true for scientific research. No matter how much we discover or quantify, there are always deeper and different ways to understand the world. But the fact that it goes far beyond human understanding does not make it worthless. There is a great deal of value in what we do understand. This is half of an answer.

What Jason and Vivian "miss," or see only dimly, is the nature of what I'm calling mystery. We see this reflected even in the title of the play, *Wit*. Early in the play, when Vivian refers to Donne's poetry as "... a metaphysical conceit, it's wit" (00:09:40), her teacher sternly contradicts her. Vivian never comes to understand the truth her teacher wished to impart. This is also the point where Vivian is told to go out and be with friends. Vivian goes back to the library.

There are different kinds of paradoxes. Some are more purely intellectual. For example, if God is all-powerful, can God create a rock so heavy that even God cannot lift it? Either God is limited by not being able to create such a rock, or God is limited in being unable to lift it. Whichever answer one gives, it means that God is not all-powerful.

I refer to these as "intellectual" paradoxes because they are primarily intellectual and abstract. They cannot be solved, but that doesn't mean that they don't have something to teach us. In this case, it can help us to reflect on whether our concepts of God make sense. It can help us to quantify the limits of the intellect. It can help us to be humble in our assertions about the nature of God and reality.

Far more interesting, however, are the sort of paradoxes I like to term "mysteries." *A mystery is a paradox of human experience that, while it cannot be "solved," speaks in some fundamental way to who and what we are. Moreover, while it cannot be solved, it can be engaged. In that engagement, it deepens and enriches our fundamental selves.*

Example: Communication and Intimacy

Consider something as simple as communication. Can you read someone's mind? Is your experience of what they tell you ever really the same as their experience? Even with your closest life partner, how is real understanding even possible?

loving. The purpose here is not to come up with a "perfect" solution. Rather, it is to engage the "mysteries" in ways that deepen and enrich our thinking and ourselves. To get at this issue, we begin with one of the basic questions of any religion: Why would a loving God allow bad things to happen to good people?

Note that, if we grant that God is simultaneously all-loving, all-knowing, and all-powerful, we can't resort to saying that it was beyond God's power, that it was a mistake, or that God could not have prevented it. Given this, there are at least three standard responses that are likely to be offered.

1. God Gives Us Trials and Hardships to Help Us Grow.

This would be consistent with the qualities we have suggested and it may well be true part of the time. However, one only has to think of diseases like Alzheimer's to realize that it's not an adequate solution. During most of the course of the disease, the victim iS incapable of learning and growing. The suffering in this case is clearly not for the sake of the one undergoing the suffering. What of those cases? Clearly this is not a full solution.

2. God Gives Us Trials and Hardships to Help Others Grow.

As before, this may account for some cases of hardship and pain. Still, the case that it is an inadequate account for suffering is, while not quite the slam dunk of the previous example, still quite strong.[8] Here, I have two concerns:

a. Say I was to take a person and torture them for years, perhaps to death. Let's also say that my

---

8 Even the first case is not a total slam dunk, as one could argue that perhaps there is some sort of spiritual growth in an Alzheimer's patient that we are unable to see. Here, we are getting so far into speculation that it's really just back to the weak sense of "The Lord works in mysterious ways." We've disengaged from the questions.

reason for doing so was based in how it might draw their family together in searching for them and cause them to become more loving and caring. Despite this reason, most would think me a monster. Yet, in cases like Alzheimer's disease, many people just "assume" that God is doing it for a greater good. For some reason, we assume both that (a) God is the one doing it (all-powerful) and (b) that it must be for the greater good (all-loving). We disengage our discernment and resort to the "cop-out" version of "The Lord works in mysterious ways." Such a notion of God appears to be beyond ethics. This may well be true. But if God is the wellspring of moral law, why would God violate himself or herself?

b. The second argument is more empirical. Supporters of the notion that God is acting for this reason can point to families that have, in fact, drawn together and been enriched in learning to care for such a loved one. Yet, as Lewis might say, this is too simplistic. Many families are torn apart by these sorts of devastating diseases and events. Consider families that face the death of a child. Years later, parents report higher rates of depression, anxiety, and divorce. Did they fail the test? In fact, *the only way one can maintain the claim that such an event was given to "help" them grow would be to say that they failed the test.* For those that failed, it's their fault that they could not live up to the test. Now again, this could in fact be true, but it's highly troubling. *This "answer" ends up blaming those who are, often, also victims.*

This second notion is consistent with saying something like: "God will never give you a trial without giving you the strength to cope with it" or "Whenever God closes a door, He opens a window." **While comforting to some, these serve as statements of failure and inadequacy to others. What these suggest is that if one fails**

Intellectually, it seems extraordinarily difficult to explain. Yet, we do communicate, connect, and understand one another on a profound level.

The very attempt at deep communication and connection, even intimacy, changes us. A real, loving relationship doesn't just exist, it *transforms* both parties. To some degree, we give ourselves over, losing ourselves (forgetting ourselves) at times in the action/activities of the relationship. Yet, there is also a return. From my rich relationships, I find that *I become more than I was* before. Somehow, my spirit is deeper and richer.

A rich marriage, or friendship, seems to take on a life of its own. If you break up, even though both parties live, it can be as if someone has died.

This is mystery. The more it is engaged, the more it has to teach us. The intellectual is only a part of the learning. The greater learning goes on in the heart, spirit, and body.

From the standpoint of the "intellect," where we are looking for an "answer," it seems inadequate. In part, because most people are looking for a "final" answer, a static conclusion.

From the standpoint of living, it is its own answer. We are deepened and enriched as we engage it. ***It is a creative, life-giving "process" rather than a static "answer."***

As we will see, the experience of mystery, while common to us all, may at times be addressed better by the language of spirituality than by science or philosophy. Yet, each has something to contribute. Paradox, in this way, speaks to the very heart of what is most fundamentally human. This is why spirituality so often uses the language of paradox. The danger, of course, is that this makes it so easily misunderstood. This is not paradox in the abstract. Again, **when one hears the phrase, "The Lord works in mysterious ways," it usually means that the speaker, instead of engaging the mystery, is copping out.** They've missed the point in the passage. Yes, the Lord works in mysterious ways, but we are called to ENGAGE that mystery, not just accept it. Unless the mystery is engaged and explored, on all levels of human capacity and experience, it is merely being dismissed or forgotten. **Engaging mystery is a fundamentally creative process that is a critical part of defining and developing our humanity.**

In *What Dreams May Come*, one hears the phrase: "Sometimes when you win, you lose" (01:15:49) and it's converse, "Sometimes when you lose, you win." This speaks to the paradox of mystery. In this case, only when Chris was willing to lose himself for his love of Annie, and Annie was willing to do the same, could they truly win. So long as one or both held back by playing to "win" in the more earthly sense of the word, they would lose.

to find or pass through the "opportunity", then one is morally lacking.

Perhaps there are richer ways to understand this?

3. God Does Not Cause Bad Things to Happen to Us Directly. They Happen Because We Have Used Our freedom to Sin, Not Just as Individuals, but Also As a People.

Again, this does not mean that God might not cause or allow some sorts of hardships for the first two reasons, but it does provide an alternative for cases wherein the first two seem inadequate. In a sense, this gets God "off the hook," because the really bad stuff is not caused by God at all but is the result of our misuse (either individually or as a whole) of the gift of freedom. Humankind, through a multitude of sinful actions, brings a great deal of misery down upon itself.

This also doesn't require that victims be blamed, at least not as individuals. While none, in Lewis's view, are entirely innocent, the child who is killed by war, a serial killer, disease, or starvation is clearly not at "fault" for what happened. By this view, God would be seen as offering to "help" the family of the Alzheimer's patient to endure the pain, but not as the "cause" of the harm. To link (in reverse) two passages from Nuland, talking about both AIDS and Alzheimer's disease:

> *I prefer to think that God has nothing to do with it. (Nuland 1995, 167) It is an arbitrary act of nature and an affront to the humanity of its victims. (Nuland 1995, 117)*

At least in the abstract, this solution appears more robust than the previous two. But does it really work? What is Lewis's core notion of freedom here?

The idea of freedom offered by Lewis is mainly the freedom to choose between God's plan for us (God's will) and one's own will. Of course, the choice is worked out in thousands of little ways but, ultimately, it's the essence of freedom; **it is *this* specific choice.**

Let us return to Boethius. If we consider not just the "all-knowing" quality of God, but also the "all-powerful," then there's a problem. Return to our analogy of time being a "bubble" in eternity. According to Christian theology, God "created" the bubble. Since God is both all-powerful and all-knowing, even before creating the bubble, God would have known that we would sin, that we would fail, and that great suffering would take place. For Lewis, this was a risk that God was willing to take in order for us to have freedom (Lewis 1980, 48). One is then forced to ask two questions:

> *First, is it possible that we could be given freedom, and yet never have made that first bad choice?*
>
> *Second, if so, then could God not have chosen a version of the bubble wherein humankind freely chose the good?*

If the gift of freedom *necessarily* meant that we would make the wrong choice, then there is something wrong with God's perfection of love, power, and knowing. *If freedom, which is a good, requires sin, which is an evil, then good, to some degree, depends upon evil. In that case, we are back to dualism: God is not "all-powerful" in the sense that most modern Christians believe.*

If we follow Lewis's rejection of dualism, *it must be possible that God could have chosen a version of the "bubble" of time wherein sin, and with it suffering, did not occur because we freely chose to follow God. If so, why didn't God just create that version of reality?* If God did not love us enough to create that version, God is ultimately responsible for our suffering.

Again, if we back off of any one of the three attributes with which we started, Boethius's and Lewis's argument works:

We will come upon other ways of naming the "mysteries" of human experience. In The Middle Voice in Hesiod, in Levinas's notion of ethical desire, as well as in our discussions of truth and faith, spirituality as interruption, and in the "tension of opposites" in *Tuesdays with Morrie*.

Perhaps, in the end, Jason was right when he said:

> **... you can't just go around thinking about all that meaning of life stuff all the time. You'd go nuts.**
> (01:20:37)

Welcome to the nuthouse.

If God is <u>not</u> all-loving, then of course God wouldn't necessarily choose the best possible version of the bubble for humanity.

If God is <u>not</u> all-knowing, then perhaps God was just unable to predict the outcome.

If God was <u>not</u> all-powerful, then perhaps it was beyond God's power to create a better alternative.

But *if we think in terms of our modern understanding of **all three qualities together**, Boethius's solution fails, and with it, **the freedom essential to both of the "other" dilemmas that Lewis addressed in** **The Great Divorce** **also fails**.*[9]

The issue can be pressed even further. If God is "perfect"—all-loving, all-powerful, all-knowing—then how could evil, even as a "distortion" of the good, get started? Once the distortions of evil have begun, one could argue that they continue as ripples in a stream, like when a pebble disturbs its stillness. But if God is "perfect," everything God created would share in that perfection and would be complete in a profound way. Thus, if there was a literal Garden of Eden and humankind resided there, they would live in perfect bliss.[10] If I am completely and utterly happy, why would I want anything different?

An easy answer is that while they were (well, once Eve was introduced) entirely content, Lucifer came into the garden and disturbed their contentment. It was then that they made the fateful choice. Unfortunately, this only shifts the problem. Yes, Lucifer acts as the pebble that disturbs the tranquility of Eden. What caused Lucifer to turn away from God? The quick answer is pride; Lucifer wanted to rule heaven. That assumes, however, that Lucifer was not created perfectly and that Lucifer was not content. Moreover, as an angel, Lucifer sat in the presence of God, in the "light" of heaven. As noted in *The Great Divorce*, nothing could be more satisfying or more fulfilling. Being able to see God, *to be in the presence of utter joy and perfection, how could Lucifer ever want to commit that first sin?*

Lewis even appears to recognize the inadequacy of this answer. He just concludes that it's the best we have (Lewis 1980, 49).

One might be tempted to argue, as Lewis suggests, that we are trying to see an answer from the wrong end of the telescope. After all, Lewis argued that if we try to

---

9 This should not be as troubling to Christians as some might think. After all, if the content of faith could be "proved" by the pure power of reason, then what would be the need for faith? But to be clear, we aren't talking about faith in a way that denies reason (or science), but in a way in which both become essential.

10 Ignoring, for the moment, that it was not in fact "perfect," since Adam started out as lonely, because that implies that God did not, in fact, make a perfect creation. This is only an issue for the biblical literalist.

see the whole, then freedom disappears. If we were to merely become "stuck" here, then Lewis would likely have us let it go.

While I think Lewis took the conversation as far as he could, Lewis would also be among the first to agree that if the situation could be further explored in a fruitful manner, it should be. Lewis stood on the shoulders of the medieval theologians, we stand on Lewis's shoulders as well. What if there are richer notions of freedom, truth, and even notions of knowing that might enrich our reflection?

Lewis argues that freedom is the manner in which we most imitate our creator. Most Christians, including non-literalists, agree that humankind is, in some crucial way, made in the image of the divine. What this means is subject to debate. Let us consider, for the sake of this argument, two attributes of God. In the Old Testament, particularly Genesis, God is characterized in many ways, but most fundamentally, with the power of creation. Similarly, in the New Testament, God is also characterized in many ways, but most essentially, one could follow 1 John 4:8: "God is Love." Might they be in some way linked? Might these guide us to a richer notion of freedom?

If one thinks about it, Lewis's notions of truth and freedom are linked. Lewis assumes a correspondence notion of truth. That is, an idea or statement is true to the degree to which it corresponds to reality. For example, if I say my hair is black and it is indeed black, then that is true. By this notion, truth is literal and absolute. On this basis, moral law must either be thought of in terms of absolutism or relativism, there is no real middle ground. Therefore, freedom is really just about a single choice, to follow the absolute or to try to become a law unto oneself.

But is freedom, understood as such, really a gift? Yes, we can clothe it in fine and noble language. But if freedom is really just the ability to sin, choose unhappiness, fail, and suffer, then what sort of gift is that? We can argue that God does not want robots to return God's love. But God, in the traditional notion, doesn't need us at all.

Why should God create suffering children, when God has the power to create the bubble of time in such a way as to allow us to bypass all that suffering and still freely choose to be God's children?

Put another way, this notion of truth suggests a corollary notion, also common for many Christians, that God has a perfect plan for each one of us. Unfortunately, due to original sin, we can't fully understand or follow that plan. If we all could follow God's plan, each of us would be supremely and perfectly happy. The earth would be a Garden of Eden.

In this scenario, freedom is really just the ability to step off that perfect path. Freedom is the ability to suffer and become miserable. **Is that really a gift?**

An Alternative Notion of Freedom

When we get to the chapter on truth, we will argue that truth, as it is lived, is more of a creative process than a set correspondence. There is a tension in Lewis's thought on this as well. While he appears to settle on truth as correspondence, there are places where he recognizes its limitation ("Because all answers deceive" [Lewis 1974, 121]), at least for our earthy intellects. Wherein do we see the power of creation? Creation (Genesis) is one of the fundamental attributes of the divine.

What if freedom is not primarily the ability to simply step on or off the path? What if we take seriously Lewis's claim that it is "the gift whereby ye most resemble your Maker …?" (Lewis 1974, 122). If we characterize God's most fundamental attributes as love and creation, then in some way perhaps freedom shares in BOTH these attributes. Freedom is not just the ability to step on or off a single path; freedom is the ability, at least to a limited degree, to create or "co-create" one's own future, to develop our faculties and use them in creative and unique ways. The term "co-create" is to acknowledge that the power is ultimately sourced in the divine and that it is done with the consent (gift) of God. Nor does it mean that there is no "goal" or that we are adrift to merely create whatever future we want. This is where love comes in.

The "goal" of developing and rising into our humanity is to generate new and creative ways to engage and care for one another, our world, and most importantly, for Lewis, God. There are limitations (boundaries) on our power of creation. But that doesn't mean that the outcomes are fixed or even entirely predictable. A tree, for example, can serve many functions, but it cannot be a person. While there are some paths (choices) that are better than others, under a creative notion of truth there is no single "best" path for one to follow.

Of course, if freedom were truly such a power of creation, certain other nuances follow. If the future was not entirely predictable, how could God be all-knowing? *Biblically*, however, *the idea that God knows all future, past, and present is not the only meaning for the term. Another meaning would be that God knows all that can be known, when it can be known.* Here, **we've popped Boethius's bubble**. The future is open, not fixed. God continues to create, in part directly, in part through us.

Can God predict the future? To a large degree, yes. In the same sense that we, with far more limited intellects and experience, can predict the sun will rise tomorrow. God is able to predict much more but not all. In this understanding, creation continues such that what is "created" cannot be entirely predicted in advance. The idea of "all-knowing" is subtly changed, but the role of freedom is enriched.

Similarly, power is re-nuanced in terms of creation. The notion of a static perfection is no longer viable (in this, we depart more strongly from Lewis; though he also appears conflicted about the notion). If the nature of God's power is genesis, then it gives forth both creation and destruction.

Destruction can be understood in many ways. Here, I'll focus on two. First, in any change, something is usually destroyed to create the new. Second, to choose one future over another is, in essence, to destroy the path not chosen. In other chapters, we cover an even more radical way through the notion of the middle voice, where genesis and destruction, activity and passivity, become one and the same. The key notion for this discussion is that the future is not fixed. There is no single "best" future (though some are better than others). Instead, we are tasked with co-creating ourselves and our futures in ways that deepen our humanity and compassion.

Lewis would be troubled by the fact that this idea reopens the possibility of a certain kind of dualism. Lewis's argument against dualism from mere Christianity, depending as it does on a correspondence notion of truth, would not apply. It's not that evil would necessarily be on the same level as good, but that if destruction is thought of as necessarily bad (which wouldn't always follow), then a certain level of "bad" would be necessary for the good.

Where, then, does one find a moral foundation? Again, let us return to the notion of love or compassion as at the heart of God. As we follow Lewis's notion of the divine, there's actually no essential reason (again, some of his most important arguments on the subject simply don't apply when examined in this way) to believe that the universe "had" to have pain and suffering. In Lewis's notion of God's perfection, it's certainly plausible that we could live in a bubble wherein we would all be perfectly happy and freely following God. Yet, in terms of our core experiences, how or where could one experience love and compassion unless one also experiences pain and suffering?

We feel sympathy for someone in pain only because we have some experience of what that is like for ourselves. If we were all just perfectly happy, there would be no place or need for compassion. Love, understood primarily as compassion, would be irrelevant.

The Jewish philosopher/theologian Emmanuel Levinas makes this point when he writes, "only a subject that eats can be for-the-other" (Levinas 1981, 74). In other words, only one who can taste, enjoy, and benefit from eating can instead choose to take bread from his or her own mouth and know what it is to give that bread to another. Only if one knows joy and pain can one relate to other beings who suffer.

For instance, if I was writhing on the floor with kidney stones, and you had never experienced or seen any sort of pain, you'd have no idea what I was experiencing. You might think I was doing a new dance, perhaps the "dead bug." *In this model, it can be argued that **some pain is essential for the highest of values—love. In fact, it is precisely because of pain and suffering that love has become the highest value. In Lewis's theology, as in many Christian theologies, that doesn't quite work.***

God remains the ground for the moral law, but moral law is understood less in terms of a fixed moral law and more in terms of a dynamic power of creation.[11] As Levinas might suggest, we are given the call to love, but the details are not specific. Any set of rules is, as Aristotle would also suggest, only a partial measure.[12] Some are very close to absolute, but others less so. We are all subject to the question of whether we are serving God in how we love one another.

Just to repeat, these are not "final" conclusions. Rather, we are *engaging* the mystery.

Conclusions

What does Lewis appear to believe that facing one's death teaches us about living? Remember that Lewis started off as an atheist based on his moral repugnance to human suffering and death. What Lewis realized, eventually, was that his very moral repugnance implied that there was some standard by which one would "morally" object to such suffering. So, **for Lewis, authentically *facing* suffering and death is the beginning of the path to faith in God**. Death, once we understand our place with God, no longer becomes a horror, but a mere transition to a better place. All of creation works backwards so that all of our suffering is "fixed" or cured.

Lewis's arguments, while powerful and instructive, are not entirely convincing. Even he recognizes some weaknesses. We used an example of illness and death— Alzheimer's disease (and an alternate notion of truth)—to illustrate some of the weaknesses in Lewis's thoughts and conclusions. We also offered an alternative understanding of freedom and knowing to address some of these weaknesses.

So, *what of the status of heaven* for Lewis? For Lewis, heaven is a natural result of a loving God for God's children. This is worth emphasizing. Many Christians focus on their "faith" in order to gain salvation, by which they mean "heaven." But to love God for the sake of gaining heaven is, in essence, to "use" God as a means to an end. As with the mother who agreed to come to heaven only to get her son back, that doesn't work. Following Lewis's thought to its logical extreme, *heaven, while a nice by-product, really shouldn't matter to the mature Christian. One should love God, and*

---

11   This is not the same as the sort of "life force" or "creative evolution" to which Lewis objects. See Lewis's note (Lewis 1980, 26).

12   Here, one might be inclined to introduce the distinction between rules and principles. Principles are much more general (i.e., always act for the greater good) while rules are more specific (thou shalt not steal). One could legitimately argue that, for Lewis, the rules are more flexible. The difference is that, for Lewis, the flexibility of the rules comes from the complexity of reality; they are very difficult to apply in some cases. In the view proposed here, it also comes from the inherent creativity of freedom.

love one's neighbor, not for what one "gets," either in this life or the next, but ultimately just for their own sake. Anything else is using "heaven" to escape one's fear of death rather than facing it.

It's also worth noting that there is a place for "keeping it simple." Part of the value of engaging this complexity is, in fact, in service to humility. The more deeply we engage these questions and mysteries, the more fully we also realize that we don't have all the answers. *For many, keeping it simple is actually a way to avoid issues and, sadly, to judge*[13] *others while not adequately questioning oneself. That sort of simplicity becomes dogmatism. On the other hand,* there is a certain simplicity that can also arise at the far side of complexity, *one which involves a richness and caring humility.* Some may exhibit this humility or care with far less "thinking" than others. But for most, we are quick to oversimplify and judge those who may be different than ourselves. Most of us would be wise to heed Lewis's observation:

Reality is not simple.

Figure Credits

Fig. 7.1: Copyright © Diego Delso (CC BY-SA 4.0) at https://commons.wikimedia.org/wiki/File:Seljalandsfoss,_Su%C3%B0urland,_Islandia,_2014-08-16,_DD_201-203_HDR.JPG.

---

13   Note that there is a difference between making judgments and being judgmental. Equivocation fallacies are not uncommon when using the two.

CHAPTER EIGHT

Buber, Truth, Chaos, and the Middle Voice

Martin Buber

MARTIN BUBER IS a Jewish philosopher who developed the idea of the I-thou and the I-it relationships.[1]

In the I-it relationship, the other person is primarily an object for one's own use or purpose. Instead of encountering the other as a "person," they are conceptualized in terms of the first person's goals. For example, if I am racist, I don't see a "person" of another color, I see an example of my stereotypes about people of that race. They are an "ideal" rather than a person.

Similar to Aristotle's friendship based on virtue, in the I-thou relationship, the other is seen as a person whose own goals or ends are to be respected, a being of infinite dignity. There is mutuality, dialogue, and respect.[2] Real relationships and lived experiences cannot be fully shoved into the boxes of ideas (Buber 1970, 65).

The reason to raise Buber at this juncture is because we are beginning, as we explore issues of truth, faith, and spirituality, to push at the edges of human thinking. This is not to say that we cannot say things "about" them. Love, for example, cannot be captured by the intellect, but there is still a great deal that can be said about love. What we are about to attempt is even more difficult, but it speaks to the heart of the mysteries of our experience. It shows up not just in philosophy, as with thinkers like Aristotle, but in all major world religions including Christianity, Judaism, Islam, Hinduism, Buddhism, and Taoism. We aren't going to fully understand this in a few chapters. At best,

---

1 There are others as well, such as the We-We and the Us-Them, but these are the two most important (Buber 1970, 13).

2 Levinas, the philosopher whose thought most underpins this book, is often compared with Buber. For example, to some degree, one could see the I-it relationship as operating on the level of need, while the I-thou relationship operates on the level of ethical desire.

that's a lifelong process. This chapter introduces some of the ideas and themes that can be developed as we move through different traditions.

Buber, for example, notes that the I-thou relationship goes beyond conception, beyond ideas. It is to meet the other in their authentic humanity, exceeding or being other than the conceptions of the mind. We can't stay there indefinitely; even good relationships move back and forth between honoring one another as persons and treating one another as objects. To a limited degree, that's ok (Buber 1970, 17). It's not that we can't also help serve one another's goals, but that even in serving one another, we aren't just an object to be used. The larger problem is when we shift too far into treating one another only as objects, as means to our ends.

For Buber, God can only be authentically approached as an I-thou. God, or whatever one terms the divine, *that greater reality beyond our human ideas about the world,* comes to us when we are "open," when we are receptive. But, as we will see in the novel *Siddhartha,* not when the divine is "pursued." Buber recognizes that *when we "pursue" rather than being receptive, we end up seeking an object that we have conceived and created.* The divine is no object; it is no "thing" at all. It can be received, but not pursued or controlled. *It can only be welcomed.*

Anything else results in idolatry.

For now, however, we turn to one of Buber's comments on the nature of human thought, on how we conceive of reality. Here, Kramer quotes Buber on **the law of non-contradiction**:

> *According to the logical conception of truth ... only one of two contraries can be true.*
> (Kramer 1988, 5; emphasis added)

For many, this is thought of as the foundational principle of logic. Others argue that there is another foundational principle—**the principle of sufficient reason**. This principle asserts that

> *for everything there must be a reason.*

The second merely claims that, for everything that exists or happens in the world, there must be sufficient reason, a "why," to explain it. I tend to agree with Heidegger that the principle of sufficient reason is more foundational than the law of non-contradiction, but both are obviously foundational to how we, as humans, think about ourselves and our world.

What if both are false?

Or perhaps, not so much false, *as limited*? For instance, while useful, what if they don't actually account for what is most basic in human experience?

Buber raises this issue when he continues that thought:

> *... the unity of the contraries is the mystery at the innermost core of the dialogue.*
> (Kramer 1988, 5; emphasis added)

In other words, at the heart of reality, perhaps the law of noncontradiction does not apply. Perhaps there is a "unity" at the heart of reality that this law denies. Consider that, for the Greeks:

To know is to divide.

In other words, the very nature of human consciousness, the part that deals with ideas, functions by dividing up the essential unity of reality.

This happens almost from birth. We are born into a confusing and chaotic word. We start with a myriad of sensations. It takes time to recognize objects, to see "things" and patterns. Why do we see the patterns we see? They are partly based in what is "real." But they are also based on our needs and faculties. For instance, if you cut my mother's umbilical cord, I feel hunger for the first time. If something is pressed against my mouth, and I suckle, then the hunger goes away. Eventually, I start to separate those "objects" in the world that relieve the pain of hunger (I learn, from my culture, to call them "food") and those that do not. I begin to divide up the world according to conceptions that serve my needs and help me flourish, or that my culture has developed for the same purpose.

These divisions, while useful, capture only a part of our reality. While some "divisions" (like food or not food) would appear common to all human cultures, in other ways, different cultures may open up (divide) the world in very different ways.

For example, anyone who is fluent in two languages knows that there are things one can say in one language that really don't translate to the other. Why? In part, because each language and culture has opened up reality in slightly different ways. Realizing this and breaking free of the hegemony of one's own cultural views is one of the values of traveling and learning about other cultures and languages.

Sometimes it's just a matter of emphasis. For example, consider the notion of "missing someone" in French:

> So you would like to think that all languages are roughly the same; different ways of saying the same thing. But in English we say I miss you, or I am missing you, which frankly reeks of target practice. The French say, rather, "Tu me manques," which is literally something like, there is a lack in me, which is you. Or, there is a hole in my being without you. I think that captures, much better, the reality of "missing" someone.[3]

At other times, it's even more substantial. For example, one fall I had a student who hailed from Africa. While raised in the United States, she still has close ties with relatives there. She tells me that she sometimes becomes very frustrated talking to them even about some of our most common ideas, such as individual freedom, because in

---

3   This example comes from a Facebook post by a colleague, Dr. Phillip McReynolds, with whom I studied at Vanderbilt.

their language, there is no word for "I." Consider how utterly differently they must view their world from how most of us view ours!

Recall Lewis's comment that "reality is not simple"? Buber agrees. We like to make it simple for our own ease (Buber 1970, 9). In fact, as Kaufman summarizes Buber:

> *Man's world is manifold, and his attitudes are manifold. What is manifold is often frightening because it is not neat and simple. Men prefer to forget how many possibilities are open to them. (Buber 1970, 9)*

In part, our tendency to divide the world into two alternatives feels easy, simple. It's tidy. We each experience a certain level of the sort of desire I once saw expressed on, of all things, a t-shirt: "I have given up my search for reality and am now looking for a good fantasy." Of course, the problem is when we convince ourselves that the fantasy is reality.

The difficult task of getting beyond this, back to a more essential richness, is something Lewis might characterize as another way of taking about how we see reality, darkly, through the lens of time. There is a rich Christian tradition[4] exploring this very issue. But here, let us start with a more basic question. If the laws of noncontradiction and sufficient reason don't always apply, if reality can be divided up in many different ways, what happens to truth?

Truth[5]

As we noted earlier, psychology tells us that reality isn't just a "given." Our minds aren't blank slates from which we imprint reality. Instead, something very different is going on. Using an abbreviated and simplified version of Heidegger's analysis of the nature of truth, we can come to an understanding of what that might be. But, we also need to be aware of what is often referred to as the "is-ought" problem. There are really two versions of this problem. One, called the **is-ought fallacy**, and it names a situation wherein, because something is currently thought of in a particular way, one believes that it has to be that way. The other, called the **naturalistic fallacy**, asserts that there is a gap between what "is" and what "ought" to be. One can't just move from, say,

---

4   I mention Christianity, as that is my tradition. That's not meant to be exclusive. For example, much of the Christian tradition on virtue comes from Aquinas, who got it from Aristotle. But Aristotle was lost to the West for generations. His work was preserved, and substantially enriched, by Islamic scholars.

5   Many passages (and the main outline of this argument) are reused, with permission, from "Talking with Students about Truth: Using Heidegger to Loosen the Grip of Literal Absolutes." *Religion and Education* 35, no. 2 (Spring 2008): 27–41.

the reality of a "table" to statements about the moral uses of the table. The reality of the table is an "is" statement, the ethics of usages in an "ought" claim. Something more is needed in order to bridge that gap.

In analyzing the nature of "truth," we need to consider both the "is" (what is real) and the "ought" (ethics, or what we should do about them). The more difficult question, and yet the one that many people appear the most certain about, is the second. We are often certain that our "moral" or ethical truths are *the* truth. Let us begin there.

If we think about the "nature" of ethical truth (i.e., what grounds truth), we are often given two alternatives:

1. There is some sort of absolute ground for ethics. (**Absolutism**)
2. There is no real ground for ethics. (**Relativism**)

Both have many forms. But for our purposes, we will start with these two:

> For *absolutism*, many would argue there are rules that exist in natural law, the mind of God, perhaps just the nature of reality. These rules exist independently of us, even if our "human" access to them is limited.

> For *relativism*, there are no laws grounded in the mind of God, nature, etc. Rather, moral rules are just "agreements" between people and cultures. They have no independent reality.

Each form has advantages and disadvantages.

With absolutism, *we have the advantage of a firm moral compass.* We may not always know exactly the right thing, but that's only because we are unaware (human limitations, choice, sin, etc.) of what the ethical rules tell us, not because they don't exist. *There is a claim that if only we would/could all follow the moral laws, then all people could be happy and fulfilled.*

There are at least two problems with this approach. First, there are significant differences between what different people, groups, and cultures believe make up the moral laws. Second, if I believe that moral law is absolute, and that it is the only guide to a good life, it is very easy for me to make the leap from the idea that I should "help" you to follow it to the idea that, if necessary, I should "force" you to do what I believe is right.

Similarly, there are advantages and disadvantages to relativism. The most important advantage is that it is *more likely to respect differences in moral sensitivity.* There can be a greater tolerance, even celebration, of differences. On the other hand, if taken to its logical extreme, one could argue that, since moral rules are just human conventions, there's no real imperative to follow them. I might only act morally in places where I am likely to be punished. If we all acted like that, we'd end up in chaos. There would be no way to measure ethical truths.

Interestingly, both can easily end up in a "*might makes right*" morality. Relativism can do so because there are no real moral laws to say how the strong should be limited. But that is at least honest. When the absolutist imposes their rules on everyone, they claim to do so "for their own good," which at least has the appearance (from the standpoint of those being coerced) of what we have been calling a **self-serving rationality**.

Of course, this isn't where either approach has to end up, though one can see the logic by which they often do. While Lewis falls into the absolutist camp, he would be sympathetic to Mill's argument that, even if we knew exactly what rules to follow, to make people follow them would be to reduce humanity to ape-like imitation (Mill 1998, 65). Mill believes that we live our lives with the goal of developing our uniquely human faculties. Since the only way to develop our faculties is to test them out, try different alternatives, and make mistakes, *freedom*, especially the freedom to make mistakes, *is the essential quality which must be honored*. Lewis would agree, though for slightly different reasons. For Lewis, of course, freedom is ultimately about the choice for or against our creator. This suggests that it is possible to be an absolutist and not seek to force one's own values on others. Similarly, an honest relativist, while he or she might just "take" what they want, would have no specific values to force on another.

As we saw earlier, Lewis takes the notion that we can argue about ethics in an interesting direction; it becomes a step in his proof for the existence of God and the preeminence of Christianity. In mere Christianity, he argues that the very fact that we have arguments about ethics, rather than fighting like animals, means that we assume, somewhere in the core of our being, that there is some common moral standard to which we both have access. Lewis, following the medieval tradition, refers to this as natural law, that part of God's law that is inscribed in the conscience of very person. The very nature of having an ethical argument presupposes such a standard. We each assume that, if we can only be clear enough, the other person will see, by virtue of having the same standard written in their conscience, that we are right. Without this assumption, there would be no point in rational discussion.

We won't go as far as Lewis in this argument. As we will see, it relies on a particular notion of truth, one that fails to go deeply into how we actually live truth. But, if we are more humble in our claims, the argument has merit. At the very least, Lewis is demonstrating that ethical argument presupposes at least two conditions:

1. some sort of common human community and language, and
2. some level of common moral standards by which to make judgments.

While both are important assumptions, the status of the "common moral standards" remains unclear. They could, for example, come from any of the following:

Implanted in us by God and existing in the mind of God.

Embedded in the nature of reality (but not, in this case, in an "intelligent" God).

Programmed into our genes by chance.

Simply a product of a common species faculties, needs, and world.

This level of argument, while interesting, is still quite abstract. Following thinkers like Soren Kierkegaard, I'm more interested in getting down to how we experience or live truth, rather than just how we think about it. As we noted in the first chapter:

> ... what good would it do me if truth stood before me, cold and naked, not caring whether I recognized her or not, and producing in me a shudder of fear rather than a trusting devotion? I certainly do not deny that I still recognize an imperative of under-standing and that through it one can work on men, but it must be taken up into my life ... (Kierkegaard 1946, 5; emphasis added)

In other words, the truths that matter to us are those that change our lives, those by which we live. It's not that other abstract truths are worthless, but they have little effect on us unless there is a way in which they make a difference in our lives.

In reality, **both absolutism and relativism speak to parts of our human experi-ence**. *Absolutism speaks to the fact that there appears to be common elements to the ethics of all major cultures, while relativism speaks to the fact that there appear to be legitimate areas of grey.* To force one to choose between these two (presented in their extreme form) is also a logical fallacy, the **fallacy of bifurcation** (also called the excluded middle). *Our actual experience suggests that there must be something between the two, something that allows for ethics without rigid rules, even if we haven't been able to name it.*[6]

To figure this out, we need to get more concrete. The approach we are using is the one raised in the first chapter, *phenomenology.* Phenomenology means allowing the phenomena of our experience, as best we can, to speak for themselves. It is similar to Aristotle's notion of observing human experience and building from the ground up rather than from ideas down. To start, we will move away from statements dealing with questions about ethics (ought) and instead to the truth of more basic statements about the "is."

---

6 Not all will agree with this statement. I think it often has more to do with personality types (or upbringing) than with actual experience. For example, if I am of a personality type that strongly needs to have a very concrete, specific, and ordered world, this might be very difficult to hear. At the same time, the very fact that there are other personality types that don't need to see the world in that partic-ular way suggests that the compulsion to view the world as absolute (i.e., not as an interpretation) is, in fact, an interpretation (even though it may be difficult for someone with such a need to acknowledge).

Level I: Correspondence

Look around the room. Perhaps there are other people there? Choose someone with a hat or an easily identifiable hair color. Ask yourself, what is that color? Here, let's assume it's a hat and that is it blue.

Is this true?

Our most common-sense notion of truth, in our society, is truth as correspondence. In other words, if my idea or statement about an object **corresponds** to the actual object, that statement or idea is true.

In this case, if I say the hat is blue and it actually is blue, then it is true.

It seems so obvious.

Let's go deeper.

What do we have to assume in order for this "correspondence" notion of truth to work? Upon what human faculty and activity does it depend?

Usually, I hear two answers to this question, both of which are correct:

1. Perception, the ability to "see" the world in terms of color.
2. A common understanding of what "blue" means (i.e., a language community).

Thinking about truth as correspondence depends upon a deeper experience and a means for perceiving the world around us, a way to measure whether our ideas and statements do, in fact, correspond to the world. But this raises a logical conundrum:

How can I know what is actual (real) in the world around me, except by my perceptions?

How can I know whether my perceptions are accurate unless I already know what is actual?

It seems like a vicious circle. I can only measure the "truth" of my perceptions if I already know the "truth" of what is in the world. But, I can only know if my knowledge of the world is accurate if I already know that my perceptions are also accurate.

We need some sort of "independent" measure that we do not have.

In logic, this sort of **circular reasoning** is a terrible thing. It is to be avoided at almost all costs. However, we aren't talking primarily about logic here, we are talking about lived experience. And when we think in those terms, something very different is going on.

We are engaged, instead, in what is called the **hermeneutic circle**.

The term hermeneutics finds its roots in the god Hermes, who served as the messenger of Zeus. For the Greeks, Zeus was the god who ruled over all others. As such, Zeus was the god who established the "order" and meaning of the universe. Hermes, as the messenger of Zeus, can be thought of as the carrier of meaning; Hermes communicated the meaning and order of (Zeus's) reality to and among others. *Hermeneutics* **is, therefore, the study of** *interpretation*, **the study of how things come to mean what they mean.**

The hermeneutic circle is a way of describing how we go about interpreting our lives and experiences, how we construct meaning. It works as follows:

The Hermenutic Circle

We are born into a confusing and overwhelming world.

We lack absolute certainly about our world.

But we are also born with certain capacities and needs. We interpret our world in ways that appear to help us to satisfy our needs.

While these interpretations may at times be wrong, so long as they are useful we don't typically question them.

We still have the capacity, if we don't become rigid, to modify our initial interpretations of the world. We can learn and grow.

What would cause us to question an interpretation? An experience of perception that appears to contradict what we previously believed.

One can think of this as a sort of "good enough" standard. We accept things as true because they appear to work for us, help us to flourish and fulfill our needs. We often end up assuming some sort of absolute certainly, but that's an additional interpretation of our experience, it's not embedded in that experience.

Level II: Perception/Revelation

As we move deeper into understanding how we *live* truth, we see that correspondence is based, at least in part, on the faculty of perception. Further, as we introduced in the first chapter via examples from psychology and perception, even the accuracy of our perceptions is highly questionable. We got out of this "logical" problem by realizing that we aren't really talking about the rules of logic, but describing how we actually live and assign truth, the hermeneutic circle. Why then have I also added the term "revelation" to this level?

There are two reasons:

> The first reason is to broaden the notion of perception by introducing a more general description. If we think about it, what does perception do for us? It *reveals* the world. Are there no other ways of revealing truths about the world that don't rely on, if we construe perception narrowly, the five senses? What of the light of the mind? Or perhaps a spiritual awareness?

> The second reason is an etymological move. Etymology has to do with the study of the origins of words, where they come from, and how their meaning changes. If we think of this stage in the more general terms of "*to reveal*," what might be its opposite?

To conceal.

This helps us to understand why the word *aletheia* is usually translated from the Greek as "truth."

Literally, *aletheia* means "*unconcealment.*" Put positively, it means, "*to reveal.*"

Taking us a step deeper, what might thinking of *aletheia* as a word for truth have to reveal to us?

Level III: *Aletheia*

This level is really just a quick stop, a transition to its root meaning. It is instructive to pause and look at what was, at one time, thought to be the root of the term. To be clear, **this is a false root**. But it is interesting nonetheless.

The false root of the term *aletheia* comes by taking out the center of the word, *lethe*. The term *lethe* shows up in both *The Great Divorce* and in *Wit*. In the first, it names a lake where an artist is asked to drink and so forget his (egoist) ownership of his art. In the second, Vivian is giving a lecture on Donne's poetry, where he calls upon a "*lethean* flood" to be forgotten, even by God. The term literally means forgetfulness or oblivion.

If one were to assume, therefore, that the "a" at the start of the word was privative (i.e., that it indicates a reversal of meaning, like a minus sign in front of a number), then instead of "forgetting" one would "remember." The meaning of "unconcealment" would be to "remember."

Part of the reason this is useful is that it helps us to distinguish between two theories of knowledge, one usually attributed to Plato and the other to Aristotle. Plato suggested that all knowledge came from eternal "forms" embedded in the heavens. We can recognize a table, for example, because the "form" of a table already exists in our consciousness, almost as a template, based on the perfect form of a "table" in the heavens. Moreover, in the Meno, Plato has Socrates argue that, since the soul is immortal, it will have had contact with, and therefore knowledge of, all things prior to entering the human body. Socrates attempted to demonstrate this by drawing key knowledge out of a slave just by skilled questions, knowledge the slave didn't (consciously) know that he possessed.

Thus, for Plato, all knowledge is recollection. We just have to "remember" for it to be unconcealed.

However, scholars eventually discerned that *lethe* was not the real root of *aletheia*. The real root was the word *legein*, which takes us instead towards Aristotle.

Level IV: *Legein*

While some translations of the word *legein* carry with them an implication of deliberation, the root of the term is "***to lay or to gather.***"

This seems utterly strange. *What has "to lay or to gather" have to do with truth?* And yet, this is the term that is translated as "truth."

One of my favorite ways of explaining has to do with why I sometimes allow students to bring a single 3 × 5 inch note card to each exam. They can write whatever they want on the card, it just has to be in their handwriting. Some students are quite inventive, even color-coding information on their cards.

My reasoning for allowing a note card is threefold. First, not everyone has the same memory for detail. What do those who lack that memory do? They know how to take notes or look it up. Here, they can take notes. Second, the very act of going through their notes, figuring out what is important, and writing it on the card is an excellent learning tool. To create a good note card they have to engage with the material in a rich and productive way. Finally, it means that no one is tempted to cheat, at least, by the usual method of sneaking in notes.

But what has this to do with *legein*?

Recall that, for Aristotle, the goal of living is human flourishing.

Why do we go to classes? Why do we read books? Why do we give up so much freedom and work so hard?

It is in the hope and expectation that this will allow us to flourish, to have a richer life. Part of this is financial. My experience is that college also helped me to make rich life choices about far more than just a job. Money does not equal happiness.

In the immediate term, however, the goal of taking a test is to do well and move on to the next stage. How does one decide what to put on the note card? ***One lays out one's books and notes, works through them, and gathers together (interprets) what is most important in terms of being successful on this exam.***

The note card represents, in a sense, one's "truth" for the exam. One developed this truth by "laying and gathering" what seems most important (an interpretation) from one's notes and experiences.

Laying and gathering, of course, most likely comes from taking in a harvest. One might cut the harvest, lay it down, gather the grains to be stored, and set aside the chaff for other uses. Here, we see *legein* as a way of answering the question of how, if we are meaning seeking and generating creatures, we create truth. **Legein names the process by which we generate truths.**

This means that our truths don't have to be absolute; they are always partial, somewhat tentative, and aimed at some goal.

This is consistent with the theory of knowledge we offered in chapter 1. Recall that, for Aristotle, ideas do not exist on their own. Rather, they are useful ways (rules of thumb?) that humans come up with to organize (gather) an otherwise chaotic and overwhelming world. Again, it begins when we are children. Perhaps, for the first time cut off from that umbilical cord, I experience hunger. Some things are presented to me that make that pain go away and I learn to call those things food. That means that I start to divide up my world, food and not food. I lay out and gather my experience of the world in ways that help me to flourish.

In modern terms, recall that we see only a tiny portion of the electromagnetic spectrum, and even of what we do see, we can retain very little. Instead, we learn to focus our attention on what seems useful to us. Useful in what ways? Again, what we experience or are taught to see as helpful, interesting, and useful for human flourishing is that which satisfies our needs in some way. For Aristotle, the notion of "laying and gathering" experiences to create truths (understood as useful interpretations of reality) is a good description of how we actually operate.

It also helps us to understand why two different people viewing the same event can see two very different things.

This is a notion of truth as a process.

A Middle Way

Earlier, we suggested that a middle way could be found between absolutism and relativism. Here, we have come to understand that truth functions, not as a "correct" correspondence between an absolute reality and our ideas, but as a creative process, a means by which we organize our experiences in ways that serve basic human needs.

If this is so, then how do we measure truth? Clearly this is not absolutism, but how is it not an extreme version of relativism?

One could use the term relativism (recall, as I noted earlier, that there are many forms), but not in its extreme form. Here, we have relativism with the possibility of standards. How does this work?

Truth, in this understanding, is not absolute (one extreme abstract correspondence notion) nor relative (another extreme interpretation of our experience), but is lived as a creative process of interpreting and understanding our experience in ways grounded in our basic nature (needs, faculties, and capacities) and in the possibilities of the world around us.

We see at least two "legs" that ground our notion of truth. One is ourselves—our human needs, faculties, capacities. The other is the world. While the world is understood as real and separate from us, experientially it's not entirely so. *Recall our definition of consciousness as a space for projecting possibilities:*

> **My world is the sum of my concrete possibilities for thought, action, and relationship beyond the physical body.**

In other words, while our worlds overlap (allowing us to work together and to communicate), how each person experiences their world is somewhat different.

Example: AIDS Education in L.A.

Consider the example of AIDS education in the ghettos of Los Angeles in the 1980s.

To illustrate this point, *assume, for a moment, that you have no religious or moral objection to sex, nor is there a fear of becoming pregnant. Assume that sex is just a great form of recreation. Then imagine you are travelling to a place where HIV is common, particularly among young people.*

Would you be willing to have unprotected sex with a stranger?

Even a very attractive stranger?

While it is, of course, much easier to make this decision while sitting at a desk, there generally aren't any takers.

Why?

The answer, invariably, is that one doesn't want to become sick or die. You have been working hard towards a future, you have goals for your life. Why put those at risk for a moment of pleasure?

Aristotle would be proud.

Clearly, AIDS education is fairly effective among college students. (At least, until one has too much to drink!) But for a long time, it was completely ignored by teenagers living in the L.A. ghettos. People just didn't seem to care about contracting HIV.

The key to understanding why is to realize that it takes, on average, eight years from diagnosis for HIV, even if untreated, to kill.

This highlights the different "world" of most college students from youths in 1980s L.A. With gang warfare and violence common at the time, most teenagers would look at the AIDS education, realize that AIDS would take eight years to kill them, and forget it. *They didn't expect to live eight more years. They had seen their older brothers and their friends killed. Why worry about a virus that would take so long to kill them?*

From an abstract point of view, my students in Iowa live in the same world as those kids in L.A. But from an experiential point of view, from the perspective of how they experienced their world and their possibilities for living in the world, it was very different.

What we bring to the table, in terms of our history, expectations, personality, etc., changes the world we live in.

It's also true that the world places limits on our interpretation of that world.

EXERCISE: THE MANY FACES OF A TREE

In another example, I have my students look out the window at a tree. I then ask them to brainstorm possible uses, values, meanings, etc., for trees. Everyone has to try and offer something unique; we get quite a list on the board (i.e., fire, lumber, food, place to play, thing of beauty, etc).

I then highlight two very different items. If no one has brought it up, I bring up the notion of a home for woodland spirits or nymphs. While this gets a laugh, I point out that this was a common belief for much of human history.

I also bring up the notion of an oxygen factory. This is a fairly modern idea. But I ask them, how sure are we that, in 100, perhaps 200 years, our descendants won't look back on our ideas about the uses of trees and laugh at us, just as we laugh at some of our ancestors.

Finally, we talk about how this tree, or some trees, are useful for some things; we can't successfully push just any interpretation on every tree. Some trees, like pine, are great for lumber. The yew tree is terrible for lumber, but great for a cancer medicine. There are also uses that no tree could serve. Say I want to marry and have children. From what we can tell, there is no tree that would make a suitable mate for that purpose.

The bottom line is that the "world" outside of us is far more complex and rich with possibilities than any human mind can capture. As Buber points out, we are often overwhelmed. To avoid this, we narrow the possibilities in useful ways. In doing so, we also cut off, failing even to recognize the manifold other possibilities for understanding our worlds. By dividing it up in one way, we preclude multiple other ways of dividing up reality. Still, however limited we are in our understanding of the world, it gives us our first way to "measure" our truths:

> One measure of a truth is its success in meeting the goals it was meant to serve— fulfilling human needs and supporting human flourishing.

This notion of truth is grounded in both our human capacities and in the concrete possibilities for thought, action, and relationships we are able to draw out of the "real" world.

Ah, but we are far from done. What of ethical truths?

For this, we have a partial answer. That is, **one way to "bridge" the "is" and the "ought" is to think in terms of a goal** (i.e., if we have a goal as our third term, then using the "is" in ways to reach that goal becomes our "ought"). **However, what grounds ethics as a goal at all?** Why bother with ethics? What part of human experience speaks to this?

Level V: *Catharsis*

If *legein* **names the process by which we generate truths, catharsis is,** in a special way, **the source of truth.** Understood correctly, it names the source of truth in at least two ways:

1. *Catharsis* names a specific human experience that gives rise to ethics.
2. Without *catharsis* as part of our experience, language, reason, and all that we associate with human culture could not develop. This means that catharsis, in helping found our language communities, is also part of the very source of our capacity to think about truth.

We will focus mainly on the first of these two assertions. We will touch here upon the second, offering a fuller treatment in the final chapter.

We introduced catharsis when we analyzed anger and forgiveness. *In psychology, catharsis is an emotional release that brings insight.* The Greek meaning of the term is somewhat different. **For the Greeks, catharsis is still an emotional outpouring, but the most essential insight it offers is a reaffirmation of the emotional bond tying together the community.** It is easiest to explain using an example. In this case, of the role of the chorus in Greek tragedy:

> In "Oedipus the King," we hear the story of a man who, without knowing it was his own family, killed his father, married his mother, and sired his own brothers. Clearly, it wasn't his intent to commit patricide or incest. In fact, upon hearing the prophecy that this would happen, he left his home so as to never become a threat to his parents. What he didn't realize was that he was adopted. Thus, by leaving home to protect his parents, he fulfilled the very destiny that he fled to avoid. Interestingly, Oedipus's primary crime is not murder, but patricide and incest.

What most people find ethically troubling about this story is the fact that Oedipus is held responsible for actions he didn't know he was committing. Yes, he killed a man on the road. But one of the man's servants struck him first. Nor did Oedipus know that the rich man with the servants was his father, the King of Thebes. Similarly, he didn't know that the Queen was his mother. Thus, while Oedipus might be responsible for the death of the traveler(s) on the road (even this is questionable, who attacked first?), the specific charges of patricide and incest should have been meaningless.

It would be easy to dismiss this problem as a lack of understanding on the part of the Greeks. After all, this happened thousands of years ago. They can't really be faulted for having less intellectual and ethical sophistication than we do today. It's too bad they didn't understand that one couldn't really be guilty for what, *through no fault of their own*, they lacked knowledge of being wrong. Of course, we understand this now. We stand on their shoulders having moved beyond their primitive understanding.

If we take this attitude, we miss the point of the tragedy. The Greeks were aware of intent as a factor in determining ethical responsibility. Given that the writer ignored this factor, and that this play came to be considered one of the great works of tragedy, there had to be a good reason. To understand why, we need to understand the difference between their world and our world.

In modern times, we have great power over nature. This is due both to our numbers and to technology. Occasionally, as with a hurricane or an earthquake, nature reminds us that we are not all powerful and that life is fragile. We were coming to believe (and still haven't entirely let go of the belief) that we are the masters of nature. Even though we now appear to be experiencing multiple 500-year storms just a few years apart, we try to ignore or use nature for our own purposes. We often tell ourselves that we are in control of nature.

The relationship of ancient peoples to nature was very different. Instead of assuming power over nature, they felt relatively powerless and in the grasp of nature. Consider the analogy of a small ship at sea during a storm. If everyone works together, all have a better chance of making it to port. We need one another. Nature is powerful, unpredictable, and merciless. Unlike us, their experience was that, due to these acts of nature, *they were often at the mercy of and responsible for events over which they had no real control.* Oedipus reflects this experience; even *though the circumstances of his sin were beyond his control, he was still responsible for the consequences.* **It is this common experience—that they were often responsible even for that over which they had little control—that was the worldview reflected in the play.**

It also helps to look to the chorus. For many modern readers, this is the tedious part of the play. We skim through it to get back to the action. But understood as an oral event, we see something very different. The audience will identify with the chorus, often knowing the part by heart, perhaps repeating it with them. The chorus provides an opportunity for the audience to take part in the tragedy, to affirm their common experience and vulnerability; to ***release that experience in a moment of catharsis reaffirms their bond as a community—the bond that, by pulling them to work together, gave them a better chance of happiness and flourishing in the face of a violent and unpredictable world.*** This moment of *catharsis* names what may be, in fact, the *source* or ground of both truth and ethics. **Catharsis, for at least some of the Greeks, spoke to the truth of the bond that united them.**

Aristotle tells us that the foundation of the *polis* (the city state or the community) is in the emotional bonds that first tie the family together. The argument, developed much more richly by thinkers like Levinas, suggests that without a primal emotional compulsion to care, nothing that we describe as distinctly human would ever develop. Why talk with one another? Why develop reason? Why form sophisticated communities? Enlightened self-interest is a factor, but it is not enough to generate the sorts of skills and attributes necessary for culture. Nor would it account for authentic self-sacrifice. I leave deeper aspects of this analysis for later. For now, I want us to reflect on how language begins, primordially, in reaching out to understand another in response to care. Without this primal compassion, we would not develop sophisticated language. Without such language, we could not have a discussion about truth. This example allows me to suggest the following: ***Truth finds one of its sources as an ethical call to care. This is both a general ground for truth and a specific ground for ethical truth.***

However, *we **find ourselves with a call to care that is given without specific cognitive content***. When I see you in pain, for example, I might feel empathy. I might be "wounded" by your pain, but that doesn't mean that I feel it as do you or that I know what to do to help. It's more a feeling than an idea, a pull to care. **How we care is a creative and often daunting project.** Ethical truths, the ideas and rules of ethics, are part of the process of figuring this out; it is a process of insight that has this *catharsis* as its source. The call to care is given to us, the rules are not. The rules of ethics are created by us.[7]

Since the call to care is given without content there are no absolute rules. One might then wonder from whence values or rules come? Again, as Aristotle suggests, we find ourselves with certain needs and capacities. It could be that the call to care is placed within us by God, evolution, or chance. That's a matter for a different debate. For the moment, it is enough to say that wherever they come from, these needs and capacities are real. They name something basic to our human experience—fulfilling human needs, supporting human flourishing, serving one another, even hurting one another. These are all parts of the *given* of our experience. This is where values come from. It is not so much a function of the mind as of the heart, the call to compassion.

On the other hand, how we deal with our needs and what rules and means we create to serve one another are also intellectual issues. We generate these by abstracting and generalizing the needs of the many. Any rules we generate, anything that can be spoken, can never adequately capture the richness and individual

---

7   Part of the reason I find Lewis's "proof" for the existence of God unconvincing is because it depends upon assuming that correspondence names the essential nature of truth. If we stay at the level of correspondence, then one could argue that the very fact that we try to convince one another of an ethical position requires us to assume some absolute standard that we can both appeal to, with which we attempt to correspond. Note how this is also much more akin to Plato's theory of knowledge than to Aristotle's. However, with the more creative notion of freedom developed at the end of the chapter on Lewis, we can think of these possibilities in ways more consistent with Aristotle and this chapter.

nature of the real and of the call to care. Again, Aristotle embodied this insight when he distinguished between the law and equity; we need judges to apply the law and realize when the letter of the law must be set aside. Jesus offered a similar insight when he criticized the Pharisees for placing rules and laws above love and compassion.

Three-Part Grounding for Truth

I'd like to suggest, therefore, that there is *a three part "grounding" for truth*. These are inputs into the creative process (*legein*) of truth. They don't provide fixed rules. Instead, they give a direction and place limits on what can be considered truth. These are:

1. **The physical world.**

   Whatever is "real" in the physical world is far greater than our minds can comprehend. In fact, the very action of the mind is to narrow that data, those experiences, in such a way as to keep them manageable. While there are far more possibilities in the "real" world than we can comprehend, they are not arbitrary. The world isn't just what we want it to be. It allows many uses, but not all.

2. **Human faculties and needs.**

   We share common faculties and needs in addition to a common "real" world. While our experiential worlds are somewhat different, we have enough in common to communicate. Our common needs and faculties contribute to a fairly common, but not absolute, vision of the world.

3. **The call to care.**

   Technically, we could call this a human faculty. However, as we will develop further, the call to care is fundamentally different than human needs. For example, needs turn inward, towards the person experiencing them. The call to care, which we will later call ethical desire, turns outwards towards others. This outward turn is essential for both truth in general and, more specifically, ethical truth. By grounding ethical truth in a call to care, an emotion, we focus just on the experience. Truth is therefore grounded (we are called to care) but not absolute (rules are created, not given).

It's worth repeating that the call to care, compassion, is in some way foundational for everything we think of as human, including the very possibility of a conversation about truth. It founds both the very capacity to think about truth and provides the specific impetus behind the development of ethical truths. This appears to be essential to the idea of a human language community we drew from Lewis.

This notion of truth opens doors to pluralism in religion, culture, and ethics, emphasizing the need for creative responses rather than fixed platitudes in how we care for one another. Because it's grounded in our concrete experience, it speaks to how we live truth in our lives. This is not a truth that stands before us, cold and naked, caring not whether we acknowledge her or not. But it's also not just whatever one wants it to be. Instead, *truth names a process by which I engage, move within, create, and interact within my world and the worlds of others. The measure of the truth of a belief is its success in integrating the whole of experience in ways that support human flourishing.*

The Role of Chaos in Hesiod's Theogony

One of the reasons we started this chapter by exploring the nature of truth, as we live it, is because it will help us to better understand this very different way of thinking about human reality. What follows is an intriguing, though *speculative*, reading of the notion of chaos as a metaphor for consciousness in the Theogony. Why speculative? Though I can provide evidence to support this reading, I am not an expert in Greek or the classics, so the scholarship that might nail this down is beyond me. However, that might not even be possible. Just as there are many ways of "dividing up" reality, one of the qualities that makes for an enduring mythology is that it speaks to many different people on many different levels. There are a number of ways in which to open up the "truth" of a good myth or story. In this case, while I will provide evidence, the main goal of the remainder of this chapter is to introduce the idea of Chaos as a metaphor for consciousness and the notion of the middle voice. As before, I am interested in how these help us identify and understand our actual human experience. They will serve as a beginning to ideas and experiences that, while not entirely accessible to the intellect, show up prominently in our analysis of the experience of spirituality.

Theogony is considered the earliest Greek creation myth. Composed between the 8th and 7th centuries B.C.E., it may even predate Homer. Much of it is thought to be synthesized from earlier stories. The fact that it is a "myth" does not mean that it is just a story. A myth endures because it transmits and helps sustain particular human, cultural, and religious truths about a people. As with many Christian denominations' attitude towards the Bible, there is no need for it to be literal.

Early in the myth, we see the birth of Chaos:

114. **Tell me, O Muses, who dwell on Olympus, and observe proper order**
115. **for each thing as it first came into being**
116. **Chaos was born first and after her came Gaia**

Several things jump out of this text. First, the Greeks were very concerned with order. Recall our example of the different worldview exhibited in *Oedipus the King*? To live in ancient times meant to be subjected to the whims of nature, luck, war, and perhaps the gods. In a world that was disorderly, even "chaotic" (here, in the modern sense of the word), the Greeks were deeply concerned with systematic order.

If they could find, even generate, an "order" to reality, perhaps they could navigate these hazards more effectively. Finding or creating that order, that "truth," was profoundly important. It was often an issue of life and death.

Second, we see a strange inversion. For the Greeks of the time, Zeus was the head God. For most modern people, or at least monotheists, the first born (if born at all) would have been God, or for a polytheists, the head God. ***If Zeus was the ultimate power, why did Chaos precede Zeus?***

The text appears to suggest that Chaos is in some way original, primary, and fundamental to the very origin of things. ***So fundamental that chaos is prior even to the possibility of the Gods.***

To understand what this might mean, it helps to understand the meaning of the term Chaos to the Greeks. To us, the term generally means disorder. But to the Greeks, there are references to at least four different meanings:

"gap" (but not a void)

"bounded interval"

"space"

"breath"

This raises some interesting possibilities. Already, we have established "space" as a metaphor for consciousness. What if the problem being raised, perhaps not in an entirely conscious way, was the issue of how WE can know the order of reality?

Heidegger raises this issue at the start of *Being and Time*, when he suggests that asking the question of "being" necessarily focuses on the question of WHO is asking. We only really understand things from our point of reference. While we can expand the range of our points of reference, we don't possess a God's-eye view.

Also, recall that for the Greeks, **to know is to divide**. The intellect only "understands" reality by dividing it up. For things we don't divide, we typically have no word. For example, if everything visible was the same shade of purple, would we even have a word for purple? Or for color? The idea of purple, or of color in general, is only useful if we are separating (dividing) objects according to different colors. Lack of a word doesn't deny that reality itself may contain an attribute, but it would not find a place in language.

Regardless of whether Zeus or any other form of God exists, we can only "talk" about them after we have started dividing up reality, after we have engaged in the actions of laying and gathering to formulate truths. In terms of our human experience (which is really the only measure we know), before even God, there must be a gap, a space, a power of dividing up reality.

This is perhaps why Chaos is born without parents. Parentage is already a division of reality, and the action of Chaos had to take effect prior to any such divisions.

What I'm suggesting is that, at the heart of the myth, the Greeks are attempting to explain their (our human) place in the cosmos. That assertion is not controversial. What is more speculative is the way in which I'm interpreting their explanation, suggesting that Chaos is, to some degree, an anthropomorphized version of an aspect of our most characteristic human capacity. Embedded in the description of our "place" in the cosmos is a description of ourselves.

The descriptions of gap, bounded interval, and space all work well with consciousness. Note how it's not just a void, but a very specific emptiness. Consciousness isn't just an abstract emptiness, it is bounded by a person's body, memories, and experiences. It is also an active space, almost always projecting possibilities for action, thought, and relationship into an experiential world.

Example: Music

Why does music resonate so well with most people? Consider the following:

> *What is more important for music, the notes or the spaces between the notes?*

If we think of the "notes" as the objects, as what is real, we will say the notes. That tends to be the way our culture assesses reality. But a cacophony of notes, without spaces between, is just noise.

Musicians are more likely to argue for the spaces than for the notes. The spaces are what allow the notes to be notes, they are a "gap" or "bounded interval" that allows for there to be music.

Others will recognize that it's really a trick question. Just as the notes need spaces to define them, so too the spaces need the notes for their bounding, their definition.

Too much space and all we have are individual sounds; the space, instead of working with the notes, becomes a void. Too little space and we have noise. Only when the two work together, each defining the other, can we have music. Music is essentially a temporal process.

Not unlike the activity of consciousness. It is an ongoing, essential, temporal process.

The last definition of Chaos strengthens this assertion. It is apparently only used once; Cicero refers to this as a meaning in one of his writings.[8] But it's not just any breath. It's the breath one holds in one's body or mouth, just before expelling it.

Breath, for many cultures, is thought of as the essence of life. Our spirit is in our breath. This is perhaps the origin, in Christianity, of the phrase "bless you" when one sneezes. Here, it was thought that, when a person sneezed, their spirit momentarily left their body with the breath. This created an opportunity for evil spirits to take residence. The blessing was to keep the spirits away long enough for the person's own spirit to return to their body.

That breath that we hold, just before expelled, has a certain intimacy about it. We are holding ourselves, our spirit, our humanity. If this serves as another meaning of Chaos, it strengthens the idea that Chaos names something fundamental and intimate about our very selves.

Middle Voice, Past Tense

Taking a step further into the passage, we find that the Greek term for the birth of Chaos is in the middle voice, past tense. What might this mean?

The middle voice does not exist in English. But we do have the passive and the active voice. The passive voice is where the subject of the sentence, and with it the emphasis, is on that which is acted upon. For example, "The cat is being petted by Tom." The active voice makes the actor the subject of the sentence. For instance, "Tom is petting the cat." English also allows a form of the passive voice (overused by students and hated by most professors!) of "the voice from nowhere." This is the passive voice without an actor. For example, "The cat is being petted" or "It is known that …"

The middle voice exists in ancient Greek, but not in English. It is where the active and passive come together. To a degree, we can illustrate it through the use of reflexive pronouns, though I don't believe the reflexive captures its full meaning (i.e., "The cat washes herself").

To get a bit closer to that "extra" not captured by the reflexive, consider Scott's translation of the Anaximander fragment. The fragment is often considered the

---

8 I apologize for not having this reference, as it is an uncommon definition. It was presented at a conference I attended but for which I no longer have notes.

earliest distinctly "philosophical" writing of which we will have access. In translation, part of it reads as follows:

... from which things arise also gives rise to their passing away ... along the lines of usage ...[9]

The Greek translates, literally, as genesis (things arising) and destruction (passing away). The parts appear to be speaking of the nature of creation. But the verb between the two is neither active nor passive, suggesting that this is not a linear event. A linear event might involve, for example, tearing something down (destruction, passing away) and then building something new (creation, arise). Here, the implication appears to be that creation and destruction are given together; they are one and the same event.

This is the sense of the middle voice that I want us to remember. Not just reflexive, but as a way of pointing to aspects of our reality that aren't neatly "divided" by intellectual thought and point to some prior unity.

By the very nature of the topic (it exists prior to thought), all concepts and explanations will be inadequate. Still, we can introduce some reasons for believing it to be so. For example, consider the idea of numbers. They are very useful in analyzing and dividing up our world. But do they not have an essential unity?

As soon as I develop a concept of "2," I imply a concept of "1." Why did I suggest "2" first? Remember the comment that if all were purple we wouldn't have a word for color? The same is true of numbers. If I perceive only unity, then I don't need a concept for it. As soon as I start dividing it up, each division implies other numbers. This suggests, in the case of numbers, at least *a unity of belonging* (i.e., it doesn't mean that everything is the same, but that all is interconnected, like a great web). When I pull on one part of a web, other parts move as well.

Another way of approximating the middle voice is as an **organic process**. An organic process, such as intercellular dynamics, doesn't just work in linear ways. Instead, there is almost a dance wherein multiple aspects of the cell work together. With microcellular biology, as with quantum physics, some of the claims of linear causation seem to fall away. It's almost as if, as Merleau-Ponty writes:

The conditioned conditions the condition. (Merleau-Ponty 1968, 22; emphasis added)

This is getting very complicated, so let's shift to something closer to our experience. Remember that, in the middle voice, the distinction between actor and acted upon breaks down; it is both active and passive at the same time. We all have at least limited experiences of this. Consider, for example, when an athlete is "in the zone." Say you're playing basketball. You've played many times. You've trained and you've practiced. Now, one day, *it feels almost as if the game is playing through you.* On one level, you are no longer in charge, you feel completely passive, receptive to whatever is needed in the moment. ***In that receptivity, you are also completely in control***, perhaps more so than at

---

9   Translation is modified from Heidegger by Dr. Charles Scott, based on class notes.

any other point in your life. When you release the ball, though far from the basket, you feel a visceral connection between yourself, the ball, and the basket. You know, even as you release, that it will be a swish. You *feel* the connection all the way to the basket.

For some, it is basketball. But it can show up in other parts of one's life. For me, it is most profoundly present in ballroom dancing. Every now and then, with a good partner, we feel that we are no longer "trying" to dance, the dance is dancing through us. The dance becomes effortless and flows through us. We are both utterly passive and utterly active.

When activity and passivity become one, one is experiencing a form that we are calling the middle voice.

Like most core human experiences, it cannot be adequately explained; it can only be experienced.

Interestingly, ***it shows up in the spiritual traditions of every major religion***.

Returning to Chaos, its birth is in the middle voice, but also the past tense.

What might this suggest?

Our contemporary notion of Chaos appears to be rooted in this more primal notion. Chaos has to exist in order to create order. Our modern notion reduces chaos to the "disorder" side of that equation. But the Greek notion appears much richer. It is middle voice in that it names a process that is nonlinear, prior to the linear divisions of the mind. It is past tense in two ways:

> First, as the capacity to divide, the naming of the space that gives divisions of thought, it is in the immediate past of every thought. It founds the very capacity for thought. It is the "gap" or "space" of consciousness.

> Second, it stretches back through human history and culture to the distant past. It is a way of talking about the possibilities for existing in the world that have been developed through time and culture and transmitted to us.

Other Evidence

While this is certainly an interesting possibility, what other evidence is there that we could think of Chaos as a middle-voiced metaphor for consciousness? I note two possibilities:

Paradox

When we point to that which founds the very possibility of the divisions of thought, any attempt to "capture" it in thought is, at best, limited. Why? Because to capture it in thought is to reduce it to one side of those "ideas" that only it can allow. If so, then to some degree, it would only be expressible via a paradox, two sides of thought that cannot be reconciled. Kirk and Raven's translation of another passage of Theogony, *if accurate*, suggests just such a paradox. Looking at lines 807–809, they point out the sources and limits of "of earth, sea, sky, and Tartaros are in Tartaros" (807–809). How can something contain itself (Kirk and Raven 1983, 40)?

Yet, when we look to line 814, we see that this is exactly where we find Chaos. When Chaos is not explicitly active, it recedes to the underworld—Tartaros. Chaos points to the paradox of a space that both contains and exceeds itself, something that doesn't "fit" into the neat divisions of thought.

The Role of Chaos in the Cosmic Order

Recall our claim that, for the Greeks, the world can be opened up in many ways. We see something of this in their mythology. While monotheistic religions stress that there is but one eternal God, the Greeks had many Gods. Moreover, there were times when even the God in charge was overthrown. Changing the ruler of a kingdom often means changing many of the rules under which the kingdom operates. The same appears to be true when changing the head God.

This is radical idea, to shift the entire "order" of the universe. But it happens twice in Theogony: once when Cronos overthrew Ouranos, and again when Zeus overthrew Cronos.

Recall also our claim that Chaos exists in the past in two ways. The first way is in the immediate "past" of very thought, as the space of consciousness that allows for that thought to appear. The second is in the more distant past, where the experiences of many become transmitted via cultures. But in a moment of such radical transition, it would seem that the very basis of that culture is being undermined or transformed. The world is being opened up in a radically new way.

If Chaos names the fundamental (creative and destructive) capacity to organize (divide) and reorganize a world, then Chaos should reappear when there is a transition from one cosmic order (way of thinking or conceiving our world) to another.

698. **For all the Titan's might, the blazing flash**
699. **of thunderbolt and lightning blinder their eyes.**
700. **Wondrous conflagration spread through Chaos, and to eyes and ears,**
701. **it seemed as though what they saw and heard**
702. **was the collision of the earth and the wide sky above.**
703. **For so vast a crash could only arise**
704. **if earth collapsed under collapsing sky** (Athenasskis 1983)

In the final battle, where Cronos is overthrown by Zeus, it seems as if all will be destroyed. Chaos reappears and becomes explicit once again.

It's also interesting to note Zeus's primary weapon, ***the lightning bolt***. What does lightning do to the sky? ***It both lights it up and divides the sky ... not unlike consciousness.***

Once Cronos is defeated, Chaos recedes back into the underworld. There are two other challenges (Typhoeus and Athena) to Zeus's authority, but both are preempted by Zeus in such a way that a major battle is avoided.

However, there is at least one obvious problem with this evidence. Ideally, just as Chaos appeared in the transition between Cronos and Zeus, so too should Chaos appear in the transition between Ouranos and Cronos. This, however, is not the case.

Of course, the fact that it isn't mentioned could be for other reasons. For example, this is the story of Zeus, told by Zeus's daughters (the muses) to Hesiod. It should, therefore, come as no surprise that the story of Zeus's assertion is told in greater detail than of what came before.

But again, while this is an interesting possibility, we don't really have enough evidence to know which is true.

Takeaways

There are really two related sets of ideas to take away from this chapter. The first has to do with truth, while the second has to do with the role of chaos and the middle voice.

By undergoing an exploration of how we experience truth, and in particular, its roots in Greek thought, we came to view truth as a creative process grounded in three things: the physical world, our needs and faculties, and the experience of catharsis as a bond of compassion. Of these, that which most separates us from the animal kingdom (though there is increasing evidence that this too is grounded, in part, in our animal heritage) is the complexity and sophistication that arises out of the experience of compassion. This founds a middle way between ethical absolutism and relativism, a manner consistent with both Aristotle and the creative notion of freedom we introduced at the end of the chapter on Lewis. One could even claim that truth is, in part, a function of the creative power of freedom.

In terms of Chaos and the middle voice, we saw Chaos as a metaphor for human consciousness. We noted how, while that which gives forth the possibility of thinking cannot itself be captured by the mind, there are still things that, tentatively, we can speak too. Moreover, just recognizing the paradox, as we will see, has much to teach us. The middle voice, like love, has to be experienced; it cannot be captured by the intellect. As we go forward in various religious traditions, we will see that the middle voice appears to play a crucial role in understanding the nature (at least, as used here) of spirituality.

CHAPTER NINE

Faith[1]

Faith … should make it possible to live with uncertainty, it shouldn't provide certainty.

Rev. William Sloane Coffin

FAITH AND TRUTH are among the most commonly used and least understood terms in American culture. In many religions, the two function less as clear ideas and instead as a sort of password or code. One is asked whether one has faith, usually in Jesus. If the answer is yes, it means that one has access to (or has accepted) ultimate truth. One is part of the club.

We have already talked about truth. Now, we apply a similar approach to faith. First, we explore some problems with common notions of faith. Second, we explore what faith means to people of faith. Third, we use this more experiential analysis, with Soren Kierkegaard in the background, to develop a more experiential definition of faith.

Section I: Heaven Can Wait

Many of us believe, implicitly or explicitly, that (1) the real purpose of this life is as a preparation for the next life, and (2) that the main reason for doing good and avoiding evil is for the sake of that afterlife. We addressed the second of these two questions with C.S. Lewis. We can ask ourselves again, do these beliefs really make sense?

---

1   Most of this is taken, with permission, from Degnin, Francis, "Talking with Students about Faith in an Era of Religious Extremes," *Religion and Education* 34, no.2 (Spring 2007): 1–26. There is also new and rewritten material.

Ask yourself:

Why is it that you choose to do good? Or choose to love?

Is the main reason for doing good so that you can go to heaven?

If the answer to the second question is yes, then are you acting for the sake of love, or are you really just trying to strike a good deal? If there is a God, wouldn't God be able to see through this tactic? Taking the issue a step further:

Unless we love for its own sake, do we truly love?

What would you choose and how would you act if you knew that there was no heaven or hell?

Shouldn't we learn to love and do good in this life for its own sake, so that heaven and hell become irrelevant?

These questions, with the ensuing discussion, help us to hone in on our true motivations for faith. Of course, some attempt to deny the premise, arguing that since heaven is a natural outgrowth of God's love and their faith, one can't separate the two. That is the point of the middle question—if you knew that there was no heaven and hell, how would you behave? Would you love God or others just for their own sake? As C. S. Lewis argues, so long as one loves God in order to get into heaven, one doesn't really love God.

It's also important to remember that, *until one has faced the possibility that it all just ends with death, one has not yet faced and accepted one's own mortality.* Every religious tradition teaches us that facing one's death is one of the most profound spiritual and psychological growth experiences. To pass over this opportunity with the belief that death is a mere transition to an afterlife is to miss the point. This doesn't mean that one can't return to a belief in the resurrection or some other form of continued existence. With C. S. Lewis, for example, heaven still awaits those who accept and love God, but only for God's own sake. As suggested by our opening quotation from Coffin, it is easy to use these beliefs to avoid authentic spiritual growth—facing, accepting, and learning how to live with uncertainty. Instead, many of us seek to convince ourselves of the "certainty" of heaven, of reducing death to a mere transition.

Could it be that "heaven" is irrelevant for a mature spirituality?

The Peaceful Death

We've raised this question a couple of times throughout this text:

What makes for a peaceful death?

Put another way:

What is necessary for one to die in peace?

What do you need?

What beliefs give you comfort?

How many of you feel that you could die in peace if you didn't believe that there would be an afterlife?

How many of you feel that only someone with faith in God and an afterlife can die in peace?

As we discussed in chapter one, these last two, while making a certain logical sense, don't hold up empirically. Instead, we return to Kübler-Ross's insights:

1. *Have I lived a rich and full life? Have I explored life and experienced much of the richness this life has to offer?*
2. *Am I surrounded by those I love, or perhaps preceded by them, so that I feel a rich connection to others? Do I feel like I've contributed to their lives and happiness and they to mine?*

Again, this is consistent with my experience as a hospital chaplain. The primary difference between those who die peacefully and those who die anxious does <u>not</u> appear to be their belief in an afterlife. Rather, those who go peacefully into that dark night are usually those who feel that they have lived a full and rich life—rich both in the sense of fulfilling experiences and deep human connections—even when they don't believe in heaven.

Conversely, some of those who most strongly assert their belief in God and heaven experience the greatest fear when dying. This is particularly true if, due to a focus on the next life, their beliefs serve to keep them from living this life to the fullest. For these people, their belief in heaven can actually make for a more painful death.

Could Belief in an Afterlife, for Some, Actually be Harmful?

It appears that belief in an afterlife is not the panacea of goodness that some assume. Not only is it an insufficient ground for moral behavior, it can lead to negative personal consequences, such as preventing one from living this life to the fullest. *I'm not arguing against the existence of an afterlife, only how an excessive emphasis upon an afterlife in one's beliefs can have negative consequences.* This may be true for the community as well as for the individual.

Consider an example from Islam:[2]

> *What is the justification, from what you've seen, the suicide bombers in Iraq offer for why they do what they do?*

This brings up questions about doing God's will, about a sure ticket to heaven, and about the belief that those they kill must be evil. Despite the claims of some politicians and news agencies, most mainstream Islamic clerics condemn such actions, noting that it's fundamentally against the teachings of the Koran. How, then, might this justification work?

The main line of argument could be characterized as follows:

1. There is but one God.
2. Everything God wants is good, all else (or most, some might be neutral) is evil.
3. God only speaks through one religion (or even just one denomination of that religion).
4. The goal of this life is to get to heaven.
5. This earth has little or no value of its own, it is just the ground for that testing.

Here, it's worthwhile to distinguish between the metaphysical *structure* of a belief and the specific *content* of the teaching. Many argue that the *content* of the Koran teaches compassion and peace. But if one believes that God is absolute, and that whatever God decides is good, one has no right to argue with the ethics of any of God's commands, even if it is mass murder. *Structure tends to overrule content.* This is further reinforced by the belief that this life is only a preparation for the next.

> *If this life only has value as a testing ground for the next life, what does it suggest about the value of this life? This world?*

---

2   Since most people find it easier to critique someone else's beliefs, and since most of my students are Christian, I begin with the example of suicide bombers in Iraq. Once the critique is understood in terms of Islamic beliefs, it becomes easier to show how it applies to the structure of Christian beliefs as well.

Whereas many of us are raised to believe that this life only has real meaning if it leads to a life eternal, we begin to see that, *if the next life is all that matters, this life has no intrinsic value of its own.* In some ways, it has no value at all.[3]

What argument, then, could one use against the suicide bomber?

If one shares the same structure, none. It wouldn't be an argument; it would merely be a claim. The claim would be

> *my beliefs about what God is telling me is right, and your beliefs are wrong.*

The problem is that, for many Christians, this is also the structure of their basic belief about reality. But not for all. This is also the case for Islam. For example, this structure, in Christianity, tends to go with the eschatological view that the Kingdom of God is to be brought about through the destruction of the world. For that reason, many Christians believe that global warming and other ecological issues aren't worth worrying about, they are just necessary steps in God's plan. For these groups, their emphasis is also often on the domination of this earth; we are given it to do with as we please.

EXERCISE: ANGEL OF LIGHT

To see if one shares the structure suggested above, consider the following example. In class, *I ask for a volunteer who seeks to be person of strong faith* (usually Christian, given where we live.) Let's call this person Derek. *Place yourself in the role of Derek.* I stand in front of you, throw my arms out wide, and say:

> *Derek, assume that I am God, or perhaps an angel of the Lord. I appear to you in a blaze of glory. If you gaze upon me, then you will be blinded. So, you must avert your eyes.*

Once his (or her) eyes are averted, I go on:

> *I come to you from on high. I do not come to you because you are worthy; none are worthy. I come to you because, in my infinite wisdom, I have chosen you. Will you hear and answer my call?*

---

3   These circumstances are often full of contradictions. For example, consider the Terri Schiavo case. One would think that Christians who shared this sort of structure (i.e., emphasis on the afterlife) would be among the first to let her go. In fact, my folks used that as an opportunity to tell us kids never to do that to them. Why not let her go to heaven? Why just keep a person's body alive? Yet, it was certain fundamentalist groups who were among the strongest advocates to keep her body alive. (It should be noted, when they did the autopsy, her entire cortex, the part of her brain that "thinks," was gone. This was also evident from scans prior to her final passing.)

With some hesitation, he usually say yes.
(I may have to remind him or her to continue averting his or her eyes.)

Do you know the clock tower in the middle of campus?

Yes.

This is God's command: Tomorrow before noon, you are to climb the clock tower. In the upper chamber you will find a loaded AK-47. When the clock strikes noon, look out the west side of the tower. You will see three people walking together. I will steady your hand and your aim.

You are to shoot and kill those three people.

There is little or no doubt in your mind that I am real. Do you do it?

You may feel some hesitation. If so, I can continue:

I shouldn't have to give you reasons, but I have mercy for human weakness.

So, I will tell you this: One of the persons shot will be the next Hitler, the others are his or her chief followers. Six billion people will die in the war that they will start. By your obedience you will have saved humanity.

Sadly, there is another side to this choice. If you fail to obey, once you see the devastation and suffering, you will be filled with remorse and self-loathing. When you die, you will burn in eternal fire. This will not be because I could not forgive you; I love you and can always forgive.

You will be unable to forgive yourself.

This is God speaking. Everything I say is good.

I've had many students, male and female, perfectly normal, kind people, who have agreed to climb that clock tower. It doesn't mean they would actually go through with it. But, at least in some cases, the logic of the demand fit so well with their theology that they could think of no reason to object. *They shared the same basic "structure" of belief as the Islamic suicide bomber.*

Others object, but get no further than the claim, "God wouldn't ask that of me." Others have said that, while they don't believe God would ever ask this, if God did, they would obey.

Others might ask how one could be sure that it was God? Lucifer was also an angel of light. It could also have been a psychotic break. How would one know?

Some argue that such a command goes against the Bible. This is a weak argument, particularly for a literalist, as the there are multiple atrocities sanctioned in the Old Testament. There have also been, and still are, atrocities committed in the name of Christ. One might also argue that what led to the atrocities was changed in the New Testament, but that is actually just a particular interpretation of the relationship between the Old and New Testaments that requires emphasizing certain passages and ignoring or explaining away others. Similarly, one might bring up the story of Abraham. Then again, God didn't actually make Abraham go through with killing Isaac, which suggests God might not here as well. Still, the problem here is that Abraham had to be willing to kill his son.[4]

There are of course other commonly accepted structures for both Christianity and Islam. I'll offer an alternative for Christianity a bit later. Here, I am reminded again of how most early Christians believed that the Bible was inspired but not literal. For many mainstream churches, the Bible represents a record of various people working out their relationship with and understanding of God, themselves, one another, and their world. As such, it would seem natural that misunderstandings would occur along the way. How does one discern which are misunderstandings? Perhaps through study, reflection, and one's own relationship with the divine. For example, the Catholic position against abortion is not based on a literal reading of the Bible. In fact, an honest literal reading would force one to conclude that the fetus is property, not a person.[5] Yet, one sees that throughout the Bible there is a general tendency towards greater respect for life. Thus, in the beginning, the Israelites only valued their own people. It was fine to massacre entire tribes, including women and children. Later, they began to understand that God didn't only love the Hebrews, but that all people were God's children. As we grew in our understanding of God, we came more and more to understand the extent of God's love.

In order to be able to defend ourselves against the rationality of the suicide bomber, it seems that we need to explore at least two tools. The first, already mentioned, is whether there are different structures than the one given above. The second, to which

---

4   Interestingly, there are biblical scholars who argue that, in the original story, Abraham did kill Isaac. The story was later "sanitized" as people's sensitivities changed. There is significant textual evidence for this point, though this doesn't constitute "proof." For example, in the oldest texts, the pronoun for coming back down the mountain is singular, as if Abraham came down alone. The claim would be that, in editing the original version, they missed correcting that pronoun. There is also tradition in the OT that the sacrifice of one's first-born son was considered extremely powerful. For example, the Israelites were on the verge of defeating the King of Moab until he scarified his first-born son, after which the tide of the battle reversed.

5   For example, if one avoids biased translations like the NIV, Exodus 21:22–24 suggests in fairly strong terms that a fetus is not a person. Here, we see that the penalty for killing a person calls for the killer to be put to death. But to strike a pregnant woman and cause a miscarriage, if no further harm is done, calls only for a fine—more like the killing of a neighbor's sheep. (The NIV changes the translation to make this problem go away.) This is further supported by Gen 2:7, which tells us that life only commences when one first takes a breath. Many (but not all) biblical literalists are against abortion. If one takes passages like these literally, they form a strong challenge to that stance (Pence 2004, 123–124). The Catholic position is also an interpretation. It's honest in that it admits its status and provides reasons.

we will now turn, is to ask the question of faith. Since each of these traditions appeal to "faith" at their core, what it is that makes for authentic faith? How might we tell the difference?

Section II: An Experiential Definition of Faith

It's one thing to discount the experience of another. It's quite another to discount one's own experience–though we often do so without realizing it. As with the Apostle Thomas, my goal is to invite us to put our fingers into our own wounds.[6] Let us see and trust our own experiences.

We are seeking a *general* understanding of faith. As with truth, I want to understand how faith functions in our lives, not just in the abstract. To get at this, there's a simple exercise:

EXERCISE: BRAINSTORMING ABOUT FAITH

Consider the following questions:

> *What is faith?*
>
> *What does faith mean to you?*
>
> *How does faith function in your life?*
>
> *What does faith do for you?*
>
> *Why do you believe what you believe?*

On rare occasions, I have someone who only wants to say that faith is their belief in Jesus and the Bible. That's a start. And that's why I have a number of questions. What does faith do? Why believe? Etc. The idea is to brainstorm about faith from a number of perspectives. In class, I chart these on the board. If we get stuck on a particular "belief," I note that, even within a particular religion, there is often wide disagreement about which belief is true. Further, if a particular belief was all there was to faith, why use the term at all? Why not just call it "true belief?" The suggestion is that belief is part of the content of faith, but that faith is really something else. What else? That's what some of the other questions help us figure out.

---

6   Using the Apostle Thomas as an example might require an explanation. Biblically, the fact that Thomas questioned Jesus's resurrection is usually seen as a sign that his faith needed strengthening. This move can be seen in at least two lights. On the surface, one can see it as a claim to believe without evidence. This is basically a power move and a call for blind faith. A richer explanation is that Thomas, having lived with Jesus, already had the evidence upon which to base his faith. It was not a call to blind faith; it was a call for Thomas to wake up to the evidence he already possessed.

By the end of the brainstorming session, we usually have some version of the following ideas on the table:

Beliefs are part of the content of faith.

Beliefs accepted by faith cannot be proven but are not just a blind leap.[7]

Faith is a relationship between evidence and experience.

Faith gives one hope.[8]

Faith gives one meaning and purpose in life.

Faith functions at the core of our being as persons.

Faith has to grow and change to be alive.

Using these, I synthesize their insights into **a general definition of faith** (or living faith):[9]

---

7   The reason I prefer the given translation from Hebrews is that it highlights the idea that, while there is no proof, there are reasons (some evidence) for taking the leap of faith in a particular direction. But I'm not sure which is the most accurate translation.

8   Hope is quite a bit more complicated than many people think. For example, is it really good to offer false hope to a dying patient or their family? It often hurts them more and doesn't allow them time to address issues they might need to before dying. Or, in the case of neocolonialism in South America, the priests would often preach hope, not for this world, but the next. The people were told that, the more they bore their trials with good cheer and offered them up to God in this life ("pick up your cross and follow me") the richer their reward in heaven. The result worked well for those in power, the poor were taught not to rise up and ask for a better life. Hope kept them in oppression.

9   Philosophically, this definition was inspired the following passage from Kierkegaard:

> Faith is the objective uncertainty
> along with the repulsion of the absurd
> held fast in the passion of inwardness,
> which precisely is inwardness potentiated
> to the highest degree (Bretail 1946, 255).

Faith is the objective uncertainty refers to the fact that those beliefs that form the content of faith cannot be proven with complete certainty. This is the source of the famous "leap" of faith. Unfortunately, many assume that the fact that there is a "leap" means that one makes this leap without evidence. *The repulsion of the absurd* suggests exactly the opposite. Given that no belief system is completely certain, there is always a leap. But why leap into one belief system and not another? Unless is it merely by chance or culture, there has to be a rationality, a way of ordering the world and one's place in it that makes sense of one's life (repulses the absurd). If one takes rationality, not as a set of abstract absolutes, but as a tool for organizing one's world to support human flourishing, then the power of faith provides a sense of purpose and place within the greater scheme of existence. This suggests that rationality, far

> **Faith is the heuristic acceptance of those beliefs as true that, while not absolutely provable:**
>
> 1. **make sense of my experience(s),**
> 2. **give purpose and meaning to my life, and**
> 3. **on their deepest level, form the core of who I am as a person.**

Let's take this definition in stages.

First, beliefs are the content of faith, but faith is more than just a belief. A belief is just an intellectual idea, while faith takes on the characteristics of an ongoing process and relationship. Relationship with what? With how one experiences the world, other people, and the divine. Living faith, authentic faith, is also heuristic. What does this mean? In this context, I took the term from computer programming. A heuristic computer program is a program that learns and adapts to experience (data and result), which changes given that experience. Living faith is faith that can grow and adapt, which can modify its beliefs based on experiences.

Why can't we just say that faith is fixed?

We've previously raised the issue of whether our minds are adequate to fully capture even the limited data of our sense experience. How much less could we ever know to "capture" the divine fullness of reality? Any idea, belief, or expression about God or spirituality is at best an approximation, always inadequate to capture that which we seek and call divine.

But this notion of faith is not just about the divine.

Why is it that I accept certain beliefs? There is no "proof" (thus the need for the famous "leap"),[10] but that's not to say that there is no evidence. I accept certain beliefs as true because, as with our discussion of truth, it's useful. It makes sense of my experiences. This is the first level of faith.

---

from being the enemy of faith, is in fact its constant companion. The question then becomes one of "which" rationality, not of rationality per se.

By using the clause *"the"* before "objective uncertainty," Kierkegaard is referring to what, in his mind, is *the* most important or the ultimate objective uncertainty—God. Changing "the" to "an" (as in *"an* objective uncertainty"), generalizes this definition of faith from religious experience to include other levels and aspects of our lives.

10   In some cases, some of the reasons for the leap may not be entirely apparent until one takes the leap—at least to test the beliefs. However, in the notion of faith that follows, we will see that this sort of process should lead to further testing, not to a dogmatic adherence to that first leap. That's where many get stuck.

Perceptual Faith

Merleau-Ponty refers to this first level as perceptual faith: faith that the evidence of our senses is accurate. Of course, that's not always the case. But, as with truth in general, we function within a hermeneutic circle. We tend not to question those beliefs that appear to work.

Still, we need to recognize that there are limits, even a leap, with perceptual faith. For example, consider the chair you're probably sitting in. Slap it. Does it feel real? Yet ask yourself:

Can anyone here prove, beyond all doubt, that this chair exists?

Of course they cannot. One only need engage in a few thought experiments. For example, have you ever had a dream that you thought was reality? Upon waking, you found out that it wasn't real. How, then, do you know beyond any doubt that you are not currently in a dream? To confuse the issue even further, have you ever had a dream where you woke up and then woke up again?

Might you still be sleeping?

Perhaps you've seen the movie *The Matrix*. How sure are you that you're not like Neo, prior to swallowing that reality pill? Or perhaps we are in the world of Descartes's evil genius, who merely uses us as playthings?

Our senses do at times fool us. While they are very limited, still, they are fairly consistent within the range of their capacities. The evidence of the "real" world is thus quite strong, just as when we are dreaming, we wake up. For most of us, the complexity, detail, and consistency of the waking world is sufficient to where we fairly easily separate it from the dream world. As for the matrix, well, unless Morpheus offers us that pill, the evidence of its reality seems quite limited.

We accept that which best makes sense of our experiences.

Perceptual faith is also the foundation of science.

Science depends upon the ability to replicate and share information derived in large part from one's senses. Perceptual faith, and thus science, differs from other levels of faith in at least two ways. First, the "leap" required to believe the evidence of one's senses is quite small. As we move away from perceptual faith, this leap will grow. Second, science deals only with evidence of the senses, knowledge that, directly or indirectly, can be *independently* tested and verified. At the heart of verification, of course, is the idea that independent researchers, running the same tests of experiments, will observe the same results.[11] Scientific knowledge is always probabilistic.

---

11 Recall the principle of non-falsification from chapter 2.

It is only as strong as the links between its evidence and the theories that explain the evidence. Moreover, scientific knowledge does not deal well with values. It works very well for explaining *how* certain things can be done, it tells us little about *what* should be done. The need for values moves us to the next two levels.

The following meme suggests a possible relationship between science and other forms of human exploration or faith:

FIGURE 9.1

Purpose versus Meaning

To understand the importance of the difference between these two ideas, it is helpful to analyze the common saying:

Everything happens for a reason.

Please, **NEVER say this to a person suffering from a serious illness or injury**, *unless you know them very well and are sure that this will comfort them.* When I ask, in a class, about how many would feel comforted by this saying, only about a third of the hands go up. If I ask, instead, how many would be angered by someone saying this to them, I often get about as many. Why?

For many people, the saying is hurtful. If I have cancer, I may hear that I am being punished.

Or I may feel, and this is likely to be true, that it's not really about comforting me, it's about comforting the person saying it. Which, when I am the one who is ill, seems rather objectionable.

Consider another phrase, *"I'm sure everything will work out fine."* Someone once said that to me when I was going in for a serious surgery. I couldn't resist asking her, "Oh, are you a doctor? Have you examined me? Do you know this disease? Perhaps you have a gift for telling the future?"

Perhaps the best example for understanding this problem is a friend of mine who was raped. After she "recovered," she used the experience to help other women in similar situations. She became a very good counselor.

Here's the question:

> ***Was she raped in order to make her a good rape counselor?***

Or to put it another way:

> ***Did God cause her to be raped for that purpose?***

Such a claim seems both highly objectionable and insensitive.

> ***Either the claim that "everything happens for a reason" is trivial*** (*all it means is that there is a cause for every event*) ***or it means exactly what these objectionable questions imply, that the rape was really a "good" thing because it was allowed to happen for a greater purpose.***

What we actually see in the claim "everything happens for a reason" is a fundamental confusion and linkage between purpose and meaning.

> **Purpose refers to the reasons why (from *before*) something happened.**

> **Meaning refers to the interpretations and values we give to the event *after* the fact.**

The phrase, "everything happens for a reason" seamlessly links the two. This means that, for my friend who was raped, because something good came out of it, the rape was actually a good thing. This is nonsense. It devalues the experiences of millions of people who have undergone real tragedies.[12]

---

12   This is not to say that there aren't people who, having undergone tragedy, still find this comforting. That's how they give meaning to, and find peace with, the event.

If the two are not linked, we can accept tragedy as real. ***The rape was not a good thing; nothing can make it "good." However, our responses to it can ensure that something different, and good, comes out of it.*** This is part of the nature of redemption. Camus writes this about the plague. Given how common rape is in our world, it applies here as well:

> What's true of all the evils in the world is true of the plague as well. It helps men to rise above themselves. (Nuland 1995, 200)

Linking the two in this way has other consequences as well. For example, it would no longer make sense to refer to humans "meaning generating" creatures. Why? Because the meaning would be "fixed" by the purpose, which would in turn be fixed by the previous purpose that created it, and so forth. Where, then, is there room for free will? Creativity?

In fact, much of psychotherapy is based on the gap between purpose and meaning. Consider *Cognitive-Behavioral Therapy*. It works on the principle that memories, feelings, and valuations are malleable. What does this mean? Just because I experienced something as hurtful and damaging in my past doesn't mean that I have to remain stuck there for all time. I can go back to those memories, reframe them, and see the experiences behind them in new ways. I can change how I feel about the experience and how those memories affect me as a person. This only works because meaning is not fixed.

There's even a theological problem with linking the two in this way. If purpose and meaning are seamlessly linked, then God becomes responsible, not just for the good, but for all the evil in the world. If God wanted to prepare my friend to help others, if that was God's purpose, then it was God's *intent* to cause that horrible act. On the other hand, if we separate the purpose and meaning, then the "purpose" could simply be the intent of the criminal, while God could instead be thought of as helping the victim to both recover and to bring something good out of a terrible ordeal.

The point is, meaning and purpose, while related, are not the same. There may be times when the meaning I ascribe to an event is the same, or nearly the same, as the reason (purpose) I initiated the event. But not always. Moreover, some things may not have a "purpose," they may only have a "cause."[13] Even those things or events can have meaning.

What has purpose and meaning to do with faith? This really ties together with the third function, that of providing our core values and sense of self.

Our faith is whatever we hold as our most important core beliefs, that which both guides our choices and how we interpret our experiences. For many, this means a religious tradition, but it doesn't have to. By this definition, an atheist would have faith, just not in a God. There are people of many faiths whose understanding of the divine

---

13   Look for the poem by Angelus Silesius in the chapter on Hinduism and Buddhism.

is so different from ours, at least on the surface, as to be hardly recognizable to one another. *This is where our values arise.* Thus, if you recall, I suggested that science had a great deal to say about how nature works, but much less to say about what we should do with that knowledge. This speaks to the level where we make those decisions. The "leap" is far greater than with science because the evidence is not as clear. It speaks to something deep at our core, something fundamental to our humanity.

Living Faith, Idolatry, Relationship to Science, Truth

It should be fairly obvious that **faith is another way of talking about truth**. More specifically, faith is another way of talking about **the hermeneutic circle**. Part of the relationship between these deeper levels of faith and science should already be clear—faith operates in each, though as the level deepens, so too does the leap. Another way to think about the relationship between faith and science, or religion and science, comes from a quote I recall, but cannot place, from my first BA in religion. I believe it comes from Gordon Allport, though I've been unable to locate the exact reference:

> *While anything that denies science is not likely to be true, anything that stops with science is not likely to be the whole truth.*[14]

The value of Allport's insight is that it clearly recognizes a space for both science and a truth that is greater than, or different from, that of science. However, assuming that there is one God, it would seem very odd that God would place the two in direct conflict. While science does not provide all the answers, any faith statement that contradicts science appears suspect.

Consider, for example, the debate over intelligent design. The "Of Pandas and People" version of intelligent design is clearly in conflict with evolution. In reality, this version is just creationism redressed in an attempt to make it past the Supreme Court decision ruling that creationism, because it was a view favoring a particular religion, violated the establishment clause of the constitution.[15] Unless one holds to a very literal view of the Bible, the argument seems silly. Many denominations hold a version of intelligent design that is compatible with evolution. For example, they argue that God, in creating evolution, nudged it subtly in various ways. We may not be able to detect the nudges, but it doesn't mean they aren't there. God could be acting through evolution.

---

14 I can't guarantee that the quote is exact, but at least the basic idea was inspired by Allport.

15 The book was at the printers when the decision of *Edwards vs Aguillard* (1987) came down. They took the proofs and did a search and replace function to switch "creationism" to "intelligent design." See: District Judge John E. Jones III, Dover, PA. http://www.npr.org/templates/story/story.php?storyId=5063317 http://www.pamd.uscourts.gov/kitzmiller/kitzmiller_342.pdf.

This may in fact be true. The arguments for and against it, however, aren't scientific. Instead, they are theological. They are important because, in part, they help us discern what to do with the fruits of science. That still doesn't mean they belong in a science class.

Living faith, on its deepest level, calls on us to integrate *both* the knowledge of science and the knowledge that science cannot provide—*without* subordinating one to the other.

Dogmatism and Idolatry

If one of the primary characteristics of living faith is that it is open to growth and change, then **dogmatic faith is faith for which the beliefs are rigid, stuck, and closed to real growth and change**.

When one's beliefs become such that, instead of being open to new data, we try to "force" new information into old ideas, we have become stuck. Again, an atheist can be just as dogmatic about their beliefs as a Christian can be about theirs. It's about whether one is open to growth.

This does not mean that one should discard long held beliefs at the first sign of trouble. Sometimes the data is wrong. Often, the changes in one's beliefs to accommodate new information or experience are minor. But one must be open to more, to conversion. As we go further into spirituality, I argue that, in reality, we should be open to multiple conversion experiences in our lives. Each transformation should deepen and enrich us as persons.

This also relates to the Hebrew notion of *idolatry*. On the surface, most think of idolatry as the worship of false gods or idols. But what is a false idol? In the biblical tradition, anything that becomes more important than God, or gets in the way of authentic spirituality, is an idol. If one's highest value is wealth, for example, gold is one's idol. It doesn't need to be shaped into a graven image.

As Lewis might point out, the same is true even of good values, such as patriotism and love of family, when those values are so blown out of proportion as to become all consuming. This suggests a link between dogmatic faith and idolatry. In dogmatic faith, the specifics of one's beliefs have become one's idol. In fact, if one's scripture becomes more important than the reality of which the scripture speaks, even scripture can become an idol.

Grounding Faith

How is such faith to be grounded? This question depends upon one's personal experiences with life and the divine. Some will come to believe that God's rationality merely exceeds human intellect but is not different in kind. Others, in line with the Hebrew notion that even the name of the divine is unpronounceable, may opt for a more radical vision such that the divine is in some way "wholly other" than the products of the mind. Others may not want to talk about religion at all. None of these approaches renders faith or its grounds "irrational." In the first case, one may conclude that the ground is suprarational. In the second case, following thinkers like Levinas and Merleau-Ponty, the ground may be prerational. In fact, one of the oldest tenants of Christianity is that *faith perfects reason*. The task then becomes one of recognizing the nature and limits of this ground and of reason, not of dismissing it.

A Different Structure for Christianity

As should have been clear, the basic "structure" illustrated above, and adopted by *some* of the followers of both Islam and Christianity, has a strong tendency towards extremism. If whatever God tells one to do is good, and if the world has no intrinsic value of its own (with which to resist commands of destruction), it is very hard to have a rational argument with the suicide bomber or the Christian terrorist. We can disagree with them, but there's not a strong foundation for that disagreement.

If, on the other hand, all lives have value and the world has value, then we have part of a foundation for opposing the ideology of extremism. If the value of this earth is not just as a testing ground, then acts that involve killing others or damaging the earth are not acts to be taken lightly. Moreover, if our notion of faith creates an appropriate place for reason instead of opposing reason, then we have the building blocks necessary for a rational objection.

Some of those building blocks come from the nature of faith itself. The use of reason and compatibility with science get us out of the starting gate. Another comes from the notions of dogmatism and idolatry. It's no longer just my belief verses yours; I can show how my beliefs fit together into a whole and are open to growth. If your beliefs are not, then it's probably dogmatism rather than faith.

Let's take another step towards constructing a very different structure for Christianity.[16]

In the earlier structure, one of the implicit ideas is that only at the end of the world can the Kingdom of God be established. That's not the only major interpretation of what it means to bring about the Kingdom of God. The **stewardship model** has a very different structure.[17]

---

16   I believe there are similar structures in Islam, but I don't have the expertise to explain them clearly.

17   Among many others, it appears that Pope Francis operates on the stewardship model.

Stewardship Model of Christianity

1. **Everything that God creates is intrinsically good, including the earth.**
2. **We are given the earth, not to dominate, but as stewards to care for it.**
3. **The Kingdom of God was given with the gift of the Holy Spirit (not waiting for end times).**
4. **It is the task of each of us to allow the Holy Spirit to work though us, bringing the Kingdom of God into this life and world.**
5. **Work is founded on love and respect for all of God's creatures and creation.**
6. **As stewards, we do not force our views on others, but gently witness, through the example of our lives, what it means to love God, one's neighbor, and God's creation.**

In this structure, the afterlife serves as a "bonus" from a loving God, but it does not change how we live this life. A Christian, under this model, would behave the same whether there was an afterlife or not.

It should be clear that this structure is far less susceptible to the sort of extremism of the other structure. It denies the basic premises of the more eschatological model. For example, that the only purpose of this life is to get ready for the next, that this world has no intrinsic value, and that God can change his or her mind in irrational ways. Moreover, it gives clear directions to care, gently, for the earth and its other inhabitants. Forced conversion is out, gentle witness is in. If God created all of us as intrinsically valuable, then to kill another should only be done with great need (i.e., perhaps self-defense).

Both models have strong biblical support. This is part of the reason why one's upbringing has such a strong influence on which model one adopts. Part of this has to do with the interpretation one has been taught while the other part has to do with one's life experiences and temperament.

Of course, there is little this sort of analysis will do to "stop" someone with a strong and determined ideology. Still, we can focus on alternative ways of understanding faith and spirituality that emphasize care and growth. Moreover, if we recall the example of the city in Denmark—the city that reached out to those at risk for terrorism rather than isolating them or dealing with them in fear—we are far more likely to bring peace and love (The Kingdom of God) into the world under this second model. There are many on the margins who would be open to a loving hand, or who, having realized the folly of their ways, would take a chance to return to normal society.

What Is Missing?

This definition of faith, while general, allows for an emphasis upon a personal relationship with the divine and upon one's own experiences. For this reason, it is more easily taken up by members of our culture, particularly at the phase in life of many college students. We also see how faith is another way of talking about truth. But it should also be noted that this **notion of faith only begins to touch on the interruptive nature of a mature spirituality**. That notion will be more easily understood through Eastern spirituality, though it applies to Western spirituality as well. The quote from Coffin, a Christian pastor, with whom we began this chapter, points in that direction:

> *Faith ... should make it possible to live with uncertainty, it shouldn't provide certainty.*

This will become clear when we get to the distinction between psychology and spirituality. In simple terms, what Coffin is saying is very similar to C.S. Lewis. That is, if the reason I go to church and do good is to get to heaven, then it's really about me and not about God. The "uncertainty" of which Coffin writes has to do with the interruptive effect of spirituality. Part of this has to do with the power of growth verses dogmatism. The other part has to do with the power of placing ourselves in service to that which is greater than ourselves without regard to what we get from it. This chapter focused on some important aspects of faith; it does not (if that is even possible) provide a whole picture. We still have much to do.

> *Whether one believes in religion or not, whether one believes in rebirth or not, there isn't anyone who doesn't appreciate kindness and compassion.*

Dalai Lama

Figure Credits
Fig. 9.1: Copyright © 2016 Depositphotos/Nik_Merkulov.

CHAPTER TEN

Minority Report

REREADING GILGAMESH AFTER LEVINAS[1]

WE'VE EXAMINED THE oldest creation myth in Western civilization. It seems appropriate, before moving on to Eastern thought, to explore what the oldest epic story in Western civilization has to say about the problem of death. This is, of course, the Epic of Gilgamesh. But this is about more than just the epic. The epic also offers us a way to more fully develop Levinas's thought, which will be critical to understanding how love might be the ultimate rational act.

The Epic of Gilgamesh attempts to answer the question of how, given the finality of death, one might find happiness, meaning, and value in this life. Many commentators argue that the text provides two separate, though ultimately unsatisfactory, alternatives.

The first solution is fame. If I build lasting monuments or perform heroic acts, then I can live forever in the memories of others. Early in the epic, we see this solution in the building of the walls of Uruk and in the slaying of Humbaba. Yet, with the death of his dear friend, Enkidu, Gilgamesh concludes that fame is ultimately empty. He wants his friend back. Even more, he fears his own demise. So he journeys to the end of the earth to find the two humans who have been granted immortality by the gods. Once there, he discovers that theirs was a unique circumstance that he could not hope to repeat.

The second solution is to eat, drink, and be merry. He is also told to love his wife, hold his children close, and be satisfied with the simple joys of living. Since Gilgamesh's culture did not believe in a robust afterlife, this was the best to which one could aspire. Gilgamesh, at last ***resigned*** to his mortality, accepts his role as ruler and shepherd for his subjects.

---

1   Reprinted, with permission, from Sage Open, July–Aug 2016, with formatting and other minor modifications. Original article can be found at: http://sgo.sagepub.com/cgi/reprint/6/3/2158244016657858.pdf?ijkey=Xz1fn37EzzQWsUQ&keytype=finite.

Why Seek an Alternative? Using Levinas to Understand the Epic

What is troubling about this interpretation is that these "solutions" are so easily dismissed. For our culture, wherein many believe that this life only has meaning in the context of some ultimate, eternal afterlife, such a dismissal makes sense. Even those who don't share a belief in an afterlife may tend towards the assumption that "primitive" cultures have little to teach us in this regard. Taken in terms of the epic's culture, were these solutions really so inadequate? Why did this story endure?

When looking at *Theogeny*, we noted that a characteristic of great literature is that it speaks to human experience in a multitude of ways. It's possible that the story is intended to reflect upon the many ways in which nature does not, ultimately, satisfy human desires. It seemed facile to use this to dismiss the possibility of a richer reading of the solutions proposed by the epic. Looking deeper, we may find resources on par with, and even richer than, some of our modern ways of addressing these questions.

It's not that the solutions offered here are absent from the literature. It's just that many commentators believe, as does Kramer, that "none of [them] holds any real promise" (Kramer 1988, 100). Even George, one of the epic's great scholars, appears to discount what may prove to be a key moment in the epic—downplaying shifts in the death of Enkidu and explaining care for one's subjects as "duty" to the gods (George 1999, xxxvii; George 2003, 504). Though George may at times fall prey to this tendency, for the most part, he rises above it. George is exactly right when he notes that the epic has often been understood as a "vehicle for reflection on the human condition" (George 2003, 527). Gilgamesh endured as an epic because it spoke, on multiple levels, to the lives of the people who created it.[2]

Part of the reason these solutions are so easily discounted may be that they are usually understood as isolated, static categories. Just as Gilgamesh undergoes a process of transformation throughout the epic, so too do these two solutions. By the end of the epic, they may well become aspects of a single, transformed solution, one that is richer in its implications for human life and happiness than our current reading. Such a transformation can only be understood if we moderate at least two fairly common assumptions. First, the modern assumption that all human behavior can be understood as some form of egoism or self-interest. Second, the assumption that this

---

2   There is controversy on this point. Some believe that the epic existed primarily in written form for the court and intellectual elite. While we lack the evidence to be certain, George argues in favor of a wider oral tradition. (See George 2003, 18–21; 34–39.) Even if the former were true, it still appears that it would have held such a position with the court. Also, it's worth noting that the sections on both the flood and the afterlife were not considered parts of the main body of the epic but were side stories. Here, we are focused on what is called the "standard" version.

life can only have meaning in terms of an infinite continuation of that self. Levinas, operating out of both the Greek and Hebrew traditions, can help us to see that these are not the only alternatives.

Why Levinas? First, Levinas operates out of the Hebrew tradition, which is not only from the same part of the world as the epic but may also have shared a common source with Ecclesiastes. This suggests that there may have been similarities between aspects of these traditions. In fact, a crucial passage of the epic for making the link to Levinas's thought is one that closely parallels a passage in Ecclesiastes. Second, as a phenomenologist, Levinas focuses on those basic experiences that define us as human. This is consistent with the possibility that the epic is meant to describe basic aspects of our human condition. Specifically, Levinas argues that at the heart of our humanity is the recognition of a powerful, yet fragile, pre-intellectual experience of care. This is an experiential claim. If accurate, this affective call to care—particularly for those who are most vulnerable—lies at the heart of both ethics and the development of everything we think of as human. This includes the capacities of speech, reason, freedom, self, morality, and even particular forms of violence.[3] While this experience is prerational, if Levinas is correct, some form of this experience should be found in every culture.

For example, it has been argued that this call, while not fully articulated, surfaced in Greek medicine underlying important aspects of the Hippocratic Oath (see Degnin 2007). In Gilgamesh, its implications are even more radical.

1. First, it provides a new way of viewing the solution of the epic—that the meaning of life and happiness are found, not primarily in intellectual beliefs, but within rich emotional and embodied relationships of care.
2. Second, if accurate, this suggests that an excessive focus on individual afterlife can, at times, be a product of intellectual abstraction, born of an attempt to replace real relational connections in a desperate bid for certainty.[4]

---

3 Because there are various schools of thought as to how to read Levinas, and because the differences between schools is not crucial for this thesis, I've left the more detailed development of these themes to other works. Here, I focus mainly on themes, such as the distinctions between need and desire, which appear as common to any interpretation of Levinas's work. To serve a wider audience, I've also avoided the use of most technical language.

4 *Even if one believes in an afterlife, the epic has much to teach us.* One thing I suggest to my students is to set aside their belief in an afterlife, at least for the first part of my Death and Dying course, because facing that fear had a lot to teach us. My own experience, which includes service as a hospital chaplain, suggests that those who use their belief in an afterlife to escape their fear are more likely to be dogmatic and judgmental. On the other hand, the psychology and spirituality of those who face that fear, embrace it and learn from it, is much different. Their beliefs are, in important ways, transformed. *The epic can be read as a story of facing that fear.*

Regardless of the actual status of an afterlife, an excessive dependence on such beliefs, far from being a realistic source of meaning in this life, might actually serve to undermine it. It might also undermine any reasonable and compassionate ethics. One need only consider the many atrocities, both historical and modern, that have been justified in order to earn said afterlife. In fact, some studies suggest that nonreligious people may in fact be more motivated by compassion than those who profess to be religious.[5] What Gilgamesh learns, and can teach us, is that the meaning of life, and the source of ethics, can be found right here in the call to care.

This also ties to a second reason why Levinas is particularly useful in rereading the epic. As both a student of Heidegger and of Judaism, Levinas provides both a powerful critique of aspects of Western philosophy and a bridge between insights of his Jewish heritage and Western thought. This bridge is particularly suggestive in terms of the epic. Not only were the Hebrews neighbors to the cultures that spawned the epic, but there is evidence that Hebrew scriptures shared common textural resources with the epic—particularly the flood narrative and Ecclesiastes (Jones 1990). Finally, there was a similar worldview in terms of an afterlife. *Early Judaism, as with some sects today, found meaning and value in life without recourse to an afterlife. Understanding this worldview could provide resources for understanding this aspect of the epic.* But for this, we need to turn to the text of the epic.

Reading the Text

Consider the attitude of the epic towards human mortality:

> *As for man, [his days] are numbered,*
>
> *whatever he may do, it is but the wind,*
>
> *… exists not for me … (George 1999, 19 [text lost]).*

George then compares this with a text from Ecclesiastes 3:19–20:

> *… as one does, so dies the other.*
>
> *They all have the same breath …*

---

5   It should be noted that these studies do not mean that religious persons are less generous than nonreligious persons. For example, it could be (as other studies suggest) that religious people are more generous as a whole, but their generosity is a lifestyle choice, and this study focuses on immediate situations. Thus, the study only appears to support the claim that, in these sorts of immediate situations, compassion appears to play a larger role for nonreligious persons. The value of this sort of study is in recognizing that generosity and compassion are not exclusive to religious people (Salsow et al. 2013).

… all is vanity …

… all are from dust, and all turn to dust again.

Both focus on the ephemeral nature of human life; we are but breath or wind. If this is so, **what gives one meaning and value in life? In the beginning, the epic suggests fame, either by great works or heroic deeds.** Gilgamesh does both, beginning with the great wall and temples of the city:

Meaning of Life: Two Kinds of Fame

Climb Uruk's wall and walk back and forth.

Survey its foundations, examine the brickwork!

Were its bricks not fired in an oven?

Did the Seven Sages not lay its foundations? (George 1999, 2)

As long as the city endures, so too would the memory of its builder. To ensure this, Gilgamesh had the story of his life and deeds inscribed on the wall. But this was not enough. Gilgamesh's desire for the second sort of fame guided his decision to kill the protector of the forest:

I will conquer him in the Forest of Cedar:

Let the land learn Uruk's offshoot is mighty!

Let me start out, I will cut down the cedar,

I will establish for ever a name eternal! (George 1999, 20)

Early in the epic, Gilgamesh's focus was on his own needs. Due to his great strength and endurance, he terrorizes his own people, exhausting the men in games and demanding the right to sleep with brides on their wedding nights:

The young men of Uruk he harries without warrant,

Gilgamesh lets no son go free to his father,

by day and night his Tyranny grows harsher … (George 1999, 3).

… Lets no girl go free to her bride [groom] … (George 1999. 4).

Since none could stand against Gilgamesh, Enkidu was created in response to the pleas of the people. He was intended to become a friend and companion to Gilgamesh, to provide a healthier outlet for Gilgamesh's "enthusiasm," and to teach Gilgamesh to care. Enkidu begins more as wild beast than man. His strength is comparable to

Gilgamesh's but he is of a substantially different temperament. Whereas Gilgamesh is like a spoiled child, caring only for himself, Enkidu began as a caretaker for the other beasts, springing them from hunter's traps and protecting them from harm. Enkidu exhibits a natural compassion that is, in the beginning, merely latent in Gilgamesh. Seduced and civilized by the temple priestess, Shamhat, Enkidu loses the trust of the wild beasts but gains the benefits of civilization. He becomes Gilgamesh's close companion.

But first, Enkidu challenges Gilgamesh. In part, Enkidu's challenge to Gilgamesh was that of any alpha male asserting dominance. From the text, we see that there was more. Upon arriving in Uruk, he is told that Gilgamesh is about to claim "first night," the right to sleep with a new bride before her groom. George's claim that Enkidu's "face paled in anger" (George 1999, 15) suggests that Enkidu was not motivated only by the desire to show dominance, but by a sense of moral outrage. Even without that claim, the fact is that his first act upon arriving in Uruk was one of compassion for the vulnerable. He stood between Gilgamesh and the bride Gilgamesh intended to despoil.

> For the goddess of weddings was ready the bed,
>
> for Gilgamesh, like a god, was set up a substitute.
>
> Enkidu with his foot blocked the door of the wedding house,
>
> not allowing Gilgamesh to enter.
>
> They seized at the door of the wedding house,
>
> in the street they joined combat ... (George 1999, 16).

In the battle that followed, Gilgamesh prevailed, but only just. Upon meeting, for the first time, someone who could stand against him, he found someone he could love and respect. They became fast friends.

The arrival of Enkidu can be seen as a relief to the citizens of Uruk in at least two ways. First, as a companion and equal to Gilgamesh, Enkidu distracts Gilgamesh from seeking to entertain himself at the expense of his people. But there is much more. *The arrival of Enkidu began a process of transformation on the part of Gilgamesh. Just as children need boundaries in order to learn to care, so too Gilgamesh needed an equal to help set those boundaries.*[6] Gilgamesh, for all his power, was bored—he abused his own people in a vain attempt to entertain himself.

---

6 It's interesting how often the "gods" in these stories act like spoiled children. For example, George refers to a passage wherein the goddess Ishtar is scorned as "like an angry child ..." (George 2003, 474). With so few limits on their power and pleasure, they need never grow up.

The gods divine with remarkable insight what is at the root of the trouble: Gilgamesh's superior energy and strength set him apart and make him lonely. He needs a friend, someone who measures up to him and can give him companionship on his own extraordinary level of potential and aspiration. (Jacobson, 1990)

Thus Enkidu, while submitting to Gilgamesh, won the battle in two crucial ways. First, he won the respect and love of Gilgamesh. Second, we never hear again that Gilgamesh sought the right of first night. Enkidu succeeded in his defense of the vulnerable.

The defense of the vulnerable, the capacity to care, is, for Levinas, the key humanizing trait. In this sense, Enkidu, even in his beast-like state, began the epic the more human of the two. Levinas argues that it is precisely the inversion of normal power relationships, this strange capacity of the vulnerable to evoke the power of compassion, that is at the heart of all we characterize as human. The experience is fragile and pre-rational. Fragile because it doesn't always happen and because it is easily swept aside. This differs from self-interest—enlightened or not—in that the focus of self-interest is the ego, the needs of the person. Levinas speaks to a capacity to set those needs aside, to place oneself in service to another. He calls this counter impulse desire (Levinas 1968, 117). Sometimes it's just a moment: I see another person or creature in pain, and for an instant, I forget myself, feeling only a desire to relieve that suffering. It's not that one's own needs are unimportant. In fact, as Levinas writes, only a being who can eat can know what it is like for another to go hungry; only a being who can feel pleasure and pain can care (Levinas 1981, 74). It's rather that, to become fully human, the needs of the one must be balanced, and at times subordinated, by care for others. To be clear:

Needs and Desire

Needs: Are robust and basic to us all. They point "inward," to caring for oneself, and to the satisfaction of basic human "needs" such as food and shelter.

Desire: Is more fragile, in the sense that it is more easily "lost" or overwhelmed by needs. Desire points "outwards," towards caring for and serving others. However, if nurtured, it can become strong enough to even overcome basic needs.

It should be emphasized that, without need, there might be no desire. One must be able to experience needs (and their satisfaction) not just to understand another's specific needs, but even to understand the concept of need. In a "perfect" world, where there were no needs, there would also be no space for compassion.

Understood in these terms, Gilgamesh won more than a physical battle. Through Enkidu, Gilgamesh first experienced limits, even pain, and gained a companion he respected and loved. This began a process by which he would, in stages, learn to live beyond his own selfishness. Gilgamesh was now vulnerable. He was also no longer bored.

To clarify how this changes the epic's answer to meaning in life, it helps to jump ahead to the second solution. Here, Gilgamesh, despondent after the death of Enkidu, is seeking the help of the one person who escaped mortality. In an older version of the story, he receives the following advice from Shiduri, the goddess/alewife:

Meaning of Life: Sieze the Day

But you, Gilgamesh, let your belly be full,

Enjoy yourself always by day and by night.

Make merry each day

Dance and play day and night!

Let your clothes be clean,

let your head be washed, may you bathe in water!

Gaze on the child who holds your hand.

Let your wife enjoy your repeated embrace! (George 1999, xxxvi).

George notes the close parallel to Ecclesiastes 9:7–9:

Go thy way, eat thy bread with joy,

and drink thy wine with a merry heart …

let thy garments be always white …

live joyfully with the wife whom thou lovest … (George 1999, xxxvi).

It's passages like these that suggest a common origin for both texts. Both begin with eating and drinking, taking joy in life's simple pleasures like wearing clean garments, and end with loving one's family. But it seems to me that the real import of these passages has been discounted. It's easy for those in our culture to notice the "eat, drink, and be merry" message. This parallels our notion of self-interest and Levinas's notion of the value and motivation of need. Such an interpretation is characteristic of Gilgamesh's behavior at the start of the epic. Yet, it's important to *notice that, even prior to receiving this advice, the epic had already declared the inadequacy of said interpretation. Why then bring it up?* Perhaps the lack is not in the "solution," but in Gilgamesh's, and our, understanding.

Because our culture focuses primarily upon self-interest, we tend to read both parts of Shiduri's advice in terms of self-interest. That's not necessarily the case in either Shiduri's speech or the passage from Ecclesiastes. It's possible that these passages address both aspects (need and desire) of human experience.

Need is addressed in the exhortation to eat, drink, and be merry.

Desire is addressed in the exhortation to love one's wife and child.

Consider that the reference to *clean clothing* reminds one, not of the isolated individual, but of the member of a community. For an ancient culture, *cleanliness was a sign of being part of a greater community.* Only those who were part of a community typically had the energy to spare from survival to worry about such cleanliness. Further, as part of the community, one was expected to care for more than just oneself. Thus, following the death of Enkidu, Gilgamesh wandered the wild clad only in the skin of a lion. This was where Gilgamesh was, in a sense, lost to both himself and to civilization. When he is reclothed in garments that will not dirty until he reaches home (a place where they could be cleaned), he is reborn and recivilized.

If everything in life is reduced to need, human meaning is reduced to a search for the service and survival of the ego. But if Levinas is correct, that which makes us distinctly human is our ability to also care for others—at times, prior to and more than for ourselves. In this reading, meaning is not found in the preservation of the ego, even if that preservation is into an eternal thereafter, but in the joining of a rich life in the giving of oneself to others. The real import of the passage is the balance[7] between the two parts, the second of which Gilgamesh will understand only at the end of his journey.

The Death of Enkidu

There are few passages more suggestive of this possibility than the scene of Enkidu's death. When Enkidu is told he is going to die, he becomes bitter, cursing all those who led him out of the forest to his death. Then the god Shamash speaks to Enkidu:

> *O Enkidu, why curse Shamhat the harlot,*
>
> *who fed you bread that was fit for a god,*
>
> *and poured you ale that was fit for a king,*

---

7   By "balance," I don't mean to infer a symmetry between need and desire, as Levinas would emphasize the asymmetry of the relationship between the self and other. (That gets into important, but very technical distinctions.) In this case, the term is merely intended to emphasize that each is of value and has a place in our lives.

who clothed you in a splendid garment,

and gave you as companion the handsome Gilgamesh?

And now Gilgamesh, your friend and your brother,

[will] lay you out on a magnificent bed,

[on] a bed of honor he will lay you out,

[he will] place you on his left, on a seat of repose,

[the rulers] of the underworld will all kiss your feet.

The people of Uruk [he will have] mourn and lament you,

the [thriving] people he will fill full of woe for you.

After you are gone his hair will be matted in mourning,

[clad] in the skin of lion, he will wander the wild (George 1999, 58–59).

This speech turned Enkidu's heart, so that his anger was stilled, and he blessed those whom he had just cursed:

Enkidu heard the words of Shamash the hero,

… his heart so angry grew calm,

… [his heart] so furious grew calm.

"Come, [Shamhat, I will fix your destiny!]

[My] mouth [that] cursed you shall bless [you] …" (George 1999, 59).

Why did Enkidu die in peace? There appear to be two possibilities.

In terms of the more common reading of the epic, one might argue that Enkidu, having been reassured that his name would live forever, could now rest in peace knowing that he had achieved the only form of immortality possible for mortals—living a rich life and dying famous.[8] Yet, *it is precisely with the death of Enkidu that Gilgamesh comes explicitly to reject both fame and a life of pleasure as adequate*

8   Foster, for example, refers to the sun god's "hollow promise … of a fine funeral," apparently recognizing the incongruity of the passage without seeing a way to make sense of it (Foster 2001, xxii). George offers a couple of possibilities for Enkidu's reversal, such as mirroring society's ambivalence about prostitution or as a commentary on the arbitrariness of the destiny of every mortal (George 2003, 481). None of these seem satisfactory.

solutions to happiness. This strongly suggests that these self centered solutions miss the point of the epic.

Instead, following Levinas's notion of desire, it seems to me that Shamash's speech reminded Enkidu of how deeply his friend would suffer upon his death and how much the gifts they had shared meant to them both. ***It was Enkidu's love and compassion for others, so characteristic of his life, which mitigated his anger and allowed Enkidu to die in peace.*** Enkidu would live on. It wasn't for the sake of personal fame. Instead, it was for the sake of the love he had shared and the positive impact of Enkidu's life upon those whom he had come to love. In this way, we will see that both "solutions" are transformed. Whereas at the beginning of the epic, both (fame and living a rich life) are separate and self-centered, with Enkidu, they become a single, other-centered solution, based on how they care for one's loved ones.

This reading finds support in Gilgamesh's response to Enkidu's death. Gilgamesh's love for Enkidu opens a door to love, but Gilgamesh only came to understand its meaning in stages. While his grief was authentic, on some level, what made Gilgamesh inconsolable was that he was still focused on himself:

> For his friend Enkidu Gilgamesh
>
> did bitterly weep as he wandered the wild:
>
> "I shall die, and shall I not be as Enkidu?"
>
> Sorrow has entered my heart! (George 1999, 70)

Gilgamesh's Wanderings

Gilgamesh's love of Enkidu had rendered him vulnerable to pain. But instead of turning that pain toward care and honor for others, he turned inward upon himself. He continued to pursue life and relationships as acts of aggression, something to be dominated and won, and not something calling for engagement and a profound surrender of the self for the sake of others. The journey that completes the epic was needed for Gilgamesh to complete these lessons. Along the way, he met various gods, goddesses, and their servants, initially discarding their wisdom, but also experiencing how his natural aggression acted against his goals.

For example, while he intended to intimidate the Ferryman as a show of power, his destruction of the "stone" poles[9] on the Ferryman's boat actually rendered them unable to cross the sea (George 2003, 499). Gilgamesh had to cut new poles and find new strategies to assist the Ferryman. When he arrives at the home of Uta-napishti,

---

9 Or stone crew, depending upon which translation. Either way, the intent of the passage appears to remain the same.

the only human to win eternal life, his intent had been to wrestle the secret from him by force. Instead of finding a heroic figure, greater than life, he finds an ordinary man. And at this point, he loses his desire to dominate Uta-napishti. Gilgamesh is coming to learn prudence and, perhaps, a bit of humility:

> I look at you, Uta-napishti:
>
> Your form is no different, you are just like me ...
>
> I was fully intent on making you fight,
>
> but now in your presence my hand is stayed. (George 1999, 88)

While at the home of Uta-napishti, he is given and fails additional tests, coming even further to grips with his mortality and his limits. Gilgamesh is disappointed but resigned to his fate. This is where many commentators leave us. While the transformation of the two solutions is not as clean as with the death of Enkidu, there are at least four pieces of evidence that it occurs.

Evidence of Gilgamesh's Transformation

First, in the prologue to the standard edition, the poet writes: "He came a far road, was weary, found peace ..." (George 1999, 1).

Second, he is given a garment that will not become soiled until he reaches home and is again able to receive clean clothing (George 1999, 98). This clothing, replacing the animal pelts he had been wearing, serves as a symbol that he has been recivilized (transformed) and is ready to rejoin the human community.

Third, there is the pivotal position in the story of Enkidu's death as the event that launched the journey—still our strongest piece of evidence.

Fourth, there is the record of Gilgamesh becoming a wise and beloved ruler following his return.

Of course, the epic externalizes this fourth item as the will of the gods. But rather than simply taking the epic at its word, let us return to the insight that these motifs could be ways of expressing inner spiritual and cultural truths. If Levinas is correct, *it is precisely care that forms an internal relationship of meaning. In other words, just as the capacity for care precedes rationality, so too the meaning of life is something that must be experienced; it must be felt in the lived connections with others.*[10] Of

---

10 This argument would be lacking if it did not include mention of the loss of the plant of rejuvenation. In a sense, this was Gilgamesh's consolation prize. If he found and ate this plant, he wouldn't live forever but he would at least regain the youth and vigor lost on this long journey—another indication of

course, we don't want to die. But an obsessive desire for an afterlife, as evidenced by Gilgamesh, is not in fact the means to happiness. It may instead be a path to misery.

At the end of the epic, Gilgamesh returns home, ready to take up his position as ruler. But he is no longer the ruler he was at the beginning of the epic. He has become a humble, wise man. When he returns with the Ferryman at his side, he takes him again to the walls of Uruk:

O Ur-shanabi, climb Uruk's wall and walk back and forth!

Survey its foundations, examine the brickwork!

Were its bricks not fired in an oven?

Did the Seven Sages not lay its foundations?

A square mile is city, a square mile is date-grove,

a square miles is clay-pit, half a square mile the temple of Ishtar:

three square miles and a half is Uruk's expanse. (George 1999, 99)

The words echo the beginning of the epic. Has Gilgamesh simply resigned himself to the notion that such fame is the only immortality available to humankind? Or has the meaning of the passage changed? George, even without the benefit of Levinas's thought, names and objects to the common view:

It is often supposed that [these lines] reveal in Gilgamesh an acceptance that he will make do with the immortal renown brought to him by building the city's wall. That is too specific a view. For while the epilogue begins by taking the audience in their imagination up on the wall once more, the last two lines make it clear that the poet fixes our gaze firmly on what the wall encloses. ... (George 2003, 526)

The gaze is fixed, not on the wall itself, but on whom the wall shelters. It's no longer primarily about Gilamesh, but about those for whom he cares.

---

how an obsessive search for immortality achieves its opposite (George 2003, 505). Oddly, upon obtaining the plant, he doesn't eat it right away, allowing time for it to be stolen away by a snake. Perhaps he wanted to save it for the old man? Perhaps he wanted to test and see if it was poison? We can't really be sure. But, recalling that there are many themes woven throughout the epic, my best guess is that it serves another purpose. For example, see (George 2003, 523–526).

Transforming the Man and the Message

Just as Gilgamesh undergoes a series of transformations, so too do these "solutions." Both begin as egocentric pursuits—Gilgamesh starts as a tyrant and a hedonist. The reason neither fame nor living well is satisfying is because both solutions are focused on himself—his ego—not on his connection and service to others. Through a series of transformations that occur throughout the text, Gilgamesh discovers a deeper, richer way of life. He discovers the value of care. It is this value, this embodied connection, which provides the unifying force for the two solutions and the only authentic means for human satisfaction. Once discovered, Gilgamesh ceases to live primarily for his own pleasure. Personal fame, while still desired, loses importance. The joy he takes in daily life, the simple pleasures and human connections become sources of real satisfaction. Even living on in the memory of others is transformed from a focus on personal accomplishments to a focus on service.

The story ends with Gilgamesh showing the wall to the Ferryman, but its meaning and emotional tenor have changed. It is no longer primarily about his personal pride, though he still takes pride in and would like to be remembered for the accomplishment. Its deeper value, that which has become of greater importance to Gilgamesh, is how well it shelters his people.

Thus both "meanings" are transformed:

Seize the day! (Eat, drink, and be merry.)

It is no longer just about personal pleasure, but about the joy of caring for one's family, one's children, and one's neighbors.

Fame! (Living on in the memory of others through monuments or enduring walls)

It is no longer primarily about his personal fame, but about the wall's value in sheltering his people.

Fame! (Living on in the memory of others through great deeds)

It is now about having contributed to their lives and well-being, not just about personal immortality.

Perhaps another way of thinking about this would be to ask the following question: If you had a choice between:

1. being "forgotten" but having made the lives of your children and their children richer and happier for your passing; or

2. you could be one of the most famous people to ever live, so that almost all people would know your name, but this name would be "Hitler";

which would you choose?

> *If you would choose to be "forgotten," but having made life better for your loved ones, then the epic speaks to you.*

Thus, for the epic:

> "Egoistic" pleasure instead becomes focused on the pleasure of service or being part of a community.

> "Egoistic" fame shifts from merely leaving a legacy to leaving a legacy of care.

This then shifts to a single solution, where

> *the meaning of life is found, not in living forever (either immortality or in an after-life), but in the concrete relationships by which we live and give of ourselves in this life.*

It's not that Gilgamesh doesn't also seek his own pleasure and it's not that he doesn't still want to be remembered. These needs are now placed in the larger context of this desire to serve his people and to be a wise and kind ruler, rather than a tyrant.

Given that we know so little of the language and culture, we cannot be sure that this reading is any more "correct" than other readings. As is true of any great literary work, it addresses the human condition from a rich variety of avenues. The value of reading the epic in the light of Levinas's thought is that Levinas offers us evocative ways to approach difficult problems in the text, particularly Enkidu's strange change of heart upon his death.

From another angle, this also parallels an insight recorded by Kübler-Ross, a pioneer in the study of death and dying:

> *To rejoice at the opportunity of experiencing each new day is to prepare for one's ultimate acceptance of death. For it is those who have not really lived—who have left issues unsettled, dreams unfulfilled, hopes shattered, and who have let the real things in life (loving and being loved by others, contributing in a positive way to other people's happiness and welfare, finding out what things are really you) pass them by—who are most reluctant to die. (Kübler-Ross 1975, xi; emphasis added)*

As I've said previously, I've seen this working as a hospital chaplain. Again, it's also not one's belief in an afterlife that correlates most strongly with whether one goes peacefully into that great beyond. It's really the two things named by Kübler-Ross:

First, whether one feels that one has lived a rich and full life (seize the day).

Second, whether one is surrounded by those one loves and feels as though one has made positive contributions to their lives, and they to yours.[11]

For those who have listened to the insights of the epic, this "truth" should come as no surprise.

---

11   Again, I'm not making any claims about the existence or nonexistence of an afterlife.

CHAPTER ELEVEN

Siddhartha

AN INTRODUCTION TO EASTERN SPIRITUALITY

THUS FAR, WE have dealt primarily with elements of Western religions, both ancient and modern. This chapter marks a shift wherein we begin to focus more on the insights of certain Eastern traditions. It's not that we will leave Western thought behind. Rather, we will work to blend some of the insights of Eastern thought and spirituality with those of the West, bringing them together to understand more fully the two primary themes of the course.

We start with a novel as a way of easing into these insights. Prior to writing *Siddhartha*, Hesse spent years studying Hindu and Buddhist scriptures. He also spent years in semi-seclusion, attempting to experience for himself what the scriptures described. But Hesse was born German and raised in Europe. The result is a blending of East and West that, via story, allows the Western reader to ease into the differences that appear to undergird Eastern approaches to death, life, and spirituality.

We should begin our study of Eastern thought with some of the usual observations. For example, both Hinduism and Buddhism, like Christianity, Judaism, and Islam, are not single disciplines. Just as with Western religions, there are many variations within these and other Eastern approaches. Like before, the idea is to provide some of the fundamentals, as well as offer some critiques, but this is in no way a comprehensive survey of Eastern or Western thought.

A second observation is that this story, like every other story we have watched or read, is a journey of transformation. For this reason, one should expect Siddhartha's understanding of himself and his path to change during the course of his life. This may seem obvious but it's worth highlighting here for a different reason. When faced with a system of thought so different than one is used to, the search for understanding might tempt one to grab onto early statements as if they are the whole truth of that approach. In other words, be careful to take statements in context rather than as absolute claims. Some will remain true until the end of the story, others will be challenged and transformed.

A third observation is to remind ourselves of natural biases like **confirmation bias** and **the fundamental attribution error**. For the most part, we will try to reduce this effect by presenting some of the more "philosophical" and coherent versions of these traditions, but even here, it would be easy to "dismiss" them based on our criticisms. The richer move is to recognize criticisms of both Western and Eastern thought and to consider what both, together, have to teach us.

A final comment to remember is that translations don't always carry the full meaning. For example, in the West, "understanding" is usually thought of in terms of the intellect or the mind. *In Hindi*, however, a word that is usually translated as "understanding" *often means an embodied or intuitive notion, not just or even primarily intellectual.* Similarly, if you read the passages from Kramer, you will see that he uses the translation "death is an illusion" (Kramer 1988, 32). But *the word that is translated as "illusion" could also mean "appearance."* The implications are profoundly different. Expanding on this will both illustrate my point and give the reader a bit of background from which to approach the novel.

Example: Krishna and Arjuna: *The Bhagavad Gita*

The *Bhagavad Gita* is one of the two founding texts of Hinduism. The basic story comes as "a dialogue between Krishna, the divine teacher, and Arjuna, the warrior disciple" (Kramer 1988, 31). A civil war is about to begin between Arjuna's family and another family, cousins, who had stolen land belonging to Arjuna's family. Arjuna, the warrior disciple, has been raised from childhood to defend the family and, in this case, take back the land.

On the eve of battle, Arjuna is beset by doubts. This is just a piece of land. To take it back, he will have to kill, not just anyone, but his own relatives. Now that he is face to face with the situation, "the land seems less important to him than preserving the lives of his family and friends" (Kramer 1988, 31). The question he asks Krishna is whether he should fight.

It's a powerful ethical argument. If we listen only to Kramer's response, we would have reason to doubt the ethical foundation of Hinduism. Because Kramer's response, while technically accurate, fails to emphasize the real point. In part, this is based on translation. Krishna tells Arjuna:

1. It is duty (*dharma*) to fight.
2. "Death is an illusion."
3. "Death … is natural and unavoidable."
4. "Only union with the Brahman is real."
5. "Only identity with the True Self (Atman) is real." (Kramer 1988, 32)

For those who have not studied Hinduism, the last two points may appear to be in contradiction, but this isn't the case. The term "Brahman" can be thought of as their notion of "God." For the Hindu, it's more like a great sea of spiritual energy, less "personal" than most Western notions of God. *The "Atman" is part of the Brahman, a spark or droplet of spiritual energy that has left the sea and now exists to animate a being.* The **Atman** is the spiritual energy that animates each one of us. Both are part of the same reality.

This does not mean that the Atman is to the Hindu what the soul is to a Christian. What travels from lifetime to lifetime via reincarnation is, for the Hindu, not just the Atman, but also the Jiva. While the Atman is impersonal, the Jiva can be thought of as one's personality and character, that which defines us as individuals. *If one is looking for an analogue to the Christian idea of the soul in Hinduism, it would be the Atman plus the Jiva.* It's also worth noting that travel via reincarnation is just an intermediate stage. The ultimate goal is to get off the "wheel" of reincarnation and allow the Atman to merge back into the Brahman. At that point, the Jiva is stripped away. For the Hindu, the Christian notion of heaven is still on the "wheel" of reincarnation. It's a stage, not the ultimate goal. In fact, from a Hindu perspective, Christianity, when it focuses on individual heaven, is really missing the point. It's too egocentric.

Returning to the passage, consider the first three points. The third, that death is natural, is not problematic when taken on its own. The fact that death is natural and unavoidable doesn't mean that it needs to be hastened, nor does it mean that killing is just.

The second is problematic. If "Death is an illusion," what does it mean for ethics? What does it mean to kill? The sense of the word "illusion" is "not real" (Kramer 1988, 32), which is exactly how Kramer takes it. But if death isn't real, then killing someone isn't real either. By this notion, even murder is no big deal.

This is limited, to some degree, by the first condition. *Dharma can be translated, roughly, as doing what is right.* There is, therefore, a limit on killing (i.e., if it's not one's duty). *One is called, in deciding one's duty, to weigh whatever good or justice is to be achieved against the taking of a life.* The problem is that, *with this translation, the value of life doesn't carry much weight. It becomes very easy to justify taking a life for even relatively small injustices.* After all, death isn't real.

It seems that Krishna isn't all that compassionate a God. He seems utterly unconcerned with the value of human life.

Krishna goes on to deepen his concern with dharma or duty. What makes something one's duty? How does one know one's duty? One comes to know one's duty by "yoking" oneself to one's deepest inner self (*similar to the notion of* **discernment** *in Christianity*), to the divine. There are a variety of ways to do so, but they fall into three general categories:

Bhakti yoga: "Emotional, self-surrendering to the divine."
Jnana yoga: "Intellectual, intuitive, metaphysical contemplation."

Karma yoga: "Physical, self-sacrificial, detached activity" (Kramer 1988, 33) usually focused on service.

Arjuna, as a warrior, is focused on *karma yoga*. The goal of all three practices, however, is to allow one to be guided by one's true self, the Atman, the spiritual core in each of us.

What we have here is a resource for why killing might be bad. Not killing in general—remember, death is just an illusion. It's just that it might be against my inner guidance to kill you in this particular moment. In this weak formulation, Kramer appears to miss the point.

A major theme of Hinduism, as with most religions, is that reality happens on many levels. Kramer, as is natural for someone not part of that tradition, appears to have read this part on a fairly literal level.[1]

But *Krishna also operates on deeper levels, he sees what is hidden in Arjuna's heart.* Kramer's translation misses this crucial point.

All his life, Arjuna has been training for battle, though he has never fought in a real war. While his training would have involved risks of injury or death, it was not the same as a battle where his opponent's goal was to kill him. As the leader, he will be their ultimate target.

Arjuna was afraid.

Arjuna wasn't willing to admit his fear of death, even to himself. Instead, **he comes up with a noble sounding pretext, a self-serving rationality, to explain why they shouldn't go to war**: It wasn't about him, it was about valuing human life over land.

Krishna saw through Arjuna's self-deception. Krishna's advice, then, was less about what to do and more about "why" to do it. Put more radically, ***Krishna wasn't focused on having Arjuna fight per se, he was focused on having Arjuna be self-honest and make whatever choice for the right reasons.*** Krishna's main focus was on getting Arjuna to look within, not on the specific choice.

How does the translation of "death is an illusion" help to hide this alternative? First, if death is an illusion, it merely discounts Arjuna's argument. It also offers a certain comfort, on two levels. First, you're not "really" killing them. Second, by contrast, you won't "really" die. It relieves the fear not through self-honesty, but by convincing oneself that the object of one's fear isn't real.

What if the better translation is something like "**appearance**"? *The term "appearance" suggests that there is more to the reality than is on the surface. But it doesn't deny that the surface is also real.*

---

1 This does not appear to be typical of Kramer's reading, which is, particularly with Buddhism, subtle and profound.

Death is "real," it's just not exactly what it appears to be.

This is consistent with the Hindu notion that reality has depth and levels. It also does not deny that some teachers may, in fact, say that death isn't real. But the meaning is more subtle than simple illusion.

By acknowledging that death is "appearance" (real, but not exactly as it appears on the surface), Krishna is giving weight to Arjuna's argument. If death is truly an illusion, then the taking of a life is a minor thing. If it is real, and if life is thought to be a value, then *only a duty of great importance can justify the taking of a life*.

The stakes are now high and with them, the call to discernment all the more urgent. Arjuna will not go to war merely for a piece of land. Instead, his decision will be based on the question of whether this involves issues of justice important enough to risk the loss of life.

We can see how complex understanding someone else's scriptures can be. In a sense, it's really no different than the complexity of understanding one's own scriptures. It's just that we were raised to believe our own. When faced with what looks like a "problem" in someone else's scripture we are far more likely to simply say it's a problem, failing to explore further. Meanwhile, if it is "our" scripture, we are far more likely to search for ways to resolve, dismiss, or explain such a problem away.

As we move to our primary text, consider the following themes:

1. What is the role of self-deception? What is its connection to pride?
2. How many times must Siddhartha "start again"? How does this relate to the Christian notion of being like a little child?
3. What is the role of both experience and intellect? How do they relate?
4. In the end, how and why does Siddhartha's attitude towards enlightenment change?
5. Why doesn't Govinda achieve enlightenment?

Siddhartha

Siddhartha was born the son of a **Brahmin** (not to be confused with **Brahman**). In the caste system of the time, the Brahmin were most commonly in charge of the temples. Siddhartha, even among this highly educated caste, stood out as extraordinarily intelligent, handsome, and gifted. His closest friend was **Govinda**.

In time, Siddhartha became dissatisfied with merely studying the holy teachings. He began to feel that the love of home, friends, and family and the studies of the temple would not always satisfy him. He asked himself:

But where were the Brahmins, the priests, the wise men, who were successful not only in having this profound knowledge, but in experiencing it? Where were the initiated who, attaining the Atman in sleep, could retain it in consciousness, in life, everywhere, in speech and in action? Siddhartha knew many worthy Brahmins, above all, his father — holy, learned, of highest esteem. ... but even he who knew so much, did he live in bliss, was he at peace? (Hesse 1951, 7)

Hesse is highlighting the difference between intellectual and experiential knowledge. Right at the beginning of the text, Hesse is making it clear that this is about more than intellectual knowledge. The goal, realizing (becoming fully conscious of) the **Atman** (the spiritual spark that is the core of each of our existences) while still alive, is what many term "enlightenment." For reasons we will explore later, the term cannot be precisely defined. ***For the moment, we will simply refer to enlightenment as being "awake," taking in and accepting reality without self-deception***, with minimal or no filters. *Siddhartha believes,* as do many, *that to achieve this state,* while extraordinarily difficult, *is also to find ultimate peace and bliss. This alone appears to make it a worthwhile endeavor. Siddhartha determines to go after it with single-minded devotion.*

Was the Atman not within him? Was not the source within his own heart? One must find the source within one's own Self, one must possess it. Everything else was seeking—a detour, error. (Hesse 1951, 7)

Siddhartha is first drawn to the Samanas, wandering ascetics. The notion of the ascetic shows up in every religion; these are people who seek spiritual growth through denying themselves worldly or physical comforts. Some religious ascetics merely fast and live a minimal existence, others actively seek to break the hold of the physical on their lives through various self-inflicted punishments such as flogging.

But first, coming from a culture in which parents and elders are held in great respect, Siddhartha seeks the permission of his father. Initially, his father is upset and denies his request. Siddhartha, however, is determined. He remains standing, unmoving, silent unless spoken to, waiting for permission. After standing there all night, his father yields, but makes two requests.

1. "If you find bliss ... come back and teach it to me."
2. "If you find disillusionment," come home anyway. (Hesse 1951, 12)

Siddhartha never returns home.

As he is leaving, he meets Govinda.

Govinda?

If one were to choose an animal to describe Govinda, what might that animal be? Most of my students end up choosing a dog—more precisely, a puppy. As the story progresses, we see that Govinda is a wonderful, kind, and generous human being. He is cheerful, eager to please, and a follower.

Govinda follows Siddhartha into the forest.

The Samanas

Living in the forest, Siddhartha attempts to become aware of the Atman by denying all worldly comforts and pleasures. He eats just enough to sustain life. He learns the practices of fasting and self-denial. He meditates. Siddhartha's goal is to still (quiet) the "ego" (self) and to fully awake to the "Atman" (or true self). But remember, the Atman is not individualized. To realize it, one must empty oneself:

> Siddhartha had one single goal—to become empty, to become empty of thirst, desire, dreams, pleasure and sorrow—to let the Self die. No longer to be a Self, to experience the peace of an emptied heart, to experience pure thought—that was his goal. When all the Self was conquered and dead, when all passions and desires were silent, then the last must awaken, the innermost of Being that is no longer Self—the great secret. (Hesse 1951, 14)

Siddhartha was successful, in a sense. He lost himself again and again, through technique after technique, but there was always the return. It was never Nirvana, just a temporary forgetfulness.

From these repeated efforts, Siddhartha becomes suspicious. What if there is something fundamentally flawed in this approach to seeking spiritual awakening? Part of the answer, he suspects, has to do with the nature of knowledge itself:

> ... I am beginning to realize that this knowledge has no worse enemy than the man of knowledge, than learning. (Hesse 1951, 19; emphasis added)

The Banker and the Attorney

One day a wealthy banker is walking through the city. It is lunchtime, but he is on his way back to the bank. As he walks by a large church, something moves him so he steps inside. The church is empty. The banker is drawn to the altar, looks up, and is overcome. He kneels before the altar. Striking his chest with balled fists, he cries out to God:

"Oh lord, I am nothing, I am nothing ..."

He repeats the phrase many times. In the meantime, a celebrated attorney hears a noise from the street and enters the church. Seeing his friend so moved, he too is moved, kneels next to him before the altar, and, striking his chest, cries out:

"Oh lord, I too am nothing, I too am nothing ..."

A short while later, the janitor returns from his lunch. Seeing two such powerful men expressing such emotion, he kneels at the back of the church. Striking his chest, he follows the lead of the attorney:

"Oh lord, I too am nothing, I too am nothing ..."

After a while, the attorney nudges the banker. Indicating the back of the church, he whispers:

"Now look who thinks he's nothing ..."

In fact, he has come to suspect something very close to what Vivian's teacher tried to tell her in the play *Wit*.

> *Simple human truth, uncompromising scholarly standards, they're connected. …*
> (00:10:35; emphasis added)

If this "knowledge" that Siddhartha seeks is more experiential than intellectual, then too much "intellectual" learning, without a foundation in experience, can actually block one's spiritual growth.

But this is not Siddhartha's only barrier to self-awareness. Though Siddhartha learned the practices of fasting and self-denial, it's important to note another practice that Siddhartha learned from the Samanas. We can illustrate this through the story of the Banker and the Attorney:

The vice, of course, is **Pride**. It's a very subtle form of pride, disguising itself even as humility. But, as many spiritual teachers will attest, it is probably the greatest hindrance to spiritual growth.

How does this relate to Siddhartha and the Samanas? Siddhartha, while giving up everything worldly, believed himself to be "better" than those who had not made the same choices. "His gaze became icy when he encountered women, his lips curled with contempt when he passed through a town of well-dressed people" (Hesse 1951, 13). He became arrogant.

In time, Siddhartha realizes that, just as there had been no one among the Brahmins who had fully "experienced" the awakening (nirvana), so too there was no one among the Samanas (Hesse 1951, 18). Still, rumors have been circulating about one who has experienced this awaking, this nirvana. He is the one they call Gotama Buddha.[2] Govinda is eager to hear his teachings. Siddhartha, though increasingly suspicious of the value of any teaching, agrees to accompany his friend.

Gotama Buddha

When they meet the Buddha, Siddhartha is profoundly moved, but not by his teachings. Siddhartha is moved by Buddha's presence.

> *Siddhartha saw him and recognized him immediately, as if pointed out to him by a god. He saw him, bearing an alms bowl, quietly leaving the place, an unassuming man in a yellow cowl. (Hesse 1951, 27)*

Govinda needed some help to recognize the Buddha. Just below the surface, there was a powerful and compassionate presence about the Buddha. For Siddhartha, this

---

2 I'm using Hesse's spelling here (Gotama), but it is also spelled as "Gautama" Buddha.

was confirmation of what he had sought almost his entire life; it was possible to reach nirvana. Buddha was living proof.

But whereas Govinda becomes a follower (has the puppy has found a new alpha?), Siddhartha does not. Govinda is shocked that Siddhartha would not also follow the Buddha. Hesse constructs a conversation between Siddhartha and the Buddha to explain. Siddhartha asks Buddha:

> Oh Illustrious One, in one thing above all I admired your teachings. Everything is completely clear and proved. … But … this unity and logical consequence of all things is broken in one place. Through a small gap there streams into the world of unity something strange, something that was not there before and that cannot be demonstrated and proved: that is your doctrine of rising above the world, of salvation. (Hesse 1951, 32)

Buddha acknowledged that this was true, then replied:

> [The goal of my teachings] is not to explain the world to those who are thirsty for knowledge. Its goal is quite different; its goal is salvation from suffering. That is what Gotama teaches, nothing else. (Hesse 1951, 33)

I believe this illustrates a profound understanding on the part of Hesse. When we discuss Buddhism, we will see that one could argue that there is no "logical" connection between the experience of nirvana and an outpouring of compassion. In fact, one could even construct an argument that compassion should be left behind. Yet, as Kramer points out, this is not what happened:

> The essence of Buddha's spiritual realization expressed itself as unconditional, selfless compassion for all creatures even at death. Dying while still alive, Buddha discovered the art of dying before dying. …"(Kramer 1988, 47)[3]

Somehow, when one reaches the highest stage of spiritual realization, something happens. One is turned back to the world, back to a sense of profound compassion and love. Buddha, knowing that most people aren't ready to take the full step into nirvana, constructed a teaching to help reduce their suffering. No doubt, it also helped many of them spiritually. Buddha also realized that, in the end, the final step was something each person had to take on their own.

Siddhartha senses that, and asks:

> But there is one thing that this clear, worthy instruction does not contain; it does not contain the secret of what the Illustrious One himself experienced—he alone among hundreds of thousands. … That is why I am going on my way—not to seek another and

---

3   The passage finishes with "discovered the assurance that there is no reality in one's physical death." I leave that off for reasons given in the discussion of Krishna and Arjuna.

better doctrine, for I know there is none, but to leave all doctrines and all teachers and to reach my goal alone—or die. (Hesse 1951, 34)

The shift appears to be fundamental to both Hinduism and Buddhism, that **scriptures and teachers can only take one so far. But it's also found in Christianity.** This is part of the problem we discussed in the chapter on faith, where even scripture can become an idol. Even if inspired, what is really sought is the source that inspired scripture. No matter how intelligent the human mind, it can at best only begin to express the nature of physical reality, to say nothing of the divine. In the end, as Kramer writes, and as many Christian writers would agree, the goal of the various practices (yogas) and scriptures is as follows:

… when one died yogically (with mindful concentration and absorption into the Self) … at that point forms and rituals vanish, sacred texts are superseded, temples are transcended. (Kramer 1988, 35)

We pass beyond scriptures to whatever it is at their source.

This is beyond that which can be said, beyond that which can be captured in language.

In the presence of the holy one, Siddhartha regains a measure of humility. He has met someone truly beyond himself. He knows the goal can be reached. But now, when asked about others becoming monks rather than striking out on their own, Siddhartha replies:

It is not for me to judge another life. I must judge for myself. I must choose and reject. We Samanas seek release from the Self, O Illustrious One. If I were to become one of your followers, I fear that it would only be on the surface, that I would deceive myself … while in truth the Self would continue to grow. …" (Hesse 1951, 34–35)

Buddha, seeing into Siddhartha's heart, *cautions him against his own cleverness.* In turn, Siddhartha comes to a new insight. All his life, Siddhartha had been seeking to escape the (ego) self. Yet, he had never taken the time to get to know that side of himself, to understand it. This is why, in part, it kept returning. This is fundamental to much of Eastern spirituality: if enlightenment is fundamentally an experience (actually, this is problematic, but it will work for now), it can only be found through experience. Denying oneself, intellectual knowledge, and fasting, while useful skills, are not sufficient.

"He has robbed me," thinks Siddhartha, "… He has robbed me of my friend [Govinda] … But he has given me Siddhartha, myself" (Hesse 1951, 36).

Appearance versus Illusion

Siddhartha sets out to experience life. As he travels, he thinks to himself:

> *What is it that you wanted to learn from teachings and teachers? ... I wanted to rid myself of the Self, to conquer it, but I could not conquer it, I could only deceive it. ... (Hesse 1951, 38)*

By deceiving it, we return to the old theme of self-deception. Siddhartha had spent so much time and energy seeking the Atman, the Brahman, that he "lost himself along the way" (Hesse 1951, 38). Siddhartha resolves to reverse his path:

> *I will no longer try to escape from Siddhartha. ... I will learn from myself, be my own pupil; I will learn the secret of Siddhartha. (Hesse 1951, 38)*

As he settles into this resolve, something changes:

> *He looked around as if seeing the world for the first time. The world was beautiful, strange, and mysterious. Here was blue, here was yellow, here was green, sky and river, woods and mountains, all beautiful, mysterious, and enchanting. (Hesse 1951, 38)*

Return to our discussion of "**appearance**" versus "**illusion**." Previously, Siddhartha had been treating the world and self almost entirely as illusion. While the world and his "self" may not have been all of reality, or perhaps even the most important parts, they are real and important. Yes, there is more to each than is on the surface. But the surface is also real and is part of the way inside. The world is no longer illusion, it is a place of wonder and beauty.

And now, we again see a theme familiar not just to Christians, but to every religion:

> *Then suddenly this also was clear to him: he was in fact like one who had awakened or was newly born, must begin his life completely afresh. (Hesse 1951, 40)*

Or from Matthew 3:18:

> *... unless you change and become like little children ...*

The Analogy to Love

Kramer also notes how this experience, what we in the West refer to as conversion and rebirth, appears to be part of every religious tradition. He describes it as follows:

As we shall see, to die spiritually before dying is to be reborn, fearless in the face of death. A spiritual death is self-transcendence, it is getting outside prior confines of the self or, as it is analogously expressed in many traditions, is like falling unreservedly and compassionately in love. It is not a matter of choice. (Kramer 1988, 24; emphasis added)

I believe Kramer is correct in his analogy, though I might nuance it differently. To get at that difference, ask yourself, what is love?

Most people can say that they have been "in" love at some point in their lives, but few can say what love means. Clearly, infatuation is not a matter of choice. What Kramer means is much deeper. Is love really not a matter of choice?

Buddha, as we will see, preferred compassion to love. Siddhartha still used the term love but claimed that he and Buddha have the same meaning. Part of what we will explore, in the nature of spirituality, is the nature of love. Here is a simple start:

Love is when another person's well-being becomes as important, or more important, than my own.

Infatuation can start us on that road, but it cannot sustain us. We can truly love others for whom there is no infatuation or romantic connection. I can love a friend or a child.

At the same time, while I can force myself to act in loving ways, I cannot truly "force" myself to love another. This is particularly true of romantic love. In that sense at least, it is not a choice. It is a gift. But is it *only* a gift?

When I was married, one of my teachers, John Lachs[4], gave me some sage advice. I was married to a woman who felt that anything done for one's partner, if not done entirely because one wanted to give in that moment, was really just a lie. She tended to only do kind things when she felt like it.

On the other hand, I cultivated certain habits. I knew what she liked for breakfast, so even when I didn't have to get up, I often got up and made it for her. I was not a perfect husband, but I made efforts to make her life easier and to express care.

John told me that love, in this case romantic love, was both a gift and a choice. It was a gift in two ways. First, it was a gift to find one who was a good "match," the right sort of person who matched up to oneself. Second, it was a gift from the other person in their choosing to be open to the relationship and to actions that sustained the relationship. So already, one level of gift has a choice made by another involved.

Similarly, we "choose" to be open to the gift of love. It's not that we force love, but we can shut it down, along with ourselves. We also choose, *even when we aren't feeling it*, to cultivate habits of care or service to that other person. While this would be a problem if one never really "felt" that they wanted to be with and do things for the other, habitual acts of caring, when performed on both sides, go a long way toward sustaining and regenerating the goodwill that is at the heart of love.

---

4 I am profoundly grateful to John Lachs for his kindness and wisdom.

My ex understood the gift part, but not the choice. Here is where I would nuance Kramer's statement differently:

It is not *only* a matter a choice ...

There is a fine line, in spirituality and in love, between gift and choice. One cannot force either. But there is a choice both in being open to spirituality and in acting to sustain one's spirituality. The same can be said for love.

Similarly, love needs to undergo rebirths (new moments of conversion) from time to time.

Rebirth

In this moment of rebirth (conversion, spiritual death, and rebirth), Siddhartha has a lot to learn. He is restarting his life. He also has a number of things to "unlearn." One of these is spiritual pride.

Consider his interaction with the Ferryman. He has just left the Buddha, he is awash in life, and he is no longer as arrogant as he was with the Samanas. Yet, he thinks of the Ferryman, who will later become Siddhartha's teacher:

> He is like Govinda, he thought, smiling. All whom I meet are like Govinda. All are grateful, although they themselves deserve thanks. All are subservient, all wish to be my friend, to obey and to think little. People are children. (Hesse 1951, 49)

One could almost imagine Siddhartha patting the Ferryman on the head as they depart.

Siddhartha is not ready to be taught. Siddhartha needs to spend time in the world, learning about the world and himself. But it's interesting that, whereas he so readily recognized Buddha, he was unable to see the deeper nature of the Ferryman.

Like Vivian from *Wit*, and even Ivan, Siddhartha has lived most of his life in his intellect. Each has done so in somewhat different ways, but each has denied themselves basic human experiences and *lived* truths. Hinduism, even more than Christianity, has as a basic tenant that one must find truth (enlightenment, salvation) through living; one can't just bypass experience. This doesn't mean that everyone needs the same types of experiences. We are all different. But one's path cannot be done without real engagement in the world.

It might also be tempting, given what Siddhartha is saying, to take this approach as anti-intellectual. This would be a mistake. Consider, for example, the years that Hesse spent studying Hindu and Buddhist writings as well as practicing what they propose. *While reflection without experience is empty, experience without reflection is meaningless.* Like Vivian in *Wit*, we need both:

Simple human truth, uncompromising scholarly standards, they're connected. ...
(00:10:35; emphasis added)

However, in this case, the goal is also to get beyond both, to something different. As with the self, unless one also does the "work" to understand, instead of truly transcending, one will become lost in self-deception.

Siddhartha has spent most of his life developing mental discipline. Now, he needs to balance. He goes to live in the world, as others might live. There, he meets the beautiful Kamala.

Kamala

Kamala was a courtesan, a high-class prostitute. As such, her status was probably far better than most women of her time. She owned property, servants, served no one except by choice, and had freedoms that were rare for a woman of the time. Siddhartha spotted her just as he was entering the town. He was transfixed.

> He looked at that sedan chair and the woman in it. Beneath heaped-up black hair he saw a bright, very sweet, very clever face, a bright red mouth like a freshly cut fig, artful eyebrows painted in a high arch, dark eyes, clever and observant, and a clear slender neck above her green and gold gown. ... his heart rejoiced. (Hesse 1951, 51)

After this, Siddhartha had one goal. He washed, got a shave and a haircut, and made himself presentable to meet the lovely Kamala. When he is brought to her chambers, after thanking her for her beauty, he asks her to be his "friend and teacher," for "I do not know anything of the art of which you are mistress" (Hesse 1951, 53).

Kamala is pleased and impressed by the handsome Siddhartha. She is also a businesswoman. She tells him that he needs to earn money, to dress in better clothes, and to return. He asks further advice; she asks his skills. Siddhartha replies, "I think, I can wait, I can fast" (Hesse 1951, 56). Nothing else? Oh! Siddhartha replies, I can compose poetry.

For the poem he offers her, and perhaps as further encouragement, she kisses him deeply, expertly.

The conversation continues, wherein she learns that he can also read and write. This is a marketable skill. Kamala sends Siddhartha to meet the merchant, Kamaswami.

There is a wonderful example of **confirmation bias** at the end of this chapter. Kamala thinks that it is good fortune that Siddhartha met her and Kamaswami. Siddhartha believes that is has nothing at all to do with fortune. Kamala asks, what if I had not wanted to help you? Siddhartha replies:

> *But you did want. Listen, Kamala, when you throw a stone into the water, it finds the quickest way to the bottom of the water. It is the same when Siddhartha has an aim, a goal. Siddhartha does nothing; he waits, he thinks, he fasts, but he goes through the affairs of the world like a stone through water, without doing anything ... he is drawn and lets himself fall.* (Hesse 1951, 60)

Here we see a bit of the attitude of control from *What Dreams May Come*. Again, there is some truth to the claim. But it is not the whole truth. As Kamala whispers to herself:

> *Perhaps it is as you say, my friend ... and perhaps it is also because Siddhartha is a handsome man. ...* (Hesse 1951, 60–61)

Life as a Merchant

Kamaswami is similarly impressed with Siddhartha. Since reading and writing are uncommon skills, he takes Siddhartha on and teaches him the business. At the beginning, their attitudes are profoundly different:

> *Kamaswami conducted his business with care and often with passion, but Siddhartha regarded it all as a game, the rules of which he endeavored to learn well, but which did not stir his passion.* (Hesse 1951, 66)

What did stir Siddhartha was Kamala, for whom the work provided the fine clothing and presents required. While Kamaswani realized that Siddhartha didn't have the basic attitude of a merchant, he realized that Siddhartha had another gift. His very patience (waiting), kindness, and sincere listening drew others to Siddhartha. Kamaswami realized that this was another route to success.

Kamaswami came to trust Siddhartha and consult him in all major matters. In order to increase his involvement, Kamaswami gave Siddhartha a third of the profits that Siddhartha earned. This produced odd results. It didn't initially change Siddhartha. In fact, on one occasion, Siddhartha went to a village to purchase rice. When Siddhartha arrived, the rice had already been sold. Despite this, Siddhartha stayed in the village for several days, visiting, making friends, even giving children money. Kamaswami was upset at both the lost time and money. But Siddhartha merely agreed to make up the money from his own profits from other ventures.

Why was Siddhartha so successful? What was it about his approach to business? First of all, Siddhartha did work hard, he was careful and thoughtful. But work did not consume him. Siddhartha knew that making money was not an end in itself but was a means to other ends. In this case, money meant more time and learning with Kamala. For most, it would be about whatever they needed to live and be happy.

One might then ask, what was it about Siddhartha's early training that made him so successful? It wasn't just the skills, but also the *detachment*. This can be best illustrated with a story.

Detachment

Example: Denny and Bill

While I was undergoing my clinical training, a group of nurses kept trying to convince me to go dancing. It was a kindness as they knew I was undergoing a divorce. We ended up at a dance studio in Nashville.

I knew of bit of swing from college, but nothing had prepared me for what I saw when I got to the studio. These were some of the top amateur dancers in the country. Though many had not trained there, they came there to dance. It was absolutely beautiful.

It was also utterly intimidating.

I watched for a while but never got on the floor. As I left, Denny, one of the owners, came out to talk with me. He asked how I was doing and why I didn't try to dance. I told him how I felt, both about the beauty and the intimidation. Denny acknowledged that it was often intimidating at the beginning, particularly for men (since we are supposed to lead). He told me that I should feel welcome to come back anytime. If all I wanted to do was watch, then I didn't have to pay. Whenever I felt comfortable trying to dance, then I could pay.

His kindness touched me.

I started taking lessons.

After a time, Denny sold his part of the business to Bill. The story was that it wasn't really making enough to support two owners, but it may have also been about different management styles. At first, the people who were used to coming to the studio continued. Bill, however, had a very different attitude towards the business.

Denny's attitude was that, if you make it fun, then they will come. He wasn't worried about squeezing every dime out of the business, nor was he worried about whether someone might take advantage of his generosity. He was "detached" from the need to maximize his immediate profit.

Bill, on the other hand, had previously been a pawn broker. In that business, he was used to having to struggle with people trying to take advantage of him financially. He was far more focused on running it as a profit-maximizing business.

It wasn't as much fun to be with Bill. Sometimes you got a sense that he thought you were trying to take advantage of him. That didn't feel welcome. Policies began to reflect this attitude. For example, under Denny, people taking private lessons at the studio were used to being able to come in and practice for free. Bill, however, started charging floor fees for practice time. Then other fees as well. People felt that they were being nickeled and dimed.

As a result, fewer and fewer people came. The staff and the teachers also began to leave, as new policies were instituted that burdened them.

Eventually, the studio closed.

Denny, in time, opened a new studio. He made it fun to be there. He treated both staff and students well, focusing on the big picture rather than on maximizing immediate profit.

The result? It's now one of the largest and highest quality studios in the country, with multiple US champions teaching there. The students are among the most successful competitors in the country. There's also a lively social dance community. Denny ended up making far more than he ever could have had he followed Bill's practices.

The bottom line? Denny, like Siddhartha, focused on relationships. He was sufficiently able to detach (stand back from) immediate profit to see the big picture and then place the business in that context. He worked hard on the business, but it wasn't just about the money. He had a greater vision.[5]

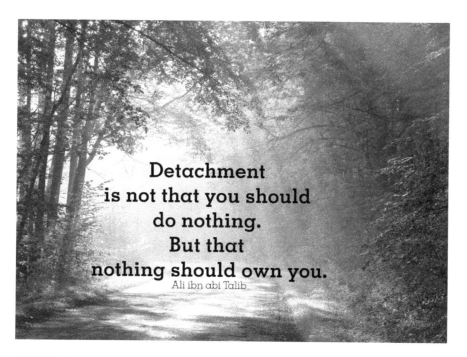

FIGURE 11.1

---

5 As an aside, Bill also found an excellent niche for himself. Instead of running a studio, he organizes and promotes events, which he does a fine job at.

Another Side of Detachment

Detachment comes in many forms and levels, some not as helpful as others. The same detachment that allowed Siddhartha to stand back from the business, and in fact to be more successful, also kept him from truly loving. Siddhartha notes that Kamala has a similar ability:

> You are like me; you are different from other people. You are Kamala and no one else, and within you there is a stillness and sanctuary to which you can retreat at any time and be yourself, just as I can. Few people have that capacity, and yet everyone could have it. (Hesse 1951, 71–71)

Kamala replies:

> Again you have Samana thoughts. ... You are the best lover I have ever had. ... And yet, my dear, you do not really love me—you love nobody. Is that not true? (Hesse 1951, 72–72)

> "Maybe," said Siddhartha wearily, "I am like you. You cannot love either, otherwise, how could you practice love as an art? Perhaps people like us cannot love. Ordinary people can—that is their secret." (Hesse 1951, 73)

The Ability of Love

For Siddhartha to learn this secret, he had to become more like other people, be born yet again anew. For this, he had to lose himself, or what he was.

> For a long time Siddhartha had lived the life of the world without belonging to it. His senses, which he had deadened during his ardent Samana years, were again awakened. ... Slowly, like moisture entering the dying tree trunk, slowly filling and rotting it, so did the world and inertia creep into Siddhartha's soul; it slowly filled his soul, made it heavy, made it tired, sent it to sleep. But on the other hand his senses became more awakened, they learned a great deal. ... (Hesse 1951, 75–77)

Siddhartha still thought of himself as different than, and superior to, his companions. This was not the case. Increasingly, he pursued property for the sake of wealth and sensation for the sake of sensation. He gambled, drank, and woke with the soul sickness of the rich, then gambled and drank again.

Overcome with self-loathing, Siddhartha eventually walks away from his life as a wealthy man. He fails to say goodbye even to Kamala, who discovers, after he is gone, that she is pregnant with his child. He wanders the forest, wishing only to end it, hoping that perhaps a tiger will chance upon him and finish the job.

Then, he reaches the river of so long ago. He is about to drown himself when he hears:

> ... from a remote part of his soul, from the past of his tired life, he heard a sound. It was one word, one syllable, ... the Holy Om. ... At that moment, when the sound of Om reached Siddhartha's ears, his slumbering soul suddenly awakened. ... (Hesse 1951, 89)

Siddhartha is horrified at what he had been about to do, but also, now, awakened to "indestructibleness of life; he remembered what he had forgotten, all that was divine" (Hesse 1951, 89).

He is also exhausted. Siddhartha falls asleep, the first deep and peaceful sleep he has experienced in years. When he wakes, there is a monk watching over him.

Govinda, now a kind monk, is worried that some ill might befall the exhausted man. So, he stops and watches while Siddhartha sleeps. Siddhartha recognizes Govinda, but it takes a while for Govinda to recognize Siddhartha. Govinda comments on Siddhartha's clothes. Siddhartha replies:

> The wheel of appearances revolves quickly, Govinda. Where is Siddhartha the Brahmin, where is Siddhartha the Samana, where is Siddhartha the rich man? (Hesse 1951, 94)

It's worth noting that here, we see the choice of the term "appearances" rather than "illusion," though this is a translation from German rather than Hindi. Moreover, while the goal is still to transcend all teachings, it worth noting that, had Siddhartha not had the teachings of his youth to fall back on, he would likely have stayed on in the nausea of his wealthy existence. Those teachings gave him the chance to be transformed.

Govinda, though confused by Siddhartha's comment, moves on, while Siddhartha again begins anew:

> Now ... I stand once more beneath the sun, as I stood once as a small child. Nothing is mine, I know nothing. How strange it is! How, when I am no longer young, when my hair is fast growing gray, when strength begins to diminish, how I am beginning again like a child. (Hesse 1951, 95)

Siddhartha is, finally, ready to recognize and let go of his pride:

> He had been full of arrogance; he had always been the cleverest, the most eager—always a step ahead. ... His Self had crawled into this priesthood, into this arrogance, into this intellectually. It sat there tightly and grew, while he thought he was destroying it by fasting and penitence. (Hesse 1951, 99)

The Ferryman (Vesudeva)

Siddhartha is powerfully drawn to the river. Somehow, he senses that, for him at least, the river can be his teacher. In his heart, he hears, "Love this river, stay by it, learn from it" (Hesse 1951, 101). The first lesson he learns immediately. He doesn't fully understand it, but he feels it:

> He saw that the water continually flowed and flowed and yet it was always there: it was always the same and yet every moment it was new. (Hesse 1951, 102)

One can't help but be reminded of the words of Heraclitus, one of the earliest Greek philosophers, who said, "One never bathes in the same river twice." This is the paradox of moving water, of identity and difference, of something that is never the same, and yet, is always the same. We face the same paradox when we think of consciousness and our metaphors of space and projection. Consciousness is the very space and play of novelty; it is where we change. Yet, it is also at the very core of our identity and how we are the same. The very temporal dynamism exhibited in both a river and consciousness, or in the moment of the ocean, is perhaps part of our attraction to water or music, which similarly exist only as temporal activities.

Drawn as he is to the water, Siddhartha remembers the Ferryman from so long ago. He decides to seek him out. Not, initially, to be his teacher, but as someone with whom he can live at peace while learning from the river. Little does he know that the Ferryman has also learned from the river. Siddhartha tells the Ferryman his story. The Ferryman gives Siddhartha a great gift, he listens:

> Vasudeva listened with great attention ... Without saying a word, the speaker felt that Vasudeva took in every word, quietly, expectantly, that he missed nothing. He did not await ... with impatience and gave neither praise nor blame—he only listened. (Hesse 1951, 104)

When Siddhartha is done, he thanks Vesudeva, who tells him that the river has spoken to Siddhartha. He offers to share his hut and work with Siddhartha and tells him that Siddhartha, too, will learn from the river. First, he will learn to listen. Then, he will learn the "other" thing.

Vesudeva is unable to name that other thing. Siddhartha will have to discover it for himself. Later, we learn that there is no such thing as time (Hesse 1951, 106). On one level, perhaps he means it is an illusion. On another, it may mean that time is not a "thing" at all, but not that it isn't real. Time is one of those "terms" that is so basic to our reality it evokes the nature of mystery. And again, looking for a quick answer is to miss the point. A mystery cannot be "solved," in part

The biggest
communication problem
is that we do not listen
to understand.
We listen to reply.

FIGURE 11.2

because it speaks to a reality that goes beyond the division of words. It can still be engaged. How?

Siddhartha learns a great deal from Vesudeva, but he learns even more from the river:

> Above all, he learned from it how to listen, to listen with a still heart, with a waiting, open soul, without passion, without desire, without judgment, without opinions. (Hesse 1951, 106)

What a gift! How often do we "listen" to one another? But our focus isn't really on listening. We listen for what we want to say next, for how we can be clever, and for something we want. Instead, we are seeking rather than listening.

Listening. This, in my mind, is a key to all spirituality. Indeed, to all philosophy. Only when we learn to listen, to be receptive, can we learn to see.

Siddhartha becomes more and more like the Ferryman. Travelers are drawn to them—their smiles, their inner peace—and tell them of their troubles. Some believe they are brothers. Years pass.

Fatherhood

The word goes out that the Buddha is dying. Many travel to see him before he passes. Among them is Kamala, who travels with her young son. As she reaches the river, she is bitten by a poisonous snake. Seeking help, they come upon Siddhartha. He cares for her, comforts her, but cannot save her. She introduces him to his son. Kamala sees something new in Siddhartha's eyes; he is different, yet the same. She asks, "Have you attained it, ... have you found peace? ... Yes, I see it. I will also find peace" (Hesse 1951, 113).

> *Kamala looked at him steadily. It had been her intention to make a pilgrimage to Gotama, to see the face of the Illustrious One, to obtain some of his peace, and instead she had found only Siddhartha, and it was good, just as good as if she had seen the other. (Hesse 1951, 113)*

Has Siddhartha become enlightened?

The next morning, after Kamala has died, Vesudeva speaks to Siddhartha. "You have not slept." Siddhartha replies, "No, Vesudeva, I sat here by the river and listened ..." Vesudeva goes on, "You have suffered, Siddhartha, yet I see that sadness has not entered your heart." "No, my dear friend. Why should I be sad? ... My son has been given to me" (Hesse 1951, 114–115).

Lest this seem cold, remember that different people use different language. For Siddhartha, being with Kamala when she died was a great honor. While Hesse uses terms like the sense of the "unity of all creation" and the "indestructibleness of every life," there is also a sense, in more Western terms, of love. He suffers, but it takes him to a place where the suffering is a witness to something else; it is witness to the gift. The suffering does not dominate Siddhartha.

As happy as Siddhartha is to have a son, the joy is not shared. Siddhartha's son is used to being rich and spoiled. Living a simple life is not what he wants or expects. This gentle man is a stranger to him. He is used to commanding servants. So, he acts out. He refuses to do work and steals from their fruit trees. He brings only sorrow and trouble to their lives (Hesse 1951, 117–118). Siddhartha is gentle and patient. He knows it was a shock to the boy and he hopes to win him over with time.

> *Siddhartha began to realize that no happiness and peace had come to him with his son, only sorrow and trouble. But he loved him and preferred the sorrow and trouble of his love rather than happiness and pleasure without the boy. (Hesse 1951, 118)*

We asked, awhile ago, if Siddhartha was enlightened. For some, enlightenment means all knowledge, a life of bliss, and the land of milk and honey (Caplan 1999, 35). But not here. Clearly, Siddhartha doesn't know how to be a father. While gentleness is important, he doesn't understand that young children also need boundaries and discipline. When his son lashes out and Siddhartha reacts only with kindness, it merely shames the boy all the more, and feeds his resentment and sense of entitlement more deeply (Hesse 1951, 120).

Vesudeva sees that the boy cannot be happy here and that he needs discipline. He tells Siddhartha that the boy is, like all, called, just not to their path. "His sorrows will not be slight. His heart is proud and hard" (Hesse 1951, 119). He advises, gently, that Siddhartha take his son to the town to be raised by Kamala's servants.

In his heart, Siddhartha knows that Vesudeva is right. Yet he cannot bring himself to let go of his son.

> ... Stronger than his knowledge was his love for the boy, his devotion, his fear of losing him. Had he ever loved anybody so much, so blindly, so painfully, so hopelessly and yet so happily? ... He could not give up his son. (Hesse 1951, 121)

In this love, Siddhartha at last becomes like the common people.

> ... He had never fully lost himself in another person to such an extreme as to forget himself; he had never undergone the follies of love for another person. ... It had seemed to him that this was the biggest difference between him and the ordinary people. (Hesse 1951, 122)

In doing so, Siddhartha is transformed. "He suffered tremendously ... and yet was uplifted, in some way renewed and richer" (Hesse 1951, 122).

Finally, the boy has enough. He steals their life savings and takes the ferry across the river, leaving it there. He discards the oar, most likely as an act of revenge. When Siddhartha wants to go after him, Vesudeva reminds Siddhartha that this is what the boy wants, that he is no longer a child, that, just as Siddhartha, he needs to find his own way.

Siddhartha searches for the boy, coming at last to the entrance of the garden where he first met Kamala. Memories come flooding back. As he stands there, he realizes:

> Siddhartha realized that the desire that had driven him to this place was foolish, that he could not help his son, that he should not force himself on him. He felt a deep love for the runaway boy, like a wound, and yet felt at the same time that this wound was not intended to fester in him, but that it should heal. (Hesse 1951, 126)

Siddhartha sits at the entrance to the garden, lost in thought, meditation, and sadness. He listens for the river, for the sound of Om. Eventually, a hand touches his shoulder. It is Vesudeva, come to bring him home.

Something more has changed in Siddhartha. The wound continues to ache. But there is something positive as well. He notices that even the wicked love their children. He now understands.

He now regarded people in a different light than he had previously: not very clever, not very proud and therefore all the more warm, curious and sympathetic. ... he now felt as if these ordinary people were his brothers ... These people were worthy of his love and [even] admiration. ... (Hesse 1951, 129 130; emphasis added)

Has Siddhartha, in a sense, become a child yet again, in another way? Another even more subtle level of pride has fallen away. Perhaps he wasn't enlightened before? *Or perhaps*, is it possible that *enlightenment comes in stages*?

Does Siddhartha even care now whether he becomes enlightened? Is that still even a concern?

Perhaps the loss of that concern is critical to the process?

If so, there is yet another stage.

Siddhartha bears his wound well, but at times it overcomes him. He reflects on his own father, and how his own disappearance must have hurt him. One day he almost returns to the town to seek his son. Catching himself, or rather, caught by the voice of the river, he returns to Vesudeva.

As when he first arrived, Siddhartha pours his heart out to Vesudeva. Vesudeva listens.[6] Again, without judgment or agenda, "absorbing his confession as a tree absorbs the rain" (Hesse 1951, 133). In this moment, Siddhartha also sees Vesudeva as for the first time; he sees him as the river, as God Himself (Hesse 1951, 133). He also realizes that Vesudeva has been waiting a long time for this moment.

When Siddhartha is finished speaking, Vesudeva takes him back to the river to listen. As Siddhartha learns to listen deeper, deeper than ever before, all the sounds and voices of the river merge into a single syllable of creation: Om. "Vesudeva's smile was radiant. ... [Siddhartha's] wound was healing, his pain dispersing; his Self had merged into unity" (Hesse 1951, 136).

From that hour Siddhartha ceased to fight against his destiny. There shown in his face the serenity of knowledge, of one who is no longer confronted with conflict of desires, who had found salvation, who is in harmony. ... (Hesse 1951, 136)

Vesudeva has been waiting for this moment. Now, he can take his leave.

Was Vesudeva enlightened?

---

6 I hope this chapter, more than any other, helps the reader to understand the value of these "close" readings of texts. Reading closely, working with and almost rewriting the text, is a form of listening to that text, a way in which so much more can be learned than by merely skimming the surface. It is a powerful and transformative skill.

Govinda

Siddhartha and Govinda meet again near the end of their lives. Something has changed. Govinda, having known Buddha, sees in Siddhartha that rare experience of having transcended all books and teachings, of having reached nirvana (Hesse 1951, 148). Govinda is conflicted. In some ways, Siddhartha appears to contradict what Govinda understands and loves about Buddha. Govinda, who has also been seeking this all his life, asks for help.

Early in the conversation, Siddhartha tells Govinda:

> *What can I say to you that would be of value, except perhaps you seek too much, that as a result of your seeking you cannot find. (Hesse 1951, 140)*

Siddhartha explains:

> *When someone is looking ... it happens quite easily that he sees only the thing that he is seeking ... Seeking means: to have a goal; but finding means: to be free, to be receptive, to have no goal. You, O worthy one, are perhaps indeed a seeker, for in striving towards your goal, you do not see many things that are under your nose. (Hesse 1951, 140)*

We see here a major shift. Early in life, Siddhartha also sought, as Kramer might put it, "a single minded passion" (Kramer 1988, 100). Kramer mentions this as part of the lesson of Gilgamesh when seeking the meaning of life. But here, we see a critique. **What if the meaning of life is not found through aggressive pursuit, but though receptivity? Through listening?** *If I am trying too hard, I see mostly what I think I am looking for (***confirmation bias***).* Remember, the mind doesn't actually capture reality. Instead, it schematizes it and creates ideas and generalities about reality. While useful, these are also limited.

This does not mean that one is entirely passive. In fact, returning to our notion of the **middle voice**, this appears to speak to that strange middle space where *passivity and activity become one*. Both the activity and the passivity are transformed; they are no longer separated. This is addressed further when Govinda asks for a doctrine or belief (Hesse 1951, 141).

> *Knowledge can be communicated, but not wisdom. ... a truth can only be expressed and enveloped in words if it is one-sided. Everything that is thought and expressed in words is one-sided, only half the truth; it all lacks totality, completeness, unity. When the Illustrious Buddha taught about the world, he had to divide it into Samsara and Nirvana, into illusion and truth, into suffering and salvation. One cannot do otherwise. ... (Hesse 1951, 143)*

Recall Siddhartha's earlier conversation with Buddha:

> *[The goal of my teachings] is not to explain the world to those who are thirsty for knowl-*
> *edge. Its goal is quite different; its goal is salvation from suffering. That is what Gotama*
> *teaches, nothing else. (Hesse 1951, 33)*

Buddha recognized this problem, just as Buddha saw the pride at the root of Siddhartha's cleverness. We saw this also in the discussion of Chaos and the middle voice, where Chaos is thought of as the creation of thought (and truth) through the dividing of the essential unity of reality.

We see hints of this idea in Aristotle. Recall the notion of **phronesis** as the ultimate virtue, the person who has so embodied the virtues into their character that they also know when to "break" the rules and make a new rule. Such a person has "transcended" the teachings.

This should help us to understand why, at the limits of human reality, words break down. Here, we can only express ourselves in paradox, mystery. Siddhartha, in what he says to Govinda, even contradicts the Buddha. The Buddha forbade his followers "to bind ourselves to earthly love" (Hesse 1951, 147). Siddhartha, on the other hand, has a very different attitude towards love:

> *I will not deny that my words about love are in apparent contradiction to the teachings*
> *of Gotama. That is why I distrust words so much, ... for I know that I am at one with*
> *Gotama. How, indeed, could he not know love, ... [He who] loves humanity so much*
> *that he has devoted a long life solely to help and teach people? ... his deeds and life are*
> *more important to me than his talk. ... (Hesse 1951, 148)*

We will explore the limits of words and ideas, particularly love, further. For now, we let this idea rest.

So far, we have seen two reasons that limit Govinda. But there is also a third, though it is subtle.

1. Seeking too hard, he is not "receptive" to what he really needs to receive.
2. As a follower, he hangs on too long to other's teachings, when one must move beyond them.
3. Govinda held on to subtle type of pride/self-deception

The last is subtle, but we see at least one point where Hesse mentions it, as a certain "contempt" for his friend's words. My thinking takes a slightly different tact. Govinda was a good person: kind, thoughtful, and compassionate. In fact, for the totality of his life, one could argue that Govinda had probably done more good for others than Siddhartha. Siddhartha, in hitting bottom, ended up giving up all his false pride. Govinda never allowed himself to risk hitting bottom, so that subtle pride had remained.

Have you ever had someone be generous and kind, but known that it wasn't really about helping you? It's not that the gift is without value but that the gift sometimes feels, well, tainted.

Lest this seem too strange, think back to Ivan Ilyich. Ivan was a "good" magistrate. He lacked mercy, but he did his job contentiously and without vindictiveness. Still, it was really all about Ivan. It was about his self-image, his image with others, and the clever and careful magistrate.

A more direct example comes from a woman I dated for a short while. People cautioned me about her. They said she was self-centered. At first, I couldn't see it. She said all the right things. More importantly, she followed through with real acts of generosity and kindness. After a while, what they were saying became clear. Even though she gave generously of her time and income, it was still mainly about her. As C. S. Lewis might put it, she loved not for love's sake, but for how it made her feel about herself. It was her way of feeling self-worth. Further, while she knew (as a strong Christian) intellectually that she couldn't "earn" heaven, on an emotional level, still, she couldn't help trying.

Govinda was likely more subtle than this, but there was an element of this sort of spiritual pride in his life. Govinda was proud of being a "good" person.

What Now?

Govinda's inability to reach enlightenment can teach us a lot about spirituality. The theme of spiritual pride shows up with both Govinda and Siddhartha. We see how subtle and powerful it can be. But we also see, perhaps, the role of the middle voice in spirituality, where it's more about a receptivity than an activity, even though that receptivity becomes a place of powerful activity. If we seek too hard, we are not receptive. If we listen in order to respond, or in order to move on, then we aren't really there. In turn, we limit our learning.

We also see that, while others can help us on a path, in the end, there are steps we must tread for ourselves. Even scripture is just a "help." If we are too much the follower, while we may lead a good life, we risk not really getting to the core of what spirituality is all about.

We also saw something weird about enlightenment. So long as enlightenment was Siddhartha's primary concern, it couldn't be done. In the end, while he did appear to be enlightened, it no longer concerned him.

It also appeared that enlightenment involves an expansion of compassion, but we aren't yet sure why, or even what enlightenment means.

These just a few of the difficult, but rich, notions we move now to explore, starting with a discussion of Hinduism and Buddhism.

Figure Credits

CHAPTER TWELVE

Hinduism and Buddhism

METAPHYSICS AND TWO FORMS OF ENLIGHTENMENT

Hinduism and the Upanishads

I have already introduced one of the founding texts of Hinduism, **The Bhagavad Gita**. Older than the Bhagavad Gita, from around 500–200 BCE, is the **Katha Upanishad**, from around 800–500 BCE.

The Upanishad tells the story of Nachiketas, who resolves to visit death and learn its secrets. He travels to Yama, "the King of Death, [who] was the first of the immortals to give up immortality in order to conqueror death as a mortal" (Kramer 1988, 28). When Nachiketas arrives at Yama's home, he finds that Yama is away. "Undeterred, Nachiketas sits quietly for three days. He neither ate nor drank, nor did he disturb the calm running of Yama's home" (Kramer 1988, 29).

Yama is so impressed by the respect of this young man that he grants him three requests. The first impresses Yama even more deeply. Nachiketas, who left home under poor circumstances, asks that his relationship with his father be restored.

From many Westerners' point of view, the second request appears to be the important one. This was "how to perform the fire sacrifice which leads one to the realm of immortality" (Kramer 1988, 29). After all, as Reverend Coffin points out, isn't the focus for a great many Christians their own salvation?

But *from a Hindu point of view, the third request is the important one.* It is so difficult that Yama at first refuses, telling Nachiketas to ask anything else. Nachiketas presses the issue. "His final question is not 'Do I survive?' but 'What survives?'" (Kramer 1988, 29).

Instead of a direct answer, Yama gives Nachiketas a sound: the mystic Om.

Let us pause here. What is this "Om" of which we heard also in *Siddhartha*? Why a sound and not just an answer?

Remember Siddhartha's concern with teachings? All are limited. *Anything which can be said is only one side of the truth, half of reality.* In Hinduism, *the sound of Om is thought to connect one to the imperishable Brahman, the spiritual all at the heart of reality. It's a sound and an activity, an experience. This is not just food for the mind.*

Of course, there are other reasons why Om might have been chosen. Done properly, the sound resonates from deep within one's stomach, up through one's chest. It vibrates the vagus nerve, the longest cranial nerve in the body. What happens when it vibrates? It releases nitrous oxide, relaxes the body, reduces inflammation in the body, helps with memory, etc. Suffice it to say, it has multiple positive effects on both mind and body. There is even a new weight loss device just approved by the FDA, which sends electrical signals through the vagus nerve. "Om" might have little to do with spiritual metaphysics, but everything to do with biofeedback loops and medicine.

Or it might have to do with both.

Returning to the third request, what survives? Nachiketas finds that it is the Atman, the eternal Self, that does not die. As we said before, the Atman is not individualized, except perhaps in the sense that each Atman (spark of the divine) exists in a different being while it is there. Our individuality (personality, character, etc.) is carried in the Jiva, which, while it does follow us from life to life, is not eternal.

This seems odd. If both the Jiva and the Atman travel from life to life, how are both not eternal? The reason has to do with reincarnation, which further has to do with Karma.

Karma can be described as a principle of justice. It's also impersonal (as in *What Dreams May Come*, there is no one sitting out there judging), but it takes the personal (Jiva) into account. To the degree that one makes "good" choices in one's life, or bears one's burdens well, one accumulates "good" karma. If one acts unjustly, is cruel, or does not accept one's burdens well, one accumulates "bad" karma. As one dies and is born again, the balance of one's karma determines where one ends up on the karmic ladder. One could end up the child of a king or one could end up an earthworm.[1]

So long as one dies without a full awareness (embodied, not just intellectual) of the true Self, the Atman, one remains on the karmic ladder of reincarnation. This doesn't just refer to our world, it could also be on another plane of existence. Some believe that one can even reach what would look very much like a Christian notion of heaven. But they wouldn't stay there forever. In time, as they "used up" their good karma, they would fall back to a lower plane of existence.

Recall how, from C. S. Lewis's perspective, other religions also have part of the truth, but only Christianity has the whole truth? From a Hindu perspective, this might be reversed. Many believe that Jesus is one of the faces of God. But instead of there being three faces and one God (the trinity), there are many more faces. Instead of there being only one "reincarnation" (to heaven or hell), there are many chances.

---

1   Consensus appears to be that philosophy professors come back as dung beetles.

Instead of "heaven" being the final goal, it's just a pleasant way station. However, if we are to be entirely consistent, while a Hindu might believe that their truth is deeper than Christian truth, they would not believe that theirs was the ultimate truth. ***Anything that can be said, any doctrine or metaphysic or idea, cannot be the whole truth.*** Phrased in this way, Lewis might also have to agree.

Thus, we see that the real goal isn't to move up the karmic ladder or to reach heaven. The real goal is to die while fully awake (enlightened). If one dies while fully realizing the Atman, as Siddhartha wished to do, one "will not be reborn at all, but will be absorbed into the ground of Brahman" (Kramer 1988, 37).

The Jiva, while it lives from life to life, ceases to exist when one dies in an enlightened state. At that point, the Atman merges into the Brahman, not unlike a drop of water falling into the ocean. The Jiva is stripped away.

First Metaphysical Objection: It Blooms Because It Blooms

In *What Dreams May Come*, we raised a concern about the nature of reincarnation. Why, once they were already in this wonderful heaven, would anyone choose to go back and risk NOT getting back to heaven and ending up in hell?

That wasn't an objection to the idea of reincarnation itself, but merely, in that particular context, to why someone would choose to be reincarnated. *This objection is different.* First, in this view, reincarnation is not an issue of choice. Second, our objection is to the notion of reincarnation itself. Consider the following:

If the only goal of the Atman leaving the Brahman is merely to return, without any knowledge or change, why does it leave in the first place? Remember, the Atman is not individualized. Once the Jiva is stripped away, it carries nothing back to the Brahman from when it left. This seems fruitless.

There appears to be a simple answer to this question, though it may not be terribly satisfying to our Western minds. We are constantly seeking reasons and purpose: the "why" of existence. But as the German philosopher Heidegger points out, our "why" is something we graft onto experience (we are meaning seeking and meaning generating creatures). It is built on a nature that is unconcerned with the "why." Heidegger quotes from a poem by Angelus Silesius:[2]

The Rose is without why;

It blooms because it blooms,

---

2 It is here that Heidegger is responding to the other candidate for the first principle of logic, that of sufficient reason. Heidegger is pointing out that the claim that "for everything there must be a reason" does not, itself, have a clear reason for its truth. It's really just a useful assumption. It also rests on nature, which just is, without giving a "why."

It pays no attention to itself;

Asks not whether it is seen.

(Heidegger 1991, 35)

In other words, **for purely natural processes, perhaps there is no "why," no overarching reason. For example, we can describe and even explain the process of water evaporating from the ocean and trace its return, but the water doesn't necessarily leave the ocean for a "purpose." It's simply a natural process.**

If this notion of reality is true, perhaps it too is simply a description of a natural process.

While this may be dissatisfying intellectually, it may be true. If so, perhaps this is part of the reason why ultimate "truth" has to be experienced in the body, not just in the mind.

Second Metaphysical Objection: Structural Violence

Based on the structure of many of their followers, there's a partial parallel one can draw between Christianity/Islam and Hinduism. The parallel has to do with the fact that each structure has both certain strengths and certain violent tendencies, though the specific strengths and tendencies differ. Before we explore this issue with Hinduism, let us review and expand on the notion in terms of Christianity and Islam.[3]

A Structural Violence in Christianity/Islam

As before, this structure does not reflect all, or nearly all, practitioners. The same could be said for what I've just outlined in terms of Eastern thought. As Lewis says, "Reality is not simple." Still, a great many practitioners in Christianity and Islam share the following basic structure of their beliefs:

1. There is but one God.
2. Everything God wants is good, all else (or most, some might be neutral) is evil.
3. God only speaks through one religion (or one denomination of that religion).
4. The goal of this life is to get to heaven.

---

3   To be clear, I'd argue that the highest practitioners of each of these religions would refuse to give in to these structures. In both Eastern and Western traditions, there is a recognition, by many, that ANY belief structure is just a tool to describe something that simply cannot be captured by the human mind. Any set of beliefs or ideas that we come up with to describe the divine are, therefore, only partially true. Thus, they are helpful in places, but if we are not careful, harmful in others.

5. This earth has little or no value of its own; it is just the ground for that testing.

As a reminder, think of the "structure" of one's beliefs as the big-picture elements, the bones that hold together the shape of a particular set of beliefs. This specific critique only applies if one holds to something like the five points above as essential to their Christian or Islamic beliefs. As previously illustrated with the stewardship model, many members of both religions structure their beliefs differently.

Content, on the other hand, involves all the other details that flesh out the body. They "fit" around the overall structure of one's beliefs. However, it's the overall structure that dominates and allows one to "interpret" the content. Thus, while the New Testament tells Christians that the most important thing is love, if that belief is on the level of content rather than structure, it can easily be explained away or dismissed. This is as true for the Christians of the Inquisition as for the suicide bombers in Islam. Both religions hold love for one's neighbor, particularly for the poor and the vulnerable, as of crucial importance. The Koran even explicitly forbids suicide (unlike the Bible, though many Christians believe that it does). Yet, *if a believer feels that God is telling them to kill others, all other directives are overcome. One has to obey God or go to hell.*

Put another way: If this life has no real value other than as a proving ground for the next, then there is nothing "intrinsically" good or bad in this world. It is really just good or bad in terms of getting to the next life. In this scenario, the value of human life is reduced to something like the "illusion" Kramer offered in his reading of the story of Krishna and Arjuna.

Of course, there are strong assertions of the primacy of love in each of these scriptures. We have seen how there is a structural tendency towards extremism. But *there are other ways in which the message is deformed, even reversed. One of these is through redefining terms.*

For example, one of the strengths of many forms of all three "peoples of the book" (Judaism, Christianity, and Islam) is the emphasis on love in terms of charity. Our focus should be on caring for the poor, the widow, and the orphan. In Catholic moral teaching, this is embodied in what is called the "**preferential option for the poor**," the belief that we are to give those most in need our first help and attention. For many Christians, including Catholics, this fundamental doctrine is given little more than lip service. How is this justified?

What has happened in some places (and many talk radio shows) is the ever-increasing notion of "tough love." Some people believe, for example, that most people are poor because they are lazy. To give them handouts would merely reinforce their behavior, which also undermines their basic human dignity.

Using this sort of argument, one may not only abstain from helping those in need, but may even feel that one is "helping" them more (tough love) by giving nothing. Thus, the basic meaning of words shifts. ***"Love" is replaced by "tough love," which*** *comes to mean "real love."* And while "tough love" does have a legitimate meaning—consider anyone who has dealt with a loved one with an addiction; or, for that matter, any parent or teacher—*its meaning is so expanded as to become an excuse for not loving at all, while still calling it love.*

It reminds me of a meme going around the internet:

> *My favorite story of Jesus was when he fed the 5,000 with five loaves and two fishes, right after each submitted to mandatory drug testing.*[4]

Redefining terms is just one way to rationalize. In another example, assume that, in addition to the beliefs I've already offered, I am a biblical literalist. If I also believe that God is a God of love, how do I reconcile the belief with passages in which the Old Testament appears to sanction genocide? One answer I've heard espoused is to claim that ordering the killing of even young children was actually a mercy on the part of God. The claim is that the people of these towns had become so diseased by sin (including sexually transmitted diseases) that killing them was a kindness. Remember that this argument is applied not only to the adults (except, on occasion, to some that helped them), but to even young or newly born children.

If I really need to reconcile my beliefs that God is all loving with religiously approved genocide, it means that I will need to find a rational sounding way to reconcile the belief with the action. It requires a classic strategy of **bad faith**, as I am lying to myself more than to others. I may do so with great intelligence and cleverness, but the real goal is not to look at the information objectively, but to find a way to prove a point. In this case, I don't really listen to other data or possibilities, except to refute them. I only listen with an agenda.

Remember the encounter between Siddhartha and the Ferryman?

Why was listening so important?

Our only real "defense" against rationalizations, including our own, is a truly open heart and mind.

For that, we need to listen without agendas.

Most early Christians believed the stories that eventually became the New Testament were inspired, but not literal. This is a view still shared by many modern denominations. For them, as for many modern-day practitioners of both Christianity and Islam, these problems would not apply. Still, it illustrates the issue of how structure can overcome content.

---

4   Interestingly, the rate of illegal drug use by those on welfare actually appears to be below that of the general population. Moreover, far from saving money (by removing abusers from the welfare rolls), these testing programs have typically cost far more than they have saved. For example, see http://www.nytimes.com/2012/04/18/us/no-savings-found-in-florida-welfare-drug-tests.html?_r=0. Accessed on August 1, 2016.

A Structural Violence in Hinduism

Hinduism, in its basic structure, avoids the most common tendency towards extremism found in the given version of Christianity and Islam. Why? Because some followers of Christianity and Islam believe that their religion (their specific version of that religion) is the only way and all others must either convert or be condemned.

Hinduism, on the other hand, holds as fundamental that there are "many ways of the mountain." No single path works for all people, each person has to find, in the end, their own way.

This doesn't mean that there aren't some Hindu sects that seek to "convert" others. It's just far less an issue than in the West. This is due, in part, to the basic structure of their beliefs. Consider the following:

1. While we can help one another to spiritual enlightenment, in the end, each person's path is their own.
2. Often, what is required of that path is great suffering and sin (mistakes, error) to realize truth.
3. We come into this incarnation based on our choices (karma) in the last incarnation.
4. We each have lessons we need to learn in each incarnation to help us move on.
5. Ultimately, the goal is to get off the wheel entirely, but it is easier to make that move from higher levels of spiritual evolution/incarnation than from lower levels.

On one level, this structure tends toward greater respect and tolerance for diversity than in the given Western belief structure. Not only must each person travel their own road, but we must be allowed (within reason) to make mistakes and even commit "sins" in order to learn. That's an advantage to this way of thinking about reality.

However, while Hinduism is less likely to sanction the same sort of extremism we see in some versions of Christianity and Islam, it has a different structural violence all its own. As we examined potential deformations of the virtue of charity in Christianity, let us also consider it in this system.

In the case of Christianity, the "tough love" argument was a redefinition, but it wasn't part of the structure of the thought. In the case of this version of Hinduism, "tough love" is actually built into the structure.

On one level, performing charitable acts such as helping the needy or the sick generates good karma. So, assume that, out of a sense of charity or compassion, I take care of you, removing some essential pain or suffering from your life. In terms of karma, have I really helped you, or myself?

My claim *could be* that, by helping you, I am denying you important lessons that you were born into this life to learn. Even if there are no specific lessons, I take away your ability to earn good karma by suffering cheerfully.

In terms of this thinking, the best thing I can do, *for your sake*, is to let you suffer. It's a classic **self-serving rationality**. In fact, *I get to feel spiritually superior for not helping those in need.*

It gets worse.

This structure helped give rise to the caste system in India. The idea was that certain people were born into this life at higher states than others. Much of this had to do with parentage, but a lot also had to do with skin tone. If you were light-skinned, you were at a superior karmic level. The really dark-skinned Indians were called the "untouchables" and were reduced to doing the dirtiest and worst jobs in society.[5]

This structure supports racism.

The problem with "structural" violence is that it is the hardest to overcome. While we see an excessive redefinition of "tough love" in some Christian circles, that's not built into the structure. The same is true for racism. Racism and slavery have often been justified in this history of Christianity, but they were not typically built into the "structure" of the beliefs.[6]

Just as with Christianity, there are multiple other deformations, but I'll offer two more examples. The first is along the lines of the values of life if death is an illusion. Consider, for example, that the ultimate goal is the stripping away of the Jiva, while the Atman cannot die. What then does it matter if an individual dies? What is important cannot die.

Another comes from the idea that great acts of self-sacrifice and devotion give one great karma. This would benefit one in the next life. One of the practices that came out of this was called **Sati**, the idea of the widow being so devoted to her husband that she would throw herself on his funeral pyre or otherwise commit suicide. The husband's family might, at times, pressure the widow, or even physically "help" her along to such an action. How would they justify it? She earned great karma. Again, this is a classic **self-serving rationality**.

It's worth noting that both the caste system and **Sati** (widow suicide) are illegal in India, but that doesn't mean that they are entirely absent.

---

5 I was recently told by a professor of religion that even the caste system wasn't really very strict until Westerners got involved. It became strict in response to pressures of British rule. This story, like all stories, is more complicated.

6 This can't be an absolute claim because different versions of the same religions often have different structures. Here, I'm just dealing with the ones I've named.

The Ethical Problem with Metaphysics

Upon pointing out the structural violence in each of these metaphysics, one can use that knowledge to try to construct a better metaphysical description of reality and spirituality. That's a worthy goal. But what if there is also another lesson? *What if the lesson is that there are no metaphysical approaches, no grand visions of the nature of reality, that are completely free of some sort of hidden violence or oppression?*

By good, I mean following Aristotle's notion of enhancing human flourishing. By bad, I mean things that cause damage, suffering, or violence (either directly to others or indirectly through social structures or by damaging the world we share).

The ease by which even relatively innocuous ethical rules or principles can be corrupted is astounding. Consider, for example, something as simple as the Golden Rule. Surely it's fairly straightforward?

> *Do unto others what you would want them to do unto you.*

It means, for most people, to treat one another with kindness and, most importantly, respect. Respect one another's wishes and self-determination, just as you would want others to respect your wishes and self-determination.

Yet, sadly, it's not all that difficult to turn the saying on its head. Say, for example, I am a member of a group who believes that only those who follow our way (well, God's way) will receive salvation. If so, I can easily say to myself: *Were I in sin and error or about to fall into eternal damnation, would I want someone to pull me out?* The answer, of course, is yes. It goes further: *If this situation is true, with the stakes so high, would I want that other person to use any means necessary to save me?* Again, given these beliefs, the answer is likely to be yes. Such a person would thus feel justified in using any means, including force, to help others to salvation, and could even claim that he or she was following the golden rule, because, if the circumstances were reversed, they would want others to do the same for themselves.

If this is so, what is our alternative? Do we just give up? The ability to make generalizations about our world is a powerful tool. Jack Caputo, a former teacher of mine, once said in class: "Who is it that had to suffer and die, which groups and ideas had to be oppressed, so that these became our self-evident truths?"[7] If it is true that our generalizations are not just imperfect, but that each contains the seeds of some form of violence, if there are no "self-evident" truths, where are we to go from here?

It turns out that we've already addressed this question, in part, in the chapter on truth. Truths are not self-evident; they are products of our meaning seeking and generating nature. We've also answered, empirically, how that can still create a space and call for ethics. That is, we share a basic experience of empathy that, while fragile,

---

7   Not an exact quote.

calls us to care for one another. We will deal more with the structure of violence in a later chapter. Here, what can we say about how to deal with this sort of violence?

In part, we can recognize and remain sensitive to Caputo's question. We cannot function, either as individuals or as a society, without making such generalizations. We need laws and principles. Instead of taking them as absolute, which involves failing to recognize those who are hurt by these chosen structures or truths, we can maintain an awareness, following Aristotle, that the ideas and laws are there to serve the greater good, not us to serve them. ***By becoming aware of the fact that we cannot eliminate all violence from society or from our choices, we can become attuned to recognizing that violence and seek to limit or moderate its impact.*** In fact, it may be that those who try hardest to pretend that their beliefs involve no inherent violence are the most susceptible to this tendency, because they will fight hardest to repress any argument, evidence, or persons who threaten their "truth" (**psychological repression**).

Moderating violence can happen in many ways. One of the most basic would be to ***ensure that no one group bears most of the burdens while another group reaps most of the benefits.***[8]

It's the call to social justice.

At the heart of it is, as in Siddhartha, *the act of radical listening.*

Buddhism

Buddhism, in its more philosophical form, has a unique resistance to violence. It does so because it is more a practice and less a metaphysics. This is not true of all forms of Buddhism. For the form we will address here, there is far less of a grand metaphysical structure than most religious beliefs.

There are conflicting stories about both the location and circumstances of Buddha's birth. Scholars suggest that he was born the son of a tribal chief who married a local princess in northeastern India, part of present-day Nepal. As with all great

---

8   For example, if we build even a "clean" coal power plant in a city or town, we know that there will be a significant increase in death, asthma, and other health issues within a certain distance (mainly downwind) of that plant. There was a recent attempt to build such a plant in my hometown of Waterloo, Iowa. The plan was to build it right on the edge of town in a poor area. The power wasn't even for use by the city. Instead, it was to supply power to Chicago. Yes, there would be a few jobs and some tax revenue to the city. But the people in the poor part of town, as is typical of such projects, would end up bearing the "health" costs of the plant.

religious figures, the stories about his life, including his early life, multiply over time. But the main legend is as follows:

When **Siddhartha Gautama** was born, there was a prophesy about his life. There were two paths: either he would become a great military leader, uniting all of India, or he would become a holy man and great spiritual teacher. Other stories only indicated that Siddhartha Gautama would leave home. In either case, the story is that his father, wanting to keep him home, and perhaps wanting to guide him towards the military option, kept him in the palace surrounded by luxury. While providing every education necessary for a young prince, he tried to ensure that poverty, sickness, old age, and death were hidden from him.

Despite living in the lap of luxury, Siddhartha Gautama felt that something was missing. But he couldn't identify it. The legend continues that he wandered out of the palace walls four times.

The first time he saw old age in the form of a very old woman.
The second time he saw illness in the form of a man with festering sores.
The third time he saw a funeral pyre, death.
The fourth time he saw a monk.

Often, it is our encounters with pain and suffering that lead us to a spiritual search. *For those who possess even a basic level of natural compassion, something in us cries out against such suffering. That is perhaps one beginning of the spiritual search.*

If this legend is true, Siddhartha Gautama's father made a critical mistake. While shielding his son from pain and suffering might have led to the result he wanted, *instead of turning Siddhartha Gautama away from the spiritual path, it only made the impact of human suffering, once witnessed, all the more powerful.* In this case, he might have done better to introduce it to his son much earlier. The result might have been the same, but it might also have been that Siddhartha Gautama would have become desensitized to the suffering.

As a comparison, I know of a woman in Nashville who, for different periods of time, sent her children to various churches, denominations, temples, etc. She herself was not religious and she wanted to pass this on to her children. Instead of shielding her children from religion in general, she sought to educate them in as many religions as possible. Moreover, she was smart enough to realize that it would be more effective to have them attend the churches for themselves.

The result? She took a risk that they might move away from her beliefs. After being exposed to so many different groups, most that claimed to be the "one" way, her children became more thoughtful and self-critical about such claims in general. She desensitized them to claims of religious exclusivity, though not necessarily to religion in general.

This might have been a better strategy on the part of Siddhartha Gautama's father. Then again, perhaps one simply cannot escape prophesy.[9]

In either case, these four trips hit Siddhartha Gautama like a ton of bricks. If he was to die, what was the point of this life? He leaves his home and seeks answers among the monks.

> *Siddhartha resolved that given the reality of old age, sickness and death, it would be better to live alone, away from the city. These human conditions raised questions in him for which he had no answers, and with which he was no longer able to continue to live. He left his ... Hindu upbringing and six years ... practiced yoga and austerities with the highest teachers ... but perceived no one to be more on the road to enlightenment than he was. (Kramer 1988, 46)*

One can observe, from this and other passages, that the name Hesse gave to his searcher was not accidental. There is a reason they both shared the same first name. It also has to do with the meaning of the name Siddhartha, which can be loosely translated as "he who has found meaning."[10]

> *Finally, with firm, deep resolve, he sat beneath a Bodhi Tree (tree of Wisdom), and resolved not to leave that seat until the insight of Supreme Enlightenment had been attained. (Kramer 1988, 46)*

Whereas I was critical of aspects of Kramer's reading of Hinduism, in the case of Buddhism, there is a subtlety and beauty to his explanation of certain key ideas that begs to be unpacked. Let us begin with the notion of desire and detachment:

> *It is crucial to understand that Buddha died not to desire itself, for one cannot live without desires, but to his attachment to desire. (Kramer 1988, 47)*

This does not mean that one does not experience desire. If I remain human, I will experience hunger. What this means, for example, is that if there is limited food, I will distribute that food, not in terms of my own self-interest, but in terms of what I can see as the greater good for all involved.

> *Most especially, he died to his desire to be enlightened ... (Kramer 1988, 47)*

Near the end of Hesse's novel, we asked several times, is Siddhartha enlightened? We also asked if the Ferryman was enlightened. Another way to ask the question is, "Do they even care anymore?"

---

9 It's worth noting that the notion of prophesy I'm implying here is very different than in most of the Old Testament. For many mainstream biblical scholars, the prophets were not generally predicting the future, but were retelling the past in terms of allegories. The purpose of the stories was to call to mind where the people had strayed from God and justice and to call them back to the same.

10 https://en.wikipedia.org/wiki/Siddhartha_(novel). Accessed on July 31, 2016.

The answer, I think, is no. As Caplan puts it:

> *Psychology deals with the human psyche, which is contained within the ego structure; spirituality deals with that which is larger than the individual, the Reality which is our very essence and foundation, of which the ego and the psyche are merely components. (Caplan 1999, 12)*

In other words, the ego considers itself enlightened (spiritual pride), whereas in true enlightenment, something very different is going on. Enlightenment is a state, a context, an experience wherein one operates out of a profound sense of the greater good, not out of one's own desires. Spirituality, understood in this way, is not the land of milk and honey.

Spirituality is the power of a greater reality to *interrupt* my agendas, ideas, and concepts about the world and call me to something else. *Spirituality is this interruption. It is experiencing that greater context.*

> *Buddha passed beyond the three states which keep humans un-liberated, namely being attached, being unattached, being non-attached. (Kramer 1988, 47)*

Again, as with desire, these categories no longer apply. We pass beyond words, scriptures, and teachings. The idea is to gain some sort of direct, fundamental experience of reality. When Buddha did so:

> *... he realized that there was nothing to be realized, and no one to realize it. (Kramer 1988, 47)*

> *Gone was his old identity; gone were his old desires and fears, gone were questions about the meaning of old age, sickness and death; gone was the one who searched. In their place was the Buddha, the one who was awake, the one who had ceased craving, the one who had died to the fear of death to become eternally present. (Kramer 1988, 47)*

Buddha rejected both the ideas of the Atman and reincarnation. The first is fairly straightforward: even the notion of the Atman is just an idea, a metaphor for explaining reality. Consider our analogy of consciousness and the river. Somehow, the river is the same, but always different. Neither category really works, though both have something to contribute.

In rejecting the Atman, it's not clear that Buddha was saying that he had a "better" idea. Rather, he appeared to be saying that all such constructs are inadequate. All are one-sided. Buddha wasn't concerned with building a better metaphysic. He was concerned with the ever-changing process, the flow of the river itself.

Buddha's response to reincarnation is a bit more complicated. Most of the time, he simply refused to answer his follower's questions on the issue. But there were rare exceptions. My favorite story is of him holding up a candle, lighting another candle, and holding the two flames apart. One may ask, is it the same flame? Kramer seeks to provide a helpful explanation (Kramer 1988, 51). Still, I think that no explanation can suffice. There is a mystery here, not to be solved, but to be engaged.

What is this mystery? What is behind it? Part of the mystery, to my thinking, is the very paradox of the river and self-consciousness. It has to do with reflecting on the very nature of time, on whether (or in what sense) it even exists at all, and whether those categories of thought even work.[11]

Pulling back from this particular abyss, let us follow Kramer in asking a different question. Why do we want to believe in reincarnation? Life after death? A heaven? **What is the question we are really asking?**

According to Kramer, Buddha would tell us that, when we ask, "*Is there life after death?*" we have confused the real question. **By focusing on this question, what we really want gets lost.** What is it that motivates us to ask this question? What is it that sent Siddhartha out on his quest?

> ... the question "Is there life after death?" is the wrong question ... It is a question which covers over the more vital one, namely, "How can I become liberated from human suffering?" (Kramer 1988, 52; emphasis added)

When we realize the fact that we will die, it makes us afraid. We suffer. We confuse the immediate experience for the more fundamental question. What we want, fundamentally, is to be relieved from human suffering. Because we associate suffering with death, we seek to be freed of death. But *it's really suffering that's at issue.*

Given this beginning, it shouldn't come as much of a surprise that Buddha, when he reached that ultimate state of enlightenment, found himself turning outward, towards others.

> The essence of Buddha's spiritual realization expressed itself as unconditional, selfless compassion for all creatures even at death. (Kramer 1988, 47)

Instead of just worrying about his own suffering, Buddha's experience of a connection to all of reality keyed into the greater suffering of all humanity, of all life. As such, he placed the rest of his life in service to reducing that suffering, to helping others.

Returning to Hesse's formulation:

---

11 Kramer addresses the illusion of time with the analogy of the motion picture. Each "frame" is fixed, but passed over a light in sequence, it creates the illusion of motion. It's a great analogy that works particularly well with process philosophy. Still, it raises other questions. For example, even though the movement of the subject of the film is clearly an illusion, it depends upon a different movement to make that possible, the movement of the frames over the light. Is that, too, an illusion? And does it require another sort of movement to make its illusion of time and motion?

[The goal of my teachings] is not to explain the world to those who are thirsty for knowledge. Its goal is quite different; its goal is salvation from suffering. That is what Gotama teaches, nothing else. (Hesse 1951, 33)

At the same time, Buddha also taught suspicion of all teachings, even his own,[12] by "constantly reiterat[ing] that religious life does not depend upon doctrines and formulations" (Kramer 1988, 47). This emphasis helps to keep many, though not all, of his followers from rigidifying his teachings into a metaphysical scheme. For Buddha, they are only guidelines.

In fact, if I were to choose what, to my thinking, is **Buddha's most fundamental teachings**, they would be:

(1) **All is impermanent.**
(2) **We must live with compassion.**

But how does the second notion, compassion, come out of the first?

From a strictly logical point of view, the two don't have to work together. From the standpoint that all of reality is in flux, that even human identity is more like the identity of a river—a paradox or mystery—how does one come to the conclusion that compassion towards the suffering of others is what we should be doing? Even if the motivation for starting this search was to relieve my own suffering, there is nothing obvious in the conclusion that takes me back towards relieving the suffering of others.

Yet, here we are. **Buddha, like many of the highest practitioners of every major religion, experiences, as a result of that spiritual conversion, a profound sense of compassion. This is an empirical claim.** If Hesse is correct, it's not love in the conventional sense. Recall that Hesse's Siddhartha values love, while Buddha appeared to teach us to avoid it. Yet, they were said to mean the same thing. What is likely here are different meanings of the term; whatever is going on at this level cannot be fully captured in words.

For example, it may be that Buddha used the term in a way that was consistent with being "attached" to a particular love, while Hesse's Siddhartha used it in a broader sense, perhaps closer to compassion. Or perhaps Hesse was referring to the need to pass through human love to get to the next stage, while what Buddha referred to was just the next stage.

Another mystery to be engaged.

For now, let us explore why it isn't logically necessary for the experience of enlightenment to turn outwards towards compassion. One way to do so is to explore two different "schemas" of ideas (or metaphysics) of enlightenment.

---

12 Buddha's specific teachings, like the Four Noble Truths and the Eightfold Path, can be found in other sources.

Personal versus Impersonal Enlightenment

What I have in mind is the new age distinction between "personal" and "impersonal" enlightenment. ***What's interesting here is not just the terms themselves, but how the meaning of a whole series of other terms changes around them.*** For example, we can talk about detachment, the nature of the world, self, the unity at the heart of all things, etc., but even where we use the same terminology, the words take on very different meanings. I use the following chart to help keep track:

TABLE 12.1

TERMS		PERSONAL ENLIGHTENMENT	IMPERSONAL ENLIGHTENMENT
Focus		Self	Others
Goal		Arrival, end point/bliss	Process/compassion
Detachment	X	Disengaged from the world	Disengaged from the ego
		Engaged with the self	Engaged with the world
Unity/Oneness	X	Identity	Belonging
Approach	X	Passive towards the world	Middle voiced/passive & active
The World	X	Illusion	Appearance
Understanding	X	Intellectual, intuitive	Embodied

The terms on the left are used by both parties for both types of enlightenment, particularly the ones with an X in the second column. Thus, it would be very easy to assume that two people are talking about the same experience, even if they are both talking about two different understandings of enlightenment. Yet, while the terms are the same, the meaning of each term is, in these cases, different. Of course, what I'm attempting here is a more precise understanding of the two approaches than even most of those deeply involved in the tradition might attempt. In part, that has to do with the fact that my training is in philosophy. And while no scheme is perfect, I reviewed this scheme with our Asian religion's specialist, who agreed with this assessment.[13]

We will begin with "personal" enlightenment. As a preliminary comment, we need to dispel any sense of "personal" and being better or worse than "impersonal." That's part of our Western heritage and it doesn't really apply here.

---

13   This was Professor James Robinson, who, sadly, passed away before the publishing of this text. In tribute to his life, despite long illness, he kept teaching (what he most loved) until the end.

Personal Enlightenment

As a close friend[14] who practices and studies under these sorts of spiritual teachers puts it, the personal enlightenment gurus are the "enlightenment now" teachers. They tell us that enlightenment is immediately available to all of us, we just have to "wake up." My friend used to work with these sorts of teachers. It worked. They could help him reach a state of utter bliss that could last for days, even weeks, at a time. They told him that, if he worked at it, he could stay there forever.

This gives us our first two terms. The focus is on waking the "true" self, while the result and the goal is utter spiritual bliss. The goal is also to be there permanently. There is no need for drugs.

Skipping over detachment for a moment (since that will be a bit more controversial), what does it mean when one says that "all is one?"

In this version of enlightenment, the tendency is to think that this oneness has the character of identity—that at the deepest heart of reality, there are no real differences. **We are NOT talking about self-identity here.** Instead, we are proposing the idea that, at the heart of things, all is identical. This feeds the next two terms. If there are no real differences, then the differences of this world are just illusions. Further, this engenders a certain passive approach to the world, because if all difference is illusion, what we "do" doesn't make any real difference.

Before going on to the other terms, let me offer an argument for viewing reality in this way. Consider our metaphor of consciousness: space. Recall that consciousness is a sort of space that allows others (images, ideas, etc.) to come to presence, to make way for the play and freedom of consciousness that defines our essential humanity. One of the goals of meditation is to "still" that space and experience it just as space itself, without anything "on stage," so to speak. What is space? It's just space. No-thing. If this names what is at the heart of reality, then all of reality is really just, well, space. *In this sense*, space is really all the same. One space is identical to all others. So, all difference might be, at the heart of reality, illusion. Just products of the play of the mind, while what's essential is the space itself.

It's a pretty strong argument.

But, in this view, what happens to ethics?

If all difference is illusion, ethics is also just an illusion. Why bother showing compassion or helping others? Differences, even suffering, are also illusion. At most,

---

14 I have to thank Dr. Michael Ackerman for much of what I have learned and experienced in Eastern thought.

we might help them to wake up, but there's no inherent necessity for even this level of care.

What, then, happens to detachment? If this world is illusion, then part of detachment is from the world. We have no obligation, no goals other than our own spiritual self-awareness, our own bliss. This is why I argue that this notion of detachment involves *disengaging from the world*—not just parts of it, but from all the ethical aspects of if as well.

My friend who works with various teachers also notes that these are the teachers who most often talk about and teach enlightenment.

My argument for the next two definitions of attachment to self and intellectual versus embodied understanding can only be understood with more information. So, we will first move on to impersonal enlightenment.

Impersonal Enlightenment

"Impersonal," in this context, does not mean cold and distant. Instead, it means focused on other rather than the self. Here, the focus is radically different. Whereas the "enlightenment now" teachers talk a lot about enlightenment, the impersonal enlightenment teachers rarely, if ever, bring up the term. Instead, they focus on growth and service.

This leads us to the different focus and goal of impersonal enlightenment. In impersonal enlightenment, the focus is not on the self, even the "true" self, but on others—service, care, reducing suffering, and compassion. Further, the emphasis on continued growth leads one to think of the goal not as a single end point (i.e., a permanent state of bliss) but as an ongoing process.

As before, I'll jump over detachment and move next to unity/oneness. In this case, think back to our discussion of Chaos and the middle voice. The oneness we described there was not that all things were the same, but that all is interconnected. Like a spider's web, if one pulls on one thread, one influences them all. Difference is real, but there is a complex unity underneath where all things "belong" to one another and all are connected.

This brings us to the world, not as illusion, but as appearance (i.e., what we see on the surface is not all there is, but it too has a certain reality). It takes us to a very different approach to the world. If the world is illusion, then we are passive and nothing we do matters. If the world is real and all is interconnected, then everything we do impacts others. My claim is that, on this level, we seek to engage the world both passively and actively. This is not unlike the middle voice, where we place ourselves in service to the greater good. We seek to understand the web and place ourselves in service to impacting it wisely.

The greater good? There really wasn't even a space for ethics under the other scheme. But in this scheme, where we can both increase and decrease real suffering, ethics is again relevant.

What of detachment? My argument is that, in impersonal enlightenment, detachment is from our egos, but we remain "engaged" in the world.[15] In what sense? For the personal enlightenment people, the goal is their own bliss. In that sense, while I'm sure they would object, I suspect they remain attached, not to some "highest" self, but to some ego, their own pleasure. By contrast, the impersonal enlightenment people remain engaged in the world. They want to serve the greater good but detach more fully from the ego; it's not about themselves.

A story my friend told me gives a sense of what this might mean. Again, he used to follow these teachers, but something bothered him about their methods. One day, at a spiritual event, he looked to one of them with his own spiritual eye. When he looked directly at him, he saw radiance and light, joy and bliss. When he looked at his feet, he saw something different. He saw a sort of dark smoke, shadows curling but being pushed down.

He took this to mean that, for these teachers, the purity of their radiance was incomplete. It was incomplete because they had taken a shortcut. Instead of dealing with their "shadow" side, their own particular darkness, and transforming it, they had just **repressed** it.

My friend now works with an impersonal enlightenment guru. She rarely talks about enlightenment. Instead, she leads a life of service and inspires the same among her followers.

This sets me to wondering if "personal enlightenment" is enlightenment at all. Can a person really stay "permanently" in that state? As Hesse pointed out with Siddhartha along the way:

> But though the paths took him away from Self, in the end they always led him back. ...
> (Hesse 1951, 15)

The last term in the schema, *understanding*, is less clear, and is based more on the analysis we will perform in the next chapter. But my suspicion is that the personal enlightenment people are still caught up in intellect and intuition, while the impersonal enlightenment people have taken it more fully into their bodies.

Not having experienced either form of enlightenment, I cannot give a definitive judgment as to whether this sort of analysis is correct. Additionally, since, as we will explore further in the next chapter, enlightenment cannot be explained, even with such experience, such a judgment would be only partially true. This is part of the

---

15 Most will also say that they wish to be detached from the world. But they are using the world in a different sense than I am here.

reason why I never ask on my exams, "What is enlightenment?" If a student left it blank, I wouldn't know whether to give them an A or an F.

What I can do, what we can all do, is evaluate these claims in a tentative manner based both on our own one experience and our ability to read about and talk with others. What we can also do is engage the mysteries and see what comes out. For that, my tendency would be to suggest the following:

Both "schemes" are partly true and partly false. They help us to think about the issue. I suspect that the impersonal enlightenment version reflects a deeper level of truth than the personal enlightenment version. Some of the reasons for this judgment should already be apparent, but we will continue to develop this point.

Given the limitations we are finding with metaphysical structures, it may be clear why certain approaches, like Zen, attempt to do away with all metaphysical beliefs. But escaping metaphysics is not all that simple.

CHAPTER THIRTEEN

Psychology versus Spirituality

IT'S NOT ABOUT ME

> *Psychology deals with the human psyche, which is contained within the ego structure; spirituality deals with that which is larger than the individual, the Reality which is our very essence and foundation, of which the ego and the psyche are merely components.*

> (Caplan 1999, 12; emphasis added)

Psychology and Spirituality: What's the Difference?

At the beginning of this book, I made a request: *set aside your beliefs, if you have them, in an afterlife.* The reason was to help each of us to face what the fear of death, as the end of all our possibilities, has to teach us. Much of that has to do with figuring out what is important for each of us in this life. But here, there is another, related question. It is to help us understand the difference between psychology and spirituality.

Psychology is usually thought of as pertaining to the study of the behavior and the mind, including the study of consciousness. The goals of psychology include not only understanding, but how to become a healthy self.

Spirituality is usually thought of as pertaining to our connection to something greater, to the ultimate nature and purpose of reality, and the meaning of life.

Caplan goes on, quoting George Feurstien:

> *Self-development, self-improvement, and even self-actualization do not amount to the spiritual life. In humanistic therapy, the self of the ego remains the guiding principle of existence, whereas in genuine spirituality it is transcended, not merely denied or negated. This all-important point must be fully appreciated. (Caplan 1999, 12)*

Psychology, *understood in this context,* **points back to the self, the ego, and the personality.**

Spirituality points to what is greater than us, the reality of which we are just a part. Spirituality can be understood in at least two ways:

1. As a sort of metaphysical existence "behind the scenes" that, in reality, is far greater than what one perceives (i.e., a battle between good and evil, heaven and hell, etc.).
2. *The experience of something "(w)holy other," the great "other" that interrupts and challenges our ideas, assumptions, metaphysical conceptions, and most importantly, interrupts our very sense of self and ego.*

The first definition of spirituality is the more common, which is why it is listed first. But the second definition is more experiential. The first is more about the interpretation of one's spiritual experiences, *the second points more to the actual experiences*. This second definition, focusing more on experience, takes us in a direction Caplan, Feurstien, and many Western writers will recognize as "authentic" spirituality.

If this is the first time one has been exposed to these sorts of ideas, they will seem alien. We will be exploring this topic from both an Eastern and Western perspective. I will start with the Western perspective since this is mainly for a Western audience and that's my own tradition.

Spirituality, understood in this second way, *is a type of human experience.*[1] It is a special class of experience that results in having one's ideas challenged, even at times shattered (conversion?). What do I mean by a "special class" of experience? It's not the experience of having someone come up with new data that causes a minor shift in direction for one's beliefs. Rather, it's a challenge that strikes at one's very core, which is embodied, emotional, and pre-intellectual. It might be a sense of uncanniness and discomfort when one sees a dead body. It might be the discomfort of seeing the pain and suffering in the eyes of someone one would rather condemn. Though one might reject this "interruption" intellectually, it presses certain questions into our very bodies. Both Ivan and Vivian had, in part, a question pressed into their bodies by the experience of illness.

---

1 There are some who would object to using the term "experience" to characterize what goes on in both psychology and spirituality. They have a point. Experience is usually thought of as something gained by the individual and incorporated into their personality. While this is also partially true of "spirituality," because, in its more radical sense, it interrupts and challenges categories of thought and personality, it's not the same. In another sense, it is an experience that should become clear as we go along.

Caplan believes confusing psychology with spirituality is a common mistake of Western spiritual thinkers. While I expect she is correct, that doesn't mean that it is true of all Western thinkers, nor that all Eastern practitioners adequately make this distinction.

For example, the following **Franciscan prayer/blessing** embodies the notion of spirituality as interruption:

> *May God bless you with a restless discomfort about easy answers, half-truths, and superficial relationships, so that you may seek truth boldly and love deep within your heart.*
>
> *May God bless you with holy anger at injustice, oppression, and exploitation of people so that you may tirelessly work for justice, freedom, and peace among all people.*
>
> *May God bless you with the gift of tears to shed for those who suffer from pain, rejection, starvation, or the loss of all that they cherish, so that you may reach out your hand to comfort them and transform their pain to joy.*
>
> *May God bless you with enough foolishness to believe you really can make a difference in this world, so you're able, with God's grace, to do what others claim cannot be done.*

The "interruption" never really stops, because all of our truths are half-truths and, therefore, restless discomfort. Moreover, the prayer also expresses the second part we noted in our discussion of Buddha and enlightenment. That is, it appears that, in its richest and deepest form, the interruptions take us to a place of great compassion for others.

We noted above that spirituality and psychology overlap. In part, this is because *they are both, at least from our perspectives, fundamental human experiences.* But there is more. *Spirituality, understood in this sense, appears to be essential for the goal of humanistic psychology: to be a healthy self.* That's a noble goal. A healthy self has an understanding of the world that allows one to function well and, hopefully, be happy. Remember, given our limited intellect and access, we always understand the world in limited terms. Even understanding another person is a strange and difficult challenge. What does this suggest?

If spirituality names a moment that "interrupts" our ideas, assumptions, and self, then "spirituality" is that which helps and enables the personality to grow and expand. Spiritual "interruption," whether through trying to understand the mystery of another's feelings or through some event in the world—being arrested by a moment of beauty or feeling pain at the suffering of an animal—is absolutely essential to a healthy personality. *But it is also more than, or different from, a mere adjunct to one's personality.*

Understanding This Difference from a Western Perspective

Christianity: Lewis

Since Christianity and Islam[2] are both rooted in Judaism, it would seem that, even if their "metaphysics" is different, the root of their spirituality would be similar, if not the same, as Judaism's. Since we already devoted an entire chapter to Lewis, I'll start by drawing out some of those similarities.

Recall that for Lewis, a mature spirituality meant that one had to love both God and one's neighbor, not for the sake of getting to heaven or some other reward, but purely for their own sake. While Lewis believed in a literal heaven, if that was the reason that one "loved," then it wasn't really love, it was just trying for a good deal. Because God loves us, heaven is a natural outpouring of that love, but it cannot be our goal. It cannot be bought or earned.

So, *for a mature spirituality, heaven should be irrelevant.*

In psychology, my primary goal is my own gain, which in this case is my own continued existence. If this is what motivates me, according to Lewis, I'll never be ready for heaven. Spirituality focuses, *not on any personal gain*, but on God and the other, on *love for its own sake*. **It focuses on the greater reality of which I am only a part.** *In a mature spirituality, I place myself in service to that reality rather than attempting to use that reality for my own ends.*

Similarly, William Sloan Coffin, former pastor for Riverside Church in New York and Chaplain for Yale Divinity School, argues that too many people go to church to gain salvation, when they should be going to church to transcend themselves (Coffin 1985). Too many have confused their continued existence (their psychology) with real spirituality (which interrupts and transcends the self). Again, if I am going to church in order to gain salvation, my focus is still upon myself and what I gain.

---

2 Islam, understood by both Islam and neutral scholars, is also a religion of love. Just as with Christian scriptures, one can easily take a line or two out of context. For example, Mohammad preached great respect for what he called the "people of the book." He didn't initially see himself as forming a new religion, but as correcting errors and abuses that had crept into Christianity and Judaism. Thus, for example, when he speaks out against the "Jews," if the passage is not taken out of context, one will realize that he was not speaking out against all Jews, but against the actions of a specific group. To say that he hated all Jews based on those passages would be, by *analogy*, to say that one who speaks out against the actions of the Westboro Baptist Church hates all Christians.

Judaism: Levinas

Recall that the Hebrews refused to allow images of the divine. Recall also that they chose the four unpronounceable letters, "YHWH," to represent their God. "Yahweh" is an alternate word chosen so we can still talk about "God" without saying God's name. Nothing we can say, no idea or word we can put into language, is adequate to understand the divine. Similarly, the idea was that no image could capture the divine. Whatever God is, our human minds are able to comprehend only the smallest parts of its mystery.

Levinas distinguishes metaphysics (understood in this context as ontology, a statement of what is real, the "world behind the scenes") from ethical *desire*[3] (desire beyond oneself, for service to care for the other, the origin of ethics).

> The first "vision" of eschatology (thereby distinguished from the revealed opinions of positive religions) reveals the very possibility of a signification without a context. The experience of morality does not proceed from this vision—it consummates this vision; ethics in an optics. (Levinas 1969, 23; emphasis his)

This is a difficult passage. To begin, Levinas is arguing, using a blend of religious and philosophical terminology, that there is a basic human experience that founds the very possibility of eschatology.[4] Part of what is important here is that *this vision is NOT dependent upon the metaphysics of any religion. In fact, Levinas argues that this is an experience that is prior to and supersedes any particular metaphysics.* To a large degree, as soon as we move to a particular vision of some sort of "world behind the scenes," to what Levinas refers to as a "positive religion," we have lost and even betrayed this vision (Levinas 1981, 4). Why? Because any particular view will still be caught up in the categories and divisions of the mind. These positive views are just interpretations of the experience.

It's not that we can function entirely without "metaphysics." After all, we need rules, principles, and generalities to help us organize and cope with the masses of data and possibilities that the world throws at us. But when we place too much emphasis upon a particular set of beliefs, those beliefs become rigid and tend to block or undermine the more fundamental experiences of which they are an interpretation. Because they tend to "capture" the divine into something we can pretend to predict and control, they are reducing that which is radically "other" to something in our own personality.

---

3 Levinas also refers to this as metaphysical desire, but he is using the term metaphysics in a somewhat different way than we are in this text. I feel that "ethical" desire better captures his meaning.

4 Eschatology is a part of theology that deals with the death, judgment, and final meaning of humankind.

We reduce spirituality to an expanded version of personality.

Levinas resists this totalizing vision with a different sort of vision:

> *But it is a "vision" without image, bereft of the synoptic and totalizing objectifying virtues of vision, a relationality of a wholly different type. ... (Levinas 1969, 23)*

Levinas wants us to understand this experience in a richer, more radical, and humbler way. He wants us to understand it in a way that holds the experience open, allowing for the experience to continue rather than coming up with specific ideas about it and using them to shut it down.

This reminds me a joke from my seminary days:

> *The problem with most religions is not that they don't have a corner on God's truth, it's that they think there's only one corner.*

Similarly, many people experience a profound religious insight, what in the West is called a "conversion" experience (Eastern religions have a similar experience, which they might call "self-awakening" [Kramer 1988, 22]) and assume that they now have the final fundamental answer. It's not that they won't keep growing, to some degree, in that direction, but that they are no longer open to the same level of radical interruption that led to the earlier conversion. They have their answer.

How many "rebirths" did we notice in Hesse's *Siddhartha*?

Psychology versus Spirituality: Detachment

How can one tell if one's "detachment" is spiritual or psychological? On a conceptual level, one can use the chart for personal versus impersonal enlightenment. In personal enlightenment, one is still "attached" to one's own bliss, to one's self, while "detached" from the world and obligations to serve others, since that is just an illusion. So long as the focus is on an aspect of oneself, we are still in the realm of psychology.

Kramer offers the following comment on detachment:

> *To live righteously, let alone die artfully, one must act without possessing any attachments to that action. ... one must act without desire or purpose, independently of the results of the action. (Kramer 1988, 34)*

How do we know we are there?

One of my favorite illustrations of this point is to take my classes through the following series of questions:

How many of you have had two friends fighting, or hurt by some sort of disagreement or misunderstanding, and have tried to intervene to help the situation?

Usually, a lot of hands go up.

How many of you have had it blow up in your face, where one or both friends ended up mad at you?

Many, even most, of the hands stay up.

As a result, how many of you have sworn never to get involved in a dispute between two friends ever again?

Some of the remaining hands stay up.

You have not yet achieved detachment.

My experience, in similar situations, is that it has "blown up" in my face perhaps one time out of five. Each time it has happened, I've been tempted to walk away from that risk forever.

But why should I deprive four others of the benefit of my help just because one gets angry at me?

If I walk away, it was really about me. It means that the success, or the failure, was really too much about me. *Detachment from the ego means that, when I act, it's not primarily about me.* It means that I try to act for the greater good and happiness of all.

This doesn't mean that I don't care if someone is helped or hurt. It just means that I don't overly judge my self-worth on the results of any particular action. Certainly, I look at patterns and try to improve my choices. I choose not to get involved in some disagreements if I realize that my involvement would probably make it worse. I try to learn how to nuance my involvement when I take action. But why, for the sake of avoiding the heartache of the occasional time it makes it worse, should I refuse to help the far greater number of times when I can really help? *My success is for the sake of those I care about, not for my ego. The same is true for my failures.*

In this example, "acting without desire or purpose" does not mean acting without intent. My intent is for the greater good. Where *I try to act without "desire or purpose" is in terms of my own ego, myself.*

Thus, detachment does not mean disengagement. Recall from earlier, when Buddha reached nirvana (enlightenment):

... [he] died not to desire itself, for one cannot live without desires, but to his attachment to desire. ... he died to his desire to be enlightened. ... (Kramer 1988, 47)

We will continue to expand on this last comment. Here, it is important to note that Kramer is using the term "desire" to refer to the wants of the ego, the realm of the personality. As Caplan put it:

... true enlightenment ... exists entirely apart from the context of ego and the arena of presumptions. The enlightened states does not presume itself to be enlightened, ego presumes itself to be enlightened. And since most people are identified with their ego, individuals also presume themselves to be enlightened. (Caplan 1999, 9)

Recall, near the end of our discussion of *Siddhartha*, when we asked if he still cared about being enlightened. This goes to that paradox. If I care too much about being enlightened, it is in the realm of the personality, the ego. If enlightenment is to be "awake" to the greater reality, it has to go beyond (and be other than) the ego.

Eastern and New Age Thinking: The Analogy of the Mountain

Caplan begins her book with an analogy of living on a mountain. The analogy moves along as one might expect. Most people live in the base of the mountain. They have decent lives there. Some do more good than bad, some more bad than good. They live and die there.

As one moves up the mountain, we see more people who seek to understand the truth of the mountain (reality) and to live according to those truths.

Next come those who more deeply recognize the nature of the mountain and seek to climb ever higher. Here, the analogy expands to include some of the difficulties in climbing or living on any mountain such as adjusting to the different air pressure, weather, etc. Interestingly, she notes that most of these individuals "strive to live lives of compassion" (Caplan 1999, 5).

Eventually, she gets to those rare persons who have climbed to the top:

They often live alone in the perspective from which they perceive the world around them, although they may have dear ones who live near them and wish to see as they do. They stand as an example that the mountain can be ascended. Some live active lives, receiving visitors, while others camp out and draw no attention to themselves. (Caplan 1999, 5)

There we have it. These are the "enlightened" ones, the rare beings who have achieved nirvana. We have arrived.

But then, Caplan goes on:

Most rare are those who, having reached the top of the mountain, descend the other side, living a life of eternal ascent and descent ... teaching the way of the mountain, helping others tie their boots, filling water bottles for them, throwing them ropes, helping them through mudslides, assisting them in scaling cliffs, encouraging them to proceed against all odds. They never stop to rest, but instead are always guiding others up the mountain. (Caplan 1999, 6)

Does this mean that there is more than one type of "enlightenment"? More than one stage? Or is it just that different people are called to do different things with the perspective gained?

If we think in terms of some of the stories and people we've already heard of, one might think of the Ferryman in *Siddhartha* as one who "camped out" and drew no attention to himself. Yet, even he led a life of service by helping those who couldn't pay to cross the river, and when Siddhartha came to him, he took him in and helped him on his spiritual journey.

Buddha or Jesus would be stronger examples of the most rare type. These are people who reach back into the world and spend their lives explicitly in service to others, helping to relieve their suffering and helping them find "truth."

Both of these examples are, to my thinking, closer to impersonal than to personal enlightenment. What of the personal enlightenment people? Where do they fit in?

Halfway Up the Mountain

Anyone who has been hiking in the mountains should be aware of a certain illusion. One sees a peak to which one aspires. One hikes for hours. Finally, it is within one's grasp. One hikes the last 100 yards, hits the top, and sees ... Crump, it's just a ridge that has been hiding a much higher peak. We still aren't even half way up the mountain (Caplan 1999, 7).

Part of the problem with religious "highs," these peak or conversion moments, isn't that they aren't real, but that, because they are so powerful and life changing we are likely to assume that we now have the "whole" truth, nothing but the truth, and that we are even ready to teach it to others. An important accomplishment, to be sure, but not the end.

Stopping halfway up the mountain feels awfully good. Instead of looking up at climbing the rest of the way, you turn around to those climbing beneath you and say, "Thank you for following me. I'm here to tell you all about the mountain. ..." (Caplan 1999, 6; quoting Jai Ram Smith)

My suspicion is that the "enlightenment now" people have climbed a fairly high ridge, but then, like so many other religious practitioners, have gotten stuck. They believe they are "there." Instead of looking further up the mountain, they look only out from the mountain. While the view is glorious, it doesn't take them onward.

Beyond the Mountain

A moment ago, I cut out part of Caplan's quote about the "most rare": those who, having climbed the mountain, descend back down, and devote their lives to helping others. Adding that part back in:

> *Most rare are those who, having reached the top of the mountain, descend the other side, living a life of eternal ascent and descent, **patiently and compassionately pilgrimaging from mountain to mountain**, teaching the way of the mountain. ... (Caplan 1999, 6; emphasis added)*

"Pilgrimaging from mountain to mountain"? Wait, we started with just one mountain, one truth. Now there are many mountains? Caplan goes on:

> *This book is not about how to get up the mountain and stay there, because ... the real path apparently has no end. The "end" of the path is not really an end, the top of the mountain not really a destination. (Caplan 1999, 7)*

What, then, did Caplan see as the purpose of her book?

> *... rather than dwelling on the subject of how to get to the top of the mountain, this book is a manual on how to avoid getting stuck. ... (Caplan 1999, 7)*

I can only applaud Caplan for this goal. It is, in part, a goal of this text as well. Similarly, note how well this works with both the chapters on faith and truth as processes rather than final end points.

What Caplan is also saying here (at least in part)—and as many Christian, Jewish, and Islamic practitioners have also realized—is that no intellectual metaphysical scheme can capture the real nature of reality, particularly the fullness of whatever we call divine and our path to that divine. For many, they call that being God. For others, it may be instead simply what is most difficult and original about being human. Which is true? All these ideas fall apart, as do fixed ideas about spiritual paths. Are we left with chaos?

There do appear to be two "constants," though descriptions vary. That is, what happens to a person when they have reached and stayed on that journey?

The first has to do with the very fact that this is a moment of spiritual interruption, where a greater sense of reality interrupts and questions my ideas of who I am and what reality should be.

The second has to do with the outcome of that interruption. As Caplan writes:

> *The great beings of past and present do not stake their flags on the top of the mountain and relish the lovely scenery, but instead a life of endless growth and service to others. (Caplan 1999, 7)*

In other words, the claim is that some form of love, empathy, or compassion is at the heart of what we discover in this journey.

These two elements appear to be the closest we can come to an essential truth.

This is an empirical claim. It may not be true. I would like to believe that it names something about the highest expression of every religion, which in turn is attempting to name that which is most fundamentally human, or humanizing, about us and our reality/experiences. Yet, if one looks at religions and scriptures, while great acts of courage and compassion have been done for the sake of those religions, so have all manner of cruelty and atrocities. Empirically, it would seem that both love and hate have equal claim to be the focus of religious and human truth. Which is more accurate and why? That's a question each must ultimately discern for themselves.

However, I have two reasons to argue for compassion. The first reason is fairly simple. Even though the historical record indicates both a great propensity towards love and towards violence in each of these religions, even most of those who choose hate usually attempt to justify their actions in terms of love, the greater good, etc. Even Hitler, for example, wrote in his suicide note that he was acting in service to his people. This suggests that love, or at least some form of the good, remains the guiding constant, though often with distorted meanings.

The second reason is more rigorous. Following Levinas, I will argue that, without compassion, nothing that we think of as characteristically "human"—self, language, freedom, rationality, culture, and even a certain kind of violence—could develop. Recalling Gilgamesh, we share "need" in common with all animals, while "ethical desire" appears to be uniquely humanizing (though I suspect it's seeds also exist in some animals). This will be the topic of the final chapter.

Here, let us follow Caplan deeper down the rabbit hole.

Notions of Enlightenment

Caplan lists eleven "definitions" of enlightenment used by various teachers. The list is not intended to be exhaustive. In fact, at best, each definition only points to an experience, they don't actually answer the question. Definitions are, by their very nature, constructs of the mind, while enlightenment has to do with a greater reality breaking down, allowing us to see the limits of our constructs. So, using definitions is a bit like a Catholic response to the Jewish notion that one cannot have images of God—that would be idolatry. The Catholic response is that one cannot have a single image of God, because God is other than any image. A variety of images can still be instructive in the search for God. Perhaps the Hindus have it right: there are many, many, many faces of God.[5]

1. ***Enlightenment is the shattering of mental constructs*** (Caplan 1999, 39).

Given what we have already discussed, this first suggestion should come as no surprise. By its very nature, we have argued that true spirituality is allowing the greater reality to break into our nice, orderly lives. Ivan Illyich had this happen when he became ill. The illness didn't "fit" into what he thought life *should* be. *It's not about what life "should" be, however, it's about what life really is.*

Enlightenment is hearing that in a deep and radical way.

It's very uncomfortable. Most of us aren't prepared to have our mental constructs shattered (Caplan 1999, 49). What we want, if Caplan is right, is fantasy:

> *… freedom from suffering, the transcendence of pain and struggle, the land of milk and honey, a state of perpetual love, bliss, and peace. … It is not only a New Age fantasy, it is the secret wish of all people. (Caplan 1999, 35)*

2. ***Enlightenment is responsiveness*** (Caplan 1999, 39).

In order to be truly responsive to a particular person or situation, one must first be open and aware. Responsiveness begins, then, with receptivity. It is as the Ferryman told Siddhartha, that he would learn to listen. Real listening is receptivity. Only by being radically receptive can we be open. Only by really listening can we become authentically responsive. One opens to reality, to others, and responds appropriately—with compassion to all, when and how it is needed.

3. ***Enlightenment is a relaxed mind*** (Caplan 1999, 40).

Recall the last meeting of Siddhartha and Govinda. Govinda speaks of seeking. Siddhartha replies:

> *What can I say to you that would be of value, except perhaps you seek too much, that as a result of your seeking you cannot find. (Hesse 1951, 140)*

Siddhartha explains:

> *When someone is looking … it happens quite easily that he sees only the thing that he is seeking … Seeking means: to have a goal; but finding means: to be free, to be receptive,*

---

5   To be clear, the Catholics believe that God has only three faces (the trinity), but that there can be many more images.

to have no goal. You, O worthy one, are perhaps indeed a seeker, for in striving towards your goal, you do not see many things that are under your nose. (Hesse 1951, 140)

If one's mind is constantly active, one cannot be truly receptive. If one cannot be receptive, one cannot be responsive.

4. ***Enlightenment is the knowledge that all things are transitory, including enlightenment*** (Caplan 1999, 41).

Caplan quotes Lee Lozowick:

In every moment, everything changes, so if you take one enlightenment experience and project it into the future, that doesn't leave the possibility for true enlightenment in each moment. (Caplan 1999, 41; emphasis hers)

Recall the two types of enlightenment. This would seem to support impersonal enlightenment, enlightenment as an ongoing process, as the richer notion. Caplan goes on, now quoting Steinitz:

Enlightenment is not any one experience. It is the knowledge—not the intellectual or cognitive knowledge but the knowledge in the body—that all things are transitory, including enlightenment, and including that knowledge. It is living from, acting from, and making choices from that knowledge. (Caplan 1999, 41)

This quote provides some context for why, in charting the different meanings of terms under "personal" and "impersonal" enlightenment, I put "embodied" under impersonal. Somehow, this is an *experience* more of the body than of the mind.

We mentioned once before that enlightenment was more a context than an absolute knowledge. In this case, the context is a profound and embodied recognition that all our ideas about reality, while helpful to some degree, are also false and harmful in other ways. What, then, is the point? Recall the comment, drawn from Caputo, about moderating violence. By being sensitive to the limits of our language and actions, we can regularly fine-tune them to be more sensitive to each moment, each person, each need.

5. ***Enlightenment is an Impersonal Energy*** (Caplan 1999, 42).

This is one place where Caplan deals with the distinction between personal and impersonal enlightenment, and where she also claims that the second is the richer.

Though this may seem strange, it's really not so different from Lewis's argument that one must love God, and the other,[6] for their own sake.

---

6 The "other" or "Other" is a term Levinas uses for the ethical call to care for other people.

Spirituality is not about me.

6. ***Enlightenment is the realization of connectedness*** (Caplan 1999, 44).

> *It has become almost a cliché to say, "Everything is connected. We are all one." Yet there is a great difference between speaking these words and realizing them ... [in] an integrated, bodily understanding. ... This realization inspires a humility that an intellectual, or even intuitive, sense of it cannot. (Caplan 1999, 44)*

Again, back to the "bodily" understanding. We are not just intellectual creatures. Perhaps not even primarily.

Buddha tells us that human suffering comes from our failure to realize our connectedness. By failing to realize this, we engage in adversarial rather than supported relationships. Morrie, in *Tuesdays with Morrie*, tells a story of the little wave. It begins with a wave bobbing about the ocean, happy as a clam, enjoying the movement, sun, and other waves. It sees something new, the shore. As it sees the other waves crash upon the shore, it becomes afraid. "*Don't you understand*," it tells the other waves, "*we are going to crash upon the shore, we are going to be nothing.*" Another wave replies, "*You don't understand. You're not a wave, you're part of the ocean.*"

It's existence as a wave was only a transitory moment, but it would go on in terms of its more fundamental reality, as part of the ocean.[7]

Part of what "humbles" me is the awareness that my ego is just a small part, not all that important. As with Lewis and the pond of *Lethe*,[8] I am no longer concerned about whether it is my accomplishment, or another's, so long as it serves the greater good.

7. ***Enlightenment is the realization that you know nothing*** (Caplan 1999, 45).

Some think that enlightenment means that one will have all knowledge and even all power. Certainly, something special happens. If Caplan is correct, those who are truly enlightened would never be foolish enough to make such a claim, even if some of their followers wanted to believe it about them.

What sort of knowledge, in addition to context, does such a person possess? It's not unlike one who has received a strong spiritual education, but is perhaps the next stage:

---

7   While this story also works for Buddhism, in terms of a more direct analogy, it seems closer to Hinduism.

8   This refers to the story in *The Great Divorce* of the artist, who needs to drink from this pond in order to forget his ego attachments to his own art. "*Lethe*" is Greek for "forget."

The individual who has received a strong spiritual education is not unlike the one who has been well educated in auto mechanics. It's not that every time the mechanic's car breaks down he instantly knows what the problem is and how to fix it on the spot, but he knows where to look, how to diagnose the difficulty. ... (Caplan 1999, 24)

It's the next stage because the person who has experienced enlightenment has something beyond the person who has merely been educated about spirituality. Still, the education does help lay the groundwork. Consider, for example, that while Hesse's Siddhartha had to leave all teachings behind, when he was ready to return to spiritual life, his spiritual education gave him a basis for that return.

8. ***Enlightenment is more easily recognized through understanding one's endarkenment*** (Caplan 1999, 45).

It's far easier, psychologically, for us to focus on our strengths, our good points. We don't want to face the difference between what we think of ourselves and what we really are. But if we don't face the shadow in ourselves, the best we can hope for is personal enlightenment, with the continued denial of both our personal shadows and the real nature of reality.

Reality, or enlightenment, is not the heavenly salvation that most people hoped it would be. There is tremendous suffering in Reality in addition to the joy, and the enlightened vision sees all of it, unable to defend itself against any aspect of it. (Caplan 1999, 52)

For this reason, Caplan notes that "the true saints, although often radiant and capable of great joy, also suffer immensely" (Caplan 1999, 52).

This is a reason for many not to want this difficult path. At the same time, recall an insight from an earlier chapter: **When one numbs oneself to pain, one numbs oneself to joy. Saints, of any religion, appear able to experience both more richly.**

This is part of the reason so many get "stuck" in personal enlightenment. This is not just joyful; it is also painful. Here, Caplan quotes Vaughan-Lee:

You can't bring them back to earth. They don't want to come. Who wants to work on the shadow and look at their own darkness and failures and inadequacies when they can be off on a spiritual cloud nine? (Caplan 1999, 27)

Approaching enlightenment though one's endarkenment may also have another advantage. As Caplan points out, one of the greatest barriers to spiritual growth is spiritual pride.[9] If one approaches enlightenment in this way, it would seem to reduce that risk.

---

9   Another is "attachments" to what we think of as spiritual truths (Caplan 1999, 36).

9. ***Enlightenment is the exception to the rule*** (Caplan 1999, 46).

This is more than saying enlightenment is rare, though that is also true. Rather, it's another suggestion of the limits of rules themselves. Rules are generated by the mind. This goes beyond what any mind can capture.

10. ***Enlightenment has degrees*** (Caplan 1999, 46).

Caplan offers a variety of possible meanings for this claim. For our purposes, it's enough to note that this version appears consistent with other claims (i.e., that one is not necessarily enlightened all the time, that enlightenment is a process, etc.). It also ties in very well with the stages that Siddhartha went through while living with the Ferryman.

11. ***Enlightenment is freedom from the spiritual path*** (Caplan 1999, 48).

Again, this is consistent with claims that have been made repeatedly. For example, Kramer pointed out that Buddha "... constantly reiterated that the religious life does not depend upon doctrines or formulations" (Kramer 1988, 47). With Hinduism, we saw that there was a point where "forms and rituals vanish, sacred texts are superseded, temples are transcended" (Kramer 1988, 35). Hesse made a similar point in *Siddhartha*. Spiritual teachings can help, but they cannot replace one's own experience. To overly venerate a spiritual text is, in Hebrew terminology, to turn it into an idol. The text becomes an idol when it becomes more important than the truths it seeks, always inadequately, to illuminate.

This is Caplan's list. But, as she points out, there is a fundamental problem with making any such list. It also has to do with why most people don't really want enlightenment. Quoting Joko Beck:

> The problem with talking about enlightenment is that our talk tends to create a picture of what it is—yet enlightenment is not a picture but a shattering of all our pictures. (Caplan 1999, 49)

Quoting Bernadette Roberts, Caplan continues:

> This is not a journey for those who expect love and bliss; rather, it is for the hardy who have been tried in fire and have come to rest in the tough, immovable trust in "that" which lies beyond the known, beyond the self, beyond union, and even beyond love and trust itself. (Caplan 1999, 13)

The Beautiful and the Sublime

Returning to Western thought, there are other ideas that could be helpful in gaining insight into this difficult topic. One of them is the idea of mystery, a puzzle or paradox that, while it cannot be solved, enriches us though the process of engaging it. In a sense, human interactions, particularly having to do with communication and intimacy, are a mystery. They don't require a final "conclusion." It's the process itself that enriches.

Two other useful categories of interruption, types of experiences that cause us to forget ourselves, but that also draw us to something greater, are the beautiful and the sublime.

The Greeks were focused on the first type, which we can call **beauty.**

I remember when I first stood in the presence of Michelangelo's *David*. I had seen pictures, even replicas, but nothing had prepared me for this. I was spellbound.

The same can be true, not just with art, but with nature. An "interruption" of beauty, so powerful that it holds us captive, engenders a sense of reverence and wonder. It is truly part of the spiritual experience.

The second category is that of the **sublime**.

Something may be just beautiful. Most beauty fits into our lives; it feeds our personalities. The beauty that holds us in awe, spellbound, also contains an element of the sublime. Most dictionary definitions hold the sublime as that which elevates thought, creating a sense of grandeur, nobility, elegance, or wonder. This appears true, when the sublime is connected to beauty.

What if the sublime is not connected to beauty?

In continental philosophy, the sublime is also thought to be a power of interruption, that which challenges and undermines meaning. When connected to beauty, it creates elevation. When taken alone, it has as much, or sometimes more, to teach us.

Beauty, even with the sublime, tends to reaffirm our understanding of our place in the universe. The purely sublime often casts that into doubt, causing us to ask life's most basic questions. *Facing one's death is sublime: It forces one to ask, what is it, if anything, which makes this life worthwhile?* For this reason, many philosophers argue that facing one's own death is the most fundamental philosophical experience. It pushes one to ask this most important question.

Levinas, however, would disagree. Prior to being able to ask the question of one's death, to even having the intellectual apparatus to understand it, is ethical desire. For Levinas, the ultimate philosophical experience, even prior to that of facing one's death, is the experience of the *other*. The specific experience of which Levinas writes is that of the vulnerable other— the poor, the widow, the orphan, the stranger.

The fact that something can move me to help another, particularly another who is ugly, diseased, horrible to see or smell, or repelling in every other way, this is a sublime interruption. It has much to teach us, but that will wait for the final chapter.

Meditation

Before leaving this topic, I want to make a couple of comments about meditation. The benefits of meditation don't require one to be religious. Previously, we noted some of the benefits of vibrating the vagus nerve through use of the sound "Om." There are many other forms of meditation, including those that involve guided imagery. Here, I'm going to comment on meditation wherein the goal is not to follow some image, but to still the processes of the mind. This form of meditation takes the "space" of consciousness and performs the difficult task of stopping it from constantly projecting possibilities.

Carl Jung argued that there are two main styles of meditation. He called one style concentration point and the other mental mindfulness. Both forms involve breathing slowly and deeply, sitting up straight but relaxed, and attempting to empty the mind.

Concentration point meditation involves using some instrument to focus one's mind. For example, one might use a candle flame or a sound. The idea is to focus one's concentration entirely on that "point" so that nothing else gets through.

Mental mindfulness takes a more relaxed approach. While some sound is allowed, the idea is not to focus the will, but to simply allow all mental distractions to "drift" away. Perhaps a thought about a paper or a project comes to mind? One acknowledges it and lets it drift away. There are many ways of performing this task; for example, some imagine that their thoughts and ideas are clouds. They let the clouds move across the sky of their consciousness until it has cleared.

In both techniques, it's important not to worry when one becomes distracted. Why? It only gives more energy to the thought. Be gentle and forgiving with yourself. Even if you were distracted for a period of time, once you catch yourself, just let it go.

Both methods appear to be effective. My own sense is that, in some ways, concentration point is easier while mental mindfulness is more effective. Why? In the beginning, it seems easier to empty the mind of future projections by filling it with something else, perhaps the image of the candle flame. Yet, one is, to some degree, using one's willpower to make the push. For that reason, what one has pushed out may want back in.

Mental mindfulness, on the other hand, doesn't push with a strong hand. It acknowledges and then releases. It takes more time to achieve the same goal, but because of how it works, it seems to be that what has been released has been released more organically. There is less to push back.

What are the values of these types of meditation?

Obviously, there are values in terms of blood pressure, anxiety, relaxation, etc. I can remember a favorite student, very smart and very cynical, who resisted my suggestion to try this for several years. Then, we did it in an exercise in class. He liked it so much that he took it up on his own.

The benefits go deeper. Here, I want to highlight some of the benefits that tie together with our discussion of the nature of consciousness from chapter one. Recall our metaphor for consciousness as a dynamic space. We understood space in the sense of allowing other things, ideas, or images to come to presence; we understood the dynamic in how it played with those ideas and images and projected them as possibilities for thought, action, and relationships in our futures.

What we are doing with this sort of meditation is "stopping" that process of projecting, at least for a time.

There are profound benefits to stopping. We tend to get "lost" in our projects, often not in the good way of a mystery. Instead, it can be more like a hamster on a wheel, racing and racing but going, well, nowhere.

By learning to "stop" the projecting of consciousness from time to time, we gain the ability to step back from our "projects" in a profound way. Perhaps a goal I've been pursuing isn't really what I want for my life? Perhaps I've just accepted it because others expected it of me? Even if my goals and projects are what I want, perhaps I'm not pursing them in the best way. Perhaps some of what I'm doing is sabotaging these goals, or I'm spending twice the time and energy I need to achieve them.

In other words, these forms of meditation, in addition to some of the usual benefits one thinks of with meditation, can also give one space to relax and make better choices about one's life.

We've seen that there are resources for understanding the distinction between psychology and spirituality in both Eastern and Western religions. We've seen more of why this distinction, like most of what is most fundamental about our reality, cannot be entirely captured by intellectual thought. Still, as Lewis might say, engaging the mystery, both intellectually and experientially, deepens and enriches our very selves, allowing us to rise into our humanity. We've also given additional reasons for why true spirituality involves a turn to compassion. We will advance this discussion further in the final chapter. Now, at last, we have the tools we need to discuss *Tuesdays with Morrie,* the book/movie that inspired the central themes of this course. This is where we go next.

Love as the Ultimate Rational Act

CHAPTER FOURTEEN

Viewing Guide

TUESDAYS WITH MORRIE

Introduction

Tuesday's with Morrie is the book/film from which all three themes of the course are drawn. It is placed near the end of the text for two reasons. While the first theme, that only when one knows how to die does one know how to live, can be explained early in the course; the second theme, how love is the only (ultimate) rational act, required significant preparation. (The third theme, dealing with self-honesty, is also easier to explain.) While all three themes will appear in our discussion, the second theme will be at the heart of this and the last chapter.

We also see a return of the theme wherein the physicality of illness pushes one to deal with certain essential truths. In this case, while it does deepen Morrie's appreciation of what he already took as important in life, Morrie's illness helps Mitch to get out of his head and realize what is really important in his life.

Tuesdays with Morrie[1] is based on the lives and conversations between Morrie, a retired sociology professor from Brandeis University in Boston who is dying from ALS, and a former student of his, Mitch. They had fallen out of touch after graduation. Mitch was a successful sports writer. His job kept him extremely busy and most of his time was spent on the road to various sporting events.

The first couple of scenes provide background information on Morrie's love of dancing and eating, as well as his general zest for life.[2] One day, the dancing

---

1 The book was first given to me by one of my own teachers and mentors, John Johnson. Dr. Johnson was then the Chief of Medicine at St. Thomas Hospital in Nashville, Tennessee. He was an amazing, thoughtful, compassionate man. The irony of the situation is that, a few years later, he was diagnosed with the same condition as Morrie. We had a few of our own Tuesdays.

2 Some readers might wonder why we are using the film rather than the book. This is one of those rare cases where I actually prefer the movie to the book. It's not just the fine

stops. We see Morrie getting into his car. He finds he can't move his legs. The car rolls backwards, gently, into a chain link fence. People in the area, mostly students, start to look up. Morrie attempts to get out of his car, but his legs won't allow him to stand. He falls onto the hard concrete.

People gather, mostly students, unsure what to do. Mitch narrates: "That was when Morrie got his death sentence" (00:03:55).

Mitch's knowledge of Morrie's illness begins while he is on the phone with his significant other, Janine. Flipping channels on the TV, he is listening with only half an ear. Janine is talking about commitment and marriage. We hear Mitch's side of the conversation:

> Because I've been in love with you for seven years. Doesn't that ... (he appears to have been interrupted) ... but in my book, that is a commitment ... do we have to talk about this now? This is the only thing we ever fight about. (interruption) ... because look at what marriage does to people, look at our married friends, look at our divorced friends ... (00:05:50)

Flipping channels, he sees his old professor being interviewed on *Nightline* by Ted Koppel. It stops Mitch in his tracks, capturing his full attention.

> Tonight, Morrie. Lessons on living. Morrie is going to die. He suffers from a disease called ALS, better known as Lou Gehrig's disease.[3] ... Morrie does not have long to live. (00:06:25)

Morrie responds:

> I'm on the last great journey here, one we all gotta take. Maybe I can teach people what to pack for the trip. Maybe my dying can be of value, something we can all learn from. Like a human textbook. ... (00:06:48)

Indirectly, Morrie is already focusing on the question that forms the first theme of the course: What does facing death have to teach us about living? There will be far more to say on the topic.

Meanwhile, the phone goes dead, Janine has hung up. Mitch settles in to watch the rest of the interview.

---

performances by Jack Lemmon and Hank Azaria, it's that, in the movie, the screen writers managed to capture the central message of the book in a single, concise scene. This same message, in the book, is dispersed through a number of chapters. Thus, while it is still easy to overlook in the movie, once seen, it comes through with a clarity not evidenced in the book.

3   Recent research has shown that Lou Gehrig probably did not have ALS (**amyotrophic lateral sclerosis**). Instead, like many athletes, he suffered from multiple concussions. One of the results of receiving multiple concussions over time, particularly if there isn't enough time between concussions to properly heal, can be severe neurological disorders. Some of these cases have the same symptoms as ALS.

Primary Characters

Morrie Schwartz	Mitch's teacher, suffering from ALS
Mitch Album	Sportswriter, former student of Morrie's, writer of the memoir
Janine	Mitch's girlfriend
Connie	Morrie's nurse
Charlotte Schwartz	Morrie's wife

Viewing Guide: *Tuesdays with Morrie*

Should I stay or should I go: (cue music)

Mitch and Janine make up, he tells her of Morrie. Sitting in a sports bar, they talk about whether Mitch should visit his old professor. Mitch is torn. Sixteen years ago, at graduation, he promised to keep in touch with Morrie.

Mitch:	It's not just Morrie, I haven't kept in touch with anybody from college. Reunions, the mail, who's got time for that stuff? (00:09:30). ... He made a really big difference in my life and I never even thanked him (00:10:00).
Janine:	You talk about him as if he's already dead. You could still go see him.
Mitch:	He's in Boston. When am I going to find time to go to Boston?
Janine:	(Voice rising) Well make time, if he meant that much to you! You know you're on the road half your life. Why can't you make time for one trip to Boston?
Mitch:	Why are you getting upset?
Janine:	Why are you making excuses? Why do you have such a problem making time in your life? (00:10:23).[4]

They are interrupted by a couple of sports fans who recognize Mitch. After they leave, the conversation continues.

---

4 When there is dialogue going back and forth like this, I may just include either the final time mark or the first and last time marks. Since there are no pages, the goal is just to make it easy for the reader to find the dialogue on the DVD version of the film.

| Mitch: | Sorry. Anyway, the truth is, it's too late. All these years I haven't sent the guy a postcard. I'm just gonna, how am I going to face him now? (00:10:38). |
| Janine: | Mitch … think … (*she has to pull him back from another distraction*) … hey! Think of him. Think about how much it would mean to him. At least call him (00:10:50). |

Observations:

First, is Janine talking only about Morrie? Of course not. This is a pattern in Mitch's life. He keeps overly "busy" to keep others, including Janine, at a distance. Her reaction is stronger because it touches on an issue that she has also experienced.

Second, as such, it's an opportunity for Janine to call Mitch out on one of his **self-serving rationalities**. Mitch is afraid that Morrie will be angry at him. Why wait until he is dying to get in touch? Did he mean so little to Mitch?

It's only an issue because Mitch is focused on himself, his own feelings. If Morrie was angry, well, that would be sad. But there's a chance that Morrie will be happy to see him, happy that he finally reached out. If Mitch's primary concern is about protecting himself, he won't take the risk, with the result of reinforcing a level of **psychological death**. If he is willing to care more about Morrie, he will take the risk.

There's an important lesson here. Many people feel awkward going up to a person who has suffered a profound loss. We don't know what to say, we are afraid of making a fool of ourselves, of being insensitive.

That's the problem. We are focused on ourselves. *Once we stop thinking about ourselves, once we place ourselves in service to the person in grief, the awkwardness drops away. It's ok to be silent. It's ok to talk. We merely place ourselves in service to whatever they need at the moment.*

Later, talking with Janine on the phone, we see that his care for his old professor (or, perhaps, his guilt for having neglected that care) has won out. In a moment of self-reflection, we hear Mitch's thoughts:

> *I lived on the phone, made dozens of calls a day. Why couldn't I make one to a dying man? The simple answer was guilt. But it was more than that. I was afraid of seeing him now. I had a thing about death. (Memory flashback from graduation where he promises to keep in touch.) I failed that promise. I also had a thing about failure. (00:11:04)*

The First Trip to Boston

Mitch decides to make a quick trip to Boston to assuage his guilt, but he is utterly unprepared for what might happen. First, Morrie gives Mitch a huge hug of welcome.

Unlike Mitch, Morrie is comfortable both with himself and with Mitch. Though Morrie is the one dying, his focus is not on himself. Morrie cares deeply for Mitch. One can see that Mitch is still uncomfortable, but he feels better for Morrie's welcome.

There is a phone call for Morrie while they are eating. Unlike Mitch, who almost always takes calls, Morrie focuses on the person who he is with. He asks Connie to take a message, because "I'm with my buddy now" (00:13:30).

There are indications of the disease. Besides the need for a wheelchair, Morrie has trouble with basic utensils while eating. They have a conversation about a class where Morrie came in, sat down, and said nothing for 20 minutes. Finally, Morrie says, "What's happening here. ... What is it about silence that makes people uneasy. ... Why do people only feel comfortable when they're filling the air with words" (00:14:23). Then, as Morrie is about to take a break for the commode, he tells Mitch:

> *You know, dying is just one thing to be sad about. Living unhappily, that's another matter.* (00:15:05; emphasis added)

Even more important, Morrie presses Mitch to face himself. After the welcome and dinner, they sit in what might be Morrie's study, talking.

Morrie:	Are you happy in Detriot? (00:15:24).
Mitch:	Yea, best town to be in for a sports writer. ...
Morrie:	Are you giving to your community?
Mitch:	I ... I ... a ... (stuttering, not sure how to answer). They're nuts for sports. That's what I give them every day in my column.
Morrie:	Are you at peace with yourself?
Mitch:	Yea, ah, I can't complain. ...

For Morrie, **these three questions appear linked**. Are you happy? Are you giving to your community? Are you at peace with yourself? Remember the suggestion that we have made before that happiness may be a byproduct of something else? Perhaps these other two questions get at what it might be a byproduct of.

Morrie shifts strategies, getting to a more specific question. Mitch used to love music, particularly piano. Morrie asks him about his music, his desire to be a pianist.

Mitch:	Yea, I gave it a shot. Then I grew up (00:16:00).
Morrie:	(Skeptical) You grew up, huh? Married, with kids?
Mitch:	Ah ... no.
Morrie:	Haven't found anybody to share your heart with?
Mitch:	No. Yes, I have, definitely.
Morrie:	Ahhh. Not enough to get married.
Mitch:	Ah, no. Well ya yes, you know, someday, but a, just when we're both ready (00:16:20).

After a few more questions, Morrie presses Mitch on his reasons:

Morrie:	... So Janine shares this "when we're both ready" thing with you? (00:16:30).
Mitch:	(with hesitation) No.
Morrie:	... I can see, Mitch, that we're going to have a great deal to talk about (00:16:40).

Mitch, in saying that they were waiting until they were "both" ready, told the truth. Logically, if either one was not ready, then the claim that they would not marry until they were "both" ready was accurate.

But he told it in a way that initially hid the fact that he was the only one who wasn't ready. Unwilling to admit his responsibility, he phrased it in a way that implied that Janine shared his inability to commit. It was a **classic pretext**, using a truth or a half truth to hide a larger lie. Morrie saw through it and pushed Mitch to admit it to himself.

Finally, Morrie turns to explaining ALS. He says, "It melts you like a candle. In my case, from the bottom up" (00:16:55). To expand on Morrie's explanation:

ALS is a progressive neurological disease than normally works from the extremities inwards. The voluntary muscles controlling the legs and arms go first, but the brain remains functional. This can be a great source of frustration for ALS patients. Their mind is as sharp as ever, but their ability to communicate with the world diminishes with each day. Eventually, if one is kept alive for a long enough time, it ends with what is called "locked in syndrome." This is a condition where one can see (if one's eyes happen to be open; one may have lost control of one's eyelids) and hear but can make no voluntary motion or utterance. It's a terrible way to live. The average life span, with medical assistance, is between two and five years after diagnosis.

Most people die, or choose to die, well before the locked in stage. The first major decision point is when the muscles controlling the lungs cease to function. At that point, a person with ALS must decide whether to go on a ventilator or be kept comfortable and allowed to die. Usually, by that time, they've had short periods of time on the ventilator, so they have a sense of what it will be like. The difference is that, this time, they won't ever come off.

After his explanation, Morrie continues:

Morrie:	But, I'm a lucky man (00:17:20).
Mitch:	You're lucky? (incredulous)
Morrie:	Yea. I still got time to learn. Time to say goodbye to the people I love. And, time to teach my final course.

Mitch:	About dying.
Morrie:	***Not about dying, about living! When you know how to die, you know how to live*** (00:17:40; emphasis reflects tone).

Herein we find the first theme of this book. ***There is no indication in the book or the movie that Morrie believes in a literal afterlife.*** We will have to see, as we go along, what Morrie means by this statement.

Mitch leaves shortly afterwards, not expecting to return. Morrie thinks otherwise. He takes a deep breath, counts how long it takes to exhale. Morrie can only count to 16. He tells Mitch: "You know it's a good thing to count your breaths now and then. Keeps you from putting things off" (00:19:00) (in other words, putting off the people who are important in your life).

Janine

Mitch is back at work, games, and press conferences. One evening, as he is finishing the day's column, Janine is waiting to go to diner. She gets up to leave and a conversation starts.

What is striking about the conversation is how Mitch, as in the first phone call, is only listening with half an ear. He is multitasking. His real attention is on finishing the article. He responds to certain key words without hearing what she is really saying. They are talking across one another.

Frustrated, she finally blurts out: "***I can't just keep going on like this, you know, waiting for you to fit me in. I ... I ... just got to think about what I want***" (00:21:40; emphasis reflects tone).

We can't always give every person all of our attention. There are too many demands on us. But as we discussed with Siddhartha, we all need people who listen, really listen, when it is important. If there is a pattern of listening, then the occasional lapse should be easily forgiven. Moreover, it was unfair, in a sense, for Janine to bring this up when Mitch was less than five minutes from the deadline for having to turn in the day's column. She even apologizes for the timing. However, to be fair to Janine, Mitch has created a life that is so "busy" it rarely allows for quality time with Janine. There are probably very few good "times" in which to bring up the issue.

When Mitch asks for time off from work, or at least to stay in Detroit, his boss refuses. In the airport on his way to yet another game or press conference, Mitch sees a gate with a plane leaving for Boston. He switches planes.

310 | Facing Death, Facing Oneself

Second Trip to Boston

Voice

When Mitch arrives at Morrie's, there are cars everywhere. At first, he is worried. Charlotte tells him, "you almost missed the funeral" (00:24:42). Then she explains that it is a living funeral. "He said he didn't want to wait until he was dead for people to say nice things about him" (00:24:48).

During the funeral, Morrie recites part of a stanza from a poem by his favorite poet, W. H. Auden.

> All I have is a voice
> To undo the folded lie ...
> The lie of authority
> Whose buildings grope the sky ...
> No one exists alone;
> Hunger allows no choice
> To the citizen or police;
> We must love one another or die (00:25:45).

The last line of this poem plays a significant role in Morrie's and Mitch's later conversations. We will return to that later. But there is another point to be made with the poem. The notion of "voice" is very similar to that used by another key writer to whom we have referred, Elaine Scarry.

Recall Scarry's claims about the relationship between pain and world. *World, if you recall, is the sum of one's possibilities for thought, action, and relationships beyond the physical body.* In this context, **"voice" is understood as the power by which we extend our agency, our freedom and possibilities, beyond the body to create our world.** A person's real voice is only, in part, what is spoken. *It comes from the core of who we are and reaches to what we aspire.*

Voice can be very powerful. For example, while most suicides have very little impact beyond those in close relation to the person committing the act, there are rare instances where one can change the world. Such was true of the origins of the Arab Spring. A street vendor in Tunisia had his livelihood taken from him by corrupt police. Leaving a note to that effect, he set himself on fire in a public street. This suicide was not the "cause" of the Arab Spring, but it was the spark that caused long simmering public resentment over oppressive political regimes to ignite.

A more precise example is provided by Scarry. Part of the very nature of torture is the collapse of one's world, so that, in part, the world of the torturer feels all the larger. This is part of the reason why the US military no longer punishes captive soldiers who sign confessions. In time, with torture, it's not about betraying one's country, the mechanisms of torture can make it such that one's country, family, and friends, psychologically, no longer really exist for them. How can one betray that which doesn't exist? In one case, Scarry writes of a prisoner who was about to break. Then, he heard a song coming from over the wall from another prisoner. He was singing to give him support. It was a like a ray of light coming into a dark room. Suddenly, his world was illuminated, expanded, and restored. He was able to hold on. This was an actual "voice" that stood against the folded lies of authority and gave back a world to one who was nearly lost.

The same analysis can apply to most abusive relationships.

Consider also the gateway to hell in *What Dreams May Come*. Some lost souls on the ships were screaming, but their mouths were sewn shut. Because they had allowed themselves to be silenced, at least about what was really important to them, they had lost the ability to have a voice.

This is not uncommon.

While I was at Vanderbilt, the chancellor was an MA in business, not an academic. He was brought in, initially for a term of about five years, to help with the financial status of the university. He did a fine job. However, not all aspects of a university should be run like a business. After he had been in the job for well over the expected five years, a petition was circulated to "thank him for his service" and to ask him to step down so that an academic could take over the reins. The organizers of the petition approached only the most senior members of the faculty, full professors at the top of the pay scale whose jobs were considered inviolate.

A number of these professors, though they agreed with the petition, refused to sign. Why? For some at least, they had spent their entire profession going along with the system, not making waves, in order to get ahead. Some probably even told themselves that, once they reached a point where their jobs were secure, they would then be able to take a stand against policies and actions that seemed to them to be wrong. Yet, as Aristotle knew too well, character is formed by decisions over time. They had lived their lives as mice. Now, though there was practically no risk, they were afraid to lend their voices to what they believed in. They had lost their voices.

This is not to say that one has to stand up for every cause, to die on every hill. No one has the time, means, or energy to right all wrongs. But if we do not, at times, stand up and take risks for causes and people we believe in, eventually, we will find ourselves unable to stand up at all.

Roaming Around Campus

After the funeral, Mitch takes Morrie out on campus. Their first conversation is about aging. Mitch asks Morrie if he ever wished he was young again. Surprisingly, Morrie says no. "I know how miserable it can be being young" (00:27:44). After a conversation about how our culture worships youth, Morrie exclaims:

> **The fear of aging reflects ... lives that haven't found meaning.** (00:28:14; emphasis added)

The same could be said for the fear of death.

They move on to a place where Morrie used to dance. It has closed. As they contemplate the decaying façade, Morrie comments: "I used to think that if I couldn't dance, I couldn't live" (00:28:36). Yet now, he takes joy in what life he has. What changed?

I remember the following email from Dr. Johnson, well into his illness:

> *I'm feeling well, but am having to adapt constantly to continuing degradation of capabilities. Had I gotten here overnight I'd be depressed. It helps to know what's in the offing and have a chance to adjust.*

Part of this has to do with reframing our world. If we have time, we can adjust to new possibilities. While illness can leave us feeling out of control, knowledge makes us feel less helpless, less out of control. This expands one's world and so reduces suffering.

This also reminds me of my friend who became quadriplegic while in graduate school. In researching the condition, I discovered that persons who end up quadriplegic (paralyzed in all four limbs) almost always want to die for the first year. After the first six months to a year, about 80% of those suffering serious spinal cord injuries change their minds, happy that they were kept alive (Wilder 2006, 83). While they can't experience many of the joys of life from before the injury, they find that there are still experiences worth living for. How does one separate the 80% from the 20%? While no measure is perfect, it appears that a reasonable ability to communicate with others is very important. It's part of being able to impact our world, to leave a legacy. *We are back to voice.*[5]

There was another important moment in that walk around campus. Mitch asks Morrie how he remains so cheerful, if he ever feels sorry for himself. Morrie replies:

> *Usually in the morning, you know, before everybody gets up. **I get so ANGRY. So bitter.** I just, **what the hell did I ever do to deserve this**! Where is the fairness? What? I cry, I rage, I mourn. And then, I detach. It's over, that's it, all over. I just look back on how I've been feeling and I say, well that's self-pity and that's enough of that for today. ...*

---

5 Earlier, we also noted that one of the primary decision points of ALS patients was whether to go onto a ventilator. When that happens, the spoken part of voice is lost to them. But much of their voice is lost before this event. In this sense, the movie is Hollywood. Morrie remains able to speak clearly until the end. In reality, it would have become progressively more difficult to speak, until only those close to you, who had been with you as your speech degraded, could understand you.

That's all the time I give it. I start thinking about the day ahead, you know. The people that are going to come to see me, the stories that I'm gonna hear. ... (00:29:23; emphasis reflects tone)

Recall our earlier claim: ***to numb oneself to pain is to numb oneself to joy.*** Morrie gives himself time for the negative emotions, but he doesn't let them dominate him. By not repressing his negative emotions, his capacity for joy, and his world, are also increased.

Nearing the end of the visit, Morrie and Mitch are back at the house. Morrie is "reveling" in the experience of having received a massage. Mitch replies that he doesn't really care for massage. Morrie comments about not understanding how some people don't like to be touched, how babies need touch so badly, and he cries.[6] Morrie asks Mitch if he cries; Mitch doesn't answer. Morrie presses further:

Morrie:	All of this makes you uncomfortable, doesn't it? The crying, the touching, I see you look away (00:32:53).
Mitch:	I guess I'm just not really a touchy-feely guy.
Morrie:	Yea, it scares you.
Mitch:	It doesn't scare me.
Morrie:	Yes, it scares you. All this does. Everything we're talking about. Death, dying.
Mitch:	There is a reason why people don't talk about these things. To spare people's feelings.
Morrie:	*To spare people's feelings? I never have understood that.* ***How can you spare someone's feelings by denying them?*** (00:33:18; emphasis reflects tone).

Here, Morrie is calling Mitch out on a very **common self-serving rationality**. Because Mitch is uncomfortable with certain feelings, he doesn't want to deal with them. *Rather than take responsibility for his own limitations, he makes it sound like an act of compassion, to spare someone else's feelings.*

This time, when Mitch leaves, there is no question about whether he wants to return. Mitch asks, Morrie replies: "Office hours are Tuesday, we're Tuesday people Mitch" (00:34:55). The reference is to when Mitch was a student, Tuesday was the day they would meet to talk.

---

6 Morrie is an emotional guy to begin with. But the greater release of emotion, the inability to hold emotions back, is also a symptom of ALS.

I Want to Be Remembered ...

While Mitch is poised for personal growth, Janine is unaware. She has waited for years and has had enough. She breaks up with him over the phone.

Time passes.

Mitch becomes a regular visitor to Boston. Usually, he brings food. He remembers what Morrie likes. Their relationship becomes increasingly comfortable. One day, he brings a recorder. Mitch tells Morrie:

Well, if you're going to keep giving me this meaning of life stuff, I want to remember it. I'd like your voice. (00:39:15)

After some banter, Mitch decides that the recorder was a bad idea and starts to put it away. Morrie stops him:

Hey, you still don't understand. I want you to remember, and I want people to know my story. (00:39:45)

Here we see a hint of one of one of the ways in which Morrie answers the "meaning of life" question, at least for himself. ***The meaning of life is to be remembered by those whom one loves, to have made a positive contribution to their lives.*** Where have we seen this before?

Psychological Death

Mitch eventually tells the story of the death of his uncle. For Mitch, he was more like an older brother than an uncle. He taught Mitch to drive, to play football, to play music. He died of cancer at 42. They never talked about it. Mitch tells Morrie that this was when he gave up music.

From Mitch's perspective, he thought he was growing up. Death made him realize that he had but a short time, so he'd better make something of himself. The problem was that he only faced it on the surface, not deep down. *They didn't talk about it. They pretended everything was normal.* Instead of authentically facing death and finding out what was really important for him, he ran.

What does this mean? One of the ways one can face death is, as we have said, to figure out what is really important in this life and to live one's life more fully. This was Morrie's way. As painful as a loss can be, *for some, the very intensity of that pain can be a testament to the value of that person in their lives.* If taken in this way, unless one gets "stuck" in that pain, it will pass, and one will be open to future relationships. In fact, it can deepen one's capacity to live and to love.

Mitch, on the other hand, never dealt with the pain of the loss. He hurt so badly that, instead of dealing with the pain and passing through to the other side, he pushed it away. ***Mitch never wanted to hurt like that again.*** Relationships put one at risk for hurt; the more one gives one's heart, the more vulnerable one becomes. So, Mitch pushed everyone away, even keeping the woman he loved, Janine, at a distance, so that he would never go through that pain again.

Mitch had chosen a form of **psychological death**.

As before, Morrie calls Mitch out on his self-deceptions:

> *You made a big success, I always knew you would. But you ran. Did you ever stop to think about what you're running from? (00:41:05)*

While Mitch changes the topic, Morrie has clearly struck a nerve. They have named the heart of why Mitch was unable to commit.[7]

To help Mitch understand his fear, Morrie tells a story of his youth. His biological mother died when he was young. He was fortunate to have gained a wonderful, loving stepmother, who balanced his father's emotional distance. At the climax, Morrie is so emotional he is having trouble breathing, but he goes on. This is a message he feels Mitch has to hear:

> *My father was afraid of love. He couldn't give it, and he couldn't receive it either. Maybe that's worse. Not letting ourselves be loved because we're afraid of giving ourselves to someone we might lose. ... (00:44:25; emphasis reflects tone)*

This was Mitch's fear as well. But now, Morrie was in respiratory distress. Mitch, unable to figure out how to use the oxygen tank, manages to call Connie.

Shortly thereafter, Mitch calls into work. His boss is furious that he isn't at the playoffs. Thinking that Mitch is at another "job," he tells Mitch to take the comp time he has built up and that they will just get along without him. They both slam down the phones.

The Physicality of Someone Else's Death

Out of work,[8] Mitch now has time for the sort of reflection he has been avoiding all his adult life. We see two profound changes, both of which were already in progress. Mitch now wants to help Morrie, even physically; whereas before, he wasn't comfortable with touch. He asks Connie to show him how to move Morrie from the

---

7 I don't think they are implying that, in order to be happy, everyone has to be married. It's just that, in Mitch's case, he was unable to make that commitment, even if he wanted too, until he dealt with old wounds.

8 Not entirely out of work, he still had his part-time TV gig.

wheelchair to the recliner. Mitch is awkward and apologizes. Instead of giving up, he promises, "I'll get better at it" (00:47:05).

What is driving Mitch to face himself is not just Morrie's words, but the sheer physicality of Morrie's illness and impending death. We saw this with both Ivan and Vivian. Unlike those two stories, Morrie was already someone who was in touch with his whole being. While illness sharpened his insights, Morrie already possessed much of that wisdom. Instead, Morrie's illness creates an opportunity for someone else.

Mitch only returns to see Morrie because Morrie is going to die. The intensity of their relationship, in the light of impending death, is as important to Mitch's self-growth as are Morrie's actual words. If not for Morrie's illness and death, Mitch might have wandered through life until, in the end, he was as lost as Ivan Ilyich.

Morrie speaks to this insight:

> *Don't look so sad because I'm going to die Mitch. Everyone's gonna die, even you. But most people don't believe it. They should have a bird on their shoulder. That's what the Buddhists do. Just imagine a little bird on your shoulder, and every day you say: Is this the day I'm gonna die, little bird? Am I ready? Am I leading the life I want to lead? Am I the person that I want to be? If we accept the fact that we can die at any time we lead our lives differently. ... If you did have a bird on your shoulder, you wouldn't put off the things closest to your heart. (00:47:40)*

Mitch takes this lesson to heart. The personal work he has done, along with the time for reflection, has helped him to both heal and to realize what he wants the most. He buys a ring and shows up at Janine's work to ask her to marry him.

Mitch never gets the chance. As they are walking to the car, he makes a crucial mistake. He tells Janine that he wants her to come and see Morrie, and that when he is with Morrie, he doesn't want to be anywhere else. This only serves to remind Janine of the fact that Mitch was always working to "fit her in," and that he had never given her that same gift. Her emotional walls come up and she drives away.

The Tension of Opposites: Love Always Wins

Morrie told another story of his father and stepmother, about how life pulls us one way or another. Later, he will expand the notion to include the fact that we learn both from what hurts us and what loves us (01:15:55). We expanded the notion further, for example, in *Wit*, by arguing that most of the interesting things about being human take place in the "grey" areas between extremes.[9] But here, Mitch asks the question, if life is pulling us one way and other, who wins? Morrie replies:

---

9 For example, Vivian, as a teacher, was completely rigid in her deadlines for students. There, we discussed the need for rules (justice, learning character and discipline for life), but also the need to balance

Love. Love always wins. *(00:55:07; emphasis added)*

This is a blatantly false claim, which Mitch sees immediately. But Morrie is a very smart, wise man. So, what might Morrie *mean* by this claim?

Mitch tells Morrie about the engagement ring, and about how he didn't even get to give it to her, despite their love for one another. Mitch recognizes what Morrie has been telling him about fearing to give himself in love. Finally, Mitch asks:

> *So, if love always wins, what the heck is the matter with us?* (00:56:47)

Morrie is not so naïve as to think that love always wins in the sense that it is always successful. Empirically, that's clearly false. Later, when Morrie tells Mitch the story of his father's death, he exclaims:

> *I won't die like he did. I'll be surrounded by love. My family and my friends, at peace.* (01:15:34)

Here, we catch another glimpse of Morrie's position on the meaning of life. Recall Kübler-Ross's insights about a peaceful death. One of the two was to be surrounded by people one loved, to feel that one has made a positive difference in their lives. Morrie is talking about love in this way.

For Morrie, love is an essential key to happiness. It may not be the only element, but without love, we cannot be fully happy. This gives us a way to logically frame Morrie's position.

> If the goal of life is happiness
>> and if love is necessary for real happiness
>>> then **love is the only way to win**.

We can see how this argument, put this way, makes Morrie's claim true: love always wins. But Morrie's way of saying it isn't very clear. *Morrie is not claiming that love is always "successful."* Rather, Morrie is arguing that **if love isn't successful, then there is no real winner.** Love is the only way to win, the only way to be truly happy.

We can also see that this suggests Frankl's notion of meaning as more important than happiness. Meaning has to do with that which extends up beyond ourselves, to something greater than ourselves. Love is a way, perhaps the most profound way, to extend that meaning.

Before moving on, it's important to note another claim, particularly because it could easily be misunderstood. Earlier, in the context of love always winning, Morrie stated:

---

that with the need for reasonable exceptions (we are all different and have different circumstances in our lives). The "grey" is this balance between rigid rules and no rules at all.

Maybe the game isn't over yet. (00:55:22)

The danger of this comment is that it can keep a person in an unhealthy, even abusive relationship, particularly if one believes the naïve formulation of "love always wins." That's not what Morrie is suggesting.

A better way of thinking about it comes in the context of Mitch himself. At this point in his life, Mitch does not know if Janine will ever come back into his life. As this is a true story, it could have gone either way. In a very real sense, Mitch had already won, regardless of whether he married Janine. Mitch was now open to love, open to life, and open to relationships. He was now able to love and give himself fully. *If it didn't work out with Janine, if their history turned out to be too long and painful for him to win her back, at least he was now capable of loving someone else.*

Love as the Only Rational Act

On the flight back, we hear Morrie's voice on tape. Mitch plays the key phrase twice.

We think we don't deserve love, that if we let it come in, we'll become soft.

... said it right. **Love is the only rational act.** *Let it come in. (00:57:38; emphasis added)*

Most people think of love and reason as opposites. Reason works on cold, hard logic. Love works on emotion. The two can work together, but how can "love" be rational?

Actually, it's not hard to make an argument for love being a rational choice. To do so, one need only *think of reason as a tool for achieving our goals.* If one of our goals is love, then one of the goals of reason would be love. This would make love a "rational" act.

It's far harder to make the case for love being the "only" rational act. Again, empirically, the statement is clearly wrong. But, again, Morrie is a pretty wise man. Is there a way of thinking about his statement that might make sense?

Instead of talking "only" in the sense of "exclusively" (i.e., that there can be no others), perhaps we could take "only" in the sense of "ultimate," the one that is most important, to which all other goals are secondary. If so, we can construct an argument similar to the one we constructed for "love always wins." Such an argument might run as follows:

IF: the goal of human life is happiness/flourishing

IF: love is somehow essential to the fullest level of human flourishing

IF: reason is a tool we use to achieve our goals

THEN: love is the ultimate rational act.

Just as we "reframed" Morrie's statement that "love always wins" to the phrase "love is the only way to win," so we are reframing Morrie's statement that "Love is the only rational act" to "Love is the ultimate rational act." We now have the second theme of this book.

Note that, if any of the three clauses is wrong, the argument falls apart. *The claim here is that love is the key element we need in order to experience the fullness of "human" happiness.* If so, *happiness is really a byproduct of love.* Staying with this formulation, if reason is a tool we use to reach our goals, and if our highest goal is happiness, and if love is the key element in happiness, then the ultimate goal of reason is really both love and happiness. It's not the only goal, but it is the most important one.

I think this captures Morrie's insight fairly well. This formulation takes love as the goal of reason. In the next chapter, we will, in a sense, reverse this argument by exploring how love is also the foundation for reason. We get there by arguing that love is part of the very foundation of every attribute we think of as characteristically human. If love is at the very foundation of our humanity, it also becomes the source, or an essential element of the source, of reason.

Janine

Mitch reaches out to Janine a second time. This time, he pours his heart out in a letter, which he leaves at her apartment along with an engagement ring. This was probably a better strategy. While the written word risks misunderstanding due to the loss of tone and expression, at least he got everything out. She could take her time to process what he wrote.

Initially, there was no response. Mitch felt like a fool. And yet … he wasn't. He had risked himself for what he wanted the most. Moreover, he had done so in a heartfelt but respectful way. He had lost, but he has also won.

In the airport on the way for yet another trip to Boston, he sees Janine. She places the ring in his hand and closes it. Mitch is confused.

Mitch: If this is a no, why didn't you just call me? (00:59:30).
Janine: Because I don't know what the answer is. Whatever Morrie did that made you write that letter, I want to see for myself (00:59:33).

When they arrive in Boston, Janine sees a transformed Mitch. Mitch, instead of being self-absorbed in his own affairs, is focused on caring for Morrie. Instead of being uncomfortable with touch, he responds naturally and effortlessly when Morrie needs oxygen, even stroking Morrie's head as he holds the mask. (Later, we will see Mitch massaging Morrie's feet and even learning how to give him a therapeutic massage.) Morrie, full of affection for Mitch, refers to him as "my helper that one" (01:02:58).

The Little Wave

While eating, Mitch asks Morrie to tell Janine the story of the ocean, the little wave. After a couple of false starts, Morrie complies:

> ... there's this little wave. And he's out there bobbing up and down and having a grand old time. Just enjoying the sunshine and ... until he sees the other waves ... crashing into the shore, so he gets scared. ... And another wave says to him, "Why do you look so sad?" And the little wave says, "Because we're gonna crash. All us waves are gonna be nothing. Don't you understand?" And the other wave says, "You don't understand. You're not a wave, you're part of the ocean." (01:01:50)

We already have a story (the little bird) from Buddhism, but one might ask, what world religion might this story best represent? Buddhism certainly applies, but it seems as though Hinduism may be a slightly better fit. Why? Buddhism applies from the standpoint that it is our illusion of separateness that leads to suffering. Our analogy to Hinduism makes the same claim. The analogy of the wave to the ocean also easily fits with our analogy of the Atman and the Brahmin, where the Atman is a droplet of spiritual energy (or a perhaps a wave?) and the Brahmin is the great ocean of the spiritual all.

Either way, it implies that Morrie may view spirituality from the perspective that an individual afterlife is irrelevant. What is most important is taking part in the greater whole.

We noted that Janine was able to see a transformation in Mitch. She saw that he was now able to give himself fully to love and commit. This is **spiritual death and transformation**. While it happens in stages, Mitch is dying to the person he was and is being reborn anew. This is taking place without specific religious doctrines.

Janine and Morrie reconcile and get engaged. Mitch eventually returns to work, but with the condition that he have Tuesdays free to see Morrie.

Solid Food

In a driving rainstorm, Mitch runs from his car to the house. As usual, he was carrying gifts of Morrie's favorite foods. When he opened the refrigerator, he saw that it was full of deli containers from previous visits. Charlotte tells Mitch that Morrie can no longer eat solid food. Mitch understands, but winces. "I'm sorry Charlotte, I just want to bring him something, you know?" (01:08:08).

For me, this story is a poignant moment for another reason. I saw one of my own friends and mentors in the same condition. Knowing it was hard for him to get out, and to make it easy on his wife, I would bring takeout when I came to visit. My visits were fewer and further between than the weekly visits of Mitch with Morrie. At one point, I suspected that he would be unable to eat solid food.

Still, like Mitch, I wanted to bring him something. I handpicked a pound of my favorite See's candies, soft centers only, hoping that he could eat them. It turned out that, so long as they didn't contain nuts, he could suck on them, allowing them to melt in his mouth.

It was a difficult visit. The paralysis had gotten to the muscles controlling speech. While he could make himself understood to his wife, I could not understand him. He sat in a wheelchair with a laptop containing a voice synthesizer, where he painstakingly pecked out each letter for the words he wanted to say. His brilliant mind was undimmed, but he could only communicate slowly and with great labor.

As I was leaving, his wife stopped me at the door. She asked me if I knew that See's were John's favorite candies. I did not. A feeling of intense gratitude washed over me. I was so happy to have been able to give him this one thing. I was also grateful for her kindness in letting me know.

When I got to my car, I cried.

A month later, he was dead.

We Must Love One Another or Die

Morrie told Mitch of the place he planned to be buried. It's under a tree on a pond, as Morrie says, "A great place to think" (01:23:38). Mitch asks, "You planning on doing a lot of thinking there?" (01:23:40). Morrie replies, emphatically, "I plan on being dead there!" (01:23:44).

For just a moment, it looked as though Morrie might be suggesting an afterlife. Instead, he pulls back. He asks Mitch to come and talk with him, to tell him his problems. Mitch comments that it won't be the same. Morrie replies, "Well I'll tell you what, when I'm dead, you talk, I'll listen" (01:23:55).

The conversation brings home to Mitch the fact that Morrie hasn't much longer to live. Mitch wonders if, once Morrie is gone, all his teaching will be wasted on Mitch. Mitch, choked with emotion, speaks:

Mitch: Nobody's like you. And if it took your death to teach me these things, then I'd rather not learn them. All the things you said? I'd give them back in one minute if this wasn't happening to you (01:24:35).

Morrie:	It's happening, it's going to happen.
Mitch:	Yea, well I don't want it to happen. I don't want you to die. That poem you're always quoting, we have to love one another or die? We die anyway, don't we? We learn to love somebody and they die, or we die, or it dies, what's the point? (01:25:03).

Mitch has just asked Morrie the meaning of life question. What is the point of it all? Here, we see Morrie's answer.

Note that I use the term "see" rather than "hear." At first, the only word Morrie speaks is "**Hold**" (01:25:07; emphasis added). With great effort, he lifts his hand just a bit, calling with that hand for Mitch to take hold. **Mitch holds Morrie's hand.**

Morrie will say more in a moment. But why this act first? As we have seen again and again, some things cannot be answered by words. As with Yama giving Nachiketas the sound of Om for an answer, **answers about the meaning of life cannot be understood unless they are first experienced in the body and in the heart.** Morrie is **showing** Mitch the answer. Only then will his speech make sense.

Mitch:	I'm sorry, I just can't accept that I don't want you to die. I guess I flunked the course, huh? (01:25:15).
Morrie:	Death ends a life, not a relationship. Poor Mitch, you still don't know how to say goodbye … Look at me. Don't you understand, you touched me. What if you hadn't come back to see me? This is the way we say goodbye …

(Morrie gestures and Mitch takes his other hand.)

Morrie:	Love you.
Mitch:	(In tears) I love you too, coach.
Morrie:	I know. You want to know something else? You always will (01:26:12).

Morrie will live on. If there is no afterlife, he will live on in Mitch, Janine, and all the other people whom he has touched, who touched him, and whose lives were made better by their time together.

For Morrie, it seems that this is enough.

It is an answer that stretches back to the dawn of humankind.

We saw it in the Epic of Gilgamesh.

CHAPTER FIFTEEN

Love Is the Ultimate Rational Act

TAKE TWO

In *Tuesdays with Morrie*, we offered the following argument for why Morrie could say that love is the only rational act.

> IF: the goal of human life is happiness/flourishing
>
> IF: love is somehow essential to the fullest level of human flourishing
>
> IF: reason is a tool we use to achieve our goals
>
> THEN: love is the ultimate rational act

As we've said before, Morrie, while a very wise man, isn't perhaps as "precise" in his language as a philosopher or a theologian might like. Saying that love is the "only" rational act is clearly false. But, when we look deeper into what Morrie might mean, it appears that "only" could be taken more in the sense of "ultimate" or "most important" than in the sense of "exclusively."

In *Tuesday's with Morrie*, when seeking one's greatest overall good, *love becomes the goal of reason. In this chapter, we will reverse that direction.* Instead of arguing that love is the ultimate goal of reason, **we will now explore how the capacity for love, understood primarily as compassion, is essential to the development of reason, to the possibility of reason itself.** If the capacity and experience of love/compassion is necessary for the development of reason, at least in our human reality, then love becomes part of the source of reason. As part of its source, every rational act would be rooted in love, even if used to deny love.

If this is accurate, it also provides a reason why love (mainly understood as compassion) appears to be the "outcome," or the highest expression of spiritual realization, in all of the major world religions.

What if reaching the highest levels of spiritual awareness is really just another way of saying that one is radically awake or open to the fullness (to whatever degree a human is capable of receiving) of reality? Then it should come as no surprise that, if the "outcome" is an awareness and outpouring of compassion, then compassion should also, in some way, be at the very root of what makes up reality, and ourselves.

There is evidence, but not proof. Still, this is a rich way of engaging and exploring the mystery.

Other than "enlightenment," this is likely to be the most complicated argument we will attempt. But it's really just another description of human experience.

Turning Points: Interruptions

We have described spirituality, not as an experience of a world behind the scenes, but as the power of something "other," *within and as part of our own reality,* "**interrupting**" and breaking through, creating the possibility of seeing reality in richer and more complex ways. We all have these experiences of breakthrough. It's not clear that all such awakenings are explicitly "ethical" in nature. These will exist for all people who are capable of ethical sensitivity. I would call them spiritual and ethical awakenings. I'll offer some examples:

Liz: How Our Mistakes Can Make Us Better People

I don't know my exact age when this happened, but I know that I was less than eight years old, because I remember the house where we lived. I was in the kitchen, alone. Our cat, Liz, was walking across the floor towards me, probably hoping for a treat.

On impulse, I picked her up, turned on the gas stovetop, and held her above the flame.

Fortunately, I didn't hold her in the flame. After a few seconds, she made a cry and jumped out of my hands.

This is the first time in my life that I recall feeling flooded with shame.

In retrospect, I don't think I was trying the hurt Liz. I really wasn't thinking at all. I was just a kid acting entirely on impulse.

The results, however, rocked me to my core. *I had just taken a creature who had done me no harm, who had showed me nothing but affection and kindness all my life, and hurt her.*

I was ashamed.

I checked Liz out, there was a bit of singed hair, but no real injury. What a relief. I cleaned off the hair and soothed her. *I never told my parents*; I was never caught.

But something in me changed. In some respects, it's important that it changed even though I wasn't caught. *I didn't change due to fear of punishment. I changed because my heart changed.*

At that point, I swore never to intentionally harm other creatures.

Since then, I've modified that to exclude bugs in the house or if there was a compelling reason. But I've never since intentionally inflicted pain on other creatures and have rescued and helped others when I could.

This was a seminal moment in my character development. There's also a choice here, though I was barely aware of making it. I could have gone the opposite way, rationalizing and justifying it to myself, perhaps even progressing to pulling the wings off of birds.

Instead, it took me in the direction of greater compassion, greater sensitivity to the suffering of others, animal or human.

The choice I made with Liz had no immediate consequences for anyone other than myself. That could have been good or bad. Good because, since I made the better choice, it was real. But if I had wanted to make a cruel choice, it would also have meant that my parents wouldn't have known to try and steer me back in a better direction. It's also possible that, had someone else known about it, I might have felt a stronger need to try to justify myself instead of just accepting blame.

We all have these seminal choices, these situations that form our character. We all respond to them somewhat differently. *If we are willing to accept responsibility, rather than justifying ourselves, we stand to grow as much or more from our mistakes as from our accomplishments.* The tension of opposites.

There's something else about this experience that I couldn't put to words then, but I can now.

Accepting my feelings of guilt, taking responsibility for the future, this is what allowed me to forgive myself. Had I not done so, I would have had to **repress** that guilt, with all the implications involved.

Jack: How Our Mistakes Can Make Us Worse People

"Jack" was a friend I knew while in my early 20s. He was talented, smart, funny, good looking, the life of every party. He was caring and idealistic, with plans to join the Peace Corps. He was dating a wonderful woman, "Julie," but they knew it wasn't a lifelong relationship. The plan was to part on friendly terms when Jack left.

The problem is that after he left, Julie discovered that she was pregnant. As a strong Catholic, abortion was not an option. She decided to raise the child on her own. Still, she felt she had an obligation to inform Jack.

This was a seminal moment, a life turning point. How would Jack react?

Instead of being supportive, Jack pressured Julie to have an abortion. He was angry, hurt, and scared. He was forced to return home because of Peace Corp policy. He was afraid that his life was being taken away from him. He tried to rally his friends, including me, against Julie.

His focus was on himself, there was no room for a woman he had once cared about or a child that was coming into the world. He was all about defending his life, his righteousness, even if that meant attacking an innocent.

Interestingly, he and his family were also Catholic. Prior to this event, they would have argued against abortion. But I learned something else from them, something that was reinforced in my own marriage. His family were wonderful, kind people. But, in talking with people who had known him since childhood, I learned that his family had never really been strict with him. They had always gotten him out of scrapes and never made him face the consequences. Here, also, they backed him unconditionally.

His parents confused unconditional love with a lack of boundaries. Without good boundaries, without consequences, most people won't develop strength of character. Without that strength, when faced with tough choices, we are more likely to choose poorly.[1] As we recall from Aristotle, we need correction and discipline as children in order to develop moral virtue.

My understanding is that Jack went into law and, at least for the next few years, was all about money. Some of our mutual friends told me that he became very cynical. So much for the Peace Corps. I think that, when he rejected Julie and his child, he also rejected that side of himself that cared for the greater good.[2] Perhaps he had never gotten beyond doing "good" for the sake of how it would look to others. I haven't spoken to him in decades. I can only hope that he's made different choices since. *We all need second chances.*

Julie, on the other hand, got so fed up with his behavior that she made him a deal. If he promised to stay completely out of their lives, then she would never pursue child support.

He got what he thought he wanted.

She got to raise their child in peace, with one loving parent.

Candy or Kindness? Ethical Awakenings

This story also begins before the age of eight. Again, I know that I was in elementary school because, in those days before fears of child abduction, I was able to walk to school or to the store by myself.

We had just been given our allowances. Having a powerful sweet tooth, the entire meaning of my existence became centered on permission to go to the store and satisfy

---

1 I've seen this dynamic many times now. In fact, whereas I used to resent my parents' demands, as a mature adult, I wrote them a letter thanking them for caring enough to punish me.

2 To be clear, I'm not saying he should have married Julie (as usual, not their real names). But he could have treated her with kindness and respect. I'm also not commenting on the morality of abortion, only on how he handled the situation.

that need. My parents, of course, saw giving us an allowance not as a means for immediate gratification, but as a way of teaching us to save and handle money. This was not part of Mom's plan.

Mom was having a bad day. I don't remember why; I just know that something was going on that made her unhappy. She was cleaning the house. I pestered her as only a young kid can do. I wore her down. In sheer exasperation, she told me, "Get out of here!"

That was all the permission I needed. I was out of the house like a shot. I wanted to be far enough away so that she couldn't call me back.

Once at a safe distance, I slowed. Then slowed again. The image of her frustration—her sadness, her pain, her face—stayed with me. It bothered me, though not in a way I could put into words. I walked slower and slower.

Finally, when I reached the store, I headed for the candy. But there, next to the candy, was a stand that had little figurines. One of these was of St. Francis, one of her favorite saints. Something crystallized, though I still didn't have words for it. It was a feeling. I bought the statue. I'm not sure whether it was choice or impulse.

I still remember how happy it made my mom. While I went back to buying candy, a start had been made. I had actually allowed care for someone else to count more than for myself.

The ability to "forget" oneself in the face of another's pain can occur on many levels. Usually, it is only a partial forgetting, where we feel drawn to care but don't fully let go of ourselves. **On rare occasions, it can be so powerful that we become lost in another's pain, completely forgetting ourselves** for a time. That pain is part of a greater reality breaking in. One such experience happened when I volunteered with an agency working with street kids in Seattle.

Street Kids in Seattle[3]

New Horizons was a Christian outreach organization that served kids (ages 18 and under) who lived and "worked" on the streets of Seattle. Most of the work, both outreach and in the center, occurred at night. But on this day, I was meeting with my mentor, a young woman with far more experience than myself. Let's call her Sally. It was a beautiful summer afternoon, and we were going to meet for lunch, where she was going to help me process my experiences.

At the time, downtown Seattle had not yet been gentrified. Abandoned warehouses and stores with doors sunk 15 feet in from the sidewalk, lined by angled glass showcases, lined the street. We were on the way to Pike Place Market. Suddenly, we saw

---

3 I published a fuller version of this story in "*Street Life*," StreetVibes, Greater Cincinnati Coalition for the Homeless, May 2004. I did not use that version in writing this short summary.

a man, a boy really, in one of these deep store fronts. He was holding a young girl, also probably about 16, up against one of those show cases, clearly against her will.

Testosterone kicked in. I yelled, "Leave her alone!" Not thinking, of course, of the fact that I was also putting Sally at risk and that, with her vastly greater experience, I should have followed her lead. The young man turned to us. As he came at us, I prepared to defend Sally and myself.

As he swung at me, I saw that there were tears streaming down his face. I tried to talk to him, but all I remember was him saying, repeatedly, "No one knows how much it hurts, no one cares."

The fight went out of me. I still blocked his swings (as best I could), but I was utterly arrested by his pain. I couldn't add to it. I just tried to talk with him.[4]

This went on until Sally left to call the police. Only then, almost as a vindication of his power, he stopped and left, his girlfriend willingly in tow. We later found that the incident had a powerful effect on the girl, but never found out where the boy ended up.

For me, it was an utterly profound and sublime experience. Never had I "lost" myself so fully. Never had I been so willing to risk myself to help another. I later described it as having seen the face of God. Not that the boy was God, but rather, that something divine spoke through his pain and suffering. In the moment, I lost myself, but there was also a return. Something changed in me, for the better.

The experience could also be described as sublime. Why sublime? Usually, we associate God or the divine with power and authority. This was something utterly different. This was, as Jesus would have said, the least among us. For the first time, I understood that, **when we are enjoined to care for the poor, the widow, the orphan, the stranger, (the migrant?), it isn't so much about what it does for them as about what it changes in us**. The sublime has to do with that which doesn't seem to fit, which calls to us and interrupts our ideas, agendas, and conceptions about the world. At that point, I **began** to realize that, if there is a divine, it speaks there. It is confusing and disrupting. If one stays with it, however, it can also be beautiful and life-giving.[5]

This is part of what Levinas is writing about. It's part of the reason why he often uses poetic and confusing language. He is trying to get away from spirituality as a "bigger" world behind our world, where ours doesn't really matter. There is a radical "absence" (space?) that calls to us from **within** our world, within ourselves, within the other. It has strong affinities to our discussion of enlightenment. In particular, **both focus on two notions: interruption as the process and compassion as the outcome. Though for Levinas, there is a focus on compassion as the source of the interruption, while that is less clear from our discussions of enlightenment.**

---

4 It's worth noting that, if he had had a weapon, or been a more effective fighter, I might have run or been more physical. Still, I took some nasty blows and limped for a couple of weeks.

5 To clarify, something beautiful can be sublime, if that beautify interrupts us in some way. But there is much that is sublime that is not beautiful.

These Magic Moments

Our lives are made up of important impulses and choices. As Aristotle tells us, while we can change our character, over time, it gets more and more "cemented" in a particular direction. What I'd like to focus on first, however, is the nature of this ethical awakening, *our human awakening*, where we first feel real compassion.

We introduced this idea in our discussion of truth. The example used there was of a child, being held by his mother during a tantrum, who hits her in a delicate spot. The child looks at his mother and sees tears of pain on her face and in her eyes.

If the child is primarily motivated by a fear of punishment, no real transformation has occurred. If, as with me and our cat Liz, it's not about fear of punishment, but real compassion, then a spiritual and ethical interruption has occurred.

Levinas's claim, which we introduced with the *Epic of Gilgamesh*, is that this sort of human moment, or at least the capacity we share to have this moment, is, in fact, fundamental to our very humanity. To understand this, let us review the notions of need and desire.

> *Need* names those impulses that serve the organism, turning inwards (i.e., food, shelter, pleasure, reproduction, etc).
>
> *Desire* (which I often prefer to call "ethical" desire)[6] refers to those impulses that turn outwards, taking us towards the service of others.

Recall that "need" is actually more basic than ethical desire (i.e., one can function on the level of need without desire). Only one who can experience needs can also experience desire. If I could not feel hunger, I could not truly empathize with another's hunger.

Partly for this reason, need is usually more robust than desire. We will often choose ourselves over another, even when the other has a greater need.

Yet, there are times when desire can overcome need, when need can be overwhelmed by compassion. And, depending upon how one cultivates one's character, the two can be brought into greater or lesser balance. For some, desire can even dominate.

Recall also that this has profound implications for the nature of heaven, God, and even the idea of a literal Garden of Eden. If love, understood here as compassion, names the highest virtue, then how could it develop without pain and suffering? If one did not experience pain, even if one saw pain in another, how could one empathize? If I could not experience hunger, how could I understand, except perhaps as

---

6 Levinas also uses the term "metaphysical desire," but he is using the term metaphysics in a different manner to common usage. It's also worth noting that these terms are translations from the French, so their common meaning is somewhat different from the English.

an intellectual abstraction, someone else's pain when undergoing starvation? In a perfect world, love, understood as compassion, would be irrelevant.

Returning to our example of the child, what is the impact of the experience of desire, of care? Let us sketch it through the development of some of our most essential human characteristics: sense of self, freedom, rationality, culture, and even, particularly, human violence.

Freedom and Language

The notion of freedom is considered essential to how we think of our humanness. Following John Stewart Mill, the most natural notion of freedom for most English-speaking Westerners could be described as **spontaneity** (i.e. *freedom is just the ability to do what I want, when I want to do it*). Simple.

That's a common Anglo-Saxon notion of freedom. But a **Germanic** notion might be quite different. For example, for Kant, *freedom has more to do with the ability to do one's duty.*

This second seems very odd. To our view, duty seems the opposite of freedom. What could they mean?

Levinas's notion is close to the Germanic idea of freedom. If we follow it through, we will see that both notions have something to contribute.

Let's begin with spontaneity.

We all know people who can't control their impulses. Such a person might risk pregnancy or an STD through unprotected sex. They might lose their temper, and lose a job or end up in jail. Perhaps they just can't resist staying up and partying, and so end up exhausted on the job site the next morning.

We refer to such people (among other things) as "*being slaves to their passions.*"

Strictly from the standpoint of spontaneity, they are free. They are doing exactly what they want, when they want. But it costs them dearly, including freedom, in terms of their futures.

If freedom is just the ability to do what one wants, my cats are usually more free than me. They come and go as they please. They sleep and eat as they want. They play. They get their messes cleaned up after them. (Dogs have masters, cats have staff. ...) They suffer very few restrictions (the kitchen counters are one). By contrast, I have to go to work, keep a schedule, and have all sorts of obligations. In fact, part of the reason I work is to keep them in kibble. By this notion, who is more free?

Somehow, we think that *there is something fundamentally different about human freedom and animal freedom.* Mill is thinking of this when he writes that most would rather be a discontented Socrates than a contented pig. Yet, if we think of freedom only in terms of spontaneity, that difference disappears.

Short-Term and Long-Term?

One way to think about "limiting" spontaneity is in terms of short-term and long-term freedom. This means that, instead of just following my impulses, I pull back from my immediate impulses far enough to see if they serve my long-term happiness. At this level, I am no longer just spontaneously acting on my impulses, but choosing which, how, and when to follow them.

This requires distance.

Say I have a strong impulse to eat a piece of cake in front of me. What slows me down? If I have never had any restrictions placed upon me, I'm likely just to follow that impulse immediately. But what if I have been punished for taking things like that in the past? Now, there is a counter impulse, the wish to avoid the unpleasantness of punishment.

These two impulses pull against one another. To some degree, I may simply follow the one that is strongest at the moment. But the fact that they pull against one another also opens up a sort of "space" between impulses, a pause between impulse and immediate action, a space for choice. This allows for a sort of distance or *separation* between impulse and action.[7]

Now that I have two fairly strong impulses, I can make a choice between them.

Some of this has to do with willpower, but not all. Often, the way to choose the less immediate impulse is to consciously strengthen that impulse (i.e., imagine the disappointment in your parents' faces, or perhaps experiences in jail). The choice is which impulse to feed, and why.

As in the Native American story:

> *Within each of us are two wolves fighting for control.*
>
> *One wolf is evil; about anger, hurt, bitterness, envy, regret.*
>
> *One wolf is good; about kindness, love, generosity, forgiveness.*
>
> *A young boy asks his Grandpa, "Which wolf wins?"*
>
> *Grandpa: "The one you feed."*

This comes back to the development of character. The more we feed particular types of impulses, the stronger those impulses become, and the easier they become to choose.

---

7   I can't help but think about the marshmallow experiments with toddlers. Kids are placed alone in a room with a marshmallow. They can eat it, but they are told that, if they refrain for a certain period of time, they will get two marshmallows. The contortions the kids experience due to the conflict within whether to satisfy that immediate desire or wait are then video taped.

Ethical Separation

There's more than one kind of "space" for a choice that can be created. We can talk about the separation from the world generated by the experience of need. That is, because I experience hunger, I realize that there is something separate in the world, food, to satisfy that hunger. We can also expand on the example of punishment and consequences. These are particularly necessary for children as it helps them to get a start on the ability to step back from those immediate impulses. It also prepares the ground for the more profound movement of separation, ethical desire.

Aristotle recognizes this in his ethics. In the beginning, children have to be disciplined to make good choices. In time, when the "habit" of good choices becomes easier, it means that a particular virtue or group of virtues have become part of your character. For Aristotle, there is still a fundamental difference between those who come to choose good acts for their own sake and those who merely choose them because it's the law or for some other external reason. Levinas attempts to explore that deeper, internal source.

Recall our example of the young child and his mother. For the first time, perhaps, something in him is moved by the fact that she is hurt. Moreover, *HE* is the one who hurt her. This is more than a fear of punishment. As with my cat, Liz, something awakens. It is care, empathy for another person. It is feeling their needs and their pain.

That feeling places a call upon me. If, in that moment, I am really open to YOUR pain, it pulls me. It **interrupts** my wishes, my goals, my needs, and it pulls at me to care for yours. For Levinas, this is the root of language—*vulnerability* to another's pain, another's needs. In that case, language begins not with the spoken word, but with the experience that calls us to language.

What does this mean? **The Latin root of vulnerability is "to be wounded."** I am wounded by your pain. I want to do something, to help. But there is a problem. Even though, because I too have experienced pain, I can feel that you are in pain, *what I feel is not the same as what you feel*. I don't really understand your pain. I don't really understand you. I don't really understand how to help. For that, I have to reach out to you. *In order to understand your needs, I have to learn and develop language.*[8]

---

8 Language begins here, not with a Hobbsean experience of enlightened self-interest, but with a profound interruption of one's spontaneity by the needs of another. While, at times, we talk to one another to manipulate someone for our own gain, that's not all language is about. In fact, it's hard to understand how language and communities would ever get started if all we had was self-interest—the stronger would just take from the weaker. Once we have sophisticated language, then the "weak" can use it to unite against the strong. But, as my much wiser colleague William Clohesy teaches, it seems unlikely that self-interest, on its own, would account for the initial development of communities and of language.

We see that the capacity to care is part of the source of language. But what of freedom?

Let us return to the Germanic notion. Freedom is not just about spontaneity, that would just be animal freedom. Distinctly human freedom includes an ability to separate from one's immediate impulses and care, instead, for the needs of the other. One might call this "duty," but not in the sense of rigid rules. Rather, *it is the counter impulse that balances ones needs and gives one the space to choose*. It is the interruption (note the connection to spirituality as interruption) of our impulses by the care for someone or something greater.

The call to care generates what we call *human* freedom in at least two ways:

1. As an impulse other than self-interest, it creates the ethical space within us to make a real choice. It is at the basis of our ability to choose.
2. It greatly expands our range of choices by helping to create language, human community, reason (to be argued), etc.

The first should be apparent from the argument that has already been outlined. The second, however, depends partly on what follows. Before we leave the topic of freedom, let us give that argument: if ethical desire is necessary to the heart of what we are as humans, to language, to reason, to becoming communities, then it is also necessary for all the fruits of our work as communities. Thus, for example, we now have the ability to get on a plane and fly to Hawaii. As language and technology become more and more sophisticated, they open up new possibilities for human activity and expression. We have choices, due to our human communities, that no person had 100 years ago. Hopefully, in another 100 years, our children will have even wider ranges of choices.

Justice, Reason, and the Self

We have given a quick outline of Levinas's argument as to why the ethical impulse is the source of both language and distinctly human freedom. Now we move on to the issue of justice, which will also give us reason and self-identity.

Justice begins, for Levinas, *in the tension between the singularity of each ethical desire and the fact that we experience many such demands*. What do I mean singular? Each is experienced as unique. Each person is unique, with different capacities and needs. Each person speaks to that ethical moment in their uniqueness as singular, as one. Biblically, this might be expressed in Luke 12:17 or Matthew 10:30, as the notion that every hair on one's head is counted.

Justice doesn't just have to do with me and one other person, it has to do with all of the people I meet or have real or potential interactions with. On some level, these are all potential ethical obligations. The sheer number and scope of needs is over-whelming! How many of us cannot bear to watch either the "save the children" or the "save the animals" specials? For most, it's not because we lack compassion, but because we feel overwhelmed by our compassion.

Sometimes we deal with this by shutting down. We also do so by developing ways *of weighing and measuring* our obligations, ways of saying which we will respond to and which we will not. In order to do this, we need to have *common measures*. Thus, even though every student in our classrooms is unique, teachers grade all of them according to the same standard. Unless there is a "compelling" difference *of which we are aware*, we try to treat all students as if they are the same.

This brings back Aristotle's theory of knowledge. We abstract commonalities from our experiences in ways that are useful. *Abstract*, from the Latin, means *"to take away."* What is lost? That which makes them singular, unique. For example, are any two men or any two women alike? Of course not. Yet, for the sake of procreation, it is a useful way of dividing up reality. We create (intellectually) what we call universals or generalities as a means of grouping together similar experiences.

Treating a group of things as if they are the same is to create a general category about them. In another example, tomatoes and peaches are very different; yet, they are both food, even both fruits. What we are doing is "abstracting" what we view as nonessential differences and treating them in terms of a single general category. But that doesn't really mean that they are the same.

Justice, for Levinas, is that task of balancing that which cannot be perfectly bal-anced. Even though we are all unique, even though the ethical claims we each have on one another are also unique, no one person is able to respond to more than a tiny fraction of those calls. Moreover, I too have needs and a claim upon myself. The ques-tion of how to balance these claims, how to figure out which to serve, that becomes the question of justice.

These can go too far. For example, separating men and women into two categories can also be used to discriminate against one or the other, or against persons who fit into neither category.

Which leads to an interesting insight: *the same capacity that generates useful uni-versals also generates stereotypes*. In fact, it could be said that *a stereotype is just a morally objectionable universal*. We will return to this crucial insight when we get to the nature of violence.

For now, let us stay with justice. Think back to the example of the child with his mother. The very fact that we experience this call—not just to one, but to many, and *even to ourselves*—forces us to ask two fundamental questions. We've already addressed the first:

What are those needs?

Again, this part of the origin of language.

The other has to do with which needs to serve. I have to determine:

Whose needs are more important?

To do this, I not only have to understand your needs, I have to come to understand my own. For that, I have to develop an awareness of myself as separate from others. I have to come to a certain self-awareness.

Thus the demand for justice not only requires that I develop (1) an understanding of the other (through language), but also (2) a means to adjudicate different claims upon me (a rationality), and (3) an awareness of who I am, of self-identity.

To be clear, this is not to say that there aren't other critical factors. Yet even cultural anthropology has come to recognize that the capacity for compassion is just as important for human development as, for example, the opposable thumb and the complex brain.[9]

Each of these capacities—reason, language, the bonding that forms communities—are essential to the development of both self-awareness and human culture. But one might ask, if "compassion" is so central to what we are as human, how and why are we so often cruel to one another? Would not the history of war and violence speak against this thesis?

For that, we need to understand both the nature of human violence and why the ethical impulse is so fragile.

The Nature of *Human* Violence

What do we mean by "human" violence? Animals fight, but they don't try to justify their killing. Most kill to eat or protect territory. At times, some will kill while trying to play with a smaller animal. Most don't really hunt for sport.[10] They don't try to wipe out entire species. *What makes human violence so chilling is not just the technologies employed, but our ability to rationalize cruelty and even genocide.*

Levinas argues for two ways in which we do violence to one another while telling ourselves that this is ok. Recall that (ethical) desire is always "singular." Ethical desire, at its foundation, is always for THIS person in THIS situation. I see someone in their vulnerability and pain, and something in me is arrested, stopped, so that I feel pulled, even at times compelled, to care, to help. Later, we develop a sensitivity

---

9   For another description of this process, including references to cultural anthropology, see Degnin and Wood, 2007.

10   As an aside, I have no problem with hunting or killing for food, so long as it's done humanely, and the species is not endangered or self-aware. Even sport hunting, so long as it's also for food, is morally acceptable, though I'd not be likely to ever take part.

to groups and issues. But *our most basic ethical impulses and experiences are for one other at this specific time*. It is singular (one) and concrete.

For Levinas, the call of the other, the call of the vulnerable, is the ultimate spiritual insight. In his philosophical writings, he focuses only on describing it as a basic human experience. In his more spiritual and religious writings, for him, this is the most fundamental way in which the divine speaks to us.

Just as with need, which points "inward" towards the needs of the organism (food, pleasure, etc.), desire, which points outward, also happens, in its most fundamental form, prior to the intellect. It can be nurtured and enhanced, but it can also be numbed.

How can it be numbed? Remember that the root of the ethical impulse is singular: it is the experience of compassion for THIS person in THIS situation. Such an impulse doesn't always happen. But when it does, how do we block it? Levinas notes two methods, both working on the same mechanism, which I will call:

1. **Distraction / dispersion**
2. **Reflection back upon the self**

The mechanism by which this is accomplished takes us back to the difference between a stereotype and a universal. In one sense, there is no difference. They are both universals, ways of generalizing and grouping experiences or objects. In another sense, they are different. As we said, *a stereotype is a morally objectionable universal*.
Here's the clincher: *they are both created as a result of the push for justice, which in turn is generated by the ethical impulse*. In other words, as we will see, part of *the very product of the ethical impulse is the mechanism for denying that impulse*. It turns back upon itself.

Imagine, for example, that you're a guard at a Nazi concentration camp. You're not a sociopath; you are a normal, well-educated person in a challenging situation. You love your family and see yourself as a good, kind person. You also see yourself as a patriot. How do you reconcile your beliefs about yourself with the atrocities you are, if not committing directly, at least supporting?

Scarry, at the end of her analysis of torture, gives an example of the first method.

> *Concentration camp guards, according to Bruno Bettelheim, repeatedly said to their prisoners, "I'd shoot you with this gun but you're not worth the three pfenning of the bullet," a statement that had so little effect on the prisoners that the constant repetition was unintelligible to Bettelheim until he realized that it has been made part of the SS training because of its impact on the guards themselves. (Scarry 1985, 58)*

Scarry is describing how, whenever a guard began to feel the stirrings of compassion for their prisoners, they **distracted** themselves from what they were doing. At times, the pain and suffering of their prisoners would "interrupt" them in their jobs; they would start to feel compassion for this person in their vulnerability and need. *To stop that feeling, they told themselves, again and again, that this wasn't really a person.* It had a human form, but it was really subhuman. *It wasn't even worth the cost of a bullet.* This allowed the feelings, and the energy, to **disperse**.

What we are seeing, therefore, is how **one can use an intellectual schema, or set of ideas, a universal, to block one's natural compassion**. For most people, if they do it repeatedly, it becomes easier and easier. (*It becomes the wolf they feed.*) We can numb ourselves to ethical desire.

When we place an intellectual idea between us and another person, instead of seeing them in their singularity (as an ethical call upon us), we see them only as an example of a category.

This mechanism is not just at the heart of Nazi agenda, it's at the heart of racism, sexism, and most of the ways in which we dehumanize other persons and groups of persons.

Of course, it comes at a cost, not just for the victims, but for the guards. We can't numb ourselves in one area of our life and keep the rest of our lives fully alive, but we can separate them to a surprising degree. Thus, we have a Nazi physician who performed horrific experiments on his victims and yet wrote sensitive poetry to his daughter.

Scarry also provides an example of the second type, this time quoting Hannah Arendt. Note that Arendt refers to the sort of compassion to which Levinas refers as "animal pity."

> *Hence the problem was how to overcome not so much their conscience as the animal pity by which all normal men are affected in the presence of physical suffering. One trick used by Himmler—who apparently was rather strongly afflicted with these instinctive reactions himself—was very simple. ... It consisted in turning these instincts around, as it were, in directing them towards the self.*
>
> So ***instead of saying: What horrible things I did to these people!,***
>
> *the murderers would say:*
>
> ***What horrible things I had to watch in the pursuance of my duties, how heavily the task weighed upon my shoulders!*** (*Scarry 1985, 58; emphasis and spacing added*)

In other words, instead of feeling sorry for their victims, the guards and torturers found a way to feel sorry for themselves, to reflect that compassion back upon themselves.

This can be a bit complicated, but the main argument is as follows:

The Nazi's argued that "survival of the fittest" was nature's way of protecting each species. That is, if the weak survived and procreated, the species would become weaker rather than stronger. In that case, it would eventually fall prey to other species or natural disasters. The same is true for humans. With the advent of civilization, however, humans are now keeping their weak alive. Worse, the weak are procreating faster than the strong. This resulted, so they believed, in "subhuman" species of humans. If these subhumans were allowed to continue breeding and mixing with the remaining "pure" stock, it would eventually degrade human stock to the point where the human race, as a species, would collapse.

It didn't matter that this was a very distorted reading of evolution, it was plausible enough to form a **pretext** for the "final solution" (killing those classified as subhuman). Himmler, and many of the guards carrying out this genocide, were still troubled by the pain they were causing. This solution, while also using a set of ideas about the nature of reality to block their natural compassion, had the effect, instead of dispersing the energy of that compassion, of *reflecting* it back upon themselves. *One hears in the guards' statements almost a sense of tragic nobility.* To paraphrase:

> *Look at the burden I had to bear for the future of the human race, for our children.*
> *A lesser man could not have carried out such a difficult, ugly, but necessary task.*

We see here a classic **self-serving rationality**. It doesn't actually need to be true. It only has to sound plausible enough for us to use it to lie to ourselves.

One can clearly see how and *why ethical experience can be so fragile.*

1. Need is more fundamental: one can experience needs without ethical desire, but not the reverse.
2. Ethical desire, by its very nature (as singular), generates the very mechanism for its denial (treating others in terms of categories) by generating the call to justice. This becomes what we have termed distinctly *human* violence.
3. While the capacity for compassion appears to be necessary for the development of human culture, language, etc., once developed, these capacities and tools can be used for other purposes. For instance, to serve selfish needs or violence rather than one another.[11]

---

11   For example, while a group of sociopaths might never develop language on their own, a sociopath growing up in a society where language, culture, and reason are already developed can do quite well. They can learn these tools and use them to their advantage, even if they would not have developed them on their own. Most sociopaths aren't serial killers. A difference is that, while they can even learn to mimic compassion, they don't feel any emotional pull towards care or ethics. They act in purely self-interested ways, even manipulating others through the appearance of kindness. One of my former business ethics colleagues, Donna Wood, pointed out a disturbing statistic: the number of sociopaths

This "reversal" of ethical desire is not a must, but it is a strong tendency. We need universals and generalities in order to function. It is easy, therefore, to get lost in ideas, rules, and laws rather than seeing what they are intended to serve. At the same time, this only heightens Caputo's call to moderate the violence that these rules and ideas generate. It becomes an issue not of perfection, but of balance. Moreover, it offers a striking suggestion.

Closing Remarks

Rising into Our humanity

While on one level we want to acknowledge and respect the basic humanity of all people as a given, on another level, *Levinas's thought implies that our life task is not just to take our own humanity as a given, but to spend our lives rising into and developing our personhood, our humanity*. It works well with what we have seen as the two common factors in a peaceful death:

1. **Have I lived a rich and full life? Have I explored life and experienced much of the richness this life has to offer?**
2. **Am I surrounded by those I love, or perhaps preceded by them, so that I feel a rich connection to others? Do I feel like I've contributed to their lives and happiness and they to mine?**

Does it seem like we've come full circle?

These two factors speak to a person who has lived a rich and full life, who has expanded their world by living with and for others. **Happiness**, for such a person, is likely, but it **appears to be more a byproduct than a direct goal**.

A byproduct of what? There are many factors that make for a happy life. But, at least since about the 12th century in Western thought, the most important appears to be a life that has a connection to something greater than oneself. The evidence appears to support the notion that, while one can feel that one's life is meaningful but not really happy, it is rare that one can be happy without feeling that one's life is meaningful. One could also argue that the richest key to a meaningful life, to connecting emotionally (more than just intellectually) to something greater than oneself,

---

among Wall Street CEO's is about four times the rate in the general population. We've allowed them great influence in structuring our society.

is found in our capacity for empathy and compassion, the ability to place ourselves in someone or something else's shoes (or paws, etc.)

There are many who would give up their own happiness for the sake of others they love. Unless they are doing so as a form of self-deception (as with some of the Lewis's ghosts), they are far more likely to end up happy than most others. Moreover, even when people are somewhat "unhappy," either due to mistakes or misfortunes that led to a difficult life, such people appear to bear those troubles more easily.

What of Spirituality?

The notions of the "other" and ethical desire connect closely with the idea of spirituality as **interruption**, as well as with the notion of **compassion** as appearing at the highest level of spiritual awareness. Though not all spiritual practices place compassion at the origin, Levinas's approach provides an account of how compassion (and a more impersonal enlightenment notion of belonging) is at the heart of reality. Further, it accounts for how it is so fragile and why we so easily do violence to one another.

We should also recall, and here again Levinas would agree, that there are aspects of this that cannot be captured in words. For example, singularity, by its very nature, is violated by words (generalities). Yet that doesn't mean we can't "engage" that mystery and explore what it might have to teach us. When speaking of such difficult experiences, we need to focus on understanding what is behind the words rather than just taking apart the logic of the positions.

Spirituality, if Levinas is correct, speaks to us (interrupts us) most fundamentally through the pain and needs of others. Will we respond to the poor, the widow, the orphan? The stranger, the migrant? Or will we find a way to use our reason to block that compassion? Will we come to realize, in our body and soul even more than our minds, that such a response is not only life-giving to them, but essential and life-giving to us as well? Will we answer the call, or will we seek to shut it down?

Where Do We Go from Here?

We've conducted an exploration of some of the resources—literary, historical, theological, philosophical, psychological—available for thinking about how death can teach us about living. These are meaning of life questions. It's not enough to understand them intellectually, though that too is important. We must take them into our lives as embodied, emotional beings.

Simple human truth, uncompromising scholarly standards, they're connected ...

In the end, while looking for clues in those that came before us can aid us in our own search, for each of us, the search is ultimately personal. While there appear to be some common themes to how one ends with a happy life, we must each engage the mystery and work out the specifics for ourselves.

Will we engage the mysteries?

Will we rise into our humanity?

Reflection/Study Questions

FACING DEATH, FACING OURSELVES

Chapter 1: Facing Death: Coming to Know Oneself

1. What are the two primary life patterns that correlate most closely with a peaceful death?
2. Why does the belief in an afterlife not always correlate with a peaceful death?
3. What is the value in setting aside, at least for a time, one's belief in an afterlife?
4. What are the three primary themes of the book?
5. What are the subthemes or goals?
6. Explain, in concrete terms, the meaning of the first theme.
7. Explain what is meant by consciousness as a dynamic space of possibilities. How is consciousness a projection? How is this essential to who we are as people?
8. How does one use the notion of "projection" to explain how to experience one's death?
9. What is the value of studying other people's answers to the "meaning of life"? What are the limitations?
10. Explain the golden mean and provide an example from one of the virtues.
11. What is the most important moral virtue? How does it relate to the law versus equity and Aristotle's theory of knowledge?
12. Explain Aristotle's understanding of the role of society and government, as well as the impact of an excessive imbalance of wealth (see footnote).
13. Explain the multipoint summary at the end of the discussion of Aristotle. Focus particularly on the question of whether happiness is the real goal, or a byproduct of seeking something else (meaning? connection?) in life.

14. What does it mean to "school one's passions," and why is this important?

15. Why is it important to "test" our intellectual beliefs about the world and our observations of real and diverse human experiences?

16. Explain what is meant by the claim that we are "meaning-seeking and meaning-generating creatures." Why is this important?

17. What is Frankl's explanation of why meaning is more essential than happiness?

Chapter 2: Self-Deception: Detecting When One Is Lying to Oneself

1. Why is it important to "know" oneself? Why is this so important that it is basically a third theme to the book? How is it necessary to achieving happiness?

2. Explain and provide examples of each of the common ways in which we tend to misunderstand ourselves and our world. Start with the two general categories (self-serving rationalities and pretexts), then proceed to the more specific mechanisms:

    a. Self-identity

    b. Confirmation bias

    c. Fundamental attribution error

    d. Self-fulfilling prophesies

    e. Psychological repression

3. Explain the "signs" that one might be engaged in such behaviors? What was the exercise we noted under self-identity?

4. Explain the examples from the footnotes: For instance,

    a. Trickle-down versus middle-class tax cuts

    b. The multiplier effect

    c. The Laffer curve

5. Be able to name and explain the common informal fallacies identified in the chapter.

Chapter 3: *The Death of Ivan Ilyich*

1. What are the major "themes" we see repeated throughout Ivan's life?
2. What are the three forms of death we described from Kramer? Explain each.
3. When Ivan was promoted, he left behind his old friends and found a new circle more suited to his status. What was his method for disengaging from old "friends"? When Ivan complained after he was passed over for promotion, how did colleagues, both above and at his level, treat him?
4. When Ivan ran into a colleague on the train to St. Petersburg, he got everything he thought he wanted. What did he get? In this case, why might this have been a bad result?
5. How did the celebrated physicians treat Ivan? How did Ivan want to be treated? How did this parallel the treatment of Ivan to prisoners on the docket?
6. When Ivan failed to get better from his illness, what self-serving rationality did his wife use to avoid feeling sorry for him?
7. How did Ivan's relationship with Gerasim differ from that of his family and friends? Why is it that Gerasim was able to comfort him but not them? Use Scarry and the inverse relationship between pain and world to explain your answer.
8. What are the three strategies/levels (in this text) for expanding one's world? How does each effect suffering?
9. What bound Ivan to the agony was not the pain itself, but his own self-deception. What was he lying to himself about? Relate this to the third "theme" of the course.
10. Under what conditions was the celebrated physician finally willing to give Ivan a straight answer? Why? How does this relate to why police sometimes ask "complex" questions? ("Why did you do it?")
11. What does the phrase, "He who has a why can bear almost any how" suggest about what is most important in life? (Relate this to Frankls' comments from chapter one.)
12. If Gerasim is an example of the second type of "world expansion" relieving suffering, what is the example of the third and most important type? (Hint: See chapter 12 of the novel.)
13. How and where do we find Kramer's examples of both psychological and spiritual death in Ivan?
14. Explain Aristotle's three forms of friendship. Which applied to Ivan's relationships, and why?

Chapter 4: Anger, Depression, Suicide: Lessons from Grief

1. What are Kübler-Ross's stages? Briefly explain each.
2. What are the two most common elements, according to Kübler-Ross, in someone who is likely to die at peace? (Hint: so that acceptance is not the "booby prize.")
3. Are there levels of depression that do not appear to have a "positive" value? What is needed for those levels/types of depression?
4. Explain the positive values and roles of denial.
5. Explain the positive values and roles of anger. Be sure to explain the deeper issues. (Hint: emotional release is not enough.)
6. Explain the nature and essential roles of forgiveness.
7. What is the specific danger of forgiveness? (Hint: What did we say forgiveness is "not"?)
8. Explain the various positive values and roles of depression. In particular, how does depression relate to the first theme of the book?
9. What is the primary indication that one of these stages has become unhealthy?
10. What is the difference in ratio between men and women on antidepressants? While they can be beneficial, what are some of the risks as discussed in the chapter?
11. What might it mean when someone who has been depressed seems at peace?
12. Why are individuals more likely to go through with suicide when the depression starts to lift? (Pay particular attention to the discussion of one's assumptive world.)
13. Why is suicide described as a "self-absorbed" act as opposed to a "selfish" act?
14. Why should one not give too much credence to an angry suicide note? How is it related to pain and world?
15. How does Scarry's distinction between pain and world explain "cutting"?
16. In the discussion of acceptance, we contrasted two different ways of facing one's loss. Explain both.
17. What types of losses don't fit into the two "different" ways, and what resource did we note for people dealing with this other type of loss?
18. What do persons who experience depression often seek even more than happiness?
19. How do these insights relate to our two central turning points in *The Death of Ivan Illyich*? (Hint: giving and receiving compassion.)
20. Be able to identify and explain the Four Pillars of Meaning.

Chapter 5: Viewing Guide: *Wit*

1. What key question/answer was missing from the "informed consent" conversation at the beginning?
2. Why did the attending wait until after Vivian had signed the consent document to emphasize the difficulties of the treatment?
3. Explain the meaning of the phrase, "Simple human truth, uncompromising scholarly standards, they're connected." What is the connection? Why is this important?
4. Why should one exercise extra caution when coming to a teaching hospital in the months of July, August, and September?
5. What was Vivan's relationship with her friends and colleagues? Compare these with Ivan's relationships. Provide examples.
6. At one point, Susie (the nurse) tells Jason (the fellow) that they need to reduce the dose. What is Jason's response? Consider this in terms of a self-serving rationality and pretext.
7. When Jason has the "cancer is awesome" conversation with Vivian, she then reflects on how she refused her own students the "touch of human kindness." How does this story relate to both Aristotle and the tension of opposites? What ethical dilemma does this highlight for any teacher, and how did Vivian fail?
8. Why did Vivian pinch her IV rather than just press the call button?
9. Susie came to parallel the role of one of the characters relating to Ivan. Which character? Explain the parallel with examples.
10. Analyze, in detail, the last scene where the attending is with Vivian. This was the best example of a self-serving rationality in the play. How and why is the phrase, "she's earned her rest" self-serving, rather than a real expression of care on the part of the physician?
11. What does the change in the willingness of cancer doctors to tell their patients they have cancer between the 1960s and the 1980s suggest about self-serving rationalities?

Chapter 6: Viewing Guide: *What Dreams May Come*

1. At the graveside, Chris (in spirit) reaches out to Annie and tells her he's never going to leave her. Yet, just seconds later, he says goodbye. Recount that scene and explain his change of heart.

2. What are the two approaches to loss noted in the text after the above scene?

3. What are the changes in beliefs noted by Aries between modern Christians and early Christians?

4. What are the two "earthly" explanations offered for the experience of the "light at the end of the tunnel" and "one's life passing before one's eyes"?

5. At various places, there are problems with the notion of a heaven wherein everything is exactly what you would want. What are those problems?

6. Explain the response to the argument that the physical world is an illusion.

7. Why do people who commit suicide go to hell? What is "hell" in this view of reality? What role does self-honesty play?

8. Why are many of the images of hell "inverted" (reversed, turned upside down) from our normal ideas? What is the author trying to say?

9. What does it mean to "stay" in hell? What will happen to Chris?

10. Describe in detail the scene that leads to the establishment of Chris and Annie's "double D" anniversary.

   a. Relate this to Gerasim in Ivan Ilyich. Remember to use Scarry's levels of expanding one's world and the inverse relationship between pain and world.

   b. How might this explain why Annie remains "fragile" after coming out of the asylum?

   c. What was the lie that Annie held on to?

   d. What were the two reasons Annie came back to regular life?

11. Describe in detail the scene that leads to Annie and Chris escaping from hell.

   a. Relate this to the experience with Ivan's son. Use Scarry.

   b. What is different about this "return" to life for Annie, as opposed to the return from the asylum? Why does she no longer appear fragile?

12. What does Annie mean by "Sometimes when you win, you lose" and "Sometimes when you lose, you win"? What does this suggest about the nature of reality and, in particular, spirituality?

13. What is the danger of this "happy ending"?

14. At the very end of the story, Annie and Chris were considering being reborn, just one last time, before returning forever to heaven. There were at least two troubling aspects to this decision. Explain:

   a. the problem with going back, just one more time, for that "first kiss" and to find one another again, and

   b. the risk of going back in general.

15. What do these two "problems" suggest about whether this is a satisfactory view of reality?

Chapter 7: Three Theological Questions: Analyzing C. S. Lewis's *The Great Divorce*

Basic questions:

1. What is Lewis's attitude toward other religions? How does Aquinas's notion of natural law found Lewis's belief? How does Lewis believe that Christianity differs from other religions?
2. What are the distinctions between eternal, natural, and human law?
3. What is Lewis's argument for the primacy of the truth of Christianity? Explain the logical fallacy involved. (Hint: see footnote and the chapter on truth.)
4. For Lewis, what is the relationship between faith and reason?
5. What does Lewis mean when he says that reality is not simple? How is Lewis "humble" about the relationship between intellect and faith, while still holding the value of both?
6. What is the role of self-deception in evil? Provide an example from your own life.
7. Explain each of Lewis's arguments for the following from *The Great Divorce*:
   a. If God is all-loving, how can God condemn people to hell?
   b. If God is all-powerful, how can evil (as a power other than God) exist?
   c. If God is all-knowing, how can there be free will?
8. Explain the role of freedom for each of the three main arguments from *The Great Divorce*.
9. What is purgatory, if it exists, and what is its role?
10. What is the role of heaven, for Lewis, and what is the goal of life that facing one's death has to each us? What is the problem of having heaven as the "goal" of one's religion?

Advanced questions:

11. Moving now to the critique of Lewis, explain the three responses, along with their limitations, to the problem of "why an all-loving God allows bad things to happen." For example:
    a. God gives us trials to help us grow.
    b. God gives us trials to help others grow.

    c. Bad things happen because of sin, not God, but God helps us bear the burden.

12. Once we no longer consider each of the attributes of God (question 7) in isolation, what happens to Lewis's solution to the problem of freedom? What happens to Bioethius's answer?

13. Explain the problem of how "evil," as Lewis and many understand it, could even get started given an all-powerful, all-knowing, all-loving creator.

14. Explain the alternate notion of freedom (as a power to co-create and love).

    a. How does this notion answer our earlier critique?

    b. How is the notion of "all-knowing" modified to make this solution work?

Chapter 8: Buber, Truth, Chaos, and the Middle Voice

Buber:

1. Explain the difference between the I-it and the I-thou relationships.
2. What are the two competing "principles" for the primary foundation for logic?
3. Why does Buber object to these two principles, not as always being wrong, but as too limited to address what is most fundamental?
4. Explain the implications of the claim, "To know is to divide." Why do we divide the world up into our concepts? What do we lose by doing so? What do we gain?
5. What are the implications, in terms of knowing "the" truth about reality, of the claim that the world is far too complex for any human mind to capture?

Truth:

6. Explain the various levels of truth, paying particular attention to Legein and Catharsis.
7. What is the nature and role of the hermeneutic circle?
8. While this truth is not "absolute," what are the three grounds we offered for truth? Which, in particular, grounds ethics? Explain.
9. What is the difference between Aristotle's and Plato's theories of knowledge?
10. Consider how this more creative notion of truth fits with the alternative notion of freedom discussed with C. S. Lewis.

Chaos and middle voice:

11. What are the four meanings of Chaos? How might this be used to argue that Chaos is a metaphor for consciousness?
12. Why was Chaos born first, even before Zeus, the chief God, or any other Gods?
13. Explain the analogy of music.
14. What is the middle voice? How does it differ from passive and active voice?
15. What are the two ways in which we read the birth of Chaos as "past tense, middle voice"?
16. Why does the fact that Chaos is presented as a paradox support the argument that Chaos may name the power of consciousness? (Hint: Kirk and Raven.)

Chapter 9: Faith

1. Explain the argument, repeated here from Lewis, that "heaven" is irrelevant to a mature spirituality.
2. What is the difference between the structure of a set of ideas and the content of the texts?
3. What is the "structure" of the metaphysics of the suicide bomber? Does it differ from the structure of many Christian sects, for example, those engaged in violence against other religions? (Note that many in both Christianity and Islam do not share this structure.)
4. What is an alternate structure for Christianity? (Hint: stewardship)
5. Repeat and explain our definition of faith.
   a. Explain each element of the definition, as well as the following ideas:
      i. Perceptual faith
      ii. Living faith
      iii. Dogmatic faith
      iv. Idolatry
6. What is the difference between purpose and meaning? Why is this important?
7. How does this definition of faith reconcile science with other forms of faith?
8. What do we suggest is still missing from this definition?

Chapter 10: Minority Report: Rereading Gilgamesh after Levinas

1. What is the "standard" solution that readers suggest for the meaning of life in the epic? (Hint: two solutions, one of which has two parts.) Provide examples from the text.

2. What is the biblical text that may share a common source with parts of the epic? Provide an example.

3. Explain and distinguish Levinas's notions of need and desire. Using the text from Shiduri, explain how this allows us to read this text differently than it might have been read otherwise.

4. How might the solutions to the meaning of life have changed, by the end, from an "ego"-centered to an "other"-centered solution?

5. Provide several examples of how Gilgamesh learns humility. (Hints: death, stone poles, inability to stay awake, etc.) What is the value of his learning this humility?

6. What are the four primary arguments (evidence) for why we should understand the epic in this way? (Pay particular attention to the details of the death of Enkidu as well as Gilgamesh's journey and transformation.)

7. What might the epic have to warn us about an excessive focus on an afterlife?

8. What are the two factors that appear to correlate most closely with a peaceful death?

9. In the end, what does the epic suggest that facing death teaches us about the meaning of life?

Chapter 11: *Siddhartha*: An Introduction to Eastern Spirituality

The Bhagavad Gita:

1. What was Arjuna's **self-serving rationality** for not fighting? How did Krishna respond?

2. What are the different implications if one translates from Hindi the word "appearance" instead of "illusion"?

3. What are the Atman and Jiva, and how do they correlate to the Christian notion of the soul?

4. If being reincarnated to ever higher levels is not the final goal of human life/spirituality, what is the ultimate goal?

Siddhartha:

5. Siddhartha leaves his home in order to seek enlightenment. After his time with the Samanas, what conclusion does he draw?
6. What primary "vice" does Siddhartha exhibit while with the Samanas?
7. Why does Govinda end up following Buddha, but Siddhartha does not?
8. Explain our discussion of Kramer's analogy between love and spirituality.
9. How do we connect Siddhartha's journey to Vivian's comment, "Simple human truth, uncompromising scholarly standards, they're connected"?
10. Explain why Siddhartha is so successful as a merchant. (Hint: detachment.)
11. Why are Kamala and Siddhartha able to practice love, but not truly love?
12. Siddhartha undergoes multiple "rebirths." Name several key ones.
13. When Siddhartha gives up his money and goes off to die, what saves him? With whom does he now come to learn?
14. What is the value of listening?
15. What does Kamala see in Siddhartha as she is dying?
16. Explain Siddhartha's relationship with his son. How does this transform Siddhartha?
17. Near the end, was Siddhartha still concerned with becoming enlightened?

    a. Was Siddhartha enlightened?

    b. Was the Ferryman enlightened?
18. At the end, Govinda and Siddhartha meet. Govinda sees in Siddhartha what he saw in the Buddha but is troubled by Siddhartha's language. What is the difference? Why?
19. What are the three reasons why Govinda may not have reached enlightenment?

Chapter 12: Hinduism and Buddhism: Metaphysics and Two Forms of Enlightenment

Hinduism:

1. In the Upanishads, Yama grants three boons. From our typical Western perspective, which is the most important? Which is most important from an Eastern perspective? Why?
2. Why does Yama give Nachiketa the sound "Om," rather than just answering his question?

3. Explain how karma and reincarnation are related.
4. What is the first objection to the ultimate goal of the Atman? What answer was offered?
5. Earlier, we illustrated a certain structural violence shared by some Christian and Islamic followers. We also offered a more "content"-oriented violence, the redefinition of Love. We then contrasted this with a different structural violence in Hinduism. What are these arguments? Is it possible that any set of beliefs, if followed too far, might have violent implications?
6. How can even the golden rule be distorted?

Buddhism:

7. Recount the primary legend of Buddha's early life.
8. What does it mean that Buddha died, not to desire itself, but to his attachment to desires?
9. What is the difference between psychology and spirituality? (See also the next chapter.)
10. Coffin writes that too many Christians go to church to seek salvation (eternal life). Similarly, Buddha saw this search as the wrong question. What is the real question about what we seek? What is important about finding that question?
11. What did I suggest are Buddha's two most fundamental teachings?
12. Explain the differences between "personal" and "impersonal" enlightenment as well as their implications (part of which is finished in the next chapter.)

Chapter 13: Psychology versus Spirituality: It's Not about Me

1. What is the stated difference between psychology and spirituality? Despite these differences, how are the two related? Why is spirituality, understood as interruption, necessary for a healthy psychology?
2. Why do we need metaphysics? Why must we also be careful to limit our reliance on such beliefs? Why does believing too much in a particular metaphysics tend to lead to violence?
3. Explain the two notions of detachment.
4. Review the various notions of enlightenment. What does this imply about the ability to capture them in words?

5. How does both beauty and the sublime also "interrupt" us? What is the value of this interruption? Is this another aspect of what we have been calling "spirituality"?

6. Even taken from a non-spiritual perspective, what are the positive effects of meditation? Relate this to our notion of consciousness.

Chapter 14: Viewing Guide: *Tuesdays with Morrie*

1. Consider the scene in the sports bar. Mitch is trying to decide whether to go see Morrie.

   a. What self-serving rationale does Janine call Mitch out on?

   b. What does the scene suggest about how Mitch uses his life to distance relationships?

   c. What perspective do we offer on being "uncomfortable" talking about death or grief?

2. What were the reasons Mitch offered, in his own self-reflection, for why he was afraid to face his old professor?

3. In their first meeting, what does Morrie tell Mitch is worth being sad about besides dying?

4. Morrie asks Mitch the following three questions. How are they linked? What does this suggest about the nature of happiness?

   a. Are you happy?

   b. Are you giving to your community?

   c. Are you at peace?

5. Explain the self-serving rationality Mitch uses when asked about when he and Janine will get married. (Hint: "When we're both ready.")

6. Despite having this disease, Morrie claims he is lucky. Explain. (Hint: first theme of the book.)

7. Fear of death is akin to fear of aging. In the case of the latter, what does Morrie suggest for those who fear?

8. Despite the fact that Morrie is cheerful most of the time, he has his "early morning moments." Why is this important? Why it is healthy? Relate this to the chapter where we discussed depression.

9. What is Morrie's response to Mitch's claim that we don't talk about death in order to "spare people's feelings"? (Hint: How is this a self-serving rationality?)

10. In the scene with the tape recorder, we see a first hint of Morrie's view of the meaning of life. What is that hint?

11. Consider the story of the loss of Mitch's uncle.

    a. How did Mitch react to that loss?

    b. How has it continued to affect his life?

    c. How does Morrie's story of his own father parallel Mitch's story?

12. Mitch is now out of work. It gives him time to reflect. When this happened to Ivan Ilyich it was sheer misery and he learned nothing from it. What is different with Mitch?

13. Recount and explain the point of the Buddhist story of the bird on one's shoulder.

14. Recount and explain the point of the story of the little wave. What religion does that seem to reflect most closely? Why?

15. Morrie claims that "love always wins." Clearly, this is false. But in what way did we figure out that it might be true? Explain.

    a. Even if Janine never comes back to Mitch, in what way had Mitch still "won"?

16. When Morrie talks about dying "surrounded" by love, how does this correlate to Kübler-Ross's insights?

17. What is a danger of a naïve reading of "love always wins"?

18. Morrie claims that "Love is the only rational act." This is confusing, and again, clearly wrong. But he's a pretty wise man. How did we reinterpret the statement (see the second theme of the book) in a way that might make it true? Reproduce the basic argument.

19. Going back to the poem, "we must love one another or die," we see the scene where Morrie has just described his burial plot. Mitch objects to the line in the poem, in tears, and says, "We all die anyway. What's the point?" Mitch has essentially asked Morrie what he views as the meaning of life.

    a. What does Morrie DO in response to Mitch's question?

    b. Why does Morrie do something first, and only then explain? (Hint: Yama and "Om")

    c. How does the difference in their understanding of the notion of "die" in the poem differ? (Hint: equivocation between psychological and physical death.)

20. In the major stories we've already discussed, what response to the "meaning of life" question appears closest to Morrie's? Be able to explain, in concrete detail, how the answer in this other story relates to Morrie's answer.

Chapter 15: Love Is the Ultimate Rational Act: Take Two

1. For Levinas, what is the difference between "need" and "desire"?
2. Explain how love is a key source of our capacities for:
   a. Reason (Hint: justice)
   b. Language
   c. Self
   d. Freedom (in two ways)
   e. Community
3. How is love also the source for two particular types of human violence? (Hint: universals, justice, stereotypes.) Explain:
   a. Distraction/dispersion
   b. Reflection
4. What three reasons were given as to why ethical desire is fragile?
5. How does this notion connect to our notion of spirituality as interruption?

References

Album, Mitch. 2003. *Tuesdays with Morrie*. Buena Vista Home Entertainment.

Aries, Phillippe. 1974. *Western Attitudes towards Death: From the Middles Ages to the Present*. John Hopkins University Press.

Bretall, Robert, ed. 1946. *A Kierkegaard Anthology*. Princeton University Press.

Boethius, Ancius. 1999. The Consulation of Philosophy. Penquin Classics.

Buber, Martin. 1970. *I and Thou*. Translated by Walter Kaufmann. New York: Simon & Schuster.

Coffin, William Sloan. 1985. The Words of Rev. William Sloan Coffin. *Fresh Air*, http://www.npr.org/templates/story/story.php?storyId=5342517.

Caplan, Mariana. 1999. *Halfway Up the Mountain: The Error of Premature Claims to Enlightenment*. Arizona: Holm Press.

Degnin, Francis. 2007. "Levinas and the Hippocratic Oath: A Discussion of Physician-Assisted Suicide," *Journal of Medicine and Philosophy* 32, no. 2.

Degnin, Francis. 2007. "Talking with Students About Faith in an Era of Religious Extremes," *Religion & Education* 34, no. 2 (Spring).

Degnin, Francis. 2008. "Talking with Students About Truth: Using Heidegger to Loosen the Grip of Literal Absolutes," *Religion & Education* 35, no. 2 (Spring).

Degnin, Francis, and Wood, Donna. 2007. "Levinas and Society's Most Vulnerable: A Philosopher's View of the Business of Health Care," *Organizational Ethics: Healthcare, Business, and Policy* 4, no. 1 (Spring/Summer).

Degnin, Francis. 2106 "Minority Report: Re-reading Gilgamesh After Levinas," *Sage Open* (July-Sept) 1–8. http://sgo.sagepub.com/content/spsgo/6/3/2158244016657858.full.pdf?ijkey=Xz1fn37EzzQWsUQ&keytype=finite.

Etkind, Marc. 1997. *... Or Not to Be: A Collection of Suicide Notes*. New York: Riverhead Books.

Foster, Benjamin, trans. 2001. *The Epic of Gilgamesh*. London: Norton Critical Edition.

Frankl, Victor. 2006. *Man's Search for Meaning*. Boston: Beacon Press.

George, Andrew, trans. 1999. *The Epic of Gilgamesh*. London: Penguin Classics.

George, Andrew, trans. 2003. *The Babylonian Gilgamesh Epic: Introduction, Critical Edition, and Cuneiform Texts*. Oxford University Press.

Gilligan, Carol. 1993. *In a Different Voice: Psychological Theory and Women's Development*. Harvard University Press.

Hesse, Herman. 1951. *Siddhartha*. Translated by Hilda Rosner. New Directions Publishing.

Heidegger, Martin. 1991. *The Principle of Reason*. Translated by Reginald Lilly. Indiana University Press.

Hesiod. 1983. *Theogony, Works and Days, Shield*. Translated by Apostolos Athenasskis. John Hopkins University Press.

Hoffer, Eric. 1951. *The True Believer: Thoughts on the Nature of Mass Movements*. Harper and Row.

Jacobson, Thorkild. 2001. "And Death the Journey's End: The Gilgamesh Epic." In *The Epic of Gilgamesh*, translated by Benjamin Foster, 183–207. London: Norton Critical Edition.

Jones, Bruce. 1990. "From Gilgamesh to Qoheleth." In *The Bible in the Light of Cuneiform Literature*, 349–379. Edwin Mellen Press.

Kirk, Raven, and Schofield, Malcolm. 1983. *The Presocratic Philospohers*. Cambridge University Press.

Kramer, Kenneth. 1988. *The Sacred Art of Dying: How World Religions Understand Death*. New York: Paulist Press.

Kübler-Ross, Elizabeth. 1975. *Death: The Final Stage of Growth*. New Jersey: Prentice-Hall.

Levinas, Emmanuel. 1969. *Totality and Infinity*. Translated by Alphonso Lingis. Martinus Nijhoff Publishers.

Levinas, Emmanuel. 1981. *Otherwise than Being or Beyond Essence*. Translated by Alphonso Lingis. Martinus Nijhoff Publishers.

Lewis, C. S. 1974. *The Great Divorce*. New York: Macmillan.

Lewis, C. S. 1980. *Mere Christianity*. Happer Collins.

Merleau-Ponty, Mourice. 1968. *The Visible and the Invisible*. Translated by Alphonso Lingus. Northwestern University Press.

Mill, John Stewart. 1998. *On Liberty and Other Essays*. Oxford University Press.

Neeld, Elizabeth Harper. 2003. *Seven Choices: Finding Daylight After Loss Shatters Your World*. Pocket Guide, Centerpoint Press.

Nuland, Sherwin. 1995. *How We Die: Reflections on Life's Final Chapter*. New York: Vintage Books.

Oken, Donald. 1961. "What to Tell Cancer Patients: A Study of Medical Attitudes." *JAMA* 175, no. 13: 1120–1128.

Pence, Gregory. 2004. *Classic Cases in Medical Ethics*, 4th ed. McGraw Hill.

Roach, Mary. 2003. *Stiff: The Curious Life of Cadavers*. W. W. Norton & Company.

Sarte, Jean-Paul. 1956. *Being and Nothingness*. Washington Square Press.

Saslow, Laura, Willer, Robb, Feinberg, Matthew, Piff, Paul, Clark, Katharine, Keltner, Dacher, and Saturn, Sarina. 2013 "My Brother's Keeper: Compassion Predicts Generosity More Among Less Religious Individuals." *Social Psychology and Personality Science* 4, no. 1: 3–38.

Scarry, Elaine. 1985. *The Body in Pain: The Making and Unmaking of the World*. Oxford University Press.

Smith, Emily. 2013. "There's More to Life Than Being Happy." *The Atlantic*, January 9, https://www.theatlantic.com/health/archive/2013/01/theres-more-to-life-than-being-happy/266805/

Tolstoy, Leo. 1981. *The Death of Ivan Ilyich*. Translated by Lynn Solotaroff. Bantam Books.

What Dreams May Come. 1998. Directed by Vincent Ward. Polygram Films.

W. H. Auden. 1940. *Another Time*. Curtis Brown, Ltd.

Wilder, Esther. 2006. *Wheeling and Dealing: Living with Spinal Cord Injury*. Vanderbilt University Press.

Wit. 2001. Directed by Mike Nicols. HBO Films.

Index

CPSIA information can be obtained
at www.ICGtesting.com
Printed in the USA
SHW022311210120
291FS